NONPERFORMING LOANS IN ASIA AND EUROPE— CAUSES, IMPACTS, AND RESOLUTION STRATEGIES

Edited by

John Fell, Maciej Grodzicki, Junkyu Lee, Reiner Martin, Cyn-Young Park, and Peter Rosenkranz

DECEMBER 2021

ASIAN DEVELOPMENT BANK

ADB

Contents

Tables, Figures, and Boxes

Tables

Figures

Foreword

The coronavirus disease (COVID-19) pandemic hit the global economy hard, triggering major recessions worldwide. While large-scale expansionary fiscal and accommodative monetary policies have thus far prevented a financial crisis, the risk of a surge in nonperforming loans (NPLs) remains significant across Asia and Europe especially once policies normalize and regulatory forbearance measures phase out. Banks entered this pandemic better prepared than in past crises—amid stronger regulation, supervision, and capital buffers—but increasing NPLs can still undermine economic recovery and upend financial stability.

This book synthesizes key lessons from past experiences of sustained buildup in NPLs and the policy implications. It is a collaborative project by the Asian Development Bank and the European Central Bank, and the volume's lessons draw from a wide range of regional and country case studies and empirical analyses. These findings and policy implications can help lay the foundations for financial and economic stability in Asia, Europe, and beyond.

Accumulations of distressed assets and their slow resolution have been among the hallmarks of previous financial crises. Such overhangs heavily constrain bank financing—the major source of corporate financing in Asia and Europe—and thus undermine economic activity. These experiences emphasize the need for decisive and comprehensive policy action to help manage NPLs swiftly.

Legal and economic framework conditions conducive to NPL resolution are essential and should address demand-side, supply-side, and structural constraints. Among the elements of these NPL resolution "ecosystems" are enhanced data quality and well-defined strategies for developing secondary NPL markets that address information asymmetries and entry barriers to these markets.

The regional and country case studies also look at the role of asset management companies (AMCs) in NPL resolution. Such "AMCs" can play a very positive role, but only if they are properly set up and run. Recent technological advances also offer promising solutions, including ways to improve, analyze, and store data. Electronic NPL trading platforms likewise hold much promise, facilitating the development of secondary NPL markets.

In addition, the important role of regional financial cooperation in NPL resolution is growing, especially in the wake of increasing financial interconnectedness. In Europe, common rules, institutions, and a joint action plan have helped tackle NPLs. While in Asia, region-wide financial regulations do not exist yet, regional strategies and frameworks can help to promote data and product harmonization to deepen regional NPL markets.

We are grateful to the authors, contributing researchers, and editors of this volume for bringing such important and timely issues into discussion. We also hope that this collective effort will help policy makers become better prepared to deal with clear and present NPL risks in the aftermath of the pandemic recession.

Luis de Guindos
Vice-President
European Central Bank

Yasuyuki Sawada
Chief Economist
March 2017–August 2021
Asian Development Bank

Acknowledgments

This book was prepared by the Regional Cooperation and Integration Division (ERCI) of the Economic Research and Regional Cooperation Department (ERCD) of the Asian Development Bank (ADB), in collaboration with the European Central Bank (ECB). It was supported by the ADB technical assistance project Strengthening Asia's Financial Safety Nets and Resolution Mechanisms (TA 9497), financed by ADB's technical assistance special fund, the People's Republic of China Poverty Reduction and Regional Cooperation Fund, and the Republic of Korea e-Asia and Knowledge Partnership Fund.

The editors are grateful to all contributors to this book. Without their valuable contributions, this book could not be finalized. The strong support, such as sharing NPL policy and operational experiences by Bruno Carrasco, Director General of ADB's Sustainable Development and Climate Change Department, is greatly acknowledged. The editorial team is also grateful for helpful feedback of participants of the following events: International Public AMC Forum (IPAF) Research Meeting on Effectiveness of NPL Resolution, Financial Safety Net Strategies, and NPL Market Development in Hanoi in November 2018; ERCD and Sustainable Development and Climate Change Department–Finance Sector Group Joint Seminar on NPL Market Development Strategies and Frameworks in Asia at the ADB headquarters in Manila in November 2019; ADB Bangladesh Resident Mission, SDCC-FSG, and ERCD: Policy Workshop on Resolving Nonperforming Loans Puzzle: Learning from International Experiences in Dhaka in November 2019; and the ADB–ECB Workshop on NPL Resolution in Asia and Europe at the ADB headquarters in Manila in February 2020.

Peter Rosenkranz (economist, ERCI, ADB) and Paulo Rodelio Halili (senior economics officer, ERCI, ADB) coordinated the production of this book under the overall supervision and guidance of Cyn-Young Park (director, ERCI, ADB), with support from Marilyn Aure Parra (senior operations assistant, ERCI, ADB) and Monica Melchor (consultant, ADB).

Eric Van Zant edited the manuscript. Michael Cortes created the cover design and implemented the typesetting and layout. Lawrence Casiraya proofread the report, while Marjorie Celis handled the page proof checking with assistance from Carol Ongchangco (operations coordinator, ERCI, ADB) and Paulo Rodelio Halili. The Printing Services Unit of ADB's Corporate Services Department and the Publishing Team of the Department of Communications supported printing and publishing.

Editors

John Fell is Deputy Director General for Macroprudential Policy and Financial Stability in the European Central Bank (ECB). He is also the chair or co-chair of several international working groups, including the Eurosystem's Macroprudential Policy Group, and the European Systemic Risk Board's Instrument Working Group and its Task Force on Stress Testing. Between 2003 and 2010, he was Head of the ECB's Financial Stability Division and editor of the ECB's Financial Stability Review, which he continues to direct. Prior to joining the ECB in 1998 as a Principal Economist, he held various positions at the European Monetary Institute and the Central Bank of Ireland.

Maciej Grodzicki is an Adviser in the Systemic Risk and Financial Institutions Division of the European Central Bank (ECB). He works extensively on issues in the euro area banking sector, including asset quality, bank profitability and consolidation, and calibration of capital buffers for systemically important banks. He has been actively contributing to the European debate on the resolution of nonperforming bank assets. Previously, he was involved in several European Union-wide stress testing exercises, the 2014 ECB comprehensive assessment, and economic adjustment programs in Cyprus and Portugal. Prior to joining the ECB in 2010, Maciej worked for 4 years at the National Bank of Poland.

Junkyu Lee is Chief of the Finance Sector Group, Sector Advisory Service Cluster, Sustainable Development and Climate Change Department, Asian Development Bank (ADB). He is an economist with seasoned policy-making experience and knowledge in financial development and stability, and international economic policies. Since 2013, he has been leading policy and operational discussions on Asia's banking sector stability, nonperforming loan resolution, and capital market development in ADB. As a former Group of Twenty (G20) finance advisor, he also has deep policy-making experience with macroprudential policy, capital flows management measures, and financial development policy in the G20 Finance Process and the Association of Southeast Asian Nations (ASEAN)+3 Finance Process.

Reiner Martin is Lead Economist at the Joint Vienna Institute, where he is developing applied training courses for public sector officials on a range of financial and macroeconomic topics. His research is focused on nonperforming loan resolution, macroprudential policy, and stress testing. Until August 2018, he was deputy head of the Macroprudential Policy Division of the European Central Bank (ECB). Prior to this, he was deputy head of the ECB's Stress Testing Division and headed the ECB financial sector teams for Cyprus, Spain, and Slovenia. He holds a doctor of philosophy (PhD) degree in economics from the University of Hamburg and master's degrees in economics and political science from the Universities of Sussex and Bristol.

Cyn-Young Park is Director of the Regional Cooperation and Integration Division (ERCI) in the Economic Research and Regional Cooperation Department (ERCD) of ADB. She manages a team of economists to examine economic and policy issues related to regional cooperation and integration. During her career at ADB, she has been a main author and contributor to ADB's major publications. Prior to joining ADB, she served as economist at the Organisation for Economic Co-operation and Development. She received her PhD in economics from Columbia University. She holds a bachelor's degree in international economics from Seoul National University.

Peter Rosenkranz is an Economist in ADB's Regional Cooperation and Integration Division. His knowledge work focuses on financial development, stability, integration, and cooperation in Asia. This includes research on nonperforming loan resolution, US dollar funding conditions, regional financial safety nets, and financial technology. He supports ADB's participation in regional policy forums (e.g., ASEAN/+3, Asia-Pacific Economic Cooperation, and Asia-Europe Meeting). Previously, he was an advisor at the Deutsche Gesellschaft für Internationale Zusammenarbeit and a market infrastructure expert at the European Central Bank. He holds a PhD in economics from the University of Zurich.

Authors

Douglas Arner is Kerry Holdings Professor in Law, University of Hong Kong.

Emilios Avgouleas is Chair of International Banking Law and Finance, University of Edinburgh.

John Fell is Deputy Director General, Macroprudential Policy and Financial Stability, European Central Bank.

Evan Gibson is a Post-Doctoral Research Fellow, Faculty of Law, University of Hong Kong.

Edimon Ginting is Country Director, Bangladesh Resident Mission (formerly Deputy Director General, Economic Research and Regional Cooperation Department, Asian Development Bank at the time of writing).

Maciej Grodzicki is Adviser, Systemic Risk and Financial Institutions Division, European Central Bank.

Ivan Huljak is Principal Advisor, Croatian National Bank.

Junkyu Lee is Chief, Finance Sector Group, Sector Advisory Service Cluster, Sustainable Development and Climate Change Department, Asian Development Bank.

Alexander Lehmann is a Nonresident Fellow, Bruegel.

Reiner Martin is Lead Economist, Joint Vienna Institute.

Diego Moccero is Senior Financial Stability Expert, Macroprudential Policy, European Central Bank.

Edward O'Brien is Adviser, Directorate General Macroprudential Policy and Financial Stability, European Central Bank.

Cosimo Pancaro is Team Lead, Stress Test Modelling Division, Financial Stability and Macroprudential Policy Directorate, European Central Bank.

Cyn-Young Park is Director, Regional Cooperation and Integration Division, Economic Research and Regional Cooperation Department, Asian Development Bank.

Daekeun Park is Professor, Hanyang University.

Peter Rosenkranz is Economist, Regional Cooperation and Integration Division, Economic Research and Regional Cooperation Department, Asian Development Bank.

Key Messages and Overview

John Fell, Maciej Grodzicki, Junkyu Lee, Reiner Martin, Cyn-Young Park, and Peter Rosenkranz

Key Messages

High and persistent levels of nonperforming loans (NPLs) have featured prominently in recent financial crises. This book traces NPL trends during and after the Asian financial crisis, the global financial crisis, and the European sovereign debt crisis. It examines the economic impact of high NPLs. And it compares the effectiveness of NPL resolution strategies across countries in the two regions. The book distills important lessons from regional and country experiences using case studies and empirical investigation to identify the best ways to resolve NPLs. These findings can be invaluable in charting a course through the financial and economic fallout of the coronavirus disease (COVID-19) pandemic to recovery and sustained financial stability in Asia, Europe, and beyond.

Persistently high NPLs can significantly undermine bank lending and economic growth. This calls for swift and comprehensive policy action as such distressed assets build up. Past crises have shown that elevated NPLs can have long-lasting effects on financial sectors, still weighing on banks' balance sheets years after the initial turmoil has passed. Preventing such "NPL hysteresis" is particularly relevant for most Asian and European countries, given their mostly bank-dominated financial systems.

Another characteristic of Asian and European financial systems is their deep and increasing interconnectedness. While providing many benefits, such as regional risk diversification, interconnectedness can also amplify propagation of financial shocks across national and regional boundaries. A sharp increase in NPLs in one country can easily spill over to neighboring countries through a range of financial and economic channels. Swift NPL resolution mechanisms are therefore important for domestic and for regional financial stability and economic growth.

The book identifies a wide range of available NPL resolution options. Yet, it also reveals the numerous supply- and demand-side impediments and structural problems that complicate or even preclude the use of some of these options, thus slowing resolution.

Supply-side challenges stem from banks' reluctance to take the losses that NPL resolution entails. This relates to both the "on-balance-sheet resolution of NPLs" and "off-balance sheet" approaches, i.e., NPL sales. Both of these options can often lead to recovery values that are below NPL net book values. In other words, NPL resolution often implies losses on the loan book, hurting bank profitability in the short term and reducing bank capital levels. Such NPL-related losses are exacerbated if the workout capacity within the originating bank is insufficient and if there is a lack of demand for NPLs on the secondary market. Being reluctant or unable to sustain NPL-related losses, banks often prefer to retain NPLs on their books, hoping that the loans will become "performing" again or that the value of the underlying assets recovers. Asian and European case studies reviewed in the book, however, show that these hopes are often unfounded and that "extend-and-pretend" approaches ultimately result in even more severe balance sheet losses for the banks.

Demand-side impediments are often multifaceted. First, banks tend to have more information about the net present value of NPLs than potential investors, creating information asymmetries between potential buyers and sellers. Second, transaction costs for resolving or selling NPLs are often significant, further reducing NPLs' net present value. Such transaction costs relate, for example, to the costs of valuing underlying collateral, the legal costs of recovery, or the notary and other fees associated with NPL sales on the secondary market. Such demand-side impediments tend to drive down the price that potential investors are willing to pay, widening bid-ask spreads, that is, the price NPL investors offer and the price that originating banks are able or willing to accept. Frequently, the bid-ask spread becomes insurmountably wide, curtailing transactions, as seen on many Asian and European secondary NPL markets.

Insufficient quantity and quality of data about NPLs is one factor impeding NPL supply and demand, resulting in NPL market failures. Although banks typically have more and better information about nonperforming exposures than potential investors, their information is often still insufficient to clearly establish the best possible resolution strategy. Potential investors face even more severe data constraints, creating additional due diligence costs and uncertainty about the net present value of NPLs. This then drives down bidding prices and discourages potential transactions.

Finally, important structural challenges impede NPL resolution in both Asia and Europe. Poor legal frameworks, insufficient judicial capacity, and opaque and lengthy collateral enforcement and insolvency proceedings delay recoveries in asset values and add to recovery costs. They add to banks' costs to resolve NPLs and widen the bid-ask spreads, reducing NPL transactions on the secondary market. Out-of-court procedures can help to overcome some of these structural challenges and to speed up the NPL resolution process, but their effectiveness across countries in Asia and Europe has varied significantly. Some countries also have legal barriers in place, restricting or even prohibiting potential investors from entering and actively participating in secondary NPL markets.

Given these challenges, the book discusses several policy options and measures to enhance and accelerate NPL resolution in Asia and Europe.

The lack of readily available data about NPLs can be addressed in various ways. A comprehensive definition of distressed assets that is comparable across countries helps to create transparency about the magnitude of the problem. Moreover, it helps to enable regional solutions to NPL problems. In Europe, the European Banking Authority published technical standards on NPLs in 2015, going a long way in this direction. In Asia, experience is more heterogeneous. Especially during crises and heightened market uncertainty, asset quality reviews and solvency stress tests can help increase transparency, supporting NPL resolution. NPL disclosure requirements for banks and standardized NPL data templates can reduce information asymmetries and foster secondary market development.

Experience in the Asian and European countries shows that the internal workout of NPLs by the originating bank is usually part of the solution. The efficiency of this "on-balance-sheet" workout depends crucially on regulatory and supervisory rules, guidance, and incentives. Ensuring sufficient provisioning appears particularly important. Sufficient provisioning prevents the supply-side constraint of banks unwilling or unable to take the losses of NPL resolution.

A complementary option to the resolution of NPLs on banks' balance sheets is the development of secondary NPL markets, where the originating banks can sell nonperforming assets to specialized investors. In most countries in Asia and Europe, various demand, supply, and structural challenges still constrain the secondary NPL market. Authorities in both regions are thus pursuing policy reforms to address NPL market failures and to stimulate supply and demand.

Securitization is one, specific form of secondary NPL market transaction. It usually involves sovereign guarantees for at least some NPL security tranches in order to increase investor confidence and to provide clarity about the recoverable value of the underlying NPLs. To be effective, however, securitization requires a certain market size and level of sophistication. This option may therefore not be viable for smaller European countries and Asian developing economies with less sophisticated financial markets. In addition, government-guaranteed securitization schemes can imply significant contingent risks for public finances.

The book also details the role and experiences with asset management companies (AMCs), often also referred to as "bad banks." Especially during crises, AMCs can effectively support NPL resolution by providing a "bridge to the future." They can prevent NPL fire sales by banks at the trough of the market, reduce financial uncertainty, and stabilize the provision of loans to the economy. In sum, they can offer significant potential benefits for both banks and taxpayers. To realize these benefits, however, AMCs need to be properly designed and managed. Asian and European case studies in the book reveal differences in the design and use of AMCs across the two regions, particularly in the role of government and how to establish them (permanent versus temporary AMCs). While Asia has numerous examples of permanent public AMCs, Europe largely set up temporary AMCs and tried to encourage private sector participation.

A more recent approach to facilitate secondary NPL markets is the establishment of NPL transaction platforms—either nationally or regionally. Such platforms are a low-cost and complementary approach to reduce information asymmetries between originating banks and potential NPL investors, thus supporting NPL market development. Their success appears to depend mainly on market size, framework conditions, and the right incentive structure.

The potential benefits of regional cooperation in Asia and Europe are also discussed in the book. Given that most financial sectors in Asian and European countries are relatively small, regional cooperation can offer potentially sizable benefits. In Europe, regional financial cooperation works mainly through common rules, the so-called *Acquis Communautaire*, and European institutions such as the European Banking Authority, the European Central Bank, and the European Commission. The European Union (EU) Action Plan for NPLs and its update in December 2020 are good examples of regional cooperation in NPLs.

In Asia, regional financial cooperation gained momentum after the Asian financial crisis, especially in the ASEAN+3 region. The International Public AMC Forum is one example of voluntary private sector-driven cooperation to share knowledge and experience in NPL resolution within member economies, although membership remains limited. Additional regional efforts to promote data and product harmonization, as well as to strengthen financial market infrastructure, could help deepen NPL markets in Asia and in Europe.

The role of the state in NPL resolution, meanwhile, differs markedly across Asia and Europe. State involvement is more limited in Europe (e.g., bail-in requirements, state-aid rules). By contrast, a more flexible approach is taken in Asia, although it is well understood that public involvement should be well targeted and not exacerbate an extend-and-pretend approach to NPLs. It remains to be seen to what extent the COVID-19 pandemic—a crisis in which the financial sector is not the source of the problem but part of the solution—may change these perspectives and approaches.

One of the key findings of the book is that no one-size-fits-all approach is effective in NPL resolution. Context-specific, bespoke combinations of resolution approaches are the best way forward. That said, the NPL resolution experience of the range of Asian and European economies reviewed in this book identifies several important lessons and best practices. Thorough analysis of country-specific situations is needed to identify which of these lessons and best practices can be deployed in a particular context.

COVID-19 and its aftermath will likely result in a substantial increase in NPLs in both Asia and Europe. This may destabilize financial systems, compromise swift post-pandemic economic recovery, and threaten financial stability. Large-scale fiscal stimulus packages have thus far helped prevent corporate defaults amid COVID-19, while regulatory forbearance has relieved pressure on banks in addressing NPLs. However, once temporary relief is lifted, corporate defaults are likely to materialize, and banks could become exposed to rising NPLs. Consequently, countries in both Europe and Asia should prepare for the likely increase in NPLs by tackling existing weaknesses in their NPL management and resolution frameworks.

Sound macrofinancial positions can help mitigate the stress on banking sectors and credit markets when entering a crisis. Banks should be encouraged to identify distressed assets early on, adopt realist c assumptions in provisioning, and ramp up capacity to offer adequate workout solutions. In addition, remaining obstacles for the further development of secondary NPL markets need to be tackled. In some jurisdictions, this may require major reforms of legal frameworks, which may prove impossible to complete ahead of the likely increase in NPLs. Nevertheless, authorities should continue to pursue and even accelerate such reforms. They should also identify and implement the remaining "quick wins" that can help streamline NPL resolution and develop markets for distressed assets.

Overview

This book is divided into four parts. Part 1, *Summary of NPL Trends and Lessons from Three Decades of Crisis Resolution in Asia and Europe* (Chapters 1–2), investigates the main trends in NPLs in Asia and Europe over the last 30 years and distills the key lessons. Part 2, *Empirical Analyses of the Macrofinancial Implications of NPLs in Asia and Europe* (Chapters 3–4), examines the main determinants of NPLs and their macrofinancial impact. It also empirically analyzes the effectiveness of resolution approaches. Part 3, *Country Case Studies on NPL Resolution in Asia and Europe* (Chapters 5–6), looks in more detail at country-specific NPL resolution practices across Asia and Europe to draw insights on effective responses to rising distressed assets. Finally, Chapters 7–8 in Part 4, *Policy Strategies for Nonperforming Loan Resolution and Market Development in Asia and Europe,* examine the policy implications of NPL resolution strategies in Europe and Asia. They suggest promising ways forward for NPL resolution in Asia, Europe, and beyond.

Part 1: Summary of Nonperforming Loan Trends and Lessons from Three Decades of Crisis Resolution in Asia and Europe

In **Chapter 1**, *Maciej Groazicki, Reiner Martin, Cyn-Young Park*, and *Peter Rosenkranz* summarize NPL trends in Asia and Europe over the last 3 decades. While a certain amount of distressed assets is a normal feature of any banking sector, elevated levels of NPLs can pose major problems for financial sectors, threatening instability for the economy as a whole. Rapid credit growth and persistently high NPL levels often precipitate financial crises. During and after the Asian financial crisis in the late 1990s, NPL levels rose sharply across several East and Southeast Asian countries. A decade later, the euro area saw a significant elevation in NPLs, prompted by the global financial crisis and later the European sovereign debt crisis. This chapter highlights the main features of NPL developments in the two regions, flagging commonalities and considerable heterogeneity in NPL developments between and within the regions.

In **Chapter 2**, *Douglas Arner, Evan Gibson,* and *Emilios Avgouleas* draw lessons from 3 decades of banking crisis resolution. In the aftermath of three major crises, a broad array of approaches were adopted to combat the increase in distressed assets. The responses ranged from outright bailouts of troubled banks to bank closures and liquidation. By analyzing the NPL resolution responses to the three major crises, the chapter provides additional insight into the commonly held belief that bank bailouts constitute an inefficient use of public funds or that they give rise to moral hazard concerns. The analysis suggests that, when properly set up, AMCs can facilitate banking sector recapitalization. The conditions of the bailout, mode of bank restructuring, conditions accompanying fiscal subsidies, and the proper setup of AMCs are important in enhancing the effectiveness of bailouts. The chapter argues that during systemic financial crises or crises caused by exogenous factors where moral hazard concerns are minimized, a combination of balance sheet restructuring and set up of AMCs comprises an optimal response. This is particularly relevant for the present pandemic.

Part 2: Empirical Analyses of the Macrofinancial Implications of Nonperforming Loans in Asia and Europe

In **Chapter 3**, *Daekeun Park, Junkyu Lee,* and *Peter Rosenkranz* review the macrofinancial linkages of NPLs and investigate the effectiveness of resolution policies. Utilizing a novel NPL dataset constructed from bank-level S&P Global data, the authors examine episodes of sharp reductions in NPL ratios and find that these can be accounted for by faster growth and less volatility in financial markets. Additionally, a probit framework reveals that the establishment of public AMCs can sharply reduce NPL ratios and is consequently a key element in NPL resolution. Estimated average treatment effects, moreover, show that episodes of sharp reductions in NPL ratios are associated with favorable macroeconomic conditions, highlighting the macrofinancial implications and feedback effects of NPLs.

In **Chapter 4**, *Ivan Huljak, Reiner Martin, Diego Moccero*, and *Cosimo Pancaro* utilize a panel Bayesian vector autoregression (VAR) model to examine the impact of NPLs on bank lending and macroeconomic conditions in the euro area. The paper has three main findings. First, an exogenous increase in the change in NPL ratios in the euro area tends to depress bank lending volumes, widen bank lending spreads, and prompt a fall in real gross domestic product (GDP) growth and residential real estate prices. A corollary to this is that an exogenous change in real GDP growth constrains bank lending and real estate prices, widens lending spreads, and leads to an increase in NPL ratios. Second, shocks to the change in NPL ratios explain a relatively large share of the variance of the variables in the VAR, particularly for euro area countries that experienced a large increase in NPL ratios during the recent crises. Finally, a reduction in banks' NPL ratios can improve macroeconomic and financial conditions. Research underpins the relevance of effective policy measures to hasten NPL resolution.

Part 3: Country Case Studies on Nonperforming Loan Resolution in Asia and Europe

In **Chapter 5**, *Junkyu Lee, Peter Rosenkranz*, and *Edimon Ginting* review case studies of NPL reduction policies implemented by selected ASEAN+3 economies, focusing on the (i) operation of AMCs; (ii) financial sector restructuring and bailouts; (iii) insolvency reforms and resolution frameworks; and (iv) prudential tightening, including loan classification and provisioning stringency during and after the Asian financial crisis. The case studies provide the basis for constructing a novel dataset of NPL reduction variables for the empirical part of this chapter. The empirical analysis of the effectiveness of reduction policies using a dynamic panel dataset of 78 banks from 6 Asian countries during 2002–2017 suggests that among the range of possible NPL resolution policies, the establishment of public AMCs has proved most effective.

In **Chapter 6**, *Alexander Lehmann* presents European country case studies on NPL resolution and NPL market development. Immediately after the European sovereign debt crisis, NPL resolution was hampered by slow economic recovery and prolonged recessions in several economies in the euro area periphery. Slow and belated national reforms further delayed recovery. Between 2014 and 2019, more assertive euro area bank supervision and EU-wide bank regulation helped set the stage for a regional framework that became more conducive to NPL resolution. When combined with national reforms, this strengthened EU framework helped significantly reduce NPL ratios in euro area countries. The case studies highlight lessons, including the importance of comprehensive definition of distressed assets, provisioning guidelines, and supervisory guidance to banks on NPL management as preconditions for effective resolution.

Part 4: Policy Strategies for Nonperforming Loan Resolution and Market Development in Asia and Europe

In **Chapter 7**, *John Fell, Maciej Grodzicki, Reiner Martin,* and *Edward O'Brien* examine why NPL resolution in Europe after the European sovereign debt crisis was initially very slow. They take stock of the key elements of a comprehensive NPL resolution approach and elaborate on the benefits of European regional cooperation. The authors highlight the regional dimension of NPLs in Europe even if not all countries are affected to the same extent and stress the need for a comprehensive approach to ensure a speedy resolution of distressed assets. This encompasses supervisory, macroprudential, and structural measures and coordination across European countries. They also make the case that system-wide national AMCs can help to meaningfully reduce large, systemic NPL stocks in the region. Resolution strategies require well-developed legal and administrative frameworks, sound lending standards, and strong macrofinancial policies to promote post-crisis recovery. The importance of these frameworks and interventions is expected to mount as the present pandemic persists.

In **Chapter 8**, *Junkyu Lee, Cyn-Young Park, Daekeun Park,* and *Peter Rosenkranz* propose frameworks and strategies for developing NPL markets nationally and regionally in Asia and the Pacific to strengthen financial resilience and promote financial development. The chapter discusses the demand-side, supply-side, and structural impediments to NPL market development and draws on lessons from country case studies on developing NPL markets in Asia. This policy chapter presents elements of a forward-looking strategy to develop NPL markets and NPL resolution frameworks in Asia and the Pacific, including the need for an enabling legal and judicial environment, strengthened supervision, and the role of out-of-court corporate workouts. It also discusses options for establishing public AMCs and/or NPL trading platforms, utilizing securitization schemes, while also highlighting the role of regional cooperation as part of a holistic strategy for the development of distressed asset markets in Asia.

Abbreviations

AMC	–	asset management company
ASEAN+3	–	Association of Southeast Asian Nations+3, includes the 10 members of the ASEAN (Brunei Darussalam, Cambodia, Indonesia, Lao People's Democratic Republic Malaysia, Myanmar, the Philippines, Singapore, Thailand, and Viet Nam) plus the People's Republic of China, Japan, and the Republic of Korea
BCBS	–	Basel Committee on Banking Supervision
BIS	–	Bank for International Settlements
BOT	–	Bank of Thailand
BRRD	–	Bank Recovery and Resolution Directive
CAR	–	capital adequacy ratio
CESEE	–	Central, Eastern, and Southeastern Europe
COVID-19	–	coronavirus disease
CRR	–	Capital Requirements Regulation
EA ratio	–	equity-to-assets ratio
EBA	–	European Banking Authority
ECB	–	European Central Bank
ECB SDW	–	European Central Bank's Statistical Data Warehouse
ESM	–	European Stability Mechanism
ESRB	–	European Systemic Risk Board
EU	–	European Union
FEVD	–	forecast error variance decomposition
FROB	–	Fund for Orderly Bank Restructuring (in Spain)
FSB	–	Financial Stability Board
GACS	–	Fondo di Garanzia sulla Cartolarizzazione delle Sofferenze, a securitization guarantee issued by Italy's Ministry of Economics and Finance

GDP	–	gross domestic product
GMM	–	generalized method of moments
IBRA	–	Indonesia Bank Restructuring Agency
IFRS	–	International Financial Reporting Standard
IMF	–	International Monetary Fund
IPAF	–	International Public AMC Forum
KAMCO	–	Korean Asset Management Corporation
LA ratio	–	loans-to-assets ratio
MPP	–	macroprudential policy
NAMA	–	National Asset Management Agency (in Ireland)
NFC	–	nonfinancial corporation
NPL	–	nonperforming loan
OECD	–	Organisation for Economic Co-operation and Development
OUSA	–	subsidiary established by commercial banks to manage NPLs in Kazakhstan
PRC	–	People's Republic of China
RBS	–	Royal Bank of Scotland
ROE	–	return on equity
SAREB	–	Sociedad de Gestión de Activos Procedentes de la Reestructuración Bancaria (Assets Arising from Bank Restructuring), Spain's asset management company
SME	–	small and medium-sized enterprises
SNB	–	Swiss National Bank
SOE	–	state-owned enterprise
SPV	–	special purpose vehicle
SSM	–	Single Supervisory Mechanism
TAMC	–	Thai Asset Management Company
TARP	–	Troubled Asset Relief Program (in the US)
UK	–	United Kingdom
US	–	United States
VAMC	–	Vietnam Asset Management Company
VAR	–	vector autoregression
VDATC	–	Vietnam Debt and Asset Trading Corporation
VIX	–	Volatility Index

PART

1

*Summary of Nonperforming Loan Trends
and Lessons from Three Decades
of Crisis Resolution in Asia and Europe*

1

Trends of Nonperforming Loans in Asia and Europe

Maciej Grodzicki, Reiner Martin, Cyn-Young Park, and Peter Rosenkranz[1]

1.1 Introduction

Nonperforming loans (NPLs) are an almost permanent feature of any banking sector. But in certain conditions, they become a serious problem for financial sectors and economies. Indeed, rapid credit growth followed by persistently high NPLs often accompany financial crisis. In East and Southeast Asia, NPLs rose sharply during and after the Asian financial crisis in the late 1990s, whereas the peak of the European NPL problem—particularly the euro area—was associated with the global financial crisis starting in 2008 and the subsequent euro area sovereign debt crisis, which began in 2010.

This chapter highlights the main features of NPL developments in Asia and Europe over the last 3 decades, examining both their commonalities and considerable heterogeneity between and within the regions.

NPLs are an unavoidable part of the banking business, although prudent bank lending standards can go a long way in making sure that only a small fraction of loans become nonperforming during their lifetime. Trying to avoid NPLs completely, however, appears almost impossible and would likely result in undesirably low levels of credit and economic activity, notably in most Asian and European economies, which are still characterized by relatively bank-centric financial systems.

[1] The views expressed are those of the authors alone and do not necessarily reflect the view of the Eurosystem or its members, the Joint Vienna Institute, or the Asian Development Bank. The authors thank Monica Melchor and Alyssa Villanueva for their excellent research assistance.

Banks are the main providers of corporate finance, both in Asia and in the euro area. In 2019, bank credit to firms relative to gross domestic product (GDP) stood at over 120% in Asia, exceeding the combined contributions of corporate bonds and stock markets to corporate financing (Figure 1.1). In the euro area, loans to nonfinancial firms fluctuated around 65% of GDP for most of the last decade, having increased from just over 50% in 1999. Despite having more than doubled in terms of GDP over the last 20 years, the corporate bond market remained a small part of corporate finance in both regions.

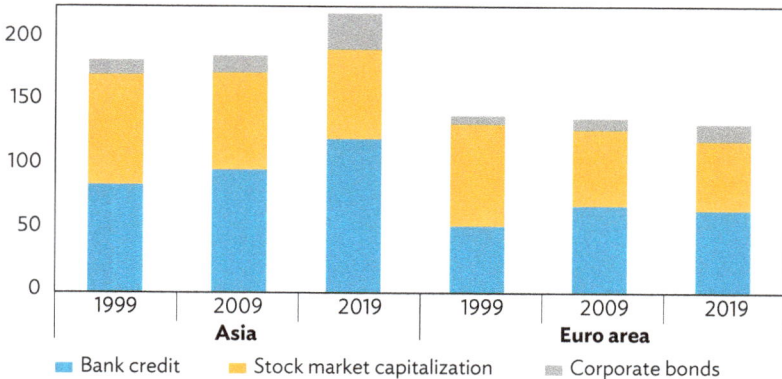

Figure 1.1: Corporate Financing Asia and Euro Area
(% of GDP)

GDP = gross domestic product.
Notes:
(i)   Asia includes Australia, India, Indonesia, Japan, Malaysia, the Philippines, the People's Republic of China (PRC), the Republic of Korea, Thailand, and Viet Nam.
(ii) The euro area includes Austria, Belgium, Cyprus, Estonia, Finland, France, Germany, Greece, Ireland, Italy, Latvia, Lithuania, Luxembourg, Malta, Netherlands, Portugal, Slovak Republic, Slovenia, and Spain.
(iii) 1999 corporate bond data as of 2000 for Malaysia, the Philippines, the Republic of Korea, Thailand, and Viet Nam. 1999 stock market capitalization data as of 2000 for Viet Nam; as of 2003 for the PRC and India. 1999 bank credit data as of 2000 for Japan; as of 2001 for the Philippines; as of 2002 for Australia; as of 2003 for Indonesia and Thailand.
(iv) 2009 corporate data as of 2010 for India. 2009 stock market capitalization data as of 2010 for Indonesia.
Sources: *AsianBondsOnline;* CEIC; Haver Analytics; European Central Bank Statistical Data Warehouse; national sources (accessed September 2020).

The dominance of bank finance in Asia and the euro area underpins the importance of efficient NPL resolution frameworks in these regions. Banks burdened with high NPLs may be unable to financially intermediate and thus support economic activity, while market-based finance may not yet be sufficiently well-developed to substitute for them. As other chapters show, empirical evidence from both Asia and the euro area suggests that high NPLs tend to reduce bank lending and economic activity. Preventing elevated NPLs, particularly over an extended period, is therefore an important public policy objective.

The chapter provides a high-level review of NPL developments across Asia and the euro area over the last few decades. More specifically, the two regional sections of this chapter look at correlations between NPLs and key economic indicators (such as GDP growth and interest rates), at the structure of the NPL stock in Asia and the euro area, and at key features of the regional secondary NPL markets. It thus provides a background for the subsequent analytical and policy-oriented chapters of the book.[2]

We find that regional economic crises played a key role in the buildup and subsequent decline of NPLs in the two regions. Asia experienced a major peak in NPLs in the aftermath of the Asian financial crisis, and it took nearly a decade for NPLs to return to pre-crisis levels. In the euro area, the surge in NPLs was related to the global financial crisis and the subsequent euro area sovereign debt crisis, which started in 2008 and 2010, respectively, and severely affected several euro area countries, mainly in Southern Europe. Underneath these high-level NPL trends, however, are often very heterogeneous context-specific NPL developments, shaped by a range of idiosyncratic economic and political factors.

1.2 Developments in Asia

The Asian financial crisis of 1997–1998 was a watershed moment for NPLs and financial sector development. In a little over a year after the outbreak of that crisis, the aggregate GDP of Indonesia, Malaysia, the Philippines, the Republic of Korea, and Thailand fell by 30%. Consequently, NPL ratios in Southeast Asia rose significantly, with Indonesia and Thailand experiencing NPL ratios higher than 40% in 1998 (Table 1.1). NPL ratios in the crisis-hit economies came down to considerably lower levels in a decade, due to strong post-crisis reforms, a combination of micro- and macroprudential policies, and sound macroeconomic conditions. In most other Asian economies, NPL ratios were also under control by the late 2000s.

---

[2] Comparative analyses of NPLs over long periods are constrained by a lack of comparable data across countries as well as changes in the definition of NPLs over time. For most Asian and European countries, NPL data series start in the 1990s, although there are often material differences in the definitions used (for example, see the metadata for NPL figures collected as part of the International Monetary Fund's Financial Soundness Indicators [IMF 2006]). The European Banking Authority (EBA) in 2013 published a harmonized NPL definition for the member states of the European Union (EBA 2013). No comparably uniform definition exists for the chapter's Asian economies.

Table 1.1: Evolution of Bank NPLs in Asia
(% of gross loans)

Economy	1997	1998	1999	2000	2001	2002	2003	2004	2005	2006	2007	2008	2009	2010	2011	2012	2013	2014	2015	2016	2017	2018	2019
Central Asia																							
Afghanistan														49.9	4.7	5.0	4.9	7.8	12.1	11.1	12.2	8.9	
Armenia		6.0	8.0	17.5	24.4	9.9	5.4	2.1	2.0	2.4	2.4	4.3	4.9	3.0	3.4	3.7	4.5	7.0	8.0	6.7	5.4	4.8	5.1
Azerbaijan						28.0	21.5	15.1	9.5	7.2				3.5	4.7	6.0	5.7	4.5	4.4	5.3	13.8	12.2	5.1
Kazakhstan						11.9	8.4	4.3	3.3	2.4	2.7	7.1	18.9	20.9	20.7	19.4	19.5	12.4	8.0	6.7	9.3	7.4	8.1
Kyrgyz Republic		10.1	30.9	30.9	13.4	13.3	11.2	8.0		6.2	3.6	5.3	8.2	14.8	9.4	6.6	5.1	4.2	6.7	8.5	7.4	7.3	7.7
Tajikistan				5.2	3.0	5.1	5.2	3.6	3.3	1.1	0.7	2.3	44.3	7.6	6.8	6.4	8.6	11.6	17.2	26.6	21.6	21.2	
East Asia																							
Korea, Rep of.					2.8	1.9	2.0	1.6	1.0	0.7	0.6	0.9	0.8	1.1	0.9	1.0	1.2	1.0	1.0	1.1	0.9	0.7	0.6
Mongolia	19.7	31.0	50.5	21.9	6.7	5.1	4.8	6.4	5.8	4.9	3.3	7.2	17.4	11.5	5.8	4.2	5.3	5.0	7.4	8.5	8.5	10.4	10.1
PRC		28.5		22.4	29.8	26.0	20.4	13.2	8.6	7.1	6.2	2.4	1.6	1.1	1.0	1.0	1.0	1.2	1.7	1.7	1.7	1.8	1.9

continued on next page

Table 1.1 (continued)

Economy	1997	1998	1999	2000	2001	2002	2003	2004	2005	2006	2007	2008	2009	2010	2011	2012	2013	2014	2015	2016	2017	2018	2019
South Asia																							
Bangladesh		40.7	41.1	34.9	31.5	28.1	22.1	17.5	13.2	12.8	14.5				5.8	9.7	8.6	9.4	8.4	8.9	8.9	9.9	8.9
India	14.4	14.7	12.8	11.5	10.4	9.1	7.2	4.9	3.3	2.5	2.3	2.5	2.3	2.2	2.7	3.4	4.0	4.4	5.9	9.2	10.0	9.5	9.2
Maldives																20.9	17.6	17.5	14.1	10.6	10.5	8.9	9.4
Pakistan	24.0	23.0	26.0	24.0	23.0	22.0	17.0	12.0	9.0	7.3	7.4	9.1	12.2	14.8	16.2	14.5	13.0	12.3	11.4	10.1	8.4	8.0	8.6
Southeast Asia																							
Cambodia	7.2	16.2	14.5	12.4	8.4	14.8	13.9	10.3	7.8	9.9	3.4	3.7	4.8	3.1	2.3	2.2	2.3	1.6	1.6	2.1	2.1	2.0	1.6
Indonesia		48.6	32.9	34.4	31.9	24.0	6.8	4.5	7.3	5.9	4.0	3.2	3.3	2.5	2.1	1.8	1.7	2.1	2.4	2.9	2.6	2.3	2.4
Malaysia	4.1	18.6	16.6	15.4	17.8	15.9	13.9	11.7	9.4	8.5	6.5	4.8	3.6	3.4	2.7	2.0	1.9	1.7	1.6	1.6	1.6	1.5	1.5
Philippines	4.7	12.4	14.6	24.0	27.7	14.6	16.1	14.4	10.0	7.5	5.8	4.6	3.5	3.4	2.6	2.2	2.4	2.0	1.9	1.7	1.6	1.7	2.0
Thailand		42.9	38.6	17.7	11.5	16.5	13.5	11.9	9.1	7.8	7.6	5.6	5.2	3.9	2.9	2.4	2.3	2.3	2.7	3.0	3.1	3.1	3.1

NPL = nonperforming loan, PRC = People's Republic of China.

Note: White cells denote nonperforming ratios less than 5%, yellow between 5% and 10%, and orange higher than 10%. Blank cells mean data are not available.

Sources: Asian Development Bank calculations using data from Bank of Mongolia; CEIC Database; International Monetary Fund Financial Soundness Indicators. https://data.imf.org/; and World Bank World Development Indicators. http://databank.worldbank.org/data/reports.aspx?source=world-development-indicators (accessed June 2020).

However, in the aftermath of the global recession of 2008, distressed assets and the accompanying elevation in default risks and financial vulnerabilities increased in some countries, particularly in Central and South Asia, and in Mongolia. The NPL ratio reached 10.1% in Mongolia, due to a fall in prices of coal and natural resources after the global recession. A resurgence in these economies' NPL ratios was a cause for concern, as high NPLs can destabilize banking systems and undermine economic growth.

Examination of how NPL ratios evolved over the past 3 decades reveals two distinctive peaks during the Asian financial and global financial crises, especially for subregions affected directly by each crisis (Figure 1.2). The Asian financial crisis hit Southeast Asia hardest, while the euro area sovereign debt crisis a decade later hit Central Asia hardest.

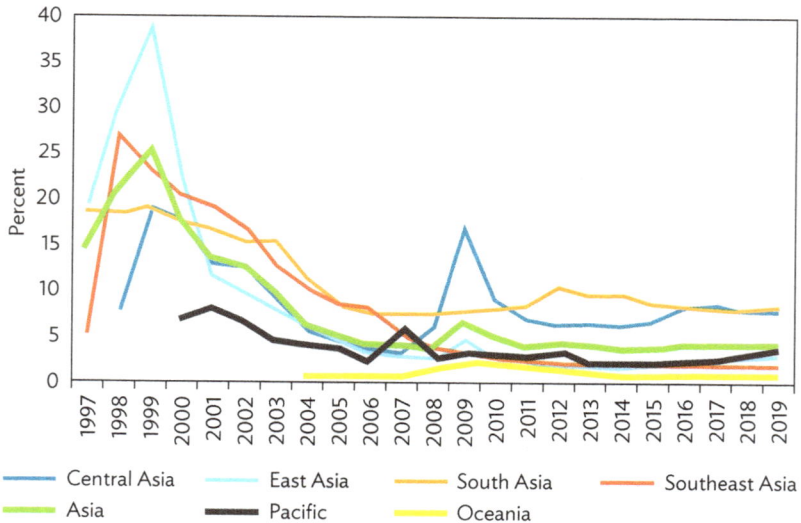

Figure 1.2: NPL Ratio by Subregion, 1997–2019

NPL = nonperforming loan.
Notes: Central Asia includes Armenia, Azerbaijan, Georgia, Kazakhstan, the Kyrgyz Republic, Tajikistan, and Uzbekistan. East Asia includes Hong Kong, China; Japan; Mongolia; the People's Republic of China; and the Republic of Korea. Oceania includes Australia. The Pacific includes Fiji and Papua New Guinea. South Asia includes Bangladesh, India, Maldives, Pakistan, and Sri Lanka. Southeast Asia includes Cambodia, Indonesia, Malaysia, the Philippines, Singapore, Thailand, and Viet Nam. Simple averages are reported.
Sources: Asian Development Bank calculations using data from Bank of Mongolia; CEIC Database; International Monetary Fund Financial Soundness Indicators. https://data.imf.org/; State Bank of Viet Nam; and World Bank World Development Indicators.http://databank.worldbank.org/data/reports.aspx?source=world-development-indicators (accessed September 2020).

On average, NPL ratios are lowest in East and Southeast Asia, at around 2%, together with Oceania and the Pacific. In Central and South Asia, NPL ratios remain relatively high, at 8%–10%, although they came down from the peak during the global financial crisis and the recession.

Notably, NPL ratios showed different patterns subregionally as they declined. In East Asia, the initial reduction was fast (falling from 39.5% to 11.9% in only 2 years) reflecting decisive post-Asian financial crisis reforms and political commitments. But in Southeast Asia, ratios went down more gradually (falling from 27.7% in 1998 to 12.8% in 2003 and taking another 5 years to come down to 3.6% in 2008), underscoring challenges of addressing high NPLs. Without direct crisis impact (and possibly no urgency and political will), NPL problems tend to persist even longer. In South Asia, the NPL ratio peaked at 19.4% in 1999 but was brought down to only 15.4% in 2003 and again to 7.5% in 2008. In Central Asia, the NPL ratio also came down slowly from its peak of 19.5% in 1999 to 9.0% in 2003 and again to 3.3% in 2007, before resurging to 17.4% in 2009 in the aftermath of the euro area sovereign debt crisis and a global recession. These experiences altogether also highlight the importance of timely resolution of NPL problems to avoid NPL overhangs.

In most economies that experience high NPLs, adverse macroeconomic conditions are important factors. The global financial crisis and the recession that followed exposed the vulnerabilities of the banking systems in many countries in Central Asia. Bank credit also grew rapidly in many of them in the years before the global financial crisis, spurred by favorable macroeconomic conditions. In 2008–2009, global oil prices fell sharply, however, undermining corporate profits and economic outlooks. NPLs rose sharply, compromising banking sector health and slowing the recovery with credit constraints.

These crisis episodes highlight the importance of macrofinancial linkages. Credit risks rise as macroeconomic conditions deteriorate and interest payments rise. Conversely, a deterioration in banks' balance sheets may feed back into the economy as banks tighten credit conditions. While the macroeconomic impact is significant for NPL ratios, bank-specific factors cannot be overlooked.

The coronavirus disease (COVID-19) crisis magnifies concerns over NPL overhangs. Countries' NPL ratios are expected to rise significantly with the unfolding of the pandemic and may well persist beyond the crisis period unless managed in a timely manner. These expectations call for policy measures to cushion the impact of COVID-19 on the banking sector and the economy in general.

Figure 1.3 illustrates the negative relationship between NPLs and economic growth, hinting at the possible harmful real economic effects associated with NPLs. From 2000 to 2017, changes in NPL ratios and GDP growth across different Asian subregions were negatively correlated. During the same period, Asian economies saw a positive relationship between the change in the NPL ratio and the change in interest rates.

Figure 1.3: NPL Ratios, GDP Growth, and Interest Rates in Asia, 1997–2019

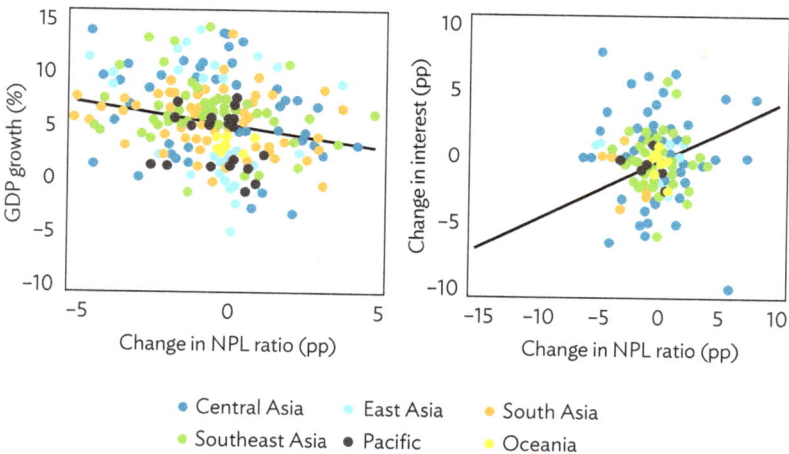

GDP = gross domestic product, NPL = nonperforming loan, pp = percentage point.
Note: Interest rates refer to central bank policy rates.
Sources: Asian Development Bank calculations using data from the Bank of Mongolia; CEIC Database; International Monetary Fund Financial Soundness Indicators. https://data.imf.org/; State Bank of Viet Nam; and World Bank World Development Indicators.http://databank.worldbank.org/data/reports.aspx?source=world-development-indicators (accessed September 2020).

Persistently high NPLs in some Asian economies might be attributed to various impediments to NPL resolution, which later chapters detail. Among these is the lack in Asia of well-developed NPL markets in which banks can dispose of distressed assets. While some economies have set up NPL markets to allow financial institutions, private asset management companies, and NPL investors to trade distressed assets, most Asian economies lack such markets due to legal, accounting, and institutional deficiencies.

A few economies have established and nurtured the growth of domestic NPL markets, however, such as the People's Republic of China (PRC), where, in 2018, the value of NPLs traded in secondary markets exceeded $56 billion (Deloitte 2019). This is comparable to values traded in the euro area. Figure 1.4 illustrates the stock of outstanding NPLs held by banks in selected Asian economies in 2016 and 2018, indicating their potential for growing NPL markets.

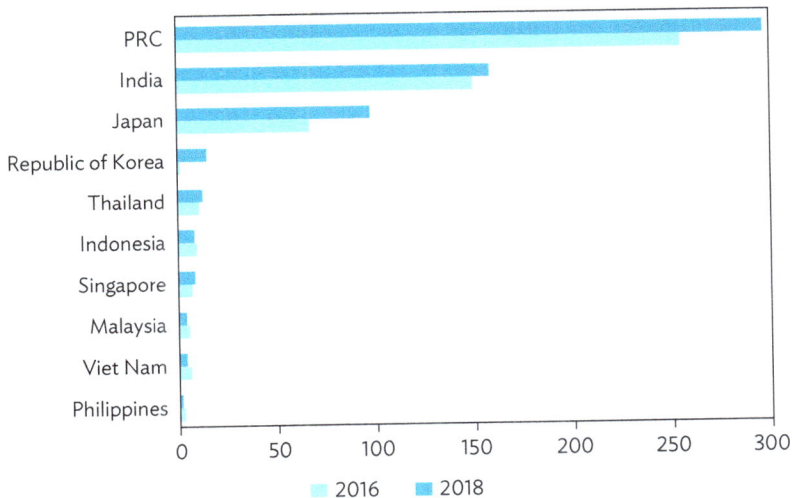

**Figure 1.4: Potential NPL Market Size
of Selected Asian Economies, 2016 and 2018**
($ billion)

NPL = nonperforming loan, PRC = People's Republic of China.
Note: 2016 NPL data was based on 2017 data for the PRC and the Republic of Korea.
Sources: Data is from Deloitte (2018) and Deloitte (2019).

1.3 Developments in the Euro Area

NPL levels in the euro area ranged between 2.5% and 5% for most of the last 2 decades, reaching their lowest levels in 2006 and 2007 (Figure 1.5). The declining trend in euro area NPLs reversed with the beginning of the global financial crisis, while the euro area sovereign debt crisis contributed to the rise from 2011. The ratio peaked in 2014 at just over 8% before gradually falling back to 2.9% by 2020.

For most of the period under review, the euro area NPL ratio remained substantially above NPL ratios in other large, advanced economies, such as the United States (US) and the United Kingdom. This suggests—as in Asia— the presence of long-standing structural weaknesses in the NPL resolution regimes in several euro area countries, e.g., relatively less efficient insolvency and debt recovery regimes. Despite recent positive developments, the euro area NPL ratio in 2020 remained about three times above equivalent ratios in Japan, the United Kingdom, and the US.

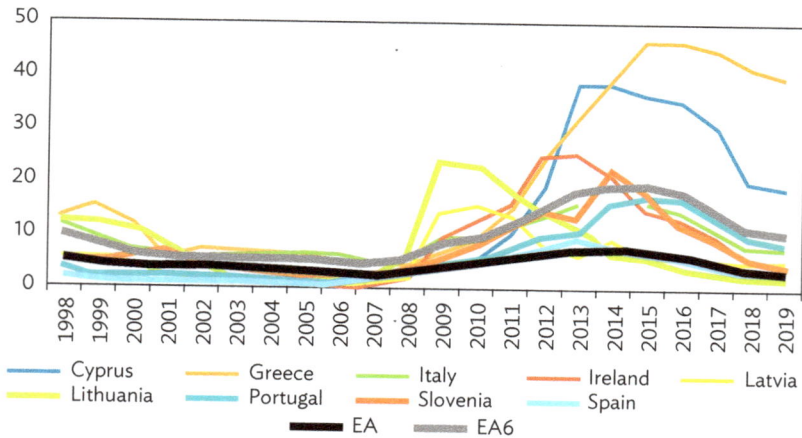

Figure 1.5: NPL Ratios in the Euro Area and Selected Member Countries, 1998–2019

EA = euro area, NPL = nonperforming loan.
Notes: The individual country series are shown only for countries where the NPL ratio exceeded the euro area average for more than 2 years. EA refers to the euro area in the constant 2019 composition. EA6 is the weighted average figure for Cyprus, Greece, Ireland, Italy, Portugal, and Slovenia. Other highlighted countries in the chart are Latvia, Lithuania, and Spain.
Sources: International Monetary Fund and European Central Bank data.

The euro area average NPL figure masks substantial differences across the 19 euro area countries. After the euro area sovereign debt crisis started, shares of nonperforming assets increased rapidly in several euro area countries. Cyprus, Greece, Ireland, Italy, Portugal, and Slovenia (the EA6 countries) all experienced double-digit NPL figures, peaking at close to 50% in Greece and close to 40% in Cyprus.[3] Spain came close to an NPL

---

[3]   Latvia and Lithuania were not members of the euro area when they experienced a large increase in NPLs, starting in 2008. They adopted the euro in 2014 and 2015, respectively. Similar to other Central, Eastern, and Southeastern European countries, the global financial crisis hit them hard (see Gardó and Martin 2010). The steep rise of NPLs in these economies was swiftly reversed, as the Baltic economies recovered and proved to be rather flexible.

ratio of 10%. Starting in 2014, NPL ratios started to decline again in all these economies, but the speed of decline varied significantly. In 2020, Cyprus, Greece, Italy, and Portugal still had NPL ratios of more than 5%.

Turning to macrofinancial conditions, Figure 1.6 illustrates correlations between GDP growth, long-term interest rates, and changes in the NPL ratios of euro area countries between 1999 and 2019.

Figure 1.6: NPL Ratios, GDP Growth, and Long-Term Interest Rates across Euro Area Countries, 1999–2019

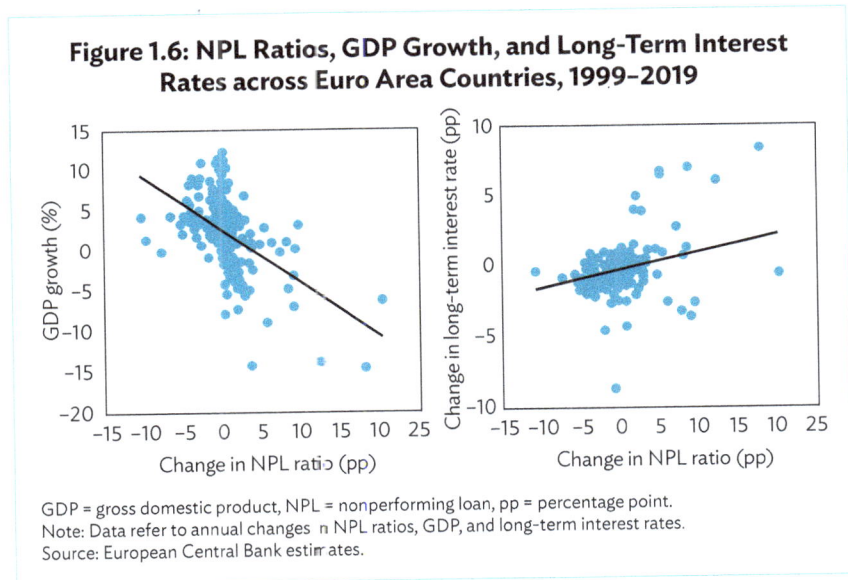

GDP = gross domestic product, NPL = nonperforming loan, pp = percentage point.
Note: Data refer to annual changes in NPL ratios, GDP, and long-term interest rates.
Source: European Central Bank estimates.

As expected, the left-hand panel shows a strong negative correlation between annual changes in NPL ratios and annual GDP growth rates. Moreover, the correlation between changes in economic development and credit defaults appears to be rather fast, given that there is no lag structure in Figure 1.6. The right-hand panel shows a positive correlation between annual changes in NPL ratios and changes in long-term interest rates. The link between increasing interest rates and rising credit defaults is, however, relatively weaker than the correlation between GDP growth and NPLs. The European patterns are in line with those in Asia.

To understand NPL patterns across euro area countries, it is useful to look in more detail at the structure of the NPL stock in the euro area—in particular, the sector composition, the age of the NPLs, and the extent to which NPLs are covered by provisions and collateral.[4]

---

[4]   On a comparable basis across all euro area countries, such detailed information is only available from 2014.

Figure 1.7 looks at the NPL composition by main asset classes—nonfinancial corporations, commercial real estate, mortgages, other retail loans, and other loans, which can be seen here as a residual item. The left- and right-hand panels show the situation in 2014 and 2019, respectively.

Figure 1.7: NPL Ratios—Contributions by Sector, 2014 and 2019

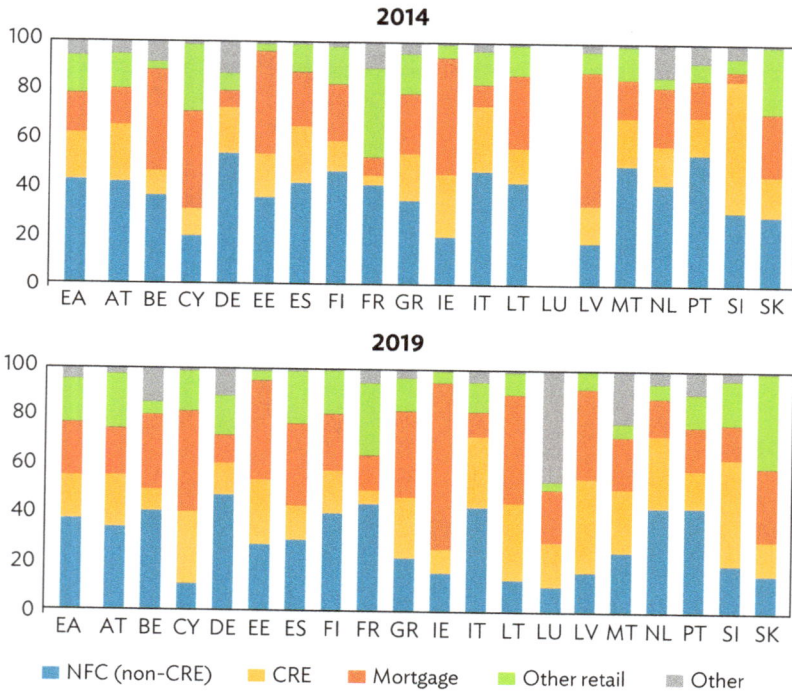

AT = Austria, BE = Belgium, CRE = commercial real estate, CY = Cyprus, DE = Denmark, EA = euro area, EE = Estonia, ES = Spain, FI = Finland, FR = France, GR = Greece, IE = Ireland, LT = Lithuania, LU = Luxembourg, LV = Latvia, MT = Malta, NFC = nonfinancial corporations, NL = Netherlands, NPL = nonperforming loan, PT = Portugal, SI = Slovenia, SK = Slovakia.
Note: 2014 data for Luxembourg is not available.
Source: European Central Bank supervisory data.

For the euro area as a whole, corporate lending—including loans backed by commercial real estate—accounted for nearly two-thirds of the NPL stock in 2014, but its share declined to about 55% by 2019. The share of mortgages, which are more challenging to work out, increased somewhat between 2014 and 2019. Differences between the euro area countries are pronounced. The share of nonfinancial corporation loans ranges from around 10% in some smaller euro area countries to above 40% in many larger economies. Comparable wide-ranging differences can be observed for the other categories, despite their smaller average share in the euro area average. Overall, the contributions by sector are very heterogeneous and suggest a need for country-specific resolution strategies.

Turning to the age structure of NPLs across the euro area, Figure 1.8 shows different NPL age brackets: (i) "unlikely to pay" loans, (ii) loans that were in arrears between 3 months and 1 year, and (iii) loans that were in arrears for more than 1 year.[5] An additional category, loans in arrears for more than 5 years, was released in 2019.

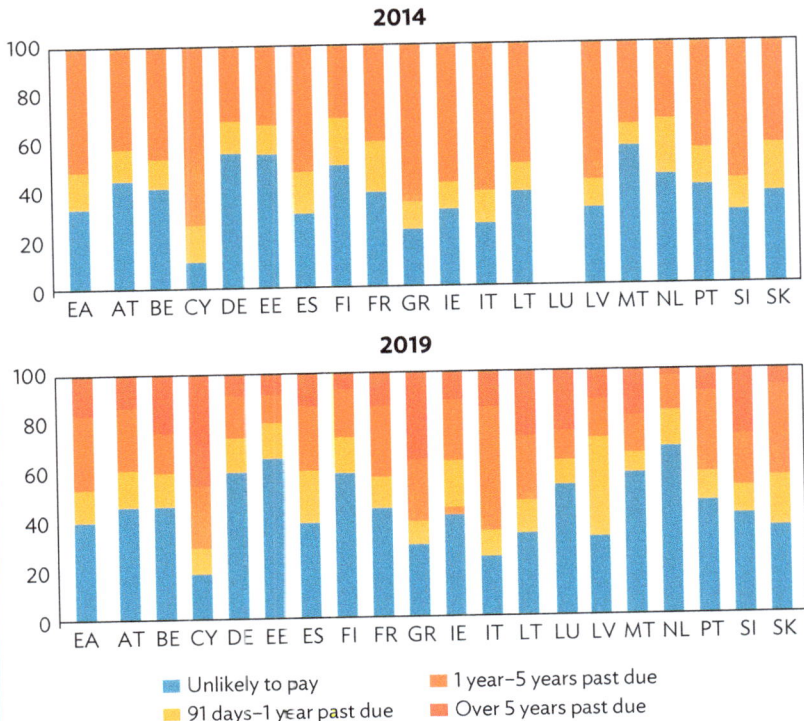

Figure 1.8: NPL Stock by Age, 2014 and 2019

AT= Austria, BE = Belgium, CY = Cyprus, DE = Denmark, EA = euro area, EE = Estonia, ES = Spain, FI = Finland, FR = France, GR = Greece, IE = Ireland, LT = Lithuania, LU = Luxembourg, LV = Latvia, MT = Malta, NL = Netherlands, NPL = nonperforming loan, PT = Portugal, SI = Slovenia, SK = Slovakia.
Source: European Central Bank supervisory data.

---

[5]   Loans classified as unlikely to pay continue to be serviced with a delay of less than 90 days and are considered nonperforming on the basis of other data about the borrower's expected ability to repay the loan. For example, classification as unlikely to pay may be triggered by a reduction in the borrower's cash flows, initiation of insolvency proceedings, or extension of forbearance measures, which would not normally be granted to a performing borrower.

Looking at the euro area as a whole, around half of the NPL stock has been in default for more than 1 year—and around 17% for more than 5 years. As the overall NPL stock halved, the share of old NPLs declined slightly between 2014 and 2019, whereas the share of unlikely to pay and recent NPLs increased slightly. Moreover, differences between euro area countries are pronounced. The share of unlikely to pay in total problem loans ranges from under 20% to almost 70%. Swift measures to cure these loans can effectively prevent a subsequent increase in the NPL ratio. In Cyprus, Greece, Italy, and Latvia, however—with NPL levels above 5%—more than half of the NPL stock is older than 1 year, suggesting that the NPL resolution process in these countries is slow and the likelihood that these loans will be resolved is particularly low.

The final structural NPL indicator is the share of NPLs covered by provisions and collateral (Figure 1.9).

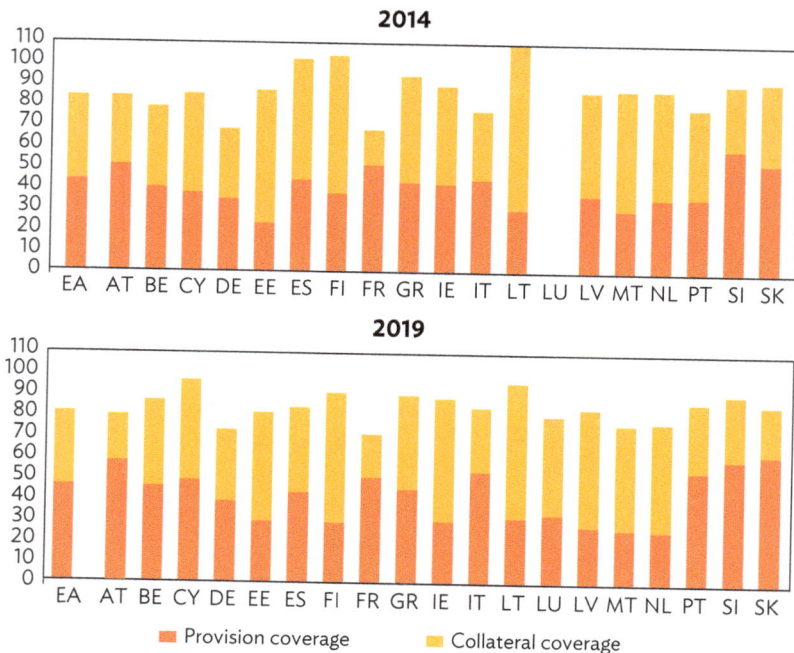

Figure 1.9: Share of NPLs Covered by Provisions and Collateral, 2014 and 2019

AT = Austria, BE = Belgium, CY = Cyprus, DE = Denmark, EA = euro area, EE = Estonia, ES = Spain, FI = Finland, FR = France, GR = Greece, IE = Ireland, LT = Lithuania, LU = Luxembourg, LV = Latvia, MT = Malta, NL = Netherlands, NPL = nonperforming loan, PT = Portugal, SI = Slovenia, SK = Slovakia. Source: European Central Bank supervisory data.

The overall coverage of euro area NPLs by provisions and collateral remained relatively stable over time In 2019, provisions stood at around 46% of NPL gross book value, with a further 34% of gross book value covered by collateral. From a bank management perspective, provisions represent a measure of incurred losses on the NPLs, while collateral provides additional protection and a source of intrinsic value of NPLs. However, the presence of collateral exposes banks to the valuation risks, often related to the state of the property market, and to uncertain costs of enforcing and disposing of collateral.[6] The relative importance of provisions and collateral differs across countries. The cross-country heterogeneity is, however, less pronounced than for other structural indicators. The share of gross book value covered by provisions has significantly increased in most euro area countries with elevated NPL ratios, suggesting that the resolution of these loans will be easier for the affected banks.

An important indicator for the agility of NPL resolution frameworks is the level of activity of the secondary NPL market—i.e., the amount of NPLs that banks are selling to other (normally nonbank) market participants. During the early years of the peak NPL period in the euro area, starting around 2009, secondary NPL markets were not very active. Even around the time when NPLs peaked in the euro area, Deloitte (2016) and KPMG (2016) highlighted that despite a stock of some 2 trillion euros in noncore assets on bank balance sheets (of which about 50% were NPLs), annual transactions only amounted to slightly more than 100 billion euros.

Figure 1.10 looks at recent secondary market NPL transactions in euro area countries with elevated NPL ratios.[7] Starting from still very low levels in 2015, NPL transactions gained traction in the second half of 2016, driven, among other things, by the strong cyclical upswing in the euro area economy from around 2015, before declining again in 2019. Most of the transactions took place in the largest NPL markets—by absolute size rather than by NPL share—Italy and Spain. Some transactions, however, were also recorded in the other high-NPL euro area countries. Regulatory pressure, which forced banks to develop NPL reduction strategies, and—in the case of Italy—government support to NPL securitizations, contributed to the increase in NPL sales.

---

[6] Collateral is highly dependent on timely and accurate valuation. Moreover, the t me needed and costs incurred to liquidate collateral vary substantially by country, depending, in particular, on the quality of the legal system and insolvency frameworks, as well as on loan documentation.

[7] Figure 1.10 data are based on publicly available information and may thus, to some extent, underestimate the true activity on the euro area secondary NPL market.

Figure 1.10: NPL Market Transactions, 2015–2019

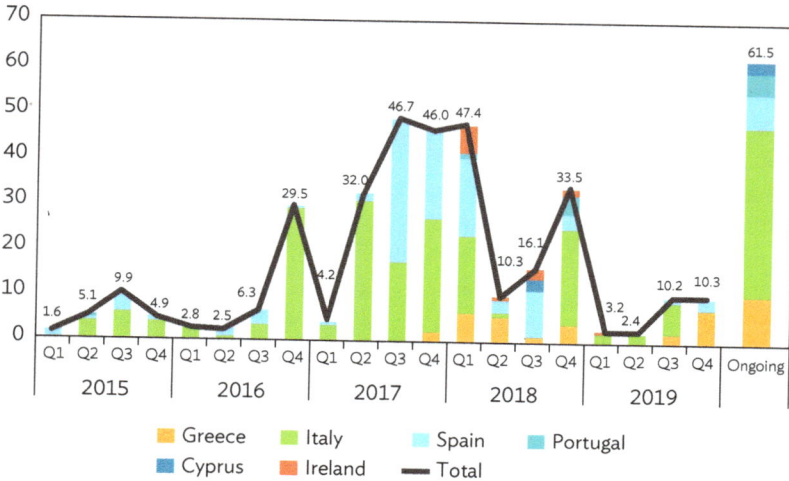

NPL = nonperforming loan, Q = quarter.
Note: Amounts in billions of euros. "Ongoing" refers to transactions which were in progress at end-2019.
Source: European Central Bank staff calculations.

Various reasons explain the lack of agility in the secondary euro area NPL market, ranging from the pricing of NPLs on banks' balance sheets, through the market structure, to framework conditions such as the length of insolvency procedures or even outright prohibitions to sell loans to nonbanks. All of these factors contribute to a gap between the price investors are willing to pay for NPLs and the price for which banks are willing to sell (e.g., see Fell et al. 2016). This so-called "bid-ask spread," along with policy options, is discussed in more detail in Chapter 7 (euro area) and Chapter 8 (Asia).

1.4 Conclusions

The regional financial and economic crises of recent decades severely affected Asian and European financial markets. Over 2 decades ago, the Asian financial crisis triggered an increase in NPLs, particularly in East and Southeast Asia. A decade later, elevated NPLs across Europe, particularly Southern Europe, followed the global financial crisis. Possible macroeconomic implications associated with a buildup in distressed assets call for investigation, as NPLs are negatively correlated with GDP and positively correlated with interest rates. This pattern played out both in Asia and in Europe.

A decade after the Asian financial crisis, NPLs declined substantially in Southeast Asia, largely owing to strengthened financial regulation, favorable economic development, and generally enhanced banking sector resilience. While NPL ratios stabilized at low levels across most of Asia during the economic boom around the mid-2000s, they spiked after the global financial crisis in many economies, especially in Central and South Asia and in Mongolia. NPL ratios also increased significantly in Europe, due to the euro area sovereign debt crisis, and have not yet returned to the pre-crisis levels, highlighting the strong persistence of NPL ratios.

NPL market development is slowly progressing as policy makers start to address the impediments to NPL management and resolution. At present, secondary markets across developing Asia are still largely underdeveloped and progress in NPL resolution is uneven. In Europe, a regional NPL market—while better developed—lacks agility, calling for policy makers to address issues in bid-ask spreads.

The current COVID-19 pandemic casts a shadow over the global economy. It exposes Asia and Europe to financial vulnerabilities, with looming problems associated with deteriorating debt quality. Policy makers need to pay close attention and prepare for possible buildups in NPLs triggered after the pandemic passes. As temporary relief measures are lifted, corporate defaults may materialize, heightening bank exposure to distressed assets. Potential rises in the NPL ratios, alongside elevated debt and default risks, are significant risks to banking sector health, which could slow economic recovery post-COVID-19.

References

Asian Development Bank (ADB). 2017. 20 Years After the Asian Financial Crisis Lessons Learned and Future Challenges. *ADB Briefs*. No. 85. Manila.

Deloitte. 2016. *Deleveraging Europe 2015–2016*. London: Deloitte.

_____. 2018. *Deleveraging Asia 2018*. London: Deloitte.

_____. 2019. *Deleveraging Asia September 2019*. London: Deloitte.

European Banking Authority (EBA). 2013. *Final Draft Technical Standards on NPLs and Forbearance*. Technical Report. Paris: EBA.

Fell, J., M. Grodzicki, R. Martin, and E. O'Brien. 2016. Addressing Market Failures in the Resolution of Loans in the Euro Area. *European Central Bank Financial Stability Review*. November. pp. 134–146.

Gardó, S. and R. Martin. 2010. *The Impact of the Global Economic and Financial Crisis on Central, Eastern and South-Eastern Europe: A Stock-Taking Exercise*. Occasional Paper 114. Frankfurt: European Central Bank.

International Monetary Fund (IMF). 2006. *Financial Soundness Indicators Compilation Guide*. Technical Report. Washington, DC: IMF.

KPMG. 2016. *European Debt Sales Report*. Amstelveen, Netherlands: KPMG International Cooperative.

2 Lessons from Three Decades of Banking Crisis Resolution: Overstating Moral Hazard?

Douglas Arner, Emilios Avgouleas, and Evan Gibson

2.1 Introduction

Banking crises are commonly caused by over-extended loan books and high leverage ratios that stress bank balance sheets when the economic cycle contracts (Geanakoplos 2009, 2010). When an economy expands, credit standards tend to be relaxed, causing asset prices to increase above so-called fundamental values. Default risk rises and banks tighten credit standards, which increases the cost of credit. Borrowers with high credit default risk are forced to deleverage by selling assets, which places downward pressure on asset prices (Brunnermeier et al. 2009). If asset sales are widespread, this will trigger fire sales and bank defaults preceding a financial crisis (Kiyotaki and Moore 1997).[1]

Over-extended loan books transform into high levels of nonperforming loans (NPLs) and the ensuing debt overhang dampens growth while the credit cycle stalls when demand for credit is greatest (Avgouleas 2015). As the economy enters recession, banks must manage balance sheet and liquidity stress, and potential insolvency.[2]

---

[1] Naturally, causality is reciprocal.

[2] Minsky (1992) and Board of Governors of the US Federal Reserve System (Federal Reserve 1970).

The measure of bank losses from NPLs is reflected on the balance sheet—normally the difference between an asset's book value (i.e., net present value plus provisions) and the ultimate recovery amount (i.e., loss given default).[3] The recovery amount is contingent on the borrower restructuring its debt contract, or the market, if the distressed asset or collateral is liquidated. Loss given default is minimized where the legal system is functioning in a pro-creditor environment (including judicial and extra judicial proceedings) and loan recovery or asset disposal procedures are not burdensome or obstructive.

If the bank adopts prudent loss-provisioning policies prior to an NPL disposal or writing-off an exposure, any loss will be absorbed by the bank's capital base. Inadequate loan-loss provisioning will hurt bank profitability because a portion of the bank's assets will become contra assets or an expense, eroding its capital reserves. High NPLs weigh on bank liquidity and, in the extreme solvency, can disrupt financial stability and economic growth (Avgouleas 2020).

In this environment, central banks can dampen credit demand by *inter alia* tightening monetary policy, raising countercyclical and other prudential requirements to restrict balance sheet growth, and place caps on loan-to-value ratios and debt-to-income limits—the core of macroprudential policy (Claessens 2014). At the same time, to understand the potential solvency risks for financial institutions and, if necessary, to take appropriate actions to stabilize bank balance sheets, regulators need the tools and expertise to identify NPLs. Ideally, regulators—in normal times—should compel banks to take preventive measures comprising: (i) high loan pre-provisioning, (ii) appropriate loan-to-income and loan-to-value ratios, (iii) macroprudential capital buffers, (iv) bail-in tools and bailable capital instruments, (v) debt service coverage ratios, (vi) NPL ratios, and (vii) limits on NPL volumes.[4]

---

[3] In the simplest terms: "Net present value is the present value of the cash flows at the required rate of return of your project compared to your initial investment, or ROI [return on investment], for a project or expenditure" (Gallo 2014).

$$NPV = \sum_{t=1}^{N} \frac{Cash\ flow_t}{(1+i)^t} - initial\ investment$$

Where "N" is the total number of time periods for the cash flow being discounted, "t" is the duration of the cash flow period, and "i" is the discount or interest rate.

[4] This chapter uses NPL ratios primarily sourced from the World Bank.

In addition to reducing the likelihood of banking failures, managing NPLs stabilizes balance sheets that will enable banks to extend new credit, which is crucial for economic activity and restoring profitability. Bank recapitalizations become tenable, reducing the likelihood of taxpayers being ultimately liable, while strengthening financial stability and reducing systemic risk. Arguably, the most effective approach to stabilizing a banking system inundated with high NPL ratios is to realize a legal transfer of NPLs to an asset management company (AMC) under a framework that is sufficiently transparent to ameliorate information asymmetries and properly structured to minimize seller's long-term loss without giving rise to egregious moral hazard. This chapter analyzes empirical evidence from three major banking crises to explain why restructuring banks' balance sheets is the most effective approach for rescuing a banking system. Examples and empirical evidence are drawn from countries most affected by banking crises in Asia, the European Union (EU), and the United States (US).

The importance of these findings cannot be underestimated, especially during the COVID-19 pandemic and its economic fallout. In the current global environment of pandemic-driven lockdowns coupled with unprecedented supply and demand shocks, a surge of NPLs is widely expected that will greatly impair the functionality of banking systems in developed and developing economies. The analysis and identification of the most effective bank stabilization remedy, the structured use of AMCs despite moral hazard risk, is of cardinal importance and at the forefront of the global financial stability debate as well as the post-pandemic economic recovery.

This chapter is divided into six sections following the introduction. Section 2.2 defines and discusses the regulatory treatment, causes, and consequences of NPLs. Section 2.3 discusses systemic bank resolution standards and moral hazard. Section 2.4 analyzes the 1997 Asian financial crisis, focusing on the resolution approaches used in Indonesia, Malaysia, the Republic of Korea, and Thailand. This includes a study of AMCs and recent resolution measures in the People's Republic of China (PRC). Section 2.5 examines the bailout of UBS, Royal Bank of Scotland (RBS), and Citigroup during the 2008 global financial crisis. Section 2.6 analyzes the 2010 eurozone debt crisis in Greece, Ireland, Italy, and Spain. Section 2.7 concludes.

2.2 Identification, Treatment, Causes, and Consequences of Nonperforming Loans

The first step in rescuing a banking system is prevention, although historically prevention alone has proved insufficient. Significant work over the past 20 years has led to the development of additional mechanisms, although there is no consensus among regulators (Weber et al. 2014). For example, views vary on the most effective approach to resolve systemically important banks (Arner and Norton 2009). When prevention is unsuccessful and NPLs increase, defining and identifying NPLs is an obvious starting point and critical for mitigating banking system weakness, but one where there is often a surprising lack of clarity.

2.2.1 Nonperforming Loans: Definition, Regulatory Issues, and Accounting Treatment

Systemizing an NPL definition is problematic because the extent of nonperformance varies, resulting in different types of delinquent loans. The Basel Committee on Banking Supervision (BCBS) focuses on exposures' delinquency status and, thus, it defines a nonperforming exposure as loans and debt securities (i) that have defaulted under the Basel II framework, (ii) are credit impaired according to the applicable accounting framework, and (iii) are more than 90 days past due (BCBS 2017). A Basel II default uses a similar definition to the International Monetary Fund (IMF)—a default on principal and interest that lasts more than 90 days.[5] In the EU, the definition is more expansive, being implemented in the post-eurozone crisis environment, which was important for harmonizing supervision across member states. The definition used by the European Banking Authority (EBA) includes the realization of collateral—(i) material exposures which are more than 90 days past due, and (ii) the debtor is assessed as unlikely to pay its credit obligations in full without realization of collateral, regardless of existence of any past-due amount or number of days past due (EBA 2014, Annex 5 [35]).

Adopting internationally accepted nonperforming exposure/nonperforming loan classifications promotes confidence in banks' financial position, credit risk, and solvency (World Bank 2002, 3). NPL classification is the most universally accepted method to identify credit exposures. Flaws in the methodology have been identified by the BCBS, notably when NPL

---

[5]　The term "nonperforming loans" is not uniform among jurisdictions. This chapter adopts the IMF definition of Bloem and Freeman (2005, 8).

definitions are determined only by *ex post* collectability—i.e., 90 days past due. Jurisdictions rarely share the same definition of NPLs (Bholat et al. 2016, 22–23), the exception being the EU. This is explained by the uniqueness of each jurisdiction's banking system and stylized qualitative factors to measure NPLs.

International Financial Reporting Standard 9 (IFRS 9) provides an internationally accepted accounting treatment for impaired assets based on forward-looking or expected credit losses. This approach comprises quantitative and qualitative measures—the timing of recording a loan loss provision and when to move NPLs and nonperforming exposures off balance sheet (Bholat et al. 2016, 36–37). Expected credit losses account for performing loans when credit risk increases, which affects bank balance sheets when credit growth and credit risk expectations increase—i.e., at the top of the credit cycle heading into a contraction.

IFRS 9 can influence capital buffers and trigger bail-in debt instruments—for example, contingent convertibles. As NPL recognition under IFRS 9 is subject to banks' discretion, incentive exists to procrastinate to avoid bail-in triggering events. The IMF recognizes this and recommends incentives to accelerate the transfer of NPLs and nonperforming exposures off balance sheet (IMF 2015). t is unclear how this will materialize in practice. For developed markets, application of IFRS 9 officially commenced in 2018, with the exception of the US, and developing markets from 2025. The introduction of IFRS 9 in Asia has been aperiodic. Hong Kong, China; Indonesia; Malaysia; the Philippines; the PRC; the Republic of Korea; Singapore; and Taipei,China are the only Asian jurisdictions to have introduced adaptations or equivalents of IFRS 9 (Deloitte 2020).

In April 2017, the BCBS released guidelines—Prudential Treatment of Problem Assets—Definitions of Nonperforming Exposures and Forbearance—to harmonize quantitative and qualitative criteria used for credit categorization and for countries with no nonperforming exposure definition. The guidelines identify criteria to upgrade an exposure from nonperforming to performing status, and the interaction between nonperforming and forbearance (BCBS 2017, 1; Bank for International Settlements [BIS] 2016, 6). This is complemented by the Standards - Regulatory Treatment of Accounting Provisions, which focus on the timing of a credit loss or when an NPL or nonperforming exposure is recorded. To overcome the problem in which IFRS 9 NPL and nonperforming exposure recognition is subject to banks' discretion, the BCBS supports the early recognition of credit losses. This approach harmonizes accounting provisions with the Basel III capital requirements, with any shortfalls deducted from Common Equity Tier 1 (BIS 2017, 1, 6–7).

Accounting classifications are important because NPLs and nonperforming exposures recorded at fair value are attributable to credit risk and therefore affect the level of loan-loss provisions and when NPLs and nonperforming exposures are written off. Valuations are procyclical because they are overstated during rapid economic expansions and understated in downturns (Bholat et al. 2016, 21). Thus, the expected credit loss seeks to smooth valuation volatility and strengthen banks' capital positions. In the EU, the Commission Regulation (EU) No 2016/2067 of 22 November 2016— amending Regulation (EC) No 1126/2008 adopting certain international accounting standards in accordance with Regulation (EC) No 1606/2002 of the European Parliament and of the Council as regards IFRS 9—gives effect to expected credit loss in IFRS 9 and recognizes the BCBS requirements.

In July 2015, the BCBS released its Guidelines for Identifying and Dealing with Weak Banks. Guidance is given on asset quality: negotiating agreements with debtors, taking possession of collateral, writing off long-term NPLs, and selling and transferring assets to AMCs. Asset recovery is to be economic, fair, expeditious, and on a net-present-value basis. The transfer of assets off balance sheet is for bank viability, management to address problems and strategies, and AMCs to maximize recovery value (BCBS 2015, 38 and 49).

2.2.2 Causes and Consequences of Nonperforming Loans

History has shown that excessive NPLs arise from a number of bad practices such as connected banking transactions (sometimes called "crony banking"), fraud, or relaxed underwriting standards. NPLs are also caused by contracting macroeconomic cycles that impact borrowers' ability to repay the loan and devalue collateral. Contracting macroeconomic cycles pose the greatest challenge since the prudential framework is not sufficient to prevent a crisis. For example, Spain was one of the worst-affected countries during the eurozone debt crisis, despite banks having sound pre-provisioning lending.[6] Spanish real estate and the economy were disproportionately inflated by the low interest rate policies of the European Central Bank (ECB), rendering dynamic provisioning measures ineffective (Jiménez et al. 2014). This provides an important moral hazard lesson for two reasons. Spain highlights the limitations of the moral hazard argument

---

[6] On the mechanics and effects of the Spanish dynamic pre-provisioning system adopted in the mid-2000s as a macroprudential measure, see Jiménez et al. (2012).

and that prudential legislation is much less potent when the macroeconomic cycle and monetary policy, rather than bank mismanagement, have inflated an NPL crisis.

An insightful econometric methodology pioneered by Klein (2013) differentiates between bank-specific and macroeconomic factors using dynamic panel regressions (see Chapter 5 for an additional literature review on the determinants of NPLs). This method was adopted by the IMF to study Italian NPLs (Weber, Kopp, and Garrido 2016). The authors ran fixed effects and "generalized method of moments" regressions of NPLs on common macroeconomic bank variables and bank-specific variables, to determine the role each played in the buildup of NPLs. The authors found that macroeconomic variables play a significant role in the accumulation of NPLs, concluding that both bank-level and macroeconomic factors have affected Italian banks' asset quality. Lower bank profitability is associated with higher NPL levels and a rapid loan book expansion due to high growth rates or low interest rates which, on average, results in lower asset quality:

Overall, the results show that the recession, which was of exceptional duration and intensity, had a profound impact on banks' asset quality, and this was exacerbated by bank-specific factors.[7]

2.2.3 Economic Consequences of Nonperforming Loans and Moral Hazard Legislation

A significant and credible body of research suggests that banking sector NPL levels can be important for credit extension and growth, an issue that is further developed in Part 2 of this book.[8] Weak bank balance sheets can dampen economic activity, especially in economies like the EU, which rely on bank financing. Studies have found that banking systems characterized by high NPLs are associated with declining credit-to-GDP ratios and GDP growth, and with increasing unemployment. A 2015 IMF study of EU bank data sourced over 5 years was consistent with these findings (Aiyar et al. 2015).

---

[7] In particular, Weber, Kopp, and Garrido (2016, 9) note: "The prolonged recession led to higher default risk for large corporates and banks, which are typically low-default portfolios."

[8] The literature on financial dependence and growth is well established: Rajan and Zingales (1998); Kashyap, Lamont, and Stein (1994). Several recent studies have looked specifically at the feedback effects of NPLs on macroeconomic performance and have reached similar conclusions (Klein 2013; Nkusu 2011; Prasad and Espinoza 2010; Bergthaler et al. 2015).

Aiyar et al. also found that high NPL ratios constrain bank capital that could otherwise be used to increase lending, reduce bank profitability, and raise funding costs—thereby stifling the supply of credit (Aiyar, Ilyina, and Jobst 2015). Reducing NPLs expeditiously is crucial to support credit growth. For this reason, the view of the European Stability Mechanism (ESM)—sole reliance on GDP growth will not lead to a substantial decline in NPL levels—is justifiable (ESM 2016, 42–43). An IMF report notes that reducing NPL levels is required for a long-term recovery following a financial crisis (World Bank et al. 2012). While the IMF has made the NPL ratio a key measurement of financial strength,[9] there is no explanation or definition of an acceptable NPL ratio. The rationale being, based on the IMF report, that NPLs on banks' balance sheets create uncertainty and weigh on the ability to resume lending, and therefore aggregate demand and investment (ESM 2016, 4).

This uncertainty relates to a bank's solvency[10]—not writing down the true value of NPLs—because the market presumes that the accounting value of capital is overstated. Regardless of how well a bank appears to be capitalized, NPLs reduce bank profitability, which is associated with illiquidity or insolvency.[11]

The explosion of NPL ratios in the aftermath of the eurozone debt crisis has been a significant cause of the anemic economic recovery. Reduced lending and the persistent impression of bank fragility weakened monetary transmission and contributed to undershooting of the ECB's inflation target, which necessitated unconventional liquidity boosting policies. NPLs suppress economic activity as overextended borrowers try to deleverage[12] and can trap resources into unproductive activities. Resolving impaired loans is tantamount to tackling debt overhang, stimulating viable firms' demand for new loans, while encouraging unviable firms to wind down (Jassaud and Kang 2015, 17; Aiyar, Ilyina, and Jobst 2015). Unclogging the bank lending channels will augment the transmission of monetary policy to the real economy.

---

[9] The IMF employs a "nonperforming loans net of provisions to capital" ratio as an indication of the extent to which losses can be absorbed before the sector becomes technically insolvent (IMF, Financial Soundness Indicators and the IMF, last updated November 2015 and referring to IMF's "Financial Soundness Indicators: Compilation Guide". 2006. Part II, [6.15]).

[10] In fact, if a separate set of variables to what the European Banking Authority uses for its stress tests is employed, the impression of vulnerability is even stronger (Acharya, Pieret, and Steffen 2016).

[11] Acharya, Pieret, and Steffen (2016). Indicatively, the authors note that: "Since the start of the Banking Union in November 2014, European banks lost nearly half their market capitalization."

[12] For example, 80% of NPLs in Italy are loans to corporates (see Jassaud and Kang 2015, 6).

These findings raise the critical question of how NPLs should be managed. A concentration of unresolved legacy loans and restricted credit supply impact on economic growth, innovation, and the Schumpeterian cycle. In the longer term, this induces the growth of unregulated or under-regulated parallel financing that can increase overall lending rather than decrease the supply of credit. A good example is the PRC, where most legacy loans are held by state-owned enterprises operating in the manufacturing sector, in contrast to technology companies that access ingenious and riskier forms of finance (from a financial stability perspective). This is especially valid for NPLs generated from gyrations in the macroeconomic cycle rather than loose underwriting standards, crony banking, or fraud. Thus, taking a too-rigid stance vis-à-vis moral hazard in relation to NPL resolution is overwhelmingly counterproductive.

Loss recognition pursuant to IFRS 9 can influence capital buffers and trigger bail-in events. Thus, bank management is incentivized to avoid triggering bail-in events (IMF 2015) and "window dress" the quality of their balance sheet. The regulator's response in such circumstances is uncertain, in contrast to resolving a single bank that has failed for idiosyncratic reasons (Avgouleas and Goodhart 2016). This is because triggering contingent convertibles or other bail-in instruments *en masse*, in a jurisdiction where issuance has been prolific (e.g., Italy), could prove disruptive in a systemic crisis or a banking system excessively burdened with NPLs (Avgouleas and Goodhart 2016).

The IMF suggested in 2015 that Italian bank managers face a number of obstacles which disincentivize the timely resolution of NPLs (Jassaud and Kang 2015). Motivated bank management coupled with timely and effective NPL resolution is key to the resumption of bank lending, tackling debt overhang, the duration and rate of NPL recovery, and mitigating bank losses. The IMF states:

> The delays depreciate the value of the NPLs, and the prices buyers are ready to pay, after discounting the delays, are not attractive for the banks. A reduction in the time to recover loans would have a positive impact in the price of NPLs (Garrido 2016).

From this framework, a series of case studies is considered that involves managing major banking crises over the past 20 years.

2.3 Systemic Bank Resolution Standards and Moral Hazard

2.3.1 International approach

Banks facing large-scale NPLs may experience a severe capital reduction. Capital write-offs can push an ailing bank into resolution. Resolution regimes, analogous to the US Orderly Liquidation Authority[13] and the EU Bank Recovery and Resolution Directive[14] (BRRD), are designed to facilitate orderly bank failures to preserve systemic stability. These regimes aim to eliminate the too-big-to-fail subsidy,[15] by curbing shareholders and managers propensity to select riskier assets.[16] Resolution regimes can utilize *ex-post* mechanisms to secure adequate funds to cover bank losses (Avgouleas and Goodhart 2015, 2016).

Publicly funded bank rescues are historically associated with moral hazard because senior unsecured creditors are typically unaffected, at the expense of the taxpayer.[17] For this reason, public bailouts are regarded as a major source of excessive risk-taking or moral hazard that represents weak monitoring by creditors. There is a widely held belief that contemporary resolution regimes can overcome this problem by eliminating public assistance or by severely curtailing access to public funds (Avgouleas and Goodhart 2019). This chapter argues that, unlike the US, and to a large extent the EU BRRD, bank resolution and NPL standards should take a less doctrinal approach by offering a pragmatic view of this problem and of temporary public funding to resolve high NPL ratios.

The Financial Stability Board Key Attributes Assessment Methodology for the Banking Sector (Key Attributes) sets out a bank resolution framework

---

[13] Title II of the Dodd–Frank Wall Street Reform and Consumer Protection Act of 2010 (Act (Pub L 111–203, HR 4173)).

[14] Directive 2014/59/EU establishing a framework for the recovery and resolution of credit institutions and investment firms OJ L 2014 173/190 or BRRD.

[15] Santos (2014); Ueda and Weder Di Mauro (2011); Li, Qu, and Zhang (2011); Morgan and Stiroh (2005).

[16] Alfonso, Santos, and Traina (2014); Brandao-Marques, Correa, and Sapriza (2013); Gadanetz, Tsatsaronis, and Altunbas (2012).

[17] Yet, bailout costs may not be accurately measured unless the cost of the alternative—instability—is also considered (Dewaripont 2014, 34). With the US Troubled Asset Relief Program, public intervention may be recovered in the long term, which makes calculating the cost of public bailouts even more complex.

for global systemically important banks, subject to preconditions.[18] As cross-border cooperation is a key component of these resolution powers, the Financial Stability Board (FSB) issued the Principles for Cross-border Effectiveness of Resolution Actions.[19]

Critically, the Key Attributes state that the purpose of an effective resolution regime:

> is to make feasible the resolution of financial institutions without severe systemic disruption and without exposing taxpayers to loss, while protecting vital economic functions through mechanisms which make it possible for shareholders and unsecured and uninsured creditors to absorb losses in a manner that respects the hierarchy of claims in liquidation (FSB 2011).

The options to resolve an unviable bank are stabilization and liquidation, which are underpinned by resolution powers:

(i)   removing and replacing senior management and directors;

(ii)   appointing an administrator;

(iii)   powers to terminate, continue, or assign contracts;

(iv)   power to purchase or sell assets;

(v)   writing down debt and restructuring bank operations;

(vi)   continuity of essential services;

(vii)   overriding shareholder rights to facilitate a merger, takeover, sale of business operations, recapitalization, or other measures to restructure or dispose of the bank's business, liabilities, or assets;

(viii) establishing a separate bridge institution or asset management vehicle to transfer run-down NPLs or difficult to value assets;

(ix)   carrying out a bail-in within resolution;

---

[18] Preconditions include:
    (i) an established framework for financial stability, surveillance, and policy formulation;
    (ii) an effective system of supervision, regulation, and the oversight of banks;
    (iii) an effective protection schemes for depositors and other protected clients or customers, and clear rules on the treatment of client assets;
    (iv) a robust accounting, auditing, and disclosure regime; and
    (v) a developed legal framework and judicial system (FSB 2016a, 13).

[19] These cover (i) statutory approaches, (ii) contractual recognition, (iii) temporary stays and early termination rights, and (iv) a bail-in tool. Contractual recognition supports cross-border resolution enforceability, for example the write down, cancellation, or conversion of debt instruments. Where bail-in instruments are governed by foreign law, bail-in recognition clauses are to support debt instruments for home resolutions (FSB 2015a, 7–8).

(x)   imposing a moratorium to suspend payments to unsecured creditors and customers; and

(xi)   effecting the closure and orderly wind down (FSB 2011, 7–8).

When bail-in tools are used to transfer impaired assets, the resolution authority's powers encompass: (i) a write-down that respects the hierarchy of claims in liquidation, equity, or other instruments to absorb losses; (ii) converting into equity or bank-under-resolution ownership instruments that respect the hierarchy of claims in liquidation; and (iii) upon entry into resolution, convert or write down any contingent convertibles or contractual bail-in instruments where terms have not been triggered (FSB 2011, 9).

All of these resolution approaches explicitly provide the public resolution authority with the power to sell or transfer bank assets and liabilities. This includes a transfer to a bridge bank or a third-party private sector buyer without requiring the consent of interested parties or creditors, nor constituting a contractual default or termination event (FSB 2011, 8). The AMC approach of selling or transferring NPLs can be an effective resolution option but requires strengthening the regulatory powers to overcome resistance from shareholders and, especially creditors, given that this will inevitably crystallize bank losses.

The FSB mandates that the private sector is the first funding choice for bank resolutions. Private and government funding conditions are designed to mitigate moral hazard and any losses incurred by the government must be recovered (FSB 2016b). It is entirely plausible that AMCs can limit the use of a public subsidy, with the Swedish AMC an excellent example. Using a fiscal contribution to cover AMC losses may be necessary when a crisis is systemic and triggered by macroeconomic developments and exogenous factors such as the inevitable surge in new NPLs from the COVID-19 economic fallout.

Conversely, bank failures can be caused by idiosyncratic factors such as management's focus on return-on-equity and bonuses, which can induce relaxed lending standards. In these circumstances, bailouts should be precluded because of moral hazard concerns. Creditors should also bear the full cost of bank losses once shareholder funds have been exhausted.[20]

From the standpoint of potential sources of funding, numerous related tools are available to reduce systemic risk. For example, global systemically important banks, which have been compared to "super polluters" that spread

---

[20] On the distinction between applying bail-in to a bank that has failed for idiosyncratic reasons and a bank resolved due to systemic upheaval, see Avgouleas and Goodhart (2015, 2019).

risk due to implicit government guarantees (Haldane 2010),[21] are subject to higher going-concern loss absorbency requirements (BCBS 2013, 3).

In addition to higher capital requirements (going-concern loss absorbency) global systemically important banks are required to hold total loss-absorbing capacity, which also captures Tier 2 capital and long-term unsecured debt. This is to ensure funds are available only for loss-absorbency and recapitalization for an order y resolution to minimize financial instability, to ensure the continuity of crit cal functions, and to avoid exposing taxpayers to losses (FSB 2015b, 5). First, total loss-absorbing capacity is a precautionary measure which supports market confidence that a global systemically important bank has adequate capital and liabilities to readily absorb losses without imposing losses on depositors and secured creditors. Second, total loss-absorbing capacity can stabilize the banking system *ex post*, since designated liabilities can be bailed in to absorb bank losses while minimizing the risk of a deposit and sec_red creditor flight, which could certainly trigger, rather than contain, a systemic banking crisis.[22]

Minimum total loss-absorbing capacity must be at least 16% of the resolution group's risk-weighted assets, which will increase to at least 18% by 2022 (FSB 2015b, 10). These requirements are in addition to the Basel III capital requirements (BCBS 2011). Presuming regulatory capital reflects a bank's approach to offsetting lending and structural reforms, including ring-fencing adopted by the United Kingdom (UK), this will render difficulties in containing moral hazard with a bail-in resolution and no public funding.

2.3.2 European Union Standards and the Single Resolution Mechanism

The main aims of the European Banking Union are to secure the safety and soundness of the EU banking system, increase financial integration and stability, and ensure consistent supervision. Centralization of prudential supervision in the EU is the first pillar of the European Banking Union; it is exercised by the ECB via the Single Supervision Mechanism. The mechanism is responsible for (i) reviews, inspections, and investigations; (ii) licensing; (iii) assessing qualifying holdings; (iv) compliance; and (v) setting countercyclical capital buffers.[23]

---

[21] See also Haldane and Madouros (2012).

[22] On the latter, see Avgouleas and Goodhart (2015).

[23] See the European Central Bank's Single Supervisory Mechanism at https://www.bankingsupervision.europa.eu/about/thessm/html/index.en.html.

Furthermore, in 2014, the EU enacted the BRRD to deal with failing banks beyond national regimes while conforming with the Key Attributes (European Commission 2014). The paramount purpose of the BRRD is to eliminate public bailouts and thus contain the "doom loop" that bound together sovereign and banking sector solvency. This avoids the mutualization of bank risk in the EU by mitigating the fiscal burden-sharing of bank losses among EU members (Avgouleas and Goodhart 2015, 13 and 26). A BRRD resolution must satisfy a number of objectives: (i) safeguarding the continuity of essential banking operations; (ii) protecting deposits, client assets, and public funds; (iii) minimizing risks to financial stability; and (iv) avoiding unnecessary destruction of value (European Commission 2014, 3).

Part IV of the BRRD specifies four resolution tools: (i) the sale-of-business tool; (ii) the bridge-institution tool; (iii) the asset-separation tool (i.e., AMCs); and (iv) the bail-in tool.[24] Bail-in tools are viewed as important to mitigating moral hazard when there is a strong reliance on bailouts. The BRRD bail-in tool allows the resolution authority to write down or convert to equity the claims of creditors in accordance with a predetermined hierarchy. This reduces the extent of a capital injection, the taxpayer burden and, in principle, acts as an additional capital buffer (ECB 2016). What is proving problematic is the BRRD requirement for banks in resolution to effect a minimum bail-in of 8% of liabilities before any contribution of public funds or from the resolution fund.[25]

The Single Supervisory Mechanism run by a Single Resolution Board is tasked with the execution of the EU's resolution regime (Avgouleas and Arner 2017). However, so far, the Single Resolution Board has used its powers only once, in the case of the resolution of the Spanish Banco Popular, which was effectively taken over by another Spanish bank wiping out the shareholders but without using the bail-in tool. This shows how difficult it is politically to use the BRRD toolbox and the Single Resolution Board resolution powers.

The ECB released guidelines aimed at reducing the exposure of systemically important banks with high NPL levels over realistic and ambitious time horizons. Although the guidance is nonbinding, regulators can opt for a "comply or explain" regime. Similar to the BCBS Guidelines: Prudential Treatment of Problem Assets—Definitions of Nonperforming Exposures and Forbearance, the ECB guidelines focus on NPLs and forbearance. In 2018,

---

[24] Chapter IV, articles 2–5, BRRD.

[25] Art. 37(10(a)) and Recs 73, 75, BRRD. For the advantages and disadvantages of this approach, see Avgouleas and Goodhart (2014).

the European Banking Authority (EBA) released Guidelines on Management of Non-Performing and Forborne Exposures. The ECB guidance and EBA guidelines limit nonperforming exposure to reporting requirements (ECB 2017; EBA 2018 6, 8, and 47). Definitions in ECB, EBA, and BCBS documents are analogous, as is the link between nonperforming exposures and forbearance. The ECB guidance and EBA guidelines provide short- and long-term options for consistent prudential treatment of distressed assets and the application of IFRS 9 and expected credit losses.

In July 2017, the EU Economic and Financial Affairs Council issued an action plan to address the problem of NPLs in the banking sector (Council of the European Union 2017).[26] NPLs were at the time almost euro (€) 1 trillion, with the highest exposure in small and medium-sized enterprises.[27]

2.4 The Asian Financial Crisis and Bank Restructuring

Asia experienced its most significant modern financial crisis in 1997–1998. Severe economic and structural imbalances leading into the crisis destabilized banking systems. This section examines the severe effects and the regulatory approaches of Thailand, Indonesia, the Republic of Korea, and Malaysia, followed by the approach of the PRC banking system restructuring. These case studies reveal that weak credit and bank governance regimes, coupled with endemically lax supervision, are rooted in a variety of causes rather than solely being a consequence of moral hazard arising from the prospect of a bailout. Radical balance sheet restructuring supported by public funds minimized taxpayer exposure and *ex-post* bank losses, which led to a resumption of lending.

2.4.1 Thailand

The easing of foreign exchange restrictions in the early 1990s enabled Thai banks to source funds internationally. Credit and reporting standards were lax. By 1996, the NPL ratio was 13% (Corsetti, Presenti, and Roubini 1998),[28] with banks holding baht (B) 487 billion of NPLs (13% of GDP) (Kawai and Takayasu 1999). The banking system rapidly unwound due to rising NPLs and a credit shortage (Nimmanahaeminda 1998).

---

[26] For more details, see also Chapter 7.

[27] Exposure in small and medium-sized enterprises was 16.7%, 7.5% in large companies, and 4.7% in households (Council of the European Union 2017, 13 and 21).

[28] Lending by financial companies equated to about a third of all commercial bank lending. Nonbank financial companies realized similar NPL ratios.

On 5 August 1997, the IMF provided standby support of $17.2 billion to restructure the financial sector by:

(i)   identifying and closing insolvent institutions,

(ii) applying blanket government depositor and creditor guarantees, and

(iii) implementing structural and regulatory reforms (Berg 1999).

In August 1997, the Financial Restructuring Package prompted the development of a private AMC framework.[29] NPLs transferred to state-owned AMCs from state-owned banks were guaranteed by the Financial Institutions Development Fund, which sustained losses.[30] In 1999, the Bank of Thailand was tasked with supervising state-owned AMCs.[31] The central bank also supported NPL transfers to private AMCs. In accordance with the Emergency Decree on Asset Management Company (1998), AMCs managed distressed assets and resolved bad debts through asset restructurings, asset sales, foreclosures, or other legal actions. Distressed debt resolution was facilitated by revised rules—NPLs were recognized after 6 months rather than 12 months and provisions were made for NPLs during bank restructurings (BOT 2000, 5 and 17).[32]

To accelerate debt restructuring, a dispute resolution mechanism was established to assist with voluntary out-of-court restructurings and to spread the debt burden between debtors and creditors. Thailand's NPL ratio reached 42.9% (1998) and NPLs rose to about B2.73 trillion in 1999—47.7% of total credit.[33] NPLs took until 2005 to fall below 10% and to 2010 to reach 3.9%.[34] Borrowings to bail out financial institutions amounted to B1.40 trillion. Emergency legislation enabled the government to issue bonds to fund the bailouts.[35]

---

[29] Bank of Thailand. Supervision Report 2001–2002, 12.

[30] Bank of Thailand. Supervision Report 2001–2002, 20.

[31] Bank of Thailand. Supervision Report 2000, 6.

[32] Bank of Thailand. Supervision Report 2000, 5 and 17.

[33] Bank of Thailand. Supervision Report 2001–2002, 32.

[34] World Bank. Bank Nonperforming Loans to Gross Loans. Data. http://www.data.worldbank.org/indicator/FB.AST.NPER.ZS?page=2.

[35] Bank of Thailand. Financial Institutions Development Fund. https://www.bot.or.th/English/BOTStoryTelling/Pages/FIDF_StoryTelling_FI.aspx.

2.4.2 Indonesia

Contagion spread from Thailand throughout Asia, with Indonesia experiencing a rapid currency devaluation (Sherlock 1998). The banking system was vulnerable from crony lending, fraud, and loose underwriting standards. On 31 October 1997, Bank Indonesia and the IMF announced a resolution package whereby performing assets were transferred from insolvent to solvent banks (Lindgren et al. 1999). The remaining banks were subject to the following conditions: (i) new investors would inject capital to cover some losses, (ii) NPLs would be restructured over 20 years, (iii) new investors pledged collateral for restructured NPLs, and (iv) investor NPL losses were covered by a Bank Indonesia loan (Enoch et al. 2001).

With NPLs remaining on-balance sheet, restructuring insolvent banks was futile (Enoch et al. 2001). On 5 November 1997, the IMF approved a $10 billion standby facility to support financial stability and banking reforms, and announced a second IMF program on 15 January 1998. This was followed by a government emergency plan involving (i) a blanket depositor and creditor guarantee, (ii) establishing the Indonesia Bank Restructuring Agency (IBRA) to rehabilitate weak banks and NPLs, and (ii) a corporate restructuring plan (Lindgren et al 1999).

The IBRA had three management functions over NPLs, investments, and a bank restructuring unit (Fung et al. 2004). This enabled the IBRA to legally sell insolvent banks' NPLs without needing approval from borrowers or bank owners (Enoch et al. 2001). In April 1998, IBRA closed 7 banks, another 7 were taken over (management was replaced in 6), and 16 banks came under IBRA control (Enoch et al 2001). Bank audits revealed widespread connected lending and 6 banks with NPL ratios approaching 55%, with one exceeding 90% (Lindgren et al. 1999, Enoch et al. 2001).

The Indonesian Debt Restructuring Agency was established to reduce short-term funding pressures and to design a distressed debt restructuring framework. Advice and mediation services were offered by the Jakarta Initiative Task Force, which eventually oversaw one-third of all voluntary corporate debt restructuring agreements (Enoch et al. 2001, 37 and 40).

Over rupiah (Rp) 400 trillion of government-issued bonds, or 35% of GDP, were issued to fund the bank recapitalization program.[36] Bank numbers halved following state closures and takeovers (Lindgren et al. 1999, 65).

---

[36] Authors' calculations referring to Enoch et al. (2001, 107).

The IBRA was responsible for Rp234 trillion of NPLs, representing 19% of GDP.[37] NPL ratios peaked in 1998 at 48.6%, before falling to 31.9% in 2001, and 6.8% by 2003 (footnote 34).

2.4.3 Republic of Korea

In 1997, the Republic of Korea's financial sector was underdeveloped, NPLs stood at 5.8%, and the banking system was heavily exposed to short-term foreign debt (footnote 34). Following a sharp drop in the won (W), the country experienced capital flight because it lacked sufficient foreign currency liquidity to meet maturing liabilities.[38] To absorb rapidly increasing NPLs, a fund was established with W3.5 trillion under the supervision of the Korean Asset Management Corporation (KAMCO).[39]

The Korea Deposit Insurance Corporation was established to resolve and restructure banks, and provided supervisors with legal control over failing banks' capital.[40] The Financial Supervisory Service[41] and the banking supervisor—the Financial Supervisory Commission—were empowered to enforce write-offs, mergers, and closures.[42] A corporate restructuring coordination committee acted as a voluntary mediator for debt restructuring (Kang 2004). The Korea Deposit Insurance Corporation supervised bank recapitalizations and KAMCO managed NPLs, with the Financial Supervisory Commission coordinating.

Viable or solvent banks' NPLs were purchased by the KAMCO fund on the condition of merger, management replacement, and downsizing.[43] This was supported by government capital injections and financed with bond issues (Kim 2006, 14–15). Banks with high NPL ratios were closed and weak banks had to submit rehabilitation plans.[44]

---

[37] Authors' calculations referring to Enoch et al. (2001, 39.)

[38] Bank of Korea. Annual Report: 1997, pp. 4 and 17. https://www.bok.or.kr/eng/bbs/E0000740/list.do?menuNo=400221.

[39] Bank of Korea. Annual Report: 1997, pp. 17, 27, and 29. https://www.bok.or.kr/eng/bbs/E0000740/list.do?menuNo=400221.

[40] Bank of Korea. Annual Report: 1997, p. 28. https://www.bok.or.kr/eng/bbs/E0000740/list.do?menuNo=400221.

[41] The administrative arm of the Financial Supervisory Commission.

[42] Bank of Korea. Annual Report: 1997. pp. 28–29. https://www.bok.or.kr/eng/bbs/E0000740/list.do?menuNo=400221; also Kim (2006) and Organisation for Economic Co-operation and Development (2001).

[43] Bank of Korea. Annual Report: 1998. pp. 38–39. See https://www.bok.or.kr/eng/bbs/E0000740/list.do?menuNo=400221.

[44] Bank of Korea. Annual Report: 1998. p. 38. https://www.bok.or.kr/eng/bbs/E0000740/list.do?menuNo=400221.

On 4 December 1997, the IMF granted the Republic of Korea $21 billion of standby credit and $36 billion on completion of the program.[45] The first IMF restructuring exercise focused on distressed banks. Legislation changed the definition of bank capital to reduce leverage and debt-to-equity ratios. The classification of assets and the BCBS capital adequacy requirements were tightened.[46] Loan-loss provisioning was abandoned and forward-looking NPL classifications adopted (Kim 2006, 16).

Financial Supervisory Commission assessments of 12 banks revealed inadequate capital adequacy ratios.[47] Between 1998 and 2002, 9 banks merged, and bank numbers fell from 33 to 19.[48] The Korea Deposit Insurance Corporation ceased operations in 2001 with recapitalizations of over W128 trillion.[49] NPL ratios peaked at 8.9% (2000) before falling to 3.4% in 2001 (footnote 34).

2.4.4 Malaysia

Malaysia's loan growth averaged 25% per annum between 1994 and 1997. Banks held 43.6% of total assets and property sector loans accounted for one-third of all loans.[50] Loan-loss provisions surged 190% to ringgit (RM) 3.96 billion during 1997, from RM1.37 billion.[51] Prior to the crisis, NPLs had been 4.1% before peaking at 18.60% in 1998 (footnote 34).

A pre-emptive crisis program was introduced to address structural weaknesses. NPLs were reclassified closer to international standards by reducing the period in arrears from 6 months to 3 months and improving detection, identification, and monitoring.[52] Exchange controls were applied to stem capital outflows.[53]

---

[45] Bank of Korea. Annual Report: 1997 p. 17. https://www.bok.or.kr/eng/bbs/E0000740/list.do?menuNo=400221.

[46] Bank of Korea. Annual Report: 1998. pp. 39, 45, and 46. https://www.bok.or.kr/eng/bbs/E0000740/list.do?menuNo=400221.

[47] Bank of Korea. Annual Report: 1998. p. 39. https://www.bok.or.kr/eng/bbs/E0000740/list.do?menuNo=400221.

[48] Bank of Korea. Annual Report: 2003. p. 58. https://www.bok.or.kr/eng/bbs/E0000740/list.do?menuNo=400221.

[49] Authors' calculations based on Bank of Korea. Annual Reports 2001 (p. 51) and 2002 (p. 49). https://www.bok.or.kr/eng/bbs/E0000740/list.do?menuNo=400221.

[50] Bank Negara Malaysia. Bank Negara Malaysia Annual Report-1997. Chapter 4, pp. 9 and 13.

[51] Authors' calculations based on Bank Negara Malaysia. Bank Negara Malaysia Annual Report-1997. Chapter 4, 3, and 9. Loan loss reserves amounted to 92% of NPLs.

[52] Bank Negara Malaysia. Bank Negara Malaysia Annual Report-1997. Chapter 4, pp. 4–5.

[53] Bank Negara Malaysia. Bank Negara Malaysia Annual Report-1998. Chapter 1, p. 4. After the depreciation of the ringgit by 40%, the government introduced exchange control measures to stabilize short-term capital flows.

In contrast to other countries in Asia at the time, Malaysia only accepted IMF technical assistance. A restructuring plan created (i) a merger plan, (ii) an AMC—Danaharta—to manage NPLs, (iii) a special purpose vehicle—Danamodal, and (iv) a Corporate Debt Restructuring Committee.[54]

Danaharta was a limited liability company owned by the central bank with the objective of maximizing NPL recovery values and purchasing unmanageable NPLs as a form of capital injection. Banks sold NPLs to Danaharta if their gross NPL ratio exceeded 10%, with the residual written down and restructured. Recapitalized banks sold NPLs to Danaharta at fair market value, funded by the government and, when market conditions allowed, the sale of bonds.[55]

Danaharta ceased purchasing NPLs in 2001 having dealt with RM52.4 billion, an expected recovery rate of 59%, and bonds totaling RM11.1 billion.[56] This fiscal backstop and NPL portfolio restructuring proved successful. By 2005, RM29 billion, or 94% of RM30.8 billion of outstanding NPLs, had been recovered, with NPL ratios dropping to 9.4%.[57]

Danamodal was responsible for bank recapitalizations. Existing bank shareholders were decimated because all losses were absorbed prior to recapitalization. In contrast to Danaharta, the central bank enforced Danamodal's powers whereby capital was only injected into viable banks on commercial terms (footnote 55) amounting to RM7.6 billion for 10 institutions.[58] Danamodal recovered RM6.6 billion by 2003 before being wound down.[59]

The Corporate Debt Restructuring Committee facilitated the voluntary restructuring of corporate debt. Recovery proceeds consisted of cash, redeemable instruments, and rescheduled debts.[60] The Corporate Debt Restructuring Committee was closed on 15 August 2002, ending Malaysia's debt restructuring program.

[54] Bank Negara Malaysia, Annual Report-1998, Chapter 4, p. 11. These were independent bodies.

[55] Bank Negara Malaysia, Annual Report-1998, Chapter 4, p. 12.

[56] Bank Negara Malaysia. Bank Negara Malaysia Annual Report-2000. Chapter 4, 14; Bank Negara Malaysia. Bank Negara Malaysia Annual Report-2002. Chapter 4, p. 116.

[57] Bank Negara Malaysia. Bank Negara Malaysia Annual Report-2004. Chapter 4, 108; World Bank. Bank Nonperforming Loans to Gross Loans. Data: http://www.data.worldbank.org/indicator/FB.AST.NPER.ZS?page=2.

[58] Bank Negara Malaysia. Bank Negara Malaysia Annual Report-2001. Chapter 4, pp. 12 and 134.

[59] Bank Negara Malaysia. Bank Negara Malaysia Annual Report-2003. Chapter 4, p. 107. Danamodal expected to recover the outstanding RM1 billion from one institution.

[60] Bank Negara Malaysia. Bank Negara Malaysia Annual Report-2002. Chapter 4, p. 115.

2.4.5 People's Republic of China
Asset Management Companies: 1998–2008

The PRC was insulated from the Asian financial crisis because its financial markets were closed, currency convertibility controlled, and GDP growth was strong. The banking system and its supervision were in transition during the crisis. Dominating the banking sector were four state-owned banks accounting for nearly two-thirds of total banking system assets.

Despite strong GDP growth, the banking system was characterized by structural weaknesses, nascent prudential supervision, and lax underwriting standards. In 1997, the NPL ratio was 20% (BIS 1999, Mo 2016). Reforms to address NPLs included (i) recapitalizing of state-owned banks, (ii) adopting international NPL classification standards, (iii) enforcing commercially viable loans, and (iv) banning local governments from influencing lending decisions (BIS 1999, 93). The last two reforms centered on strengthening credit standards and quashing connected lending. Bank recapitalizations were funded by yuan (CNY) 270 billion in government bonds (BIS 1999, 93–96).

In 1999, four state-owned AMCs were established to transfer NPLs from corresponding state-owned banks (Hsu, Arner, and Wan 2007). Transfers of NPLs in 1999–2000 amounted to CNY1.4 trillion, about 20% of the banks' combined loan book, or 18% of GDP. One estimation maintains that this was less than half of total NPLs (Ma and Fung 2002, 2).

NPLs were purchased by state-owned AMCs issuing bonds, with credit supplied by the central bank. Disposals were slow, and the recovery rate was 21% (Ma and Fung 2002, 4 and 11–12). The government decided to list two state-owned banks in Hong Kong, China and the central bank transferred CNY320 billion in NPLs to their AMCs at approximately 35% of book value (Ma 2006). To offset the banks' NPLs, $45 billion was injected to boost capital adequacy ratios and new lending (The Economist 2004). Although NPLs eventually fell to 2.4% in 2008, this reduction was attributed to very strong GDP growth, rather than AMC transfers (footnote 34).

Managing Nonperforming Loans Post-2008: An Increasing Concern

As growth rates have decelerated and levels of indebtedness have risen, NPLs have substantially increased, reaching $1.5 trillion or CNY10.5 trillion in June 2019 (PwC 2020). Yet, between 2016 and 2018, banks disposed of CNY4.4 trillion of NPLs (McMahon 2019a). As of mid-2018, the Organisation for Economic Co-operation and Development (OECD) estimated that state-owned enterprises accounted for 82% of all corporate debt (Molnar and Lu 2019, 8).

Regulatory reforms were implemented to accelerate NPL recognition. In 2018, the China Banking and Insurance Regulatory Commission introduced 90-day NPL recognition rules. It issued "window guidance" to request that the six largest banks recognize NPLs which are 60 days overdue. Reports suggest that some banks began using more stringent NPL recognition practices, for example 30 days due (Xiaomeng and Xiao 2019, Lee 2019, Leng and Zhang 2019). Nonetheless, NPL disposals have been prolonged because of understated NPL levels (McMahon 2019a).

The commission relaxed NPL recognition rules in February 2020 when the economic ramifications from the COVID-19 pandemic became apparent (Bloomberg 2020). This is contrary to the IMF policy to preserve financial stability, maintain banking system soundness, and sustain economic activity during the pandemic: "Loan classification and provisioning rules should not be eased, and it is critical to measure NPLs and potential losses as accurately as possible" (IMF 2020). The China Banking and Insurance Regulatory Commission has stated, however, that: "Saving corporates now is saving banks themselves" (Bloomberg 2020).

The PRC's NPL ecosystem is quite different to 20 years ago. There is a developed NPL market and the "Big Four" banks are not the primary source of NPLs and systemic risk. Small- and medium-sized banks (i.e., local and rural) are the biggest potential source of systemic risk because collectively they form a large segment of the banking system and have high levels of poor-quality NPLs (Xiaomeng and Xiao 2019). The "Big Four" banks have established asset investment corporations to manage the NPLs, which reduces supply and supports prices. Consequently, AMCs are managing lower-quality NPLs (McMahon 2019b).

Provincial and local governments have become involved in bank restructurings, established AMCs (more than 50) and financial asset exchanges, and have introduced credit risk regulations (Yue and Jia 2019). This is beneficial because local governments can order local state-owned banks to sell NPLs (Liu and Wu 2016).

Until May 2019, bank bailouts were rare. This changed when the People's Bank of China and the China Banking and Insurance Regulatory Commission decided to nationalize the Bank of Baoshang, the Shandong Provincial Government restructured Heng Feng Bank, and the Industrial and Commercial Bank of China and Cinda Asset Management provided the Bank of Jinzhou with a large capital injection. In contrast to bailouts being funded by the Ministry of Finance or the central bank, these bailouts were funded by the PRC's sovereign wealth fund and public AMCs (McMahon 2019c). In September 2019, the central bank stated that shareholders would be primarily responsible for future bank failures (Mitchell and Yang 2019).

2.4.6 Lessons from the East and Southeast Asian Experiences

During banking crises, balance sheets are placed under extreme stress that require restructuring through capital injections, renegotiating credit terms, and transferring distressed assets off-balance sheet. Effective bank resolution regimes require legal and regulatory frameworks, and supervision to address: (i) risk management, (ii) capital and liquidity buffers, (iii) large exposure restrictions, (iv) transparent credit standards, (v) bank restructuring frameworks, and (vi) distressed debt transfer mechanisms.

Capital adequacy ratios of up to 10% that satisfied the Basel recommendations proved insufficient to absorb high NPLs during the Asian financial crisis. When banks required balance sheet and business model restructuring to remain solvent, NPL and resolution regimes were either underdeveloped or non-existent. Indonesia, the Republic of Korea, and Thailand were forced to accept IMF support to bail out and recapitalize their banking systems.

The IMF bank resolution policies focused on closing and liquidating insolvent institutions and government guarantees. Capital restructuring was a last resort. Indonesia epitomizes the policy of closing rather than restructuring banks, with numbers halving within a few years. Bank closures reduced Indonesia's NPL ratio, yet this is attributable to closing a few banks with particularly high NPL ratios. A concentration of bank closures in Thailand did not correlate with a drop in NPL ratios in the short term. Indonesia and Thailand had the highest closures and experienced the deepest and longest disruptions to their banking systems and the most extensive use of public funds.

Resolving systemic banking crises by focusing on closures weakens confidence. Paradoxically, this was a condition of the IMF support program. To contrast, Malaysia neither requested an IMF bailout nor embarked on widespread bank closures. Instead it relied on an NPL transfer mechanism. This resulted in a more effective banking system restructuring program that maintained confidence throughout the crisis.

Indonesia's reluctance to implement reforms and promulgate legislation intensified its banking crisis and hindered NPL resolution. In contrast, the Republic of Korea's existing framework was expeditiously modified, which proved effective at mitigating rising NPLs. All jurisdictions experienced a significant reduction in NPLs and banking system stabilization following bank consolidations and debt restructuring arrangements. The timing of the responses offers a valuable lesson. For example, Thailand was slow to respond, and Indonesia was reluctant to implement reforms, which maintained banking system fragility as NPLs continued to surge.

Experience from East and Southeast Asia shows that expeditious debt restructuring and legal frameworks, rather than bank closures, proved most effective. All resolution programs involved public funding, although approaches to restructuring varied. Government guarantees were critical for stabilizing banking systems and a condition of the IMF bailouts.

The use of AMCs was instrumental in cleansing balance sheets of NPLs, strengthening capital ratios, and restarting lending to aid the economic recovery. This finding is further discussed and supported by empirical evidence provided in Chapter 5. AMCs were funded either by government capital injections or the sale of bonds. Legal and regulatory infrastructure was a prerequisite for the expeditious transfer and sale of NPLs.

There is no clear evidence of whether state-owned or private AMCs are more effective. Debt overhang from Thailand's NPL program is an ongoing problem. The PRC's state-owned AMC performance cannot be duly assessed around the time of the state-owned bank privatizations because of distortions from the extensive bank recapitalizations. More recently, the PRC has been struggling to reduce the volume of NPLs, despite the introduction of asset investment corporations and provincial AMCs.

The Korean Asset Management Corporation (KAMCO) is a good example of how a pre-existing AMC can promptly abate a potential banking crisis (from a surge in NPLs) and purchasing NPLs can be profitable despite reliance on taxpayer funding. In our view, this is an important finding. Banks need to be equipped with the tools to manage NPLs promptly to avoid distressed assets festering and balance sheets destabilizing, impairing confidence, which is apparent in some EU countries.

2.5 Bank Rescue Case Studies from the Global Financial Crisis

This section focuses on the approaches adopted during the global financial crisis in Switzerland, the UK, and the US to restructure UBS, Royal Bank of Scotland (RBS), and Citigroup. Switzerland and the UK managed guarantee-based programs rather than asset sales. The US opted for a guarantee and the Troubled Asset Relief Program (TARP) to purchase distressed assets.[61]

2.5.1 UBS

On 1 October 2007, UBS announced a write down of Swiss francs (SwF) 4 billion from investments in asset-backed securities and collateralized debt obligations (Securities and Exchange Commission 2007, Swiss Federal Banking Commission 2008).[62] Performance of these instruments was linked to NPLs—US subprime mortgages.[63]

UBS received a government capital injection of SwF6 billion, consisting of mandatory convertible notes (i.e., converting into equity) and the sale of NPLs and NPL-linked instruments, from the central bank, the Swiss National Bank (SNB 2013a). These distressed assets were then transferred to a special purpose vehicle (SPV), the StabFund.[64] The StabFund was designed to absorb UBS distressed assets and produce a return on its investments. Distressed asset purchases were financed by SNB loans and UBS equity contributions—a maximum of 10% of assets purchased up to $6 billion or

---

[61] Board of Governors of the Federal Reserve System, Troubled Asset Relief Program (TARP) Information, at http://www.federalreserve.gov/bar kinginforeg/tarpinfo.htm.

[62] The subsidiary was Dillon Read Capital Management.

[63] For a description of securitization, see Wood (2007).

[64] StabFund or Stabilisation Fund.

SwF7.2 billion. Equity contributions were designed to absorb the first 10% of losses (SNB 2013a, 2013b, 2013c).[65]

Distressed assets totaling $38.7 billion or SwF45.3 billion were sold to the StabFund between December 2008 and April 2009.[66] Asset sales amounted to $15.8 billion or SwF18.5 billion, which were used to repay SNB loans (footnote 66). The Swiss government realized a profit of SwF1.2 billion by selling its SwF6 billion UBS equity stake. UBS made the final SNB loan repayment in August 2013 and it purchased the StabFund in September 2013.

2.5.2 Royal Bank of Scotland

RBS grew dubiously through a series of aggressive acquisitions, notably the 2007 partial purchase of ABN AMRO (House of Commons Treasury Committee 2012). Following the failure of Lehman Brothers, the capital and liquidity of RBS became severely strained and NPLs rose dramatically, reaching 9% by 2013 (European Commission 2009a, Moody's Investor Services 2016).

On 8 October 2008, the UK government announced that RBS would be recapitalized. The European Commission approved the Bank of England's plan which included a guarantee under EU State Aid Rules (European Commission 2009a, 2009b). An initial sale of RBS shares (pound sterling [£] 15 billion), underwritten by the government, attracted virtually no subscribers. This forced the government to purchase most of RBS' shares—effectively a capital injection and nationalization. Bank of England emergency loans provided an additional £20 billion recapitalization (European Commission 2009b), with the government holding 90.6 billion RBS shares, or 84% of its capital (UK Financial Investments [UKFI] 2010).

On 3 November 2008, the government established UKFI to manage RBS' recapitalization and the government's investment. A condition of the RBS capital injection was participation in the Asset Protection Scheme, established to protect banks against losses on distressed assets (Asset Protection Agency [APA] 2010). RBS sought protection for £282

---

[65] The StabFund was a limited partnership consisting of two partners solely owned by the SNB: an unlimited liability partner managing the SPV, and a limited liability partner. For the SwF/$ exchange rate, see Board of Governors of the Federal Reserve, 'Historical Rates for the Swiss Franc', at https://www.federalreserve.gov/releases/h10/dat00_sz.htm.

[66] SwF/$ exchange rate averaged to 1.17:1. See Board of Governors of the Federal Reserve. Historical Rates for the Swiss Franc.

billion in assets (e.g., NPLs). The government provided a guarantee against 90% of losses above the first £60 billion (IMF 2011).

The Asset Protection Scheme operated analogous to a state-owned AMC managing bank NPLs, except that asset ownership was retained by the bank. This arrangement was quicker to implement and did not require capital injections to purchase distressed assets. There were disadvantages, however, in retaining distressed assets on-balance sheet and the bank not receiving any NPL sale proceeds. Government capital injections were required to maintain bank solvency until NPL returns were realized (National Audit Office 2010). RBS exited the Asset Protection Scheme on 18 October 2012 after removing over £1 trillion in assets from its balance sheet (HM Treasury 2015). The Asset Protection Scheme ceased operations with a £5 billion profit (APA 2012).

On 3 November 2009, the government announced that RBS would be restructured, among other things, including raising its Common Equity Tier 1 ratio above 8% (compared to 4% in 2008) and disposing noncore assets (European Commission 2009b). RBS struggled and, in July 2017, agreed with the European Commission in satisfaction of State Aid Rules to commit £835 million in new lending instead of closing branches (European Commission 2017).

In March 2020, the Office of Budget Responsibility estimated that taxpayers would incur a loss of £32 billion on the government's £45 billion bailout. At the time of writing, the UK Treasury still holds a 55% stake in RBS.

2.5.3 Citigroup

The $700 billion TARP was designed to stabilize the US financial system by purchasing distressed assets (Federal Reserve 2008).[67] TARP consisted of subprograms including the Capital Purchase Program to strengthen bank capital, among other things.[58]

Citigroup was a recipient, receiving $25 billion, and on 23 November 2008 agreed to a government bailout which included a $301 billion government guarantee on a pool of distressed assets under the Asset Guarantee Program. Distressed assets were retained on Citigroup's balance sheet.

---

[67] And the Emergency Economic Stabilization Act 2008, s 102.

[68] Federal Deposit Insurance Corporation (FDIC). 2008 Annual Report 2008. Part I, Supervision and Consumer Protection.

The terms of Asset Guarantee Program rendered Citigroup liable for the first $39.5 billion in losses. TARP and Citigroup would then absorb $5.0 billion and $0.6 billion, respectively. Subsequent losses were absorbed at $10.0 billion by the Federal Deposit Insurance Corporation and $1.1 billion by Citigroup. Losses thereafter would be serviced by the Federal Reserve Bank of New York securing a loan over the remaining guaranteed assets at 90% collateral value. [69]

To strengthen Citigroup's balance sheet, a TARP capital injection of $20 billion was exchanged for Citigroup preferred shares. This approach, the Targeted Investment Program, was adopted because standard TARP funding was insufficient to stabilize Citigroup. [70]

Citigroup's share price continued to decline precipitously, undermining the Targeted Investment Program capital injection. In July 2009, $25 billion in preferred equity obtained through TARP was exchanged for common stock. Citigroup had become partially nationalized.

In September 2009, Citigroup notified the US Treasury that it intended to repay the Targeted Investment Program and terminate the Asset Guarantee Program. Conditions included maintaining sufficient capital levels, the ability to access long-term debt markets without government assistance and raising common equity by 50% of the Treasury's redeemable equity. On 23 December 2009, Citigroup increased its capital levels by issuing 5.4 billion common shares for $17 billion and tangible equity units for $3.5 billion. The Treasury unwound its position in Citigroup's TARP, Asset Guarantee Program, and Targeted Investment Program programs on 10 December 2010, selling 7.7 billion common shares for a $12 billion profit. [71]

2.5.4 Analysis and Evaluation

In the early stages of the global financial crisis, bailouts of systemic banks were preferred to closure and liquidation, perhaps because of the lack of legally viable bail-in tools. The approach taken in the UBS, RBS, and Citigroup rescues was the antithesis of the IMF approach during the Asian financial crisis. In the global financial crisis, governments provided massive capital injections, effecting bank nationalizations, albeit structured, and importantly to avoid distressed assets being transferred onto government balance sheets.

---

[69] FDIC (2008), pp. 19–21.

[70] FDIC (2008), p. 18.

[71] 171 FDIC (2008), pp. 9, 34, 38, and 40.

Global systemically important banks became fragile from an overexposure to NPLs and/or NPL-linked financial instruments. This complicated bailouts and AMCs' capacity to sequester distressed assets from banks. RBS and Citigroup were subject to government guarantees and retaining distressed assets on-balance sheet. UBS transferred distressed assets to an AMC—a similar process to that adopted in the Asian financial crisis. Both approaches strengthened bank balance sheets and stabilized banking systems, eventually enabling banks to resume lending. Nevertheless, both programs exposed governments to bailout liability.

Rescue frameworks were sourced from existing legislation to aid prompt implementation. Participating banks signed contractual agreements with regulators to facilitate restructuring and uphold obligations. Hesitation in the UK forced the government to purchase equity in RBS after its share issue failed. This hesitation is analogous to that of Indonesia and Thailand, which undermined confidence and the success of their bailout programs.

Switzerland injected capital and took an ownership position in UBS at the beginning of its program. This restructuring approach highlights the advantage of loss control when using an AMC as opposed to a state guarantee. Regulators can control the timing of the sale of NPLs until favorable market conditions prevail, effectively mitigating losses and government liability.

In contrast, RBS and Citigroup retained distressed assets on-balance sheet, necessitating larger capital injections to strengthen balance sheets and therefore increasing state ownership, heightening potential taxpayer risk. Bank liability from the disposal of distressed assets under the UK and US asset protection (guarantee) schemes compelled banks to absorb initial losses. Distressed asset sales under a guarantee scheme are usually implemented when market conditions will not mitigate losses. Thus, an asset protection scheme guarantee approach can create inefficiencies since the risk of government liability is elevated by depressed asset markets. This can necessitate further capital injections.

The global financial crisis guarantee schemes were profitable and relatively short-lived. Despite substantial taxpayer risk, the asset protection schemes, i.e., asset price guarantee programs, were effective and efficient in managing distressed assets, stabilizing global systemically important banks, stemming creditor runs, and maintaining banking system stability.

Switzerland's central bank had a far greater exposure to potential losses than those from the UK and US guarantee schemes. Since the SNB was the AMC creditor and equity holder, if the AMC failed, the SNB would be exposed to unlimited liability. If UBS' losses were substantial, the exposure of SNB and, ultimately, the taxpayer, would shield UBS from liability. While this approach risks compromising a central bank's credibility and credit standing, there is no realistic solvency risk because central bank losses in its issued currency can be inflated and absorbed in the long run. Conversely, Switzerland's approach is more effective in strengthening banks' capital bases and more efficient since further capital raising is not necessary. For these reasons, this approach is preferable to an asset protection scheme guarantee.

2.6 The Eurozone Debt Crisis and Banking Sector Restructuring

2.6.1 The Post–2018 Regime for Bank Debt Restructuring

Before analyzing the impact of the eurozone debt crisis on the banking systems of Greece, Ireland, Italy, and Spain, the post–2018 EU bank debt restructuring regime is examined. From our analysis, one point stands out: stricken EU countries were more proactive in tackling banks' distressed debt before the implementation of the Bank Recovery and Resolution Directive (BRRD), even though the EU state aid regime has remained largely unaltered.

Once the EU, and especially the European Monetary Union, moved toward a more centralized policy for tackling NPLs, state-backed AMCs were abandoned in favor of private sector AMCs.[72] The European Council agreed in July 2017 on an NPL action plan outlining:

(i)   more intensive supervision for banks with high NPLs,
(ii) reform of domestic insolvency and debt recovery frameworks,
(iii) development of secondary markets for NPLs (i.e., distressed debt or assets), and
(iv) restructuring of the banking industry (European Council 2017).

A blueprint for member state AMCs was proposed by the end of 2017, consistent with the EU legislative framework and State Aid Rules for asset relief measures and the use of AMCs. This blueprint sets out common principles for asset, valuation and participation parameters and thresholds,

---

[72] Section IV.A. draws on Avgouleas (2020).

capital structures, and governance and operational procedures. These are applicable for private and public AMCs. In March 2018, the EU Commission submitted a package of measures together with the Second Progress Report on the Reduction of Nonperforming Loans (European Commission 2018a). The European Parliament and Council endorsed the 2018 NPL proposals by agreeing in June 2019 to pass the "banking package" into EU law with the promulgation of the Capital Requirements Regulation (CRR II)[73] and the Capital Requirements Directive. In April 2019, amendments to CRR II created a statutory prudential "backstop" which is designed to prevent under-provisioning for expected-loss NPLs.[74]

The objective of these measures is to reduce NPL ratios and future excessive NPL accumulations. These measures can be taxonomized as follows:

(i)   Augmenting market-based solutions for the massive disposal of NPLs through legal and regulatory reforms and EU-wide infrastructure that facilitates the disclosure and pooling of buyer interest and liquidity, including initiatives for pan-EU NPL platforms (European Commission 2018b).

(ii) Introducing measures to build a liquid market for distressed debt, at the domestic and EU level, including the recent initiatives by EU bodies for disclosure and transparency standardization.[75]

(iii) Expanding the microprudential framework through supervisory requirements imposed by the Single Supervisory Mechanism. First, requiring EU banks to build capability for the timely detection and effective management of NPLs. Second, establishing quantitative NPL reduction targets over the short, medium, and long terms (ECB 2017, 12–13). To achieve these targets, banks should improve NPL governance and use NPL reduction approaches as described in the ECB's Guidance to Banks on Non-performing Loans (ECB 2017, 12). Banks should go beyond strategies (i), (ii), and

---

[73] Regulation (EU) 2019/876 of The European Parliament and of the Council of 20 May 2019 amending Regulation (EU) No 575/2013 as regards the leverage ratio, net stable funding ratio, requirements for own funds and eligible liabilities, counterparty credit risk, market risk, exposures to central counterparties, exposures to collective investment undertakings, large exposures, reporting and disclosure requirements, and Regulation (EU) No 648/2012 (CRR II); and Directive (EU) 2019/878 of the European Parliament and of the Council of 20 May 2019 amending Directive 2013/36/EU as regards exempted entities, financial holding companies, mixed financial holding companies, remuneration, supervisory measures and powers, and capital conservation measures (Capital Requirements Directive).

[74] Regulation (EU) 2019/630 of the European Parliament and of the Council of 17 April 2019 amending Regulation (EU) No 575/2013 as regards minimum loss coverage for nonperforming exposures.

[75] For example, EBA (2018) and NPL transaction templates: https://eba.europa.eu/risk-analysis-and-data/eba-work-on-npls.

(iii) outlined in this taxonomy, by introducing (ECB 2017, 8–17):[76]

    (a) a hold/forbearance strategy that, depending on borrower capability and expertise, can lead to workouts;

    (b) active portfolio reductions, through sales and by writing off provisioned NPL exposures deemed unrecoverable;

    (c) a change of exposure type, including foreclosure, debt-to-equity swaps, debt-to-asset swaps, or collateral substitution; and

    (d) legal options involving insolvency proceedings or out-of-court solutions;

(iv) Strengthening prudential backstops to compel banks to provision for NPLs *ex ante* and thus have adequate capital reserves when writing off NPLs.[77] This is a proactive measure that targets future accumulation of NPLs by incentivizing banks to take *ex ante* action against NPL accumulation.[78] Hopefully, the backstop will provide a strong incentive for banks to strengthen underwriting standards and provide a disincentive against lax loan underwriting practices.

Nevertheless, with the economic impact of the COVID-19 pandemic on EU economies forecast to be severe, the European Commission sanctioned the temporary suspension of state aid restrictions.[79] This has resulted in a direct recapitalization of private sector firms by the state (Espinoza 2020). Relaxing EU State Aid Rules will inevitably be extended to the financial sector in the near future.[80] Of course, the European Commission, European Council, EBA, and ECB developed the AMC Blueprint on how to set up public and private sector AMCs, based on the four areas identified in the 2017 Action Plan (European Commission 2018c, 3), and on a liquid pan-European market for distressed bank debt exclusive of state support (European Commission 2018d). These market-based solutions are expected

---

[76] For the full articulation of the NPL reduction, governance, and write-off techniques into EU supervisory standards, see EBA (2018).

[77] For the most recent EU pronouncement of this policy, see European Council (2018).

[78] By building-up capital buffers *ex ante*, banks will reduce the provision of credit, thereby reducing credit growth in the event of a credit bubble. However, these measures will affect credit growth in other times, which will make prudential backstops a very blunt regulatory instrument.

[79] On 19 March 2020, EU Competition Commissioner Margrethe Vestager introduced the "Temporary Framework for State Aid Measures" to assist businesses accessing the liquidity and financial support to maintain viability during the COVID-19 economic downturn. The framework provides measures that do not qualify as state aid, such as financial support given *directly to consumers* and support measures under the rules for rescue and restructuring aid to meet acute liquidity needs and support undertakings facing financial difficulties. See European Commission (2020a).

[80] European Commission (2020b and 2020c), European Banking Authority (2020), and European Parliament (2020) for further details.

to be supported by the future introduction of legislation, in accordance with the EU 2019 "banking package" on the liquidation of collateral.

In the reality of the COVID-19 pandemic, the utilization of state-backed AMCs will depend on the bargaining power of member states and the volume of new NPLs. EU members with fragile banking systems, such as Greece, will introduce state-backed AMCs to manage the fresh supply of NPLs. This prediction is relevant given the survey below of AMC performance in the EU during the early stages of the global financial crisis and the eurozone debt crisis.

2.6.2 Spain

Spain experienced a property bubble prior to the eurozone debt crisis. After the bubble burst in January 2009, Spain entered recession, at which point NPLs exceeded 4% (footnote 34).

The government established the Fund for Orderly Bank Restructuring (FROB) to restructure banks. FROB was capitalized with €9 billion to takeover nonviable banks, subscribe convertible instruments to merge viable banks, and subscribe ordinary shares to recapitalize viable banks (FROB 2012, 7). The banking system reform strategy was implemented in three phases: consolidation, solvency improvement, and cleaning up balance sheets (FROB 2012, 8).

Following a second recession in 2012, Spain sought a banking system bailout of €100 billion from the European Stability Mechanism. Financial assistance was implemented through FROB in accordance with the EU State Aid Rules. Conditions included diagnosing bank capital requirements based on asset quality, transferring distressed assets to an AMC, recapitalizing and restructuring viable banks, and an orderly resolution of nonviable banks involving burden-sharing with the private sector.[81] The bailout program consisted of early intervention, restructuring, and resolution.

Banking system stress tests identified additional capital requirements which resulted in partial bank nationalizations for €38.9 billion and €2.5 billion to establish the Asset Management Company for Assets Arising from Bank Restructuring (SAREB).[82]

---

[81] European Commission. Post-Programme Surveillance for Spain. Available at http://www.ec.europa.eu/ economy_finance/assistance_eu_ms/spain/index_en.htm (visited on 31 January 2016).

[82] Bank of Spain. Financial Stability Report 11/2012. p. 40.

SAREB's purpose is to receive, manage, and dispose of distressed assets from banks in receipt of government assistance.[83] FROB has the power to transfer distressed assets from banks to SAREB for independent management.[84] Systemically important banks own 55% of SAREB, while FROB (i.e., the government) owns 45%. In exchange for distressed assets, SAREB issues government guaranteed bonds that can be used as collateral for financing (IMF 2013). Banking system NPLs at the time were about €330 billion (Bank of Spain 2013, 22). From January 2013, banks were required to hold a capital ratio of 9% (Bank of Spain 2013, 13). Spain exited the EU financial assistance program in January 2014. The NPL ratio rose to 8.4% in 2014 before dropping to 5.5% in 2016, and 3.2% in 2019 (footnote 34).

Although SAREB has reduced banks NPL ratios to manageable levels, it has posted losses for every financial year since its inception in 2014. Losses can be attributed to accounting rules imposed by the Bank of Spain on the valuation of assets. These rules require an assessment of assets individually to reflect changes in market prices. Nonperforming loan sales are not as profitable because the sale price must be above the valuation price, which has been greatly reduced by the accounting rules. SAREB subsequently slowed the sales of NPLs to stem losses (Cas and Peresa 2016, 24). The recovery of Spain's real estate sector has been critical for SAREB's profitability because 100% of its assets are held in Spain and are collateralized in real estate. Exogenous market forces and competition have contributed to SAREB's losses. Half of Spain's banking sector entities did not participate in SAREB, and thus competed with the AMC in running down exposures.

Lessons drawn from the unprofitability of SAREB suggest that the efficient use of public resources by an AMC is contingent on: (i) development of the market for NPL collateral, (ii) government policy including accounting treatments, (iii) AMC business model assumptions, and (iv) NPL supply factors.

2.6.3 Ireland

Ireland is one of the best examples of a successful implementation of a state-backed AMC which held large proportions of assets in its home market and overseas. The National Asset Management Agency (NAMA), established in December 2009, fully repaid €31.8 billion of total debt by March 2020 and

---

[83] SAREB. Half Year Report. H1 2013. SAREB is a public limited company with a 15-year lifespan to liquidate assets.

[84] See generally Bank of Spain (2012).

is expected to post a €4 billion surplus.[85] This was achieved even though NAMA bought the bulk of its NPLs at a premium over market price, based on the principle of so-called long-term economic value. This approach is analogous to that of SAREB. NPL sales were enhanced through bundling with performing loans and the number of debtors being very small. The chronicle of NAMA unfolded as follows. Ireland experienced a credit boom typified by connected lending and low credit standards that produced a highly levered banking system heavily exposed to the property market (Commission of Investigation into the Banking Sector in Ireland 2011). Illiquid wholesale funding markets coincided with a downturn in the credit and property cycles, and a collapse in the banking system (Honohan 2010). NAMA was empowered to provide capital, credit, and restructurings or reorganizations to manage asset exposures.[35] The purpose of NAMA was to address serious economic threats, and the stability of banks and the finance sector by, among other things, (i) producing an expeditious and efficient economic recovery, (ii) protecting state and taxpayer interests, (iii) restructuring banks, and (iv) restoring banking system confidence.[87]

In December 2010, Ireland accepted an IMF/EU €85 billion bailout. Key objectives of the rescue program were to identify viable banks and implement strengthening measures (i.e., downsizing and reorganization), recapitalize banks, encourage bank deposit inflows and market-based funding, strengthen banking supervision, and introduce a bank resolution framework (IMF 2010).

NAMA acquired bank NPLs prior to the IMF/EU program secured on real estate amounting to €74 billion in gross book value terms, involving 800 debtor business plans and 11,000 loans collateralized on 16,000 properties (NAMA 2011, 6). NPLs were acquired at a 57% discount over face value and below book value, yet above market value due to the long-term economic value premium. NAMA paid €31.8 billion by issuing government-guaranteed senior notes and €1.6 billion in subordinated debt securities.[88] Delays in restructuring distressed debt included legal obstacles, such as a 1-year foreclosure moratorium on defaults (IMF 2015). In October 2017, all

---

[85] NAMA. 2020. Press Statement - NAMA Redeems Last Remaining €1.064 Billion of Outstanding Debt. 2 March. https://www.nama.ie/news/press-statement-nama-redeems-outstanding-1-064-million-in-subordinated-debt.

[86] See ss12(2)(a) and (d), NAMA Act 2009.

[87] See ss2 (a) and (b), NAMA Act 2009.

[88] NAMA. Section 227 Review. (July 2014), 12.

senior debt had been redeemed (3 years ahead of schedule) and in March 2020, all subordinated debt was redeemed.[89]

Ireland exited the IMF/EU bailout in December 2013. Nonetheless, Irish banks still held a substantial volume of NPLs on-balance sheet because NAMA only purchased selective assets and NPLs kept rising. The IMF attributed this to weak accounting standards (IMF 2015), notably IAS 39—a backward-looking provisioning approach for loss accruals. Mortgage arrear resolution targets were introduced, forcing banks to sustain short-term forbearance which reduced arrears (Doherty 2016). NPLs peaked in 2013 at 31.8%, more than 2 years after transfers to NAMA began (Central Bank of Ireland 2017). This NPL peak included asset classes that were not transferred to NAMA. For context, in 2014 the NPL ratios for the three largest banks were 17%, 33%, and 45% (Fitch Ratings 2014).

The reason for establishing an AMC, which is in accordance with the BRRD, is to cleanse bank balance sheets of distressed assets.[90] NAMA had an additional requirement to redeem senior debt, which it achieved with efficiency.[91]

From 2013 to 2017, the volume of NPLs on bank balance sheet, nonetheless, fell from €80 to €30 billion. This reduction is not attributable to NAMA. Two-thirds of 2017 NPLs were derived for house purchases. Banks' mortgage books have experienced a "self-cure" because of improved economic conditions and loan restructuring efforts made by banks, supported by supervisory targets (Donnery et al. 2018). Ireland's NPL ratio fell from 11.5% in 2017 to 5.7% in 2018 (footnote 34).

2.6.4 Italy

The Italian economy prior to 2008 experienced a prolonged low-growth period because of structural economic imbalances and an inert public sector. This low-growth environment was accentuated by the eurozone debt crisis and contributed to Italy's very high sovereign indebtedness, which has hovered around 135% of GDP since 2014.

With the onset of the eurozone debt crisis in early 2010, credit conditions tightened when wholesale funding markets became illiquid and credit risk

---

[89]   NAMA. NAMA Bonds': available at https://www.nama.ie/financial/nama-bonds/.

[90]   Art 42(5) (b) and (c), BRRD.

[91]   ss10(2) and 11(d), NAMA Act 2009.

intensified. By the end of 2011, the Italian banking system's Common Equity Tier 1 averaged 9.3% and leverage was lower than comparable European banks.[92] Italy's NPL ratio was 11.7% with over half of gross NPLs being bad debts (footnote 34).

The government introduced a number of reforms:

(i)   pre-bankruptcy creditor agreements to facilitate full or partial company sales,

(ii) out-of-court dispute procedures,

(iii) frivolous cases were discouraged, and

(iv) summary proceedings were enforced.[93]

One-third of procedures lasted between 3 to 5 years.[94] Italy's high NPL levels were maintained because of prolonged credit recovery procedures.[95]

The government introduced amendments in August 2015 to increase creditor recovery rates by promoting out-of-court restructuring agreements, and forced collateral sales were simplified and shortened.[96] Tax treatments of loan-loss provisions allowed for full and immediate tax deductibility of loan write-downs and write-offs. These reforms resulted in bankruptcy and enforcement procedures being expedited.[97]

To circumvent inefficient procedures, large banks, hedge funds, private equity, and turnaround management firms have formed special purpose vehicle (SPV) partnerships targeting corporate loans. These partnerships restructure companies with for example, debt-to-equity swaps and capital injections (Jassaud and Kang 2015, 18).[98] Large banks set up internal workout units to dispose of NPLs. Progress was initially slow because Italy's NPL market was virtually non-existent prior to 2013 (Jassaud and Kang 2015, 17).

---

[92] Bank of Italy. Annual Report for 2011, 2012. pp. 143 and 144.

[93] Bank of Italy. Annual Report for 2014, 2015. pp. 110–111.

[94] Bank of Italy. Financial Stability Report No. 1 / 2016. pp. 34 and 35.

[95] Bank of Italy. Annual Report for 2014, 2015. p. 118.

[96] Bank of Italy. Financial Stability Report No. 2 / 2015. p. 38.

[97] Bank of Italy. Financial Stability Report No. 2 / 2015.

[98] For example, UniCredit, Intesa, KKR, and Alvarez & Marsal.

The banking system comprises of many small banks that are inexperienced in managing NPLs (footnote 95). In November 2015, four unviable small banks were recapitalized by the central bank's AMC and resolution fund, the National Resolution Fund, with €3.6 billion financing from the three largest banks.[99] Existing shareholders and subordinated debt absorbed losses (European Commission 2015). All four banks were restructured into bridge banks with bad debts transferred to an AMC.[100] In May 2017, the EU approved the sale of three bridge banks to UBI Banca for nominal consideration—€1. The bridge banks were burdened with high NPLs, requiring €450 million of capital (Reuters 2017). A condition of the sale obliged the National Resolution Fund to inject €810 million of capital and grant risk guarantees.

One obstacle under the BRRD bail-in rules is when NPL restructuring results in substantial losses, which require a recapitalization. Before a failing bank receives a capital injection, creditors (i.e., bondholders) must be bailed-in to the equivalent of 8% of liabilities. With retail investors constituting one-third of bondholders, any bail-in will affect a large proportion of the population and have potentially adverse consequences for the banking system and the economy (IMF 2016).[101]

After failing to raise €5 billion in capital in December 2016, the European Commission approved a precautionary recapitalization of Monte dei Paschi di Siena (Italy's third-largest bank).[102] Although the recapitalization was designed as a bail-in, in effect it was a bailout. Retail equity investors were fully compensated with new senior-ranking bonds issued by the Italian Ministry of Economics and Finance (Dipartimento del Tesoro 2016, Bank of Italy 2016).

In May 2017, two banks were liquidated under Italian insolvency law and not under the BRRD as the Single Resolution Board decided that the "public interest" criterion under the BRRD was not satisfied. A decree issued by the Italian government in June 2017 provided the legal framework for the liquidations, including public support to guarantee an orderly exit from the

---

[99] On 16 November 2015, the EU Bank Recovery and Resolution Directive was transposed into national legislation.

[100] Nuova Banca delle Marche, Nuova Banca dell'Eturia e del Lazio, Nuova Cassa di Risparmio di Chieti, and Nuova Cassa di Risparmio di Ferrara.

[101] See pp. 1, 24, 25, 27, 33, 34, 79, and 82 of IMF 2016.

[102] In 2017, the Bank of Italy identified Intesa Sanpaolo and Banca Monte dei Paschi di Siena as domestic systemically important banks, with UniCredit also being a global systemically important bank. Bank of Italy. Financial Stability Report No. 1 / 2017.

banking system. Shareholders and junior bondholders shared losses and no bail-in mechanism was used.[103]

The EU approved a further €8.1 billion (€5.4 billion net public funding) recapitalization of Monte dei Paschi di Siena in July 2017 after the bank agreed to transfer NPLs to an AMC and cap executive pay. Concerns were raised by the ECB over Monte dei Paschi di Siena's ability to maintain capital buffers. The government underwrote a €3.9 billion capital injection and converted €4.2 billion of subordinated bonds to equity which has resulted in the state acquiring a 70% ownership stake (Bank of Italy 2017, 33; Visco 2017).

Private equity funds participated in the process. KKR Credit launched Pillarstone Italy in October 2015. Pillarstone has two functions, NPL resolution and corporate restructuring (The Economist 2016). Pillarstone took on the debts of five companies including paper maker Burgo and Lediberg, theme park manager Alfa Park, telecommunications group Sirti, and the shipping company Premuda (Landini and Gaia 2016). The companies are being relaunched after Pillarstone injects capital and absorbs distressed debt sourced from Italian banks (Quarati 2016).

In February 2016, the Ministry or Economics and Finance issued a securitization guarantee (GACS) for senior notes issued by SPVs that are recipients of NPLs (see also Chapter 6). Banks access the facility for a fee. Banks are incentivized to transfer NPLs off-balance sheet because the guarantee effects a true sae, reduces risk and uncertainty, and ameliorates price discovery. Initial NPL transfers were relatively low until 2017 when a number of enormous NPL sales were finalized by Italy's largest banks. Italy's NPL ratio dropped sharply from 16% in 2017 to 8% in 2019.[104]

2.6.5 Greece

Doubts concerning the sustainability of Greek debt became apparent in the second half of 2009 as the economy entered recession and a sovereign debt crisis unfolded. Investors began to lose confidence in Greece's ability to service its bonds. In April 2010, the Greek government requested an IMF/EU bailout.

---

[103] Veneto Banca and Banca Popolare di Vicenza—both banks lacked sufficient resources to cover future losses (Visco 2017). Some retail jun or bondholders were compensated for losses.

[104] World Bank. Data. Bank Nonperforming Loans to Gross Loans. http://www.data.worldbank.org/indicator/FB.AST.NPER.ZS?page=2; and CEIC. Italy Non Performing Loans Ratio. https://www.ceicdata.com/en/indicator/italy/non-performing-loans-ratio.

Conditions of the €110 billion package included reining in fiscal spending, structural reforms to rebalance the economy, and stabilizing the banking system by among other things, establishing the Hellenic Financial Stability Fund—a private entity. Banks maintained liquidity from the Bank of Greece's Emergency Liquidity Assistance and were recapitalized through injections of fresh capital via the Hellenic Financial Stability Fund and a novel instrument called deferred tax credits (Hellenic Financial Stability Fund 2016).[105]

Twelve banks were placed into liquidation or resolved in 2013 (Bank of Greece 2014). NPLs were retained on-balance sheet, as a distressed debt legal framework did not become operational until November 2015. By 2016, the NPL ratio reached 47%, where it has remained, the second highest in the EU (EBA 2016, 12).

A number of legal framework weaknesses identified by the Hellenic Financial Stability Fund has led to the introduction of out-of-court mechanisms to facilitate negotiations between debtors, creditors, and banks, and an out-of-court workout procedure. Judicial impediments persisted because most judges lacked debt restructuring experience and there were delays in court hearings due to the volume of cases and inefficient procedural rules. The 2016 NPL law and subsequent legal amendments addressed some of these flaws, although impediments persist (Hellenic Stability Fund 2016, 2017).

On 17 May 2016, following the recapitalizations of two of the largest banks, Alpha Bank and Eurobank, KKR Credit reached an agreement to assign and manage credit and equity exposures through Pillarstone (KKR 2016). KKR utilized a similar arrangement as in Italy. In contrast to Pillarstone Italy, the European Bank for Reconstruction and Development provided a capital injection up to €50 million and Pillarstone Greece offers corporate governance advice (Reiser 2017). Pillarstone Greece was the first entity to be licensed by the Bank of Greece to manage nonperforming exposures.

In late 2019, the Greek government launched the Hercules Asset Protection Scheme (guarantee scheme) analogous to the Italian GACS; in it, banks pay a fee for a securitization guarantee of senior notes issued by SPVs that are recipients of their NPLs. The Hercules Asset Protection Scheme differs from GACS as the senior notes are not investment grade. Hercules is designed to remove €30 billion of NPLs from banks' balance sheets (European Commission 2019). Whether the bank NPL reduction targets will be achieved is doubtful considering that Greece is one of the worse-

---

[105] Also see Hellenic Financial Stability Fund. What We Do. https://hfsf.gr/en/what-we-do/.

affected economies in the EU from the COVID-19 pandemic (European Commission 2020d).

2.6.6 Analysis and Evaluation

The EU/IMF bailout programs prescribe consolidation, capital injections, government guarantees and, where possible, using AMCs to cleanse balance sheets of distressed assets. Consolidation involves mergers and downsizing rather than closures.

Ireland nationalized (i.e., recapitalized), and Spain merged and nationalized banks prior to establishing AMCs. Closure and liquidation is the last resort, in contrast to the IMF approach during the Asian financial crisis. Capital injections have been critical in maintaining bank solvency and stability.

When the property markets in Spain and Ireland collapsed, NPL ratios rose significantly, mirroring those of Indonesia and Thailand. The surge in NPLs during the eurozone and Asian crises highlights that satisfying international standards does not necessarily reflect banking system strength.

The 2006 NPL ratios in Ireland and Spain were less than 1% (footnote 34) because of the 2005 adoption of incurred loss accounting standards and securitization, which allowed banks to reduce loss provisioning (OECD 2011, 77). Italy, which used the same standard, had an NPL ratio of 6.6% in 2006, higher than the Republic of Korea and Malaysia, but significantly lower than Indonesia and Thailand (OECD 2011). This is alarming because NPLs were clearly understated. For this reason, incurred loss accounting should be avoided.

Ireland established an AMC prior to its EU/IMF bailout, similar to Malaysia in the 1990s, which has assisted in stabilizing the banking system. The favorable economic conditions that, in conjunction with restructuring efforts, led to a "self-cure" of NPLs on Irish bank balance sheets have since reverted as a result of the COVID-19 recession, causing modest increase in NPLs. Spain established an AMC, as an EU bailout condition, which has significantly reduced NPLs.

Following successive bank recapitalizations and the promulgation of NPL laws to facilitate NPL sales, Greece and Italy have achieved NPL reductions through sales to private sector investors. Delays in establishing legal frameworks to facilitate efficient NPL transfers destabilized the Greek and

Italian banking systems. Recurring delays in dealing with high NPL ratios on banks' balance sheets intensified potential insolvencies and perpetuated a vicious cycle of recession, illiquidity, and debt overhang. The subsequent introduction of GACS in Italy has been instrumental in transferring large volumes of NPLs off-balance sheet and has significantly reduced banks' NPL ratios.

In the Asian and eurozone crises, legal frameworks were severely underdeveloped. Laws were required to establish AMCs and effect efficient NPL transfers off-balance sheet. Legislation per se is not sufficient, as viable AMCs require well-functioning distressed asset markets. Deficiencies in legal frameworks and underdeveloped distressed debt markets are the most severe obstacles (Aiyar et al. 2015, 14). Successful distressed asset markets are, in turn, characterized by short legal processes (Altman 2013). Evidence suggests that domestic markets for distressed assets grow in tandem with the level of NPLs, viable AMCs (Jassaud and Kang 2015, 19), and expeditious transfer and sale mechanisms.

For structural reasons, the EU market for distressed debt is relatively illiquid. Eliminating or diminishing the profit incentive for NPL purchases produces a disincentive for private investors to participate in distressed asset markets, which constrains market development and liquidity.

Bond issues funded the purchases of NPLs from banks in Greece, Ireland, Italy, and Spain. The ownership structure and the *raison d'être* of the schemes in Ireland and Spain are similar. Both AMCs were set up with a majority private and minority government equity stakes, and both received government guarantees on senior bond funding. After paying back its debt and shrinking its balance sheet to a negligible size, thereby mitigating taxpayer exposure, Ireland's AMC reverted to 100% government ownership.[106] Spain's AMC (SAREB) is partially privatized, with Spanish taxpayers exposed to the government's 45% equity share and potential losses on the guaranteed senior bonds. The use of private sector investors in Italy is proving to be profitable and effective, with strong market growth. Greece's scheme will be tested by low bond ratings and the global COVID-19 recession which has increased NPLs.

Italy's GACS incentivizes banks to transfer NPLs because the guarantee increases prices. Banks are incentivized to securitize Italian NPLs because

---

[106] From inception, NAMA was 51% privately owned and 49% publicly owned through an SPV to limit liability. NAMA has reverted to 100% publicly owned following the final investor payment on 26 May 2020.

securitized notes are guaranteed at investment grade, lowering their funding costs and enabling a more favorable capital treatment for originating banks. Government guarantees therefore require calibration to balance the competing incentives of NPL transfers off-balance sheet and the NPL purchases by AMCs, SPVs, and private investors.

2.7 Conclusion

The IMF approach to banking crises has evolved from closing down banks to aligning with the Financial Stability Board Key Attributes: strengthening bank balance sheets. This resolution approach is designed around an orderly banking system and the continuity of vital economic functions while mitigating taxpayer exposure. Evidence from major banking crises over the past 3 decades (and bank restructuring in the PRC) supports the use of public funds where the bank rescue program focuses on the effective restructuring of balance sheets that is cost-saving in the long term rather than outright bank closures. When the threat of a banking crisis or a surge of NPLs is identified, balance sheet restructuring can be very effective in maintaining banking system stability. Reluctance or hesitation to implement reforms can intensify banking crises and undermine long-term bank solvency.

Robust capital, leverage, and liquidity buffers reduce the risk of bank failures. However, regulators can misjudge banking system strength by relying on compliance with international standards especially in the face of adverse macroeconomic conditions. Banks that are fully compliant (*ex ante*) with international standards can experience a rapid deterioration of their capital position from exogenous and endogenous shocks, including contagion from a financial crisis in another economy. When capital buffers are under stress and private funding is unavailable, the government should be allowed to make a capital injection for systemic or macroeconomic stability into a viable yet failing bank, thereby inciting market confidence. When a bank is under severe stress from systemic and macroeconomic factors, the argument against public support for fear of giving rise to moral hazard is untenable. In limited cases, state injections of capital will result in the government taking an ownership position in a systemically important bank, which may be necessary to restore market confidence. Idiosyncratic lending, however, should be avoided.

Banks need the tools to manage balance sheets promptly and to avoid NPLs undermining capital adequacy and banking system confidence. Bail-in tools can provide additional capital to strengthen bank balance sheets by converting creditor claims to equity when there is no danger of contagion, especially when the key cause of bank failure is idiosyncratic—for example, fraud (Avgouleas and Goodhart 2015). In a financial crisis, an anti-bailout bias can cause the collapse of credit markets and, the banking system, leading to widespread economic disruption. A consistent bailout approach, including cross-border cooperation, instils confidence and stability in a banking system.

It is advisable that regulators adopt a broad and uniform definition of NPLs and nonperforming exposures, for example, the Basel Committee on Banking Supervision (BCBS) definition, to capture the widest range of distressed assets. Accounting treatments should avoid fair value and incurred loss accounting which underestimate banking system vulnerability. Expected credit losses and accounting treatments, which harmonize with the nonperforming exposure definition (BCBS) provide a more accurate financial position.

A public authority must be designated to coordinate management of an NPL resolution program. This can greatly reduce information asymmetries and conflicts of interest between creditors attempting to optimize restructuring outcomes (Avgouleas and Goodhart 2017). A public authority could also supervise private sector AMCs and be tasked with the implementation of legal and infrastructural changes designed to boost secondary NPL market liquidity.

AMCs are effective at strengthening bank capital without the need for ongoing capital injections, and the timing of distressed asset sales can be controlled until more favorable market conditions prevail. Using private sector AMCs is preferable to government bailouts since government ownership and taxpayer liability is absent (or the level is significantly lower). The same may be said about AMCs with a measure of government investment that is fully recoverable. In contrast, public AMCs that do not cap public support nor incorporate a clear path to recovery of public funds can expose the government to unlimited liability, burdening the taxpayer.

A key *raison d'être* in the use of AMCs during crisis is asset valuation. Moreover, where asset classes are clearly identified for valuation and transfer to an AMC, the prospects for profitability are enhanced. From an accounting perspective, bad debts are considered uncollectable. Thus, the chances of AMC profitability are low unless bad debts are bought with a discount on the holding and transfer costs, and the selling price. This benefits the AMC at the expense of the bank when the discount is excessive.

To contrast, a guarantee places liability on the government, primarily for the bank's benefit and can assist in sustaining AMC viability. A public AMC is unlikely to satisfy the objective of ensuring the most efficient use of public resources, although in the long run this may prove to be a more efficient solution than other bailout options.

Government guarantees can be critical for banking system stability. Large exposures to NPL-linked financial instruments can complicate the design of AMCs to sequester banks from distressed assets. In these circumstances, retaining distressed assets on-balance sheet supported by government guarantees may be the preferred option. Government guarantees that retain distressed assets on-balance sheet can lack control over the timing of sales, exposing governments to substantive liability and extensive capital injections. Guarantees should only be used when banks can be returned to viability and NPL sales can be controlled.

Debt restructuring requires legislative frameworks and infrastructure. If NPL legislation or infrastructure is absent or deficient, a program should be designed that is expeditious and ideally takes an *ex ante* approach. Delays in promulgating legal support or infrastructure destabilizes banking systems by maintaining and intensifying high NPL ratios on-balance sheet.

Effective and expeditious NPL transfers depend on passing NPL legislation that builds suitable bankruptcy, arbitration, and civil procedures. These requirements should not depress NPL sales, values, or distressed asset markets. Legal infrastructure should enable all banks regardless of size to participate in the restructuring program.

To incentivize NPL transfers, government guarantees can be placed on NPL sales to private AMCs and AMC bond issues. The efficiency of NPL transfers is heightened in a market-based system because government guarantees require calibration to balance the competing incentives of transferring NPLs off-balance sheet and minimizing AMC losses from NPL sales. As guarantees expose taxpayers to liability and increase the cost of a program, fees can be charged to offset costs.

An AMC must be capable of maximizing discretionary NPL sales. Ideally, NPLs are sold when market conditions yield profit and an efficient transfer. Deficiencies in legal frameworks and underdeveloped distressed debt markets are the most severe obstacles. If the market is underdeveloped or obstructed, the government needs to design policies to create investment incentives or remove legal and regulatory obstacles. In general, legal and regulatory obstacles are those that penalize or act as a disincentive for NPL transfers, purchases, and the development of liquid secondary markets for distressed debt. The optimum market-based restructuring solution for NPLs utilizes private sector AMCs, a tax regime that promotes distressed asset markets, and a legal system that ensures the efficient and effective transfer of NPLs.

Assuming these conditions are fulfilled, AMCs can effectively cleanse bank balance sheets of NPLs, strengthen capital ratios in the long term, and enhance banks' capacity to restart lending. Where the majority of funding is sourced from the private sector (i.e., bond issues), this will act as a countercyclical relief mechanism that stabilizes a banking system overly burdened with NPLs, while mitigating taxpayer expenditure.

This is an important lesson for EU members and other policy planners, notably in Asia. Experience from past banking crises (and the PRC) suggests that when regulating NPLs and bank restructurings, a shift to balance-sheet strengthening is of the utmost importance rather than obsessing over mitigating moral hazard. Bailing out a banking system should not overestimate the latter where the causes of a crisis are systemic.

Today, given the widespread financial turbulence and surge of NPLs forecast for the global economy from the COVID-19 pandemic, focusing on balance-sheet strengthening will be paramount in the years ahead for both developed and developing countries.

References

Acharya, V., D. Pieret, and S. Steffen. 2016. Capital Shortfalls of European Banks since the Start of the Banking Union. Paper. New York University. Stern School of Business. https://12ec6960-6cef-0574-005b-9883c552e5bf.filesusr.com/ugd/ba8141_b6422566f2ca4ed39daa7e16bf8d39f4.pdf.

Aiyar, S., A. Ilyina, and A. Jobst. 2015. How to Tackle Europe's Non-Performing Loan Problem. *VoxEU.* 5 November. http://www.voxeu.org/article/how-tackle-europe-s-ncn-performing-loan-problem.

Aiyar, S., W. Bergthaler, J. M. Garrido, A. Ilyina, A. Jobst, K. Kang, D. Kovtun, Y. Liu, D. Monaghan, and M. Moretti. 2015. A Strategy for Resolving Europe's Problem Loans. IMF Staff Discussion Note. SDN/15/19. Washington, DC: IMF.

Alfonso, G., J. Santos, and J. Traina. 2014. Do "Too Big To Fail" Banks Take on More Risk? *Federal Reserve Bank of New York Economic Policy Review.* 20 (2). pp. 41–58.

Altman, E. I. 2013. The Role of Distressed Debt Markets, Hedge Funds and Recent Trends in Bankruptcy on the Outcomes of Chapter 11 Reorganizations. Paper. New York University. Stern School of Business.

Arner, D. and J. Norton. 2009. Building a Framework to Address Failure of Complex Global Financial Institutions. *Hong Kong Law Journal.* 39 (1). pp. 95–128.

Asset Protection Agency (APA). 2010. Annual Report and Accounts 2009–10. HC 259, 20.

_____. 2012. Annual Report and Accounts for the Period from 1 April 2012 to 31 October 2012. Report to the House of Commons. 12 June 2012 HC 120, 6.

Avgouleas, E. 2015. Bank Leverage Ratios and Financial Stability: A Micro- and Macroprudential Perspective. October 2015 *Levy Economics Institute, Working Paper.* No. 849. https://www.econstor.eu/bitstream/10419/146977/1/840973446.pdf.

_____. 2020. The EU Framework Dealing with Non-Performing Exposures: Legal and Economic Analysis. In D. Busch and G. Ferrarini, eds. *European Banking Union.* Oxford: Oxford University Press.

Avgouleas, E. and D. Arner. 2017. The Eurozone Debt Crisis and the European Banking Union: "Hard Choices", "Intolerable Dilemmas" and the Question of Sovereignty. *The International Lawyer.* 50 (1). pp. 29–67.

Avgouleas, E. and C. Goodhart. 2014. A Critical Evaluation of Bail-in as a Bank Recapitalisation Mechanism. CEPR Discussion Paper No. DP10065. Centre for Economic Policy Research. London.

_____. 2015. Critical Reflections of Bank Bail-Ins. *Journal of Financial Regulation.* 1 (1). pp. 3–29.

_____. 2016. An Anatomy of Bank Bail-Ins – Why the Eurozone Needs a Fiscal Backstop for the Banking Sector. *European Economy: Banks, Regulation, and the Real Sector.* Issue 2016-2: pp. 75–90.

_____. 2017. Utilizing AMCs to Tackle Eurozone's Legacy Non-Performing Loans. *European Economy: Banks Regulation and the Real Sector.* Issue 2017.2.

_____. 2019. Bank Resolution 10 Years from the Global Financial Crisis: A Systematic Reappraisal. In Douglas Arner, Emilios Avgouleas, and Steven Schwarcz eds. *Systemic Risk in the Financial Sector: Ten Years after the Great Crash.* Toronto: McGill-Queen's University Press.

Bank for International Settlements (BIS). 1999. Strengthening the Banking System in China: Issues and Experiences. BIS Policy Paper. Basel.

_____. 2016. Prudential Treatment of Problem Assets - Definitions of Non-Performing Exposures and Forbearance. Consultative document, Bank for International Settlements, Basel. http://www.bis.org/bcbs/publ/d367.htm.

_____. 2017. Regulatory Treatment of Accounting Provisions – Interim Approach and Transitional Arrangements. BIS Standards. Basel.

Bank of Greece. 2014. The Chronicle of the Great Crisis: The Bank Of Greece 2008–2013. Speech by George A Provopoulos, Governor of the Bank of Greece, Athens.

Bank of Italy. 2016. The "Precautionary Recapitalization" of Banca Monte dei Paschi di Siena. https://www.bancaditalia.it/media/approfondimenti/2016/ricapitalizzazione-mps/index.html?com.dotmarketing.htmlpage.language=1.

_____. 2017. Financial Stability Report No. 2 / 2017.

Bank of Spain. 2012. Restructuring and Resolution of Credit Institutions. Briefing Note on Royal Decree-Law 24/2012. 25 September. Madrid: Bank of Spain.

_____. 2013. Financial Stability Report 5/2013. Madrid.

Basel Committee on Banking Supervisions (BCBS). 2011. Basel III: A Global Regulatory Framework for More Resilient Banks and Banking Systems. Bank for International Settlements. pp. 62–3.

_____. 2013. Global Systemically Important Banks: Updated Assessment Methodology and the Higher Loss Absorbency Requirement. Basel: Bank for International Settlements.

_____. 2015. Guidelines for Identifying and Dealing with Weak Banks. Basel: Bank for International Settlements.

_____. 2017. Guidelines: Prudential Treatment of Problem Assets - Definitions of Non-Performing Exposures and Forbearance. Basel: Bank for International Settlements.

Berg, A. 1999. The Asia Crisis: Causes, Policy Responses, and Outcomes, October 1999 IMF Working Paper No. 99/138. Washington, DC: International Monetary Fund.

Bergthaler, W., K. Kang, Y. Liu, and D. Monaghan. 2015. Tackling Small and Medium Sized Enterprise Problem Loans in Europe. IMF Staff Discussion Note, SDN/15/04.

Bholat, D., R. Lastra, S. Markose, A. Miglionico, and K. Sen. 2016. Non-Performing Loans: Regulatory and Accounting Treatments of Assets. Bank of England, Staff Working Paper. No. 594.

Bloem, A. M. and R. Freeman. 2005. The Treatment of Nonperforming Loans. International Monetary Fund Issue paper prepared for the July 2005 Meeting of the Advisory Expert Panel.

Bloomberg. 2020. China Makes Bad Loans Disappear as Virus Pummels Banks. 27 February.

Board of Governors of the Federal Reserve, Historical Rates for the Swiss Franc. https://www.federalreserve.gov/releases/h10/dat00_sz.htm.

Brandao-Marques, L., R. Correa, and H. Sapriza. 2013. International Evidence on Government Support and Risk Taking in the Banking Sector. IMF Working Paper, 13/94. Washington, DC: IMF.

Brunnermeier, M., A. Crocket, C. Goodhart, A. D. Persaud, and H. Shin. 2009. The Fundamental Principles of Financial Regulation. Geneva Reports on the World Economy 11.

Cas, S. and I. Peresa. 2016. What Makes a Good 'Bad Bank'? The Irish, Spanish and German Experience. *European Economy Discussion Paper* 036. Luxemburg: European Commission, September 2016.

Central Bank of Ireland. 2017. Non-Performing Loans: The Irish Perspective on a European Problem. Speech from Central Bank of Ireland Deputy Governor Ed Sibley at the second annual conference of the European Systemic Risk Board (ESRB), Frankfurt, 22 September 2017.

Claessens, S. 2014. An Overview of Macroprudential Policy Tools. *IMF Working Paper* No. 14/214. Washington, DC: International Monetary Fund.

Commission of Investigation into the Banking Sector in Ireland. 2011. Misjudging Risk: Causes of the Systemic Banking Crisis in Ireland, March 2011 Report of the Commission of Investigation into the Banking Sector in Ireland.

Corsetti, G., P. Presenti, and N. Roubini. 1998. What Caused the Asian Currency and Financial Crisis? Part I: A Macroeconomic Overview. *National Bureau of Economic Research Working Paper* 6833.

Council of the European Union. 2017. Council Conclusions on Action Plan to Tackle Non-Performing Loans in Europe. Press Release, 11 July.

Deloitte. 2020. IFRS 9 in Asia: Creating a Future-ready, Optimized Bank. https://www2.deloitte.com/content/dam/Deloitte/global/Documents/Financial-Services/InsIFRS/01_IFRS9_Asia.pdf.

Dewatripont, M. 2014. European Banking: Bail-out, Bail-in and State Aid Control. *International Journal of Industrial Organisation*. 34 (1). pp. 37–43.

Dipartimento del Tesoro (Italy). 2016. Guarantee on Securitization of Bank Non Performing Loans (GACS) to Be Introduced Shortly. http://www.dt.tesoro.it/en/news/news_gacs.html.

Doherty, S. 2016. NPL Workout and Resolution in the Euro Area. Bank for International Settlements. Address by the Deputy Governor of the Central Bank of Ireland, at the Peterson Institute for International Economics, Washington, DC, 6 October.

Donnery S., T. Fitzpatrick, D. Greaney, F. McCann, and M. O'Keeffe. 2018. Resolving Non-Performing Loans in Ireland: 2010–2018. Central Bank of Ireland Quarterly Bulletin. Dublin.

Economist, The. 2004. Botox Shot: Injections of Capital May Soon Wear Off. 8 January. http://www.economist.com/node/2338716.

————. 2016. Bargain Hunt. 20 August. http://www.economist.com/news/finance-and-economics/21705341-structural-obstacles-make-italian-banks-bad-loans-hard-sell-bargain-hunt.

Enoch, C., B. Baldwin, O. Frecaut, and A. Kovanen. 2001. Indonesia: Anatomy of a Banking Crisis Two years of Living Dangerously 1997–1999. *International Monetary Fund Working Paper* No. 01/52. Washington, DC: IMF.

Espinoza, J. 2020. Brussels Considers Further Relaxation of State Aid Rules. Financial Times. 6 April.

European Banking Authority (EBA). 2014. Final Report, Guidelines on management of non-performing and forbearance exposures. 31 October. EBA.

————. 2016. EBA Report on the Dynamics and Drivers of Non-Performing Exposures in the EU Banking Sector. EBA, Paris.

————. 2018. Guidelines on Management of Non-Performing and Forborne Exposures. EBA, Paris.

————. 2020. EBA Provides Additional Clarity on the Implementation of Selected COVID-19 Policies. 21 December. EBA, Paris.

European Central Bank (ECB). 2016. Systemic Implications of the European Bail-In Tool: A Multi-Layered Network Analysis. *Financial Stability Review.* May. pp. 120–129.

————. 2017. ECB. Guidance to Banks on Non-Performing Loans. March 2017. Frankfurt. https://www.bankingsupervision.europa.eu/ecb/pub/pdf/guidance_on_npl.en.pdf?form=MY01SV&OCID=MY01SV.

European Commission. 2009a. United Kingdom Restructuring of the Royal Bank of Scotland Following its Recapitalisation by the State and Its Participation in the Asset Restructuring Scheme. 14 December. Brussels.

————. 2009b. State aid: Commission approves impaired asset relief measure and restructuring plan of Royal Bank of Scotland. Press release. 14 December. Brussels.

————. 2014. EU Bank Recovery and Resolution Directive (BRRD): Frequently Asked Questions. 15 April. Brussels.

_____. 2015. State Aid: Commission Approves Resolution Plans for Four Small Italian Banks Banca Marche, Banca Eturia, Carife and Carichieti. Press release. 22 November. Brussels.

_____. 2017. State Aid: Statement on Agreement in Principle between Commissioner Vestager and UK Government on Royal Bank of Scotland Commitment. Press release. 26 July. Brussels.

_____. 2018a. Second Progress Report on the Reduction of Non-Performing Loans in Europe. Progress report. 14 March. Brussels.

_____. 2018b. European Platforms for Non-Performing Loans. Documents accompanying the Third Progress Report on the Reduction of Non-Performing Loans and Further Risk Reduction in the Banking Union. 28 November. Brussels.

_____. 2018c. AMC Blueprint. Document accompanying the Second Progress Report on the Reduction of Non-Performing Loans in Europe. Brussels.

_____. 2018d. Third Progress Report on the Reduction of Non-Performing Loans and Further Risk Reduction in the Banking Union. 28 November. Brussels.

_____. 2019. State Aid: Commission Approves Market Conform Asset Protection Scheme for Banks in Greece. Press release. 10 October. Brussels. https://ec.europa.eu/commission/presscorner/detail/en/ip_19_6058.

_____. 2020a. Temporary Framework for State Aid Measures to Support the Economy in the Current COVID-19 Outbreak. Communication from the Commission. 20 March. Brussels.

_____. 2020b. State Aid: Commission Expands Temporary Framework to Enable Member States to further Support the Economy in the COVID-19 Outbreak. 19 March.

_____. 2020c. Coronavirus Response: Banking Package to Facilitate Bank Lending – Supporting Households and Businesses in the EU. 28 April.

_____. 2020d. State Aid: Commission Approves €2 billion Greek Guarantee Measure to Support Companies Affected by the Coronavirus Outbreak. Press release. 3 April. Brussels.

European Council. 2017. Banking: Council Sets Out Action Plan for Non-Performing Loans. Press release 456/17. 11 July. Brussels.

_____. 2018. Non-Performing Loans: Political Agreement Reached on Capital Requirements for Banks Bad Loans. Press release 815/18. 18 December. Brussels.

European Parliament. 2020. COVID-19: Revised rules to encourage banks to lend to companies and households. Press Release. 9 June.

European Stability Mechanism (ESM). 2016. ESM Annual Report 2015. Luxembourg City. pp. 42–43.

Federal Reserve. 1970. *Financial Instability Revisited: The Economics of Disaster— Fundamental Reappraisal of the Discount Mechanism*. 1970 Board of Governors of the Federal Reserve System.

_____. 2008. Troubled Asset Relief Program. TARP information from the Board of Governors of the Federal Reserve.

Financial Stability Board (FSB). 2011. Key Attributes of Effective Resolution Regimes for Financial Institutions. Basel.

_____. 2015a. Principles for Cross-border Effectiveness of Resolution Actions. Basel.

_____. 2015b. Principles on Loss-Absorbing and Recapitalisation Capacity of G-SIBs in Resolution: Total Loss-Absorbing Capacity. TLAC Term Sheet. 9 November. Basel.

_____. 2016a. Key Attributes Assessment Methodology for the Banking Sector – Methodology for Assessing the Implementation of the Key Attributes of Effective Resolution Regimes for Financial Institutions in the Banking Sector. 19 October. Basel.

_____. 2016b. Guiding Principles on the Temporary Funding Needed to Support the Orderly Resolution of a Global Systemically Important Bank "G-SIB". 18 August. Basel.

Fitch Ratings. 2014. 2015 Outlook: Irish Banks. Outlook report. New York.

Fund for Orderly Bank Restructuring (FROB). 2012. Fund for Orderly Bank Restructuring. April.

Fung, B., J. George, S. Hohl, and G. Ma. 2004. Public Asset Management Companies in East Asia – Case Studies. 2004. Bank for International Settlements. https://www.bis.org/fsi/fsipapers03cs.pdf.

Gadanetz, B., K. Tsatsaronis, and Y. Altunbas. 2012. Spoilt and Lazy: The Impact of State Support on Bank Behavior in the International Loan Market. *International Journal of Central Banking*. 8 (4). pp. 121–174.

Gallo, A. 2014. A Refresher on Net Present Value. *Harvard Business Review*. 19 November. http://hbr.org/2014/11/a-refresher-on-net-present-value.

Garrido, J. 2016. Insolvency and Enforcement Reforms in Italy. *International Monetary Fund Working Paper*, WP/16/134. Washington, DC: IMF.

Geanakoplos, J. 2009. The Leverage Cycle. In D. Acemoglu, K. Rogoff, and M. Woodford, eds. *NBER Macroeconomics Annual 2009*. Volume 24. Chicago: University of Chicago Press. pp. 1–65.

———. 2010. Solving the Present Crisis and Managing the Leverage Cycle. *FRBNY Economic Policy Review*. 16 (August). pp. 101–131.

Haldane, A. G. 2010. The 100 Billion Question. Comment given at the Institute of Regulation and Risk, Hong Kong, China. 30 March.

Haldane, A. G. and V. Madouros. 2012. The Dog and the Frisbee. Speech at the Federal Reserve Bank of Kansas City's 366th economic policy symposium. Jackson Hole, Wyoming. 31 August.

Hellenic Financial Stability Fund. 2016. Updated Analysis of Non-Regulatory Constraints and Impediments for the Development of the NPL Market in Greece. September 2016.

———. 2017. Progress Update of HFSF's Study on NPL Market Impediments. June. Athens.

HM Treasury. 2015. Rothschild Report on the Government's Shareholdings in the Royal Bank of Scotland (RBS). 10 June.

Honohan, P. 2010. The Irish Banking Crisis Regulatory and Financial Stability Policy 2003–2008. Report to the Minister of Finance by the Governor of the Central Bank. 31 May.

House of Commons Treasury Committee. 2012. Treasury Fifth Report. The FSA's Report into the Failure of RBS. London.

Hsu, B., D. Arner, and Q. Wan. 2007. Policy Functions as Law: Legislative Forbearance in China's Asset Management Companies. *UCLA Pacific Basin Law Journal*. 23 (2). pp. 129–171.

International Monetary Fund (IMF). 2010. IMF Approves €22.5 Billion Loan for Ireland. *IMF News*. 16 December. https://www.imf.org/en/News/Articles/2015/09/28/04/53/socar121610a.

———. 2011. United Kingdom: Crisis Management and Bank Resolution Technical Note. *IMF Country Report*. No. 11/228. Washington, DC.

_____. 2013. Spain: Financial Sector Reform—Third Progress Report. *IMF Country Report*. No. 13/205. Washington, DC.

_____. 2015. Ireland: Ex Post Evaluation of Exceptional Access Under the 2010 Extended Arrangement. *IMF Country Report*. No. 15/20. Washington, DC.

_____. 2016. Italy – 2016 Article IV Consultation; Press Release; Staff Report; and Statement by the Executive Director for Italy. *IMF Country Report*. No. 16/222. Washington, DC.

_____. 2020. Policy Steps to Address the Corona Virus. Policy Papers. Washington, DC.

Jassaud, N. and K. Kang. 2015. A Strategy for Developing a Market for Nonperforming Loans in Italy. *IMF Working Paper*. WP/15/24. Washington, DC: IMF.

Jiménez G., S. Ongena, J-L Peydró, and J. Saurina. 2012. Macroprudential Policy, Countercyclical Bank Capital Buffers and Credit Supply: Evidence from the Spanish Dynamic Provisioning Experiments. *Barcelona GSE Working Paper Series*. no 628. Barcelona Graduate School of Economics: Barcelona.

_____. 2014. Hazardous Times for Monetary Policy: What Do Twenty-Three Million Bank Loans Say About the Effects of Monetary Policy on Credit Risk? *Econometrica* 82 (2). pp. 463–505.

Kang, D. 2004. Key Success Factors on the Revitalization of Distressed Firms: A Case of the Korean Workouts. Korea Development Institute, 2–2. Sejong.

Kashyap, A. K., O. A. Lamont, and J. C. Stein. 1994. Credit Conditions and the Cyclical Behavior of Inventories. *Quarterly Journal of Economics*. 109 (3). pp. 565–592.

Kawai, M. and K. Takayasu 1999. The Economic Crisis and Financial Sector Restructuring in Thailand. In *Rising to the Challenge in Asia: A Study of Financial Markets: Volume 11 – Thailand*. Manila: Asian Development Bank.

Kim, K. 2006. The 1997–98 Korean Financial Crisis: Causes, Policy Response, and Lessons. Presentation at The High-Level Seminar on Crisis Prevention in Emerging Markets. Singapore. 10-11 July.

Kiyotaki, N. and J. Moore. 1997. Credit Cycles. *Journal of Political Economy*. 105 (2). pp. 211–248.

KKR. 2016. Alpha Bank, Eurobank and KKR Reach Agreement to Support Greek Companies. Press release. 17 May. KKR.

Klein, N. 2013. Non-Performing Loans in CESEE: Determinants and Impact on Macroeconomic Performance. *IMF Working Paper*. WP/13/72. Washington, DC: IMF.

Landini, F. and M. Gaia. 2016. KKR Unit Takes on Italian Shipping Company Debt from Banks. *Reuters*. 22 April.

Lee, G. 2019. China's Biggest Banks Well Prepped on Non-Performing Loans, Ready for Stricter Reporting Standard. *SCMP*. 15 May.

Leng, C. and S. Zhang. 2019. China Bank First-Quarter Bad Loans Hit 16-Year-High as Regulator Tightens Oversight. *Reuters*. 10 May.

Li, Z., S. Qu, and J. Zhang. 2011. Quantifying the Value of Implicit Government Guarantees for Large Financial Institutions. Moody's Analytics Quantitative Research Group.

Lindgren, C-J., T. J. T. Balino, C. Enoch, A-M. Gulde, M. Quintyn, and L. Teo. 1999. Financial Sector Crisis and Restructuring: Lessons from Asia. International Monetary Fund, *Occasional Paper* 188. Washington, DC.

Liu, R. and H. Wu. 2016. Carving up the Non-performing Loan Elephant. As rewritten by Han Wei. *CaixinOnline*. 8 August. https://www.caixinglobal.com/2016-08-08/carving-up-the-non-performing-loan-elephant-101011466.html.

Ma, G. 2006. Who Pays China's Bank Restructuring Bill? Centre d'Études Prospectives et D'Informations Internationales. Paris.

Ma, G. and B. S. C. Fung. 2002. China's Asset Management Corporations. *BIS Working Papers*. No 115. Basel: Bank for International Settlements.

McMahon, D. 2019a. Slow, Steady, Cheap, and Painless – Making Sense of China's Bad Loan Strategy. *Marco Polo*. 8 April. https://macropolo.org/cleanup_analysis/slow-steady-cheap-and-painless-making-sense-of-chinas-bad-loan-strategy/.

_____. 2019b. China's Major Banks Turn Inward to Deal with Bad Loans. *Marco Polo*. 21 May. https://marcopolo.org/china-bad-loans-amc-write-offs/

_____. 2019c. Is There a Method Behind Beijing's Bank Rescue Madness? *Marco Polo*. 18 November. https://macropolo.org/beijing-bank-rescue-method/?rp=e.

Minsky, H. P. 1992. The Financial Instability Hypothesis. *Levy Economics Institute of Bard College Working Paper*. No. 74. Annandale-on-Hudson: Levy Economics Institute.

Mitchell, T. and Y. Yang. 2019. China Central Bank Head Warns on Strength of Regional Lenders. *Financial Times*, Beijing. 24 September.

Mo, Y. K. 2016. A Review of Recent Banking Reforms. Bank for International Settlements. Basel.

Molnar, M. and J. Lu. 2019. State-Owned Firms Behind China's Corporate Debt. OECD ECO/WKP(2019)5. Paris: OECD.

Moody's Investor Services. 2016. The Royal Bank of Scotland Group plc – Substantial Restructuring Progress Underpins Our Positive Outlook. January.

Morgan, D. P. and K. J. Stiroh. 2005. Too Big to Fail after All These Years. Federal Reserve Bank of New York Staff Reports. No. 220. New York.

National Asset Management Agency (NAMA). 2011. Annual Report and Financial Statements. 30 June. Dublin.https://1library.net/document/zkw517mz-nationa -asset-management-agency-annual-report-financial-statements.html.

National Audit Office. 2010. HM Treasury, The Asset Protection Scheme. Report by the Comptroller and Auditor General. 21 December. London.

Nimmanahaeminda, T. 1998. Statement by the Hon. Tarrin Nimmanahaeminda, Governor of the Bank for Thailand, at the Joint Annual Discussion. Press release. International Monetary Fund, 1998 Annual Meetings. 6–8 October.

Nkusu, M. 2011. Nonperforming Loans and Macrofinancial Vulnerabilities in Advanced Economies. *IMF Working Paper*, WP/11/161. Washington, DC: IMF.

Organisation for Economic Co-operation and Development (OECD). 2001. *Insolvency Systems in Asia: An Efficiency Perspective*. Finance and Investment series Paris: OECD.

_____. 2011. OECD Economic Surveys: Ireland. Paris.

Prasad, A. and R. A. Espinoza. 2010. Nonperforming Loans in the GCC Banking System and Their Macroeconomic Effects. *IMF Working Paper*, WP/10/224. Washington, DC: IMF.

PricewaterhouseCoopers (PwC). 2020. *The Chinese NPL Market in 2020: Regulatory catalyst may lead to higher volumes.* February.

Quarati, A. 2016. Milan Stock Exchange: Deal with Pillarstone Lifts Premuda Shares. *The Medi Telegraph.* 23 April 2016.

Rajan, R. G. and L. Zingales. 1998. Financial Dependence and Growth. *American Economic Review.* 88 (3). pp. 559–586.

Reiser, A. 2017. EBRD to Invest in Pillarstone Greece. *EBRD News.* 11 May. https://www.ebrd.com/news/2017/ebrd-to-invest-in-pillarstone-greece.html.

Reuters. 2017. Fitch: Italy Bridge Banks Sale Highlights Post-Resolution costs. 20 January.

Santos, J. A. C. 2014. Evidence from the Bond Market on Banks "Too-Big-To-Fail" Subsidy. *Federal Reserve Bank of New York Economic Policy Review.* 20 (20). pp. 29–39.

Securities and Exchange Commission (SEC). 2007. UBS AG Form 6-K. Report on Foreign Issuer, Washington, 2.

Sherlock, S. 1998. Crisis in Indonesia: Economy, Society and Politics. Parliament of Australia. Current Issues Brief 13 1997–1998. April. http://www.aph.gov.au/About_Parliament/Parliamentary_Departments/Parliamentary_Library/Publications_Archive/CIB/CIB9798/98cib13.

Swiss Federal Banking Commission. 2008. Subprime Crisis: SFBC Investigation into the Causes of the Write-downs of UBS AG. September .

Swiss National Bank (SNB). 2013a. SNB Purchases StabFund from SNB. Press release. 8 November.

———. 2013b. SNB StabFund Repays Swiss National Bank Loan. Press release, 16 August.

———. 2013c. SNB's Special Purpose Vehicle for UBS Assets to be Domiciled in Switzerland. Press release. 26 November.

Ueda, K. and B. Weder Di Mauro. 2011. Quantifying the Value of the Subsidy for systemically Important Financial Institutions. *IMF Working Paper* WP/12/128. Washington, DC: IMF.

UK Financial Investments Limited (UKFI). 2010. UK Financial Investments Limited (UKFI) Update on UKFI Market Investments March 2010.

Visco, I. 2017. Address by the Governor of the Bank of Italy. Italian Banking Association Annual Meeting.

Weber, A., E. Kopp, and J. Garrido. 2016. Cleaning-Up Bank Balance Sheets: Economic, Legal, and Supervisory Measures for Italy. *IMF Working Paper*, WP/16/135. Washington, DC: IMF.

Weber, R., D. Arner, E. Gibson, and S. Baumann. 2014. Addressing Systemic Risk: Financial Regulatory Design. *Texas International Law Journal*. 49 (2). pp. 149–200.

Wood, P. R. 2007. Project Finance, Securitisations, Subordinated Debt. The Law and Practice of International Finance Series. Volume 5. London: Sweet and Maxwell Limited. pp. 111–174.

World Bank. 2002. Bank Loan Classification and Provisioning Practices in Selected Developed and Emerging Countries. *A Survey of Current Practices in Countries Represented on the Basel Core Principles Liaison Group.*

World Bank, IMF, European Investment Bank, European Bank for Reconstruction and Development, ECB, and European Commission, European Banking Coordination. 2012. Vienna Initiative - Working Group on NPLs in Central, Eastern and Southeastern Europe. March 2012.

Xiaomeng, W. and L. Xiao. 2019. Regulators Pressure Banks to Speed Up Bad-Debt Recognition. *CaixinOnline.* 12 June.

Yue, H. and D. Jia. 2019. China's Regulator Drafts Rules for Local AMCs, 16 February 2019. Caixin.

PART

2

Empirical Analyses
of the Macrofinancial Implications
of Nonperforming Loans
in Asia and Europe

3 Assessing Macrofinancial Implications and Resolution Policies of Nonperforming Loans

Daekeun Park, Junkyu Lee, and Peter Rosenkranz[1]

3.1 Introduction

Nonperforming loans (NPLs), however hard banks and their supervisors try, are an unavoidable by-product of the banking business. They burden the banks, strain their liquicity, increase their funding costs, reduce their capacity to extend new loans, and deplete their earnings. This is why resolving NPLs is regarded as essential to banking.

Empirical analysis of the determinants of NPLs examines the role of macroeconomic variables and of bank-specific factors in driving their movements. Evidence of the macroeconomic factors influencing credit risk points to the countercyclical behavior of NPLs (Klein 2013). An expansion in real gross domestic product (GDP) leads to an improvement in borrower repayment capacity, a reduction of default risk, and a decline in NPLs; economic contraction works in the opposite direction. More generally, better macroeconomic conditions—a decline in unemployment, inflation, currency depreciation, and global financial volatility, among other factors—constrain NPL ratios (Roy 2014; Ha, Trien, and Diep 2014; Lee and Rosenkranz 2019). In their examination of the bank-specific factors associated with higher NPLs in Asia, Lee and Rosenkranz (2019) point to decreased capitalization, lowered profitability, increased risk appetite, past loan growth, and fall in credit supply.

NPLs not only directly damage banks, but also eventually burden the entire economy by keeping banks from adequately performing the role of financial intermediation, slowing down overall economic activity. Empirical studies

[1] The authors thank Alyssa Villanueva, Hyewon Kang, and Monica Melchor for their excellent research assistance.

also confirm the negative macrofinancial feedback effects of NPLs. Espinoza and Prasad (2010), Nkusu (2011), De Bock and Demyanets (2012), Klein (2013), and Lee and Rosenkranz (2019) find that an increase in the NPL ratio generates a strong, albeit short-lived, negative response in economic activities such as output growth, employment, and credit growth, although the magnitude differs depending on the sample group of countries and the sample period.

Besides, a large and sustained buildup of NPLs could raise the possibility of a banking crisis, which usually develops into a nationwide financial crisis, levying a heavy toll on the entire economy. Previous financial crises have demonstrated the long-lasting negative impacts NPLs can have on financial stability and economic performance, as their effects persist beyond crisis periods. Ari et al. (2019), investigating NPL ratios in 88 banking crises since 1990, find that pre-crisis NPL problems and the severity of post-crisis recessions are closely related and argue that reducing pre-crisis vulnerabilities and quickly addressing NPL problems during a crisis are vital for post-crisis output recovery.

Consequently, the identification of policy options to effectively manage and respond to a buildup in NPLs has gained attention in recent years. Policy makers have diverse tools for tackling a large and sustained buildup of NPLs and to resolve them, including establishing public asset management companies (AMCs), asset protection schemes, and debt write-offs, together with injections of public funds to recapitalize banks. Although each of these measures can resolve NPLs from banks' loan portfolios and lower the overall NPL ratio, substantial costs are involved. These costs should be weighed against the benefit of reducing NPLs for macrofinancial issues, including economic growth, unemployment, exchange rates, and the supply of credit.

This study evaluates the effectiveness of NPL resolution policies by assessing the macrofinancial implications of NPLs. It uses a new NPL dataset constructed from bank-level NPL data provided by Standard & Poor's (S&P) Global Market Intelligence.

To do so, the chapter adopts a two-step strategy. First, the analysis investigates whether NPL resolution policy measures bring about a sharp drop in the overall NPL ratio of an economy. We focus on these sharp drops because NPL reduction tends to start with just such a precipitous decline in the overall NPL ratio. In particular, Balgova, Plekhanov, and Skrzypińska (2017) observe that among 178 episodes of NPL reduction,

143 (about 80%) began as such. Focusing on the sharp drops thus allows us to investigate policy effectiveness and the associated macrofinancial effects. Observation of NPL ratio behavior indeed reveals that, from time to time, ratios move sharply up and down. While it is possible that the factors that have proved significant in explaining the overall movements of NPL ratios also explain the sharp movements, it is also possible that not all the factors are useful in doing so. Indeed, other factors may be responsible for the sharp movements. For example, besides improved macroeconomic conditions, NPL resolution measures such as the establishment of public AMCs and injection of public funds may account for the sharp reductions.

Second, the analysis evaluates the effect of a sharp drop in an NPL ratio on the performance of macrofinancial variables by estimating the average treatment effect on the treated. NPL reductions starting with a sharp drop in the ratio are regarded as the treatment group, and the episodes of high and persistent NPL ratio as the control group. Balgova, Plekhanov, and Skrzypińska (2017) made the first attempt to measure the effects of NPL reduction measures on macroeconomic performance by estimating the average treatment effect on the treated.

In the chapter, the next section introduces the literature that empirically investigates the determinants of NPLs and that measures the macroeconomic feedback effects of NPL reduction. Section 3.3 describes the NPL ratio data. Section 3.4 estimates dynamic panel models for NPL ratios and discusses the results. In addition, panel probit models for sharp rises and sharp drops in NPL ratios are estimated. Section 3.5 measures the macrofinancial effects of an NPL reduction by estimating the treatment effect on the treated. Section 3.6 concludes.

3.2 Literature Review

Much of the existing literature on NPLs investigates macroeconomic factors and bank-specific factors rather than the adoption of NPL resolution policies. Bank-specific factors focus on the variables that may signal or influence the risk-taking practices of banks. On the other hand, macroeconomic factors focus on the variables expected to affect borrowers' debt servicing abilities. These studies find that deteriorating macroeconomic conditions—such as lower economic growth, higher unemployment or inflation rates, greater currency depreciation, sudden reversals of portfolio flows, and higher global financial volatility—tend to raise NPL ratios.

For example, Nkusu (2011), investigating the determinants of NPLs across 26 developed countries, finds that deteriorating macroeconomic conditions such as lower economic growth and higher unemployment lead to higher NPL ratios. De Bock and Demyanets (2012) use panel data consisting of 25 emerging market economies to find that lower economic growth, currency depreciation, weaker terms of trade, and lower debt-creating capital inflows deteriorate loan quality and decrease credit growth. In particular, their analysis reveals that sudden reversals of portfolio inflows are likely to be followed by a sharp deterioration in loan quality. Klein (2013), using bank-level data from 16 countries in Central, Eastern, and Southeastern Europe, demonstrates that NPL ratios are significantly affected by the unemployment, GDP growth, and inflation rates.

Lee and Rosenkranz (2019), using panel data of 165 commercial banks from 17 emerging economies in Asia, find that both macroeconomic and bank-level variables are key to explaining the evolution of banks' NPL ratios in Asia, which themselves have strong negative feedback effects on the economy (Box 3.1). In particular, higher NPL ratios are associated with higher unemployment and inflation rates, greater currency depreciation, and lower economic growth. They also find that NPL ratios tend to rise when global financial volatility is higher. Likewise, Espinoza and Prasad (2010), investigating a sample of 80 banks in the Gulf Cooperation Council region, find that NPL ratios are positively correlated with greater global financial volatility. In addition to macroeconomic factors, meanwhile, Ozili (2019) investigates the influence of financial development on NPLs. Using a global sample of country-level panel data, Ozili finds that two financial sector development proxies—foreign bank presence and financial intermediation (as measured by private credit by banks to GDP)—are positively associated with NPL ratios.

Box 3.1: Assessing the Determinants of Nonperforming Loans in Asia

To evaluate the determinants of nonperforming loans (NPLs) in Asia, a dynamic panel data model is estimated examining macroeconomic and bank-level variables. The analysis employs panel data of individual banks' balance sheets from BankScope and macroeconomic indicators from CEIC. The sample covers annual data for 1995–2014. Bank-level data consists of 165 commercial banks in 17 emerging economies in Asia, and the dataset covers more than 60%

continued on next page

Box 3.1 (continued)

of the banking sector's assets in most of the sample countries. The data on NPLs consists of 2,271 observations. Across all specifications and estimation methods, the results suggest that banks' NPL ratios exhibit strong serial correlation, with an estimated coefficient of the lagged dependent variable ranging between 0.6 and 0.9.

The results of the dynamic panel data model across all specifications underline that both macroeconomic indicators and bank-level variables play an important role in explaining the evolution of banks' NPL ratios. The real GDP growth rate, change in unemployment rate, and inflation rate have a considerable effect on NPLs. An economic slowdown raises unemployment and hampers debt servicing capacity, prompting a rise in NPLs. Higher inflation can similarly hurt debt servicing capacity as it weakens real income when wages are sticky. The VIX, exchange rate, and the Asian financial crisis dummy also have an important impact on the evolution of NPLs across banks in emerging Asia as greater global risk aversion and tighter financing conditions exacerbate a surge in distressed assets. Bank-specific factors have a statistically significant, though relatively small, effect on the buildup of credit risk. In particular, a lower equity-to-asset ratio, signifying lower capital, is associated with higher NPLs. The loans-to-deposit ratio—a measure of bank liquidity—and past excessive lending, as captured by lagged loans growth, are similarly associated with an increase in credit risk. On the other hand, increasing return on equity, signifying higher bank profitability, reduces NPLs (table).

Estimation Results Dynamic Panel Regression

VARIABLES		Bank-level variables	
Nonperforming loans (lagged)	0.697***	Equity-to-assets ratio (lagged)	−0.005
Macroeconomic variables		Return on equity (lagged)	−0.002*
Unemployment rate	0.129***	Loans-to-deposits ratio (lagged)	0.001***
Inflation rate (lagged)	0.010**		
Exchange rate (lagged)	0.000	Loans growth rate (twice lagged)	0.0004***
Real GDP growth rate (lagged)	−0.017***		
Volatility index	0.006***		
Asian financial crisis (dummy)	0.383***		

GDP = gross domestic product.
Note: Results reflect fixed effects estimation. The dependent variable is the logit transformation of the NPL ratio. *** = significant at 1%, ** = significant at 5%, * = significant at 10%.
Source: Lee, J., and P. Rosenkranz. 2019, Nonperforming Loans in Asia: Determinants and Macrofinancial Linkages, ADB Economics Working Paper Series No. 574.

Unlike these studies, Balgova, Plekhanov, and Skrzypińska (2017) evaluate the effectiveness of NPL policy measures by focusing on episodes of sharp reductions in NPL ratios. Estimating a two-part model, they investigate if policy measures such as establishing public AMCs, injecting public funds, adopting macroprudential regulations, and loosening criteria for NPL recognition reduce overall NPL ratios. They find that the introduction of AMCs is more effective than bank recapitalization in reducing NPL ratios, but that AMCs are more effective in reducing NPL ratios when used alongside bank recapitalization.

Balgova, Plekhanov, and Skrzypińska (2017) also measure the macrofinancial effects of NPL reduction policies by estimating the average treatment effect on the treated. They use the episodes of sharp drops in NPL ratios as the treatment group and the episodes of persistently high NPLs as the control group. Using propensity score matching analysis, they find that sharp reductions in NPL ratios lead to extra growth (in per capita GDP) in excess of 1.5 percentage points a year over several years.

By contrast, other empirical studies measuring the macrofinancial effects of NPLs investigate impulse response functions estimated from panel vector autoregressive (VAR) models. Panel VAR models are used to avoid the simultaneity problem arising from NPLs and macrofinancial variables affecting each other. These studies try to estimate the macrofinancial effects of NPLs in different groups of countries: Espinoza and Prasad (2010) in the Gulf Cooperation Council countries; Nkusu (2011) in advanced economies; De Bock and Demyanets (2012) in emerging economies; Klein (2013) in the Central, Eastern, and Southeastern European countries; and Lee and Rosenkranz (2019) in the emerging economies in Asia. These studies find that the rise in NPL ratios has strong, albeit short, negative effects on macrofinancial variables such as growth, unemployment, and credit expansion.

3.3   Nonperforming Loan Data and Reduction Episodes

3.3.1 The New Nonperforming Loan Dataset

We construct a country-level panel dataset of NPL ratios using bank-level data from S&P Global Market Intelligence, which is the new name of SNL Financials after its merger with S&P Capital IQ. S&P provides access to about 200 items from the financial statements of banks. It is regarded as an alternative to BankScope, which is now called Orbis Bank Focus.

The continuity of the BankScope data was not ensured when BankScope was rebranded. The new NPL dataset constructed may be regarded as an alternative to the NPL ratio available from the International Monetary Fund (IMF) Financial Soundness Indicators.

Since the S&P database provides information on NPLs at the bank-level only, the analysis computes the NPL ratio of a country by aggregating the NPLs of all the banks belonging to the country. One of the problems with constructing country-level data from bank-level data is that not all banks belonging to a country are covered by the data source. Although the S&P data covers banks across 192 countries, its coverage of individual banks differs significantly across countries and sometimes across years. As a result, only the countries where the S&P database covers at least 25% of the total assets of the entire banking sector of the country are selected. The data for the total amount of assets of the banking sector are collected from the IMF International Financial Statistics. This selection criterion leaves us with 76 countries.

3.3.2 Episodes of Nonperforming Loan Reduction

We focus on two types of episodes—NPL reductions and rises. Adapting the operational definition of an NPL reduction episode used by Balgova, Plekhanov, and Skrzypińska (2017), this analysis defines it as a period of consecutive drops in the NPL ratio, with the cumulative reduction exceeding 6 percentage points.[2] Sometimes, such a period is interrupted by a short and small rise in the NPL ratio and, thus, such a rise is not regarded as an interruption in the episode so long as it is limited to a single year and involves a relatively small rise—that is, less than a 1.6-percentage-point increase in the NPL ratio. Likewise, an NPL rise episode is defined as a period of consecutive rises in the NPL ratio with the cumulative rise exceeding 6 percentage points. These operational definitions allow us to identify 41 episodes of NPL reduction and 47 of rise from the newly constructed dataset of NPL ratios.

Among the 41 episodes of NPL reduction, 24 start with a more than 4-percentage-point drop in the NPL ratio in a single year, which this analysis calls a sharp drop in the NPL ratio.[3] Among the 47 NPL rise episodes,

---

[2] Balgova, Plekhanov, and Skrzypińska (2017) use the criterion of a cumulative reduction of the NPL ratio exceeding 7 percentage points. Use of this criterion does not affect the results of this chapter significantly.

[3] Balgova, Plekhanov, and Skrzypińska (2017) use the criterion of a more than 5-percentage-point drop. In order to increase the number of episodes of sharp drops, we adopt the criterion of a more than 4-percentage-point drop.

22 start with a sharp rise in the NPL ratio. Therefore, more than half of the episodes of NPL reduction and NPL rise start with a year of sharp movement in the NPL ratio, although more so for an episode of NPL reduction. This motivates us to focus on episodes of sharp drops in the NPL ratio to explore the determinants of the NPL ratio and to evaluate the effectiveness of NPL resolution policy measures. Figure 3.1 shows the movement of the NPL ratio for the 24 episodes of NPL reduction starting with a sharp drop in the NPL ratio.

3.4 Determinants of Sharp Movements in Nonperforming Loan Ratios

Before proceeding to analyze the determinants of sharp movements in the NPL ratio, the analysis starts by estimating a linear panel regression model:

$$\Delta NPL_{c,t} = \alpha + \beta \Delta NPL_{c,t-1} + \mu \boldsymbol{X}_{c,t} + \theta \boldsymbol{Frame}_{c,t} + v_{c,t} \tag{3.1}$$

In this equation, $\Delta NPL_{c,t}$ denotes the change in the NPL ratio of country c in year t. $\boldsymbol{X}$ is a vector of control variables which consists of country-specific macroeconomic variables and global macroeconomic variables. Country-specific macroeconomic variables include real GDP growth rate, inflation rate, rate of change in exchange rate, and rate of change in real estate prices. Global macroeconomic variables include the volatility index (VIX), rate of change in global commodity prices, and a global financial crisis (GFC) dummy.

Since the debt servicing capability of borrowers is positively affected by higher economic growth and lower inflation, the growth and inflation rates are expected to have a negative coefficient and a positive coefficient, respectively. The change in real estate prices may have opposite effects on NPLs. On one hand, property market booms are expected to enhance the debt servicing ability of borrowers. On the other, they may deteriorate the quality of loans as loan screening criteria become looser during property booms. A sharp currency depreciation is expected to increase the amount of NPLs in countries that rely heavily on external debt, as currency depreciation increases the debt service burden of foreign currency-denominated loans. Since exchange rates are expressed in units of local currency per US dollar, a positive value for the rate of change in the exchange rate implies a currency depreciation. Thus, the coefficient of this variable is expected to be positive.

Figure 3.1: Episodes of NPL Reduction Starting with a Sharp Drop in the NPL Ratio

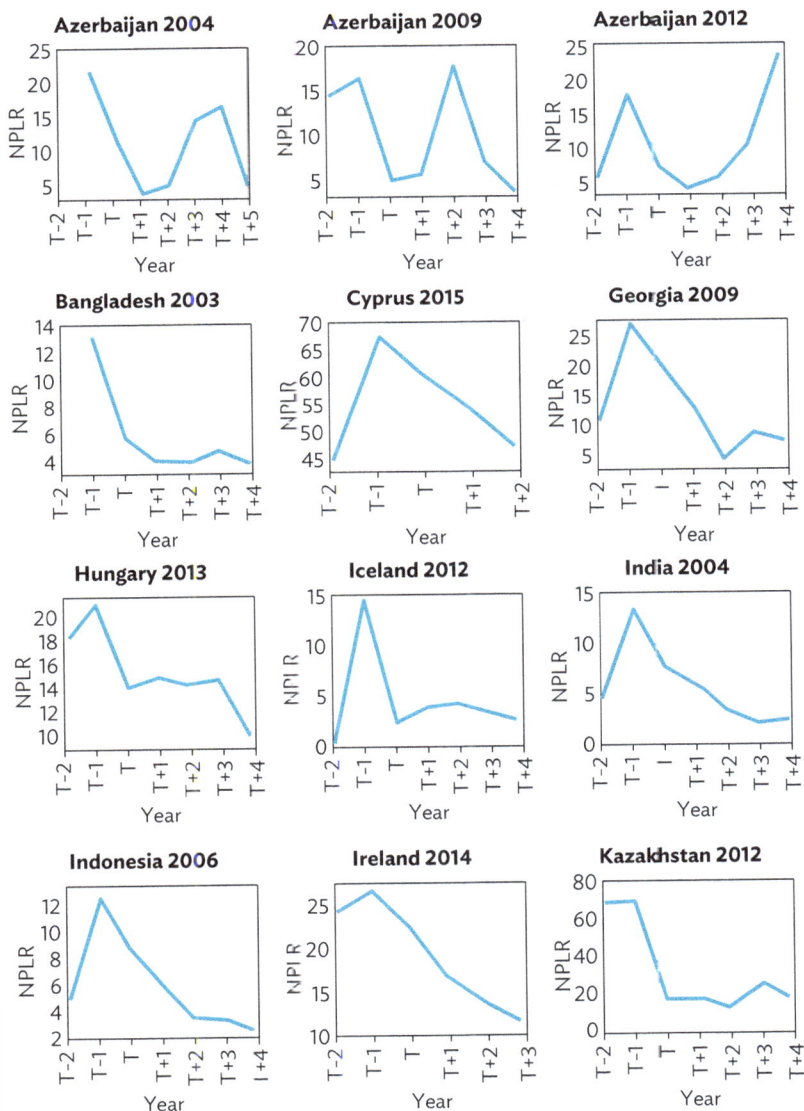

continued on next page

Figure 3.1 *(continued)*

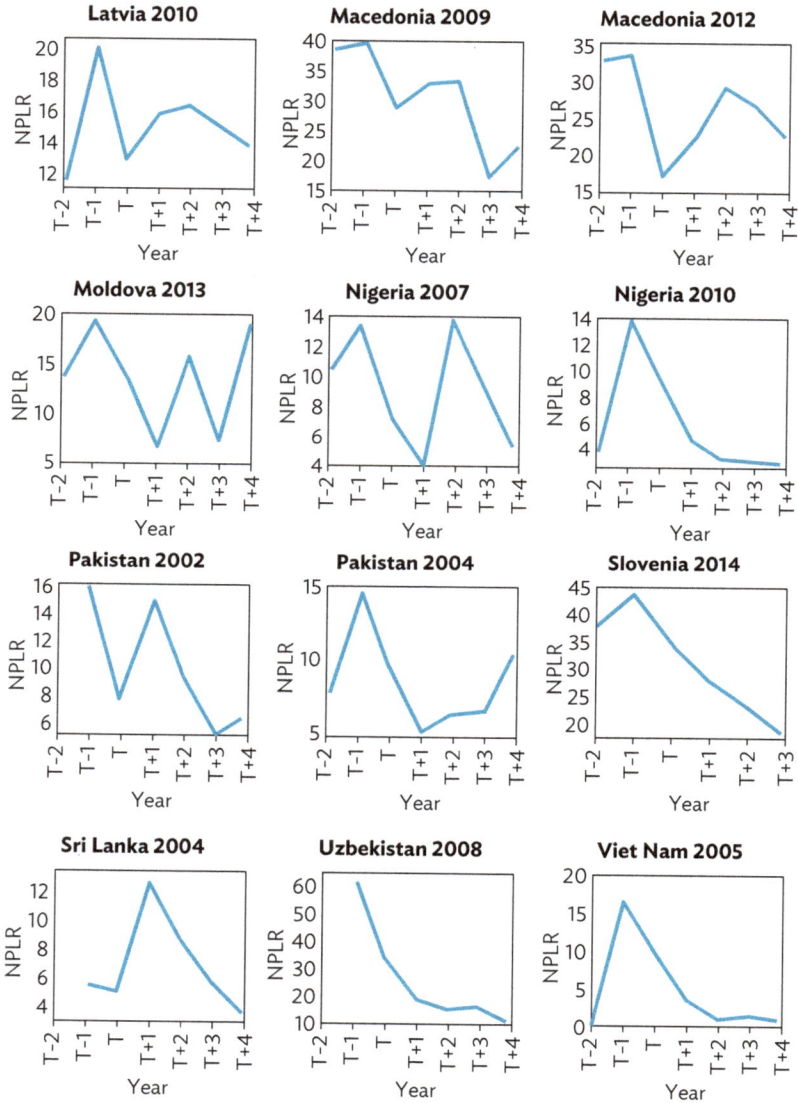

NPL = nonperforming loan, NPLR = nonperforming loan ratio.
Source: Authors' calculations using data from Standard & Poor's Global Market Intelligence (accessed August 2018).

The VIX represents market volatility and risk attitude in global financial markets. Higher financial market volatility makes it harder for borrowers with high risk profiles to have their loans rolled over. As a result, the coefficient of the VIX is expected to be positive. The GFC dummy takes a value of 1 for 2008 and 2009, and 0 otherwise, and is expected to have a positive sign. Changes in commodity prices are expected to have different effects on the loan quality of countries depending on whether these are commodity exporters or importers. Lower commodity prices will negatively affect commodity exporting countries, raising their NPL ratios.

Frame is a vector of policy dummy variables which takes a value of 1 if the corresponding NPL resolution framework was in operation during the year. We consider the existence of public AMCs, injection of public bailout funds, and strengthening of macroprudential regulations as NPL resolution policy measures. Data on public AMCs is available from the Building Better Bad Banks project by Hallerberg and Gandrud (2015). The database contains information on 139 cases of AMCs across 62 countries during 1996–2016. The data on financial sector bailouts is taken from Bova et al. (2016). The database includes 95 cases of financial sector bailouts across 66 countries. The macroprudential policy dummy takes a value of 1 if the macroprudential policy on banks is strengthened. The data is available from Cerutti, Claessens, and Laeven (2015).

Table 3.1 presents the description and data source for the variables included in equation (3.1). Table 3.2 presents the descriptive statistics for these variables. The NPL ratio data themselves are an unbalanced panel. The explanatory variables are collected from different data sources and their sample coverage differs with data availability. Table 3.3 displays the results of panel unit root tests. Both tests strongly reject the existence of a unit root for all the variables tested.

Table 3.1: Variables and Data Source

Variable	Description	Frequency	Source
Change in NPL ratio	Change in ratio of NPLs over total loans	Yearly	Standard & Poor's Global Market Intelligence
Growth rate	Real GDP annual growth rate	Yearly	World Bank World Development Indicators
Inflation rate	Commodity price index annual growth rate	Yearly	World Bank World Development Indicators
Rate of change in exchange rate	Rate of change of local currency/US dollar	Yearly	CEIC
Rate of change in real estate prices	Rate of change of housing price index	Yearly	CEIC
Volatility Index (VIX)	Chicago Board Options Exchange Volatility Index	Yearly	Bloomberg
Rate of change in global commodity price	Primary commodity prices	Yearly	International Monetary Fund
Existence of public AMCs	= 1 if a public AMC is in operation either at t, t-1, or t-2	Yearly	Assigned
Injection of public bailout funds	= 1 if a bailout exists either at t, t-1, or t-2	Yearly	Assigned
Macroprudential policy	= 1 if a positive change in macroprudential policy index occurs at t, t-1, or t-2	Yearly	Assigned

AMC = asset management company, GDP = gross domestic product, NPL = nonperforming loan.
Source: Authors' compilation.

Table 3.2: Descriptive Statistics

Statistic	Mean	S.D.	Min	Max	Observations
NPL ratio (%)	6.072	0.966	0.002	94.480	1,104
ΔNPL ratio (%)	0.273	4.579	-52.252	72.431	1,104
Growth rate (%)	3.534	3.893	-14.814	34.500	1,104
Inflation rate (%)	4.677	5.472	-4.470	59.220	1,090
Exchange rate (%)	2.967	15.713	-28.751	232.166	1,104
Property price (%)	4.362	7.453	-29.302	43.345	500
Commodity price (%)	5.129	18.418	-31.886	26.328	1,104
VIX	19.382	6.460	11.090	32.693	1,104
AMC dummy	0.568	0.496	0	1	621
Bailout dummy	0.145	0.352	0	1	801

AMC = asset management company, NPL = nonperforming loan, S.D. = standard deviation, VIX = volatility index.
Sources: Authors' calculations using data from Bloomberg; Bova et al. (2016); CEIC database; Hallerberg and Gandrud (2015); International Monetary Fund; Standard & Poor's Global Market Intelligence; and World Bank World Development Indicators (accessed August 2018).

Table 3.3: Panel Unit Root Tests
(Fisher-type unit root test)

Variable	Fisher-ADF	Fisher-PP
NPL ratio	399.99***	336.04***
Change in NPL ratio	502.24***	1149.10***
Real GDP growth	472.18***	520.76***
Inflation	400.37***	591.15***
Change in exchange rate	438.56***	788.94***
Loan growth rate	314.26***	528.34***
Change in house prices	142.98***	211.05***
VIX	233.55***	138.97***
Change in price index	268.71***	597.53***

ADF = Augmented Dickey Fuller, GDP = gross domestic product, NPL = nonperforming loan,
PP = Phillips-Perron, VIX = volatility index.
Notes: *** = significant at 0.1%. Empirical results have been derived using Stata 15 software. Reported unit root tests were conducted with one lag.
Sources: Authors' calculations using data from Bloomberg; CEIC database; International Monetary Fund; Standard & Poor's Global Market Intelligence; and World Bank World Development Indicators (accessed August 2018).

Since the lagged dependent variable is included as one of the explanatory variables in equation (3.1), the model to be estimated is a dynamic panel model. To get a consistent estimate for this dynamical panel model, this analysis uses the generalized method of moments (GMM) estimator suggested by Arellano and Bond (1991). Table 3.4 shows the estimation results for various model specifications. The results for model 1 show that only the growth rate and VIX are significant in explaining the change in the NPL ratio. In addition, the sign of the coefficient estimates is consistent with the theoretical prediction: higher growth rate helps lower NPL ratios, while higher volatility in international financial markets tends to raise NPL ratios. Other variables, such as the inflation rate, the rate of currency depreciation, and the rate of change in commodity prices that usually display significance in explaining the level of NPL ratios in previous empirical literature, fail to demonstrate significance in explaining the change in NPL ratios. Meanwhile, the coefficient of the lagged dependent variable is negative, implying that a year of a large rise (drop) in the NPL ratio is likely to be followed by a year of drop (rise) in the NPL ratio.

Table 3.4: Dynamic Panel Regression Models

Variable	(1)	(2)	(3)	(4)
ΔNPL(t-1)	-0.0724**	-0.0152	-0.0716**	-0.0051
	(-2.07)	(-0.31)	(2.04)	(-0.10)
Growth	-0.1124**	-0.0927**	-0.1178**	-0.2958**
	(-2.40)	(-2.39)	(-2.48)	(-3.78)
Inflation	0.0436	0.2599**	0.0373	-0.0360
	(0.98)	(4.69)	(0.83)	(-0.58)
Exchange rate change	0.0017	0.0001	0.0019	-0.0087
	(0.16)	(0.01)	(0.19)	(-0.65)
Property		-0.0221		
		(-1.37)		
Commodity	-0.0083	-0.0017	-0.0063	0.0057
	(-0.99)	(-1.27)	(-0.72)	(0.49)
VIX	0.1029**	0.0677**	0.0696*	0.1256**
	(4.04)	(3.95)	(1.78)	(3.62)
Global financial crisis			0.7271	
			(0.96)	
AMC				-1.8328**
				(-2.40)
Sample	902	418	902	521

AMC = asset management company, NPL = nonperforming loan, VIX = volatility index.
Note: ** = significant at 1%, * = significant at 5%.
Sources: Authors' calculations using data from Bloomberg; CEIC database; Hallerberg and Gandrud (2015); International Monetary Fund; Standard & Poor's Global Market Intelligence; and World Bank World Development Indicators (accessed August 2018).

In their analysis of determinants of NPLs in Asia, Lee and Rosenkranz (2019) find that both macroeconomic and bank-specific variables play an important role in explaining the evolution of banks' NPL ratios in Asia, which tend to be persistent in their levels (Box 3.1). Lower output growth, higher unemployment, and increased inflation are found to be associated with an elevation in NPLs. Greater global risk aversion, tighter financing conditions, and financial crises also contribute to a buildup in distressed assets. In addition, bank-specific factors are found to have a statistically significant, albeit relatively small effect in increasing credit risk. Lower bank profitability, reduced capital, and past excessive lending are associated with elevated credit risk. The present analysis reinforces the findings of Lee and Rosenkranz (2019) on the effect of output growth, inflation, and global risk aversion to credit risk.

Model 2 adds the change in property prices as an explanatory variable. The result is similar to that of model 1, except that the coefficient of inflation rate is significantly positive. Meanwhile, property prices do not affect NPL ratios significantly. As can be seen from the sample size, adding the variable of the rate of change in property prices not only changes the set of explanatory variables, but also changes the sample group. This is because the data for property prices is available only for about half of the entire sample. In model 3, the GFC dummy is added as an explanatory variable, but the result is similar to that of model 1. The GFC dummy is not significant either. It seems that the global financial crisis is taken care of by the VIX variable, as this increased sharply during that crisis.

Finally, model 4 includes the AMC dummy as an explanatory variable. A significantly negative coefficient for the AMC variable would imply the effectiveness of public AMCs in preventing the acceleration of NPL accumulation or in reducing NPLs. The estimated coefficient is significantly negative, implying that public AMCs are effective in keeping NPL ratios from rising. We also included dummy variables for public bailout funds and strengthening macroprudential regulation, but none of these variables are significant. The results of models 3 and 4 also demonstrate that currency depreciation does not have a significant effect on the NPL ratio, which is also the case in models 1 and 2.

3.4.1 Episodes of a Sharp Rise in the Nonperforming Loan Ratio

Next, the chapter looks into the determinants of a sharp rise in the NPL ratio. Investigating the factors responsible for sharp rises in the NPL ratio is of interest because economic crises, including financial and currency crises, are usually associated with a sharp rise in the NPL ratio. For this reason, this analysis looks at whether focusing on sharp movements in NPL ratio makes any difference in identifying the source of change in the NPL ratio. To focus on the determinants of a sharp rise in the NPL ratio, the following panel probit model is estimated:

$$P(SRL_{c,t} = 1) = \Phi(\alpha + \beta\Delta NPL_{c,t-1} + \mu X_{c,t} + \gamma \textbf{\textit{Frame}}_{c,t}) \qquad (3.2)$$

In equation (3.2), $SRL_{c,t}$ is a dummy variable that takes the value of 1 if a sharp rise in the NPL ratio occurs during year t in country c, and 0 otherwise. A sharp rise in the NPL ratio is defined as a more than 4-percentage-point rise in the NPL ratio in a given year. Other variables included in equation (3.2) are the same as those included in equation (3.1). The probit model is estimated with random effects and Table 3.5 presents results.

In Table 3.5, models 1 and 2 are estimated without the AMC dummy and models 3 and 4 with the AMC dummy. Models 1 and 3 are estimated with the lagged dependent variable as an explanatory variable, which is replaced by the lagged value of the NPL ratio in models 2 and 4. A major difference between the results of the dynamic panel model and those of the panel probit model is the significance of the effect of currency depreciation on the change in the NPL ratio. The estimates in Table 3.5 consistently demonstrate that a larger currency depreciation increases the possibility of a sharp rise in the NPL ratio. The results also support the general view that stronger growth lowers the possibility of a sharp rise in the NPL ratio. As for the global variables, VIX has a significant positive effect on NPL ratios, implying that larger volatility and lower risk appetite in global financial markets raise the possibility of a sharp rise in the NPL ratio. Changes in commodity prices, however, do not have a significant effect on this possibility. In conclusion, it is found that there is a difference between the determinants of a sharp rise in the NPL ratio and the determinants of changes in the NPL ratio. In particular, currency depreciation and global financial market volatility turn out to be key macroeconomic variables that explain sharp rises in the NPL ratio.

Table 3.5: Determinants of Sharp Rises in the NPL Ratio

Variable	(1)	(2)	(3)	(4)
ΔNPL(t-1)	0.1490		0.0150	
	(1.04)		(1.04)	
NPL(t-1)		0.0215**		0.0169
		(2.37)		(0.92)
Growth	-0.0248	-0.0129	-0.0246*	-0.0503*
	(-1.45)	(-0.84)	(-1.79)	(-1.63)
Inflation	0.0229*	0.2169**	0.0235*	0.0074
	(1.85)	(2.19)	(1.89)	(0.38)
Exchange rate	0.0078**	0.0068**	0.0076**	0.0081**
	(2.17)	(2.14)	(2.16)	(2.01)
Commodity	-0.0021	0.0009	-0.0021	0.0013
	(-0.54)	(0.24)	(-0.51)	(0.27)
VIX	0.0242**	0.0284**	0.0243**	0.0360**
	(2.00)	(2,71)	(2.00)	(2.44)
AMC			0.0652	0.0024
			(0.29)	(0.01)
Constant	-2.5474**	-2.5432**	-2.5751	-2.5441**
	(-8.03)	(-9.89)	(-7.73)	(-6.40)
Sample	983	1,064	983	1,064

AMC = asset management company, NPL = nonperforming loan, VIX = volatility index.
Note: ** = significant at 1%, * = significant at 5%.
Sources: Authors' calculations using data from Bloomberg; Hallerberg and Gandrud (2015); International Monetary Fund; Standard & Poor's Global Market Intelligence; and World Bank World Development Indicators (accessed August 2018).

As for NPL resolution policies, the coefficient of the AMC dummy is not significantly different from 0, meaning that public AMCs are not effective in preventing a sharp rise in the NPL ratio. We also estimated a model with the AMC dummy replaced by the public bailout dummy and the macroprudential regulation dummy, neither of which was significant.

3.4.2 Sharp Drops in the Nonperforming Loan Ratio

While it is possible that the factors that proved significant in explaining movements of the NPL ratio can explain these sharp movements as well, it is also possible that not all these factors explain sharp movements in NPL ratios. Other factors may even be responsible for these sharp movements. As a matter of fact, estimation of the probit model for sharp rises in the NPL ratio demonstrates that the macroeconomic variables that have significant effects on sharp rises in the NPL ratio are somewhat different from those that are significant in explaining general movements in NPL ratios. To see if this is also the case with sharp drops in the NPL ratio, the probit model for sharp drops in the NPL ratio is estimated and the results are presented in Tables 3.6 and 3.7.

Table 3.6: Determinants of Sharp Drops in the NPL Ratio: Models 1–4

Variable	(1)	(2)	(3)	(4)
ΔNPL(t-1)	0.0452**	0.0256	0.0406**	0.0446**
	(3.07)	(1.13)	(2.30)	(3.05)
Growth	0.0505**	0.0371**	0.0488**	0.0507**
	(2.36)	(2.25)	(2.02)	(2.35)
Inflation	-0.0395	0.0290	-0.0622*	-0.0305
	(-1.56)	(1.32)	(-1.75)	(-1.27)
Exchange rate	0.0048	-0.0017		
	(0.93)	(-0.18)		
Commodity	0.0057			
	(1.19)			
VIX	-0.0432**	-0.0638**	-0.0580**	-0.0403**
	(-2.56)	(-2.43)	(-2.47)	(-2.42)
AMC		0.9037**		
		(2.54)		
Bailout			0.1572	
			(0.44)	
MPP				-0.1226
				(-0.66)
Constant	-1.4411**	-2.1508**	-1.1151**	-1.4076**
	(-4.06)	(-3.56)	(-2.41)	(-3.84)
Sample	953	560	737	957

AMC = asset management company, MPP = macroprudential policy, NPL = nonperforming loan, VIX = volatility index.
Note: ** = significant at 1%, * = significant at 5%.
Sources: Authors' calculations using data from Bloomberg; Bova et al. (2016); CEIC database; Cerutti, Claessens, and Laeven (2015); Hallerberg and Gandrud (2015); International Monetary Fund; Standard & Poor's Global Market Intelligence; and World Bank World Development Indicators (accessed August 2018).

Table 3.7: Determinants of Sharp Drops in the NPL Ratio: Models 5–7

Variable	(5)	(6)	(7)
$\Delta NPL(t-1)$	0.0235	0.0238	0.02558
	(0.91)	(0.95)	(1.11)
Growth	0.0710	0.0518	0.0802**
	(1.60)	(1.24)	(2.16)
Inflation	0.0273	0.0272	0.0338
	(1.13)	(1.15)	(1.42)
VIX	-0.0661*	-0.0782**	-0.0689**
	(-1.84)	(-2.20)	(-2.50)
AMC	0.9112**	0.7377*	0.8648**
	(2.05)	(1.66)	(2.08)
Bailout	-0.4747	-0.6124	
	(-0.80)	(-0.99)	
MPP	0.1242		-0.4582
	(0.37)		(-0.79)
AMC*Bailout		0.5578	
		(1.29)	
AMC*MPP			0.2740
			(0.41)
Constant	-2.2274**	-1.8240**	-1.9252**
	(-2.71)	(-2.50)	(-3.08)
Sample	494	516	538

AMC = asset management company, MPP = macroprudential policy, NPL = nonperforming loan, VIX = volatility index.
Note: ** = significant at 1%, * = significant at 5%.
Sources: Authors' calculations using data from Bloomberg; Bova et al. (2016); Cerutti, Claessens, and Laeven (2015); Hallerberg and Gandrud (2015); Standard & Poor's Global Market Intelligence; and World Bank World Development Indicators (accessed August 2018).

$$P(SDL_{c,t} =1)= \Phi(\alpha+\beta \Delta NPL_{c,t-1} + \mu \boldsymbol{X}_{c,t} + \gamma \boldsymbol{Frame}_{c,t}) \qquad (3.3)$$

$SDL_{c,t}$ is a dummy variable that takes 1 if a sharp drop in the NPL ratio occurs during year t in country c and 0 otherwise. A sharp drop in the NPL ratio is defined as a more than 4-percentage-point drop in a given a year.

Model 1 is estimated with only macroeconomic variables as explanatory variables. The results show that higher growth raises the possibility of a sharp drop in the NPL ratio. Unlike the results for the panel regression model and the probit model for sharp rises in the NPL ratio, however, the rate of currency depreciation does not have any significant effects on the possibility of a sharp drop in the NPL ratio. The coefficient of VIX, however, is significantly negative, implying that stability in global financial markets is a key factor in sharp drops in the NPL ratios.

Models 2, 3, and 4 add each of the three NPL policy dummy variables: namely the public AMC dummy, the public bailout dummy, and the macroprudential regulation dummy, to the set of explanatory variables to examine the effectiveness of NPL resolution policies. The coefficient of the AMC dummy in model 2 is significantly positive, implying that public AMCs are helpful in achieving a sharp drop in the NPL ratio. Neither of the other policies, injection of public bailout funds and strengthening macroprudential regulations, however, significantly affects the possibility of achieving a sharp drop in the NPL ratio. Model 5 includes all three policy dummies as explanatory variables. It turns out that only the coefficient of the public AMC dummy is significantly positive.

Model 6 adds the interaction term between the AMC dummy and the public bailout dummy as an explanatory variable. A significantly positive value for this interaction term would imply that it is more likely for policy makers to reduce NPL ratios by implementing both policy measures together rather than adopting each of the policy measures separately. Balgova, Plekhanov, and Skrzypińska (2017) find that public AMCs are more effective in reducing NPL ratios when they are used with public bailout funds. It turns out that although the coefficient of the interaction term is positive, it is not significantly different from 0. Model 7 adds the interaction term between the AMC dummy and the macroprudential policy dummy, but the coefficient is not significantly different from 0 either.

The empirical finding that the public AMC dummy is the only NPL policy variable that consistently demonstrates significance in all of the model specifications should be interpreted with care. As a matter of fact, the result that establishing a public AMC significantly raises the possibility is not surprising. It is because it is the function of public AMCs to acquire NPLs from banks and thereby remove NPLs from banks' balance sheets. The empirical results in Tables 3.6 and 3.7 confirm the belief in this study that public AMCs have been utilized by countries to resolve a large amount of NPLs from banks' balance sheets and they were able to achieve this goal to a certain degree.

A more important question is whether lowering the NPL ratio by removing NPLs from bank balance sheets is effective in significantly improving macrofinancial performance. This will be examined in the next section.

3.5 Evaluating the Macrofinancial Effects of Nonperforming Loan Reduction

Estimation of the probit models for sharp drops in the NPL ratio demonstrates that public AMCs can be effective in sharply lowering NPL ratios in countries suffering from severe and consistent NPL problems. Given the finding that NPL resolution policies are capable of achieving a sharp drop in the NPL ratio of the banking sector of an economy, it is asked whether an NPL reduction can improve the macrofinancial performance of an economy. Following Balgova, Plekhanov, and Skrzypińska (2017), the analysis looks for the answer by estimating the average treatment effect on the treated (ATET). As equation (3.4) shows, the ATET is defined as the expected difference between the observed outcomes in the treatment group (Y_{1i}) and the counterfactual economic outcomes that would have occurred in the treatment group in the absence of treatment (Y_{0i}).

$$ATET = E[Y_{1i}|D_i = 1] - E[Y_{0i}|D_i = 1] \tag{3.4}$$

The first term in equation (3.4) is the average change in the NPL ratio in the treatment group, which is an observable quantity from the sample. Since the second term is not observable, the analysis selects episodes from the control group that closely match an episode in the treatment group. In this study, episodes of NPL reduction starting with a sharp drop in the NPL ratio, are regarded as the treatment group, and episodes with persistently high NPL ratios as the control group. We define a sharp drop in the NPL ratio as a more than 4-percentage-point drop in the NPL ratio in a single year, and a persistently high NPL ratio as one higher than 6 percentage points persisting for at least 3 consecutive years. Note that this study uses achievement of a sharp drop in the NPL ratio rather than adoption of a certain policy measure as the criterion for the treatment group. Thus, the analysis implicitly assumes that the episodes of NPL reduction starting with a sharp drop in the NPL ratio are achieved by implementation of NPL resolution measures, including introduction of public AMCs.

The selection of matching episodes from the control group is based on the estimated propensity of an episode in the control group to belong to the treatment group conditional on a set of economic characteristics. We consider different sets of economic characteristics, including GDP growth rate and inflation rate during the year of the sharp drop. In various other specifications, the analysis also matches per capita GDP at purchasing power parity, GDP growth rate during the year preceding the sharp drop, public debt-to-GDP ratio, investment-to-GDP ratio, and unemployment rate. This study focuses on two macroeconomic outcomes (GDP growth rate and unemployment rate) and two financial outcomes (rate of currency depreciation and credit creation effect measured by change in money supply [M2] as a fraction of GDP).

Table 3.8 presents the estimates of the average treatment effect on the treated for 4 years after a sharp drop in the NPL ratio. Thus, year 0 is the year in which a sharp drop in the NPL ratio occurs. As the table shows, estimates for the average treatment effect display improved macroeconomic performance in higher GDP growth and lower unemployment rates during the 4 years after the treatment, although significant improvement in the growth rate is only visible during the first 2 years. The estimates for the average treatment effect also demonstrate that sharp drops in NPL ratio through NPL resolution policies have positive feedback effects on financial variables. In particular, sharp currency appreciation (a sharp drop in the exchange rate) and larger increase in the M2/GDP ratio are achieved. A higher value for M2/GDP may imply more active credit creation by banks. These positive feedback effects, however, do not last long.

Table 3.8: Average Treatment Effect on the Treated

Variable/Effect	Year 1	Year 2	Year 3	Year 4
GDP growth rate	2.4564**	2.3006*	1.4371	-0.1777
	(0.9517)	(1.2664)	(1.3342)	(1.0323)
Unemployment rate	-1.1434*	-1.3694*	-2.1099*	-0.9036
	(0.6940)	(0.7613)	(1.1936)	(1.3655)
Exchange rate change	-13.2709*	-4.8804*	0.8324	11.5421*
	(6.8998)	(2.8478)	(3.5748)	(6.5404)
Change of M2/GDP	1.1449	1.5218**	0.0499	0.5988
	(2.2919)	(0.7437)	(1.5199)	(1.0895)
Control	40	40	37	34
Treated	37	37	35	31

GDP = gross domestic product, M2 = money supply.
Note: ** = significant at 1%, * = significant at 5%.
Sources: Authors' calculations using data from CEIC database; Standard & Poor's Global Market Intelligence; and World Bank World Development Indicators (accessed August 2018).

3.6 Macrofinancial Effects of Nonperforming Loans in Asia

Lee and Rosenkranz (2019) find evidence supporting the existence of macrofinancial feedback effects of NPLs in Asia. In particular, they find that a buildup in NPLs prompts a contraction in loans growth, increase in unemployment, and reduction in output. The other direction of causality also holds as deteriorating macroeconomic conditions contribute to a buildup in distressed assets. Box 3.2 provides more detail.

Box 3.2: Assessing the Macrofinancial Feedback Effects of Nonperforming Loans in Asia

To investigate the macrofinancial feedback effects of nonperforming loans (NPLs) in Asia, Lee and Rosenkranz (2019) employ a panel vector autoregression (PVAR) model. The analysis uses panel data of economy-level macroeconomic indicators covering annual data for 1994–2014 for 32 countries, mostly in emerging Asia. The baseline model includes (i) change in the NPL ratio, (ii) year-on-year growth rate of loans, (iii) change in the unemployment rate, and (iv) change in the monetary policy rate. In an additional specification, the unemployment rate is replaced with GDP growth.

The results of the PVAR analysis illustrate how a buildup of NPLs can affect the real sector of the economy and spill over through macrofinancial feedback effects. In particular, an increase in NPLs leads to a reduction in credit supply, a rise in unemployment, and a slowdown in overall economic activity (figure). A one-standard-deviation shock in the NPL ratio would trigger a 0.18-percentage-point contraction in the GDP growth rate, about a 3.61-percentage-point decline in the loan growth rate, and a 0.21-percentage-point increase in unemployment after a year. The corresponding figures over 3 years are 0.1, 1.5, and 0.1 percentage points. In their analysis, they also find the results are, moreover, bidirectional as macroeconomic factors can simultaneously prompt changes in the NPL ratio. Greater GDP growth and credit supply decrease the NPL ratio, while tighter monetary policy and rising unemployment increase the NPL ratio.

Estimated Impulse Response Functions to a Shock in the NPL Ratio

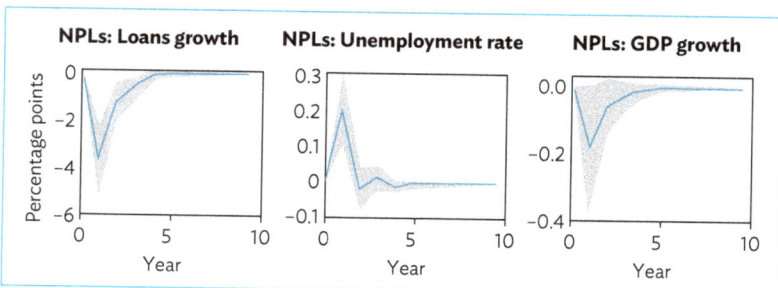

GDP = gross domestic product, NPL = nonperforming loan.
Notes: The figures correspond to impulse responses to a one-standard-deviation shock in the NPL ratio. A one-standard-deviation shock to the NPL ratio is equal to 3.5 percentage points in the baseline model, and 3.1 percentage points in specification 2. 95% confidence intervals are generated by 5,000 Monte Carlo draws.

Source: Lee, J. and P. Rosenkranz. 2019. Nonperforming Loans in Asia: Determinants and Macrofinancial Linkages. *ADB Economics Working Paper Series*. No. 574. Manila.

We also assess the macrofinancial implications of NPLs and the effectiveness of NPL resolution policies focusing on Asian countries. The Asian panel constructed from the S&P data contains 18 countries: Armenia, Azerbaijan, Bangladesh, the People's Republic of China, Georgia, India, Indonesia, Japan, Kazakhstan, the Republic of Korea, Malaysia, Pakistan, the Philippines, Singapore, Sri Lanka, Thailand, Uzbekistan, and Viet Nam. There are 23 cases of sharp drops in NPLs, and 12 out of these 23 cases are episodes of NPL reduction as defined in section 3.3.

We assess the determinants of sharp drops in NPLs by estimating a panel probit model and the results are presented in Table 3.9. Model 1 includes only macrofinancial variables as explanatory variables. The results are similar to those from the global panel. A sharp drop in the NPL ratio is more likely when the hike in the NPL ratio during the previous year is larger or when the global financial market is less volatile. The growth rate, however, is not significant, implying that higher growth does not increase the possibility of achieving a sharp drop in the NPL ratio.

Table 3.9: Determinants of Sharp Drops in the NPL Ratio: Asian Countries

Variable	(1)	(2)	(3)	(4)
ΔNPL(t-1)	0.0824	0.0616	0.0808**	0.7223**
	(2.56)	(1.46)	(2.37)	(2.91)
Growth	0.0380	-0.0122	0.0585	0.0350
	(0.56)	(-0.10)	(1.26)	(0.86)
Inflation	0.0408	0.2145**	-0.0009	0.0318
	(0.57)	(2.79)	(-0.01)	(0.66)
Exchange rate	-0.0144	0.0107	-0.0109	-0.0180
	(-0.69)	(0.53)	(-0.51)	(-0.74)
Commodity	-0.0016	-0.0074	-0.0029	-0.0001
	(-0.14)	(-0.34)	(-0.21)	(-0.01)
VIX	-0.0547*	-0.2047**	-0.0904*	-0.0530*
	(-1.91)	(-2.51)	(-1.92)	(-1.79)
AMC		0.7013		
		(1.16)		
Bailout			-0.1893	
			(-0.23)	
MPP				-0.1812
				(-0.52)
Constant	-1.1649**	-0.1903	-0.5721	-1.1313*
	(-2.05)	(-0.16)	(-0.66)	(-1.81)
Sample	227	139	158	957

AMC = asset management company, MPP = macroprudential policy, NPL = nonperforming loan, VIX = volatility index.
Note: ** = significant at 5%, * = significant at 10%.
Sources: Authors' calculations using data from Bloomberg; Bova et al. (2016); CEIC database; Cerutti, Claessens, and Laeven (2015); Fallerberg and Gandrud (2015); International Monetary Fund; Standard & Poor's Global Market Intelligence; and World Bank World Development Indicators (accessed August 2018).

Models 2, 3, and 4 examine the effectiveness of three policy measures—public AMCs, injection of public bailout funds, and strengthening macroprudential regulations—by adding policy dummies one by one. It turns out that none of these NPL policy measures were significant in achieving a sharp drop in the NPL ratio. While such a result may be interpreted to mean that these policy measures were not effective in reducing NPLs in Asia, it is also noted that these policy measures have not been actively adopted by Asian countries experiencing NPL problems. For example, public AMCs existed in only 5 of 23 cases of sharp drops in NPL ratios. Only one case was accompanied by injection of public bailout funds and seven cases were accompanied by strengthening of macroprudential regulations.

To see if a sharp reduction in the NPL ratio has been effective in improving the macrofinancial performance of Asian economies, Table 3.10 shows the average treatment effect on the treated estimated using the Asian panel. As can be seen from the table, the average treatment effect displays improved macrofinancial performance in the event of a higher growth rate, currency appreciation, and stronger credit creation, which is also the case with the global panel. Unlike the result from the global panel, however, the effect on unemployment rate is not significant. Although unemployment rate goes down during the 4 years after a sharp drop in the NPL ratio, it is not statistically significant. Although it cannot be identified what kinds of policy measures effectively reduced NPLs in Asian countries, it can be concluded that once a significant reduction in NPLs is achieved, this can improve the macrofinancial performance of the country.

Table 3.10: Average Treatment Effect on the Treated: Asian Countries

Variable/Effect	Year 1	Year 2	Year 3	Year 4
GDP growth rate	2.8392**	6.8319**	4.9166**	1.3269
	(1.3929)	(1.9194)	(2.3852)	(2.1913)
Unemployment rate	-0.7870	-0.1985	-0.7378	-0.9141
	(1.8653)	(1.5209)	(1.4824)	(1.8224)
Exchange rate change	-40.0811*	-7.9623**	-4.0174	11.5109
	(24.0658)	(2.4244)	(7.8140)	(10.3290)
Change of M2/GDP	1.1895	3.5332	3.1583*	2.8240**
	(1.3247)	(3.3450)	(1.8115)	(1.2230)
Control	11	11	11	10
Treated	14	14	13	13

GDP = gross domestic product, M2 = money supply.
Note: ** = significant at 5%, * = significant at 10%.
Sources: Authors' calculations using data from CEIC database; Standard & Poor's Global Market Intelligence; and World Bank World Development Indicators (accessed August 2018).

3.7 Conclusion

Previous empirical analyses point to the important role of both macroeconomic and bank-specific variables in driving NPLs. A deterioration in macroeconomic conditions—for example, indicated by a reduction in output growth, rise in unemployment, increase in inflation, and rise in global risk aversion—is associated with elevated credit risk. Factors influencing the risk-taking behavior of banks also play a role in a rise in distressed assets. Lower bank profitability, excessive past lending, and increased liquidity are associated with a higher NPL ratio.

Empirical evidence points to the effect of financial distress on the real economy, underlining the harmful macrofinancial feedback effects of NPLs. Analysis of the effectiveness of NPL resolution measures are therefore critical to ensuring financial stability and sustained economic growth.

This study therefore empirically evaluates the effectiveness of NPL resolution policy measures using a new NPL dataset constructed from bank-level data from S&P Global. The study focuses on episodes of sharp movements in NPL ratios because a large portion of NPL reduction episodes start with a year in which the NPL ratio drops sharply. Estimation of panel probit models reveals that while slower growth, sharper currency depreciation, and higher global financial market volatility are associated with sharp rises in NPL ratios, sharp drops in NPL ratios can be explained by faster growth and lower global financial market volatility. In particular, the empirical analysis consistently demonstrates that public AMCs can be an effective tool in achieving a sharp drop in NPL ratios and thus play a critical role in NPL resolution. Public AMCs, however, are not effective in preventing a sharp rise in NPL ratios, which implies that public AMCs are useful mostly as a crisis resolution measure.

The estimated average treatment effects on the treated underpin that a sharp drop in NPLs is associated with favorable macrofinancial effects, in line with Lee and Rosenkranz (2019), who examine Asian economies in particular. NPLs yield harmful macrofinancial feedback effects and a reduction in the NPL ratio leads to an amelioration of deteriorating macroeconomic conditions. We also undertake an empirical exercise focusing on Asian economies only. While the results are slightly less significant, they underpin the negative macrofinancial feedback effects associated with NPLs.

The significant effect of a buildup in credit risk on the real economy underlining the macrofinancial feedback effects of distressed assets calls for the swift and rapid adoption of NPL resolution measures. While this analysis suggests an effective role for public AMCs in reducing the size of NPLs, it remains important to strengthen national legal, regulatory, and supervisory frameworks and institutional capacities, as well as to build and develop a market for effectively addressing NPLs.

While the analysis abstracted from cross-border spillover effects, increasingly interlinked financial markets highlight possible spillovers and contagion from cross-border bank lending and rapid deterioration of bank asset qualities. This highlights the important role of regional cooperation to help identify and mitigate possible spillovers and cross-border contagion. Growing cross-border banking activities in Asia and the emergence of possibly systemically important regional banks further underpin the need for regional regulatory dialogue and cooperation, including cross-border resolution mechanisms.

References

Arellano, M. and S. Bond. 1991. Some Tests of Specification for Panel Data: Monte Carlo Evidence and an Application to Employment Equations. *Review of Economic Studies*. 58 (2). pp. 277–297.

Ari, A., S. Chen, and L. Ratnovski. 2019. The Dynamics of Non-Performing Loans During Banking Crises: A New Database. *IMF Working Paper*. WP/19/272. Washington, DC: IMF.

Asian Development Bank (ADB). 2017. The Era of Financial Interconnectedness How Can Asia Strengthen Financial Resilience? *Asian Economic Integration Report 2017*. Manila. pp. 96–136.

_____ 2018. Toward Optimal Provision of Regional Public Goods in Asia and the Pacific. *Asian Economic Integration Report 2018*. Manila. pp. 121–177.

Balgova, M., A. Plekhanov, and M. Skrzypińska. 2017. Reducing Non-Performing Loans: Stylized Facts and Economic Impact. Working Paper.

Bova, E., M. Ruiz-Arranz, F. Toscani, and H. Ture. 2016. The Fiscal Costs of Contingent Liabilities: A New Dataset. *IMF Working Paper*. Washington, DC: IMF.

Capiro, G. and D. Klingebiel. 1996. Bank Insolvencies: Cross-Country Experience. *World Bank Policy Research Working Paper*. No. 1620. Washington, DC: World Bank.

Cerutti, E., S. Claessens, and L. Laeven. 2015. The Use and Effectiveness of Macroprudential Policies: New Evidence. *IMF Working Paper*. WP/15/61. Washington, DC: IMF.

De Bock, R., and A. Demyanets. 2012. Bank Asset Quality in Emerging Markets: Determinants and Spillovers. *IMF Working Paper*. WP/12/71. Washington, DC: IMF.

Deloitte LLP. 2018. *Deloitte Deleveraging Asia 2018*.

Espinoza, R. and A. Prasad. 2010. Nonperforming Loans in the GCC Banking System and Their Macroeconomic Effects. *IMF Working Paper*. WP/10/224. Washington, DC: IMF.

French, K. and J. Poterba. 1991. Investor Diversification and International Equity Markets, *American Economic Review*. 81 (2). pp. 222–26.

Ha, V., L. Trien, and H. Diep. 2014. Macro Determinants of Non-Performing Loans and Stress Testing of Vietnamese Commercial Banks' Credit Risk. *VNU Journal of Science: Economics and Business*. 30 (5E). pp. 1–16.

Hallerberg, M., and C. Gandrud. 2015. *Building better bad banks: The Political Economy of Public Asset Management Companies for Resolving Financial Crises.* http://fgch.github.io/amc-site/.

Jassaud, N. and K. Kang. 2015. A Strategy for Developing a Market for Nonperforming Loans in Italy. *IMF Working Paper*. WP/15/24. Washington, DC: IMF.

Klein, N. 2013. Non-Performing Loans in CESEE: Determinants and Impact on Macroeconomic Performance. *IMF Working Paper*. WP/13/72. Washington, DC: IMF.

Lee, J. 2017. Regional Experience in Dealing with Distressed Assets in Asia. Mimeograph. Asian Development Bank.

Lee, J. andP. Rosenkranz. 2018. Case Studies on NPL Reduction Measures in the ASEAN+3 Region. Unpublished.

Lee, J. and P. Rosenkranz. 2019. Nonperforming Loans in Asia: Determinants and Macrofinancial Linkages. *ADB Economics Working Paper Series*. No. 574. Manila: ADB.

Martin, R. 2019. NPL Market Development – Challenges, Opportunities and Lessons from Europe. Presentation material.

Nkusu, M. 2011. Nonperforming Loans and Macrofinancial Vulnerabilities in Advanced Economies. *IMF Working Paper*. WP/11/161. Washington, DC: IMF.

Ozili, P. K. 2019. Non-Performing Loans and Financial Development: New Evidence. *Munich Personal RePEc Archive Paper*. No. 92338.

Park, C.Y. and K. Shin. 2017. A Contagion through Exposure to Foreign Banks during the Global Financial Crisis. *ADB Economics Working Paper*. No. 516. Manila: ADB.

Roy, S. 2014. Determinants of Nonperforming Assets in India-Panel Regression. *Eurasian Journal of Economics and Finance*. 2 (3). pp. 69–78.

4

Do Nonperforming Loans Matter for Bank Lending and the Business Cycle in Euro Area Countries?

Ivan Huljak, Reiner Martin, Diego Moccero, and Cosimo Pancaro[1]

4.1 Introduction

Nonperforming loans (NPLs) were a key policy issue in the euro area for most of the 2010s. As Chapter 1 details, NPLs in the euro area increased from around 3% at the onset of the global financial crisis in 2008 to a peak of around 8% in 2014. A key driver of this substantial growth in NPLs was the severe and protracted recession in parts of the euro area. At the same time, as Chapter 7 discusses, several market failures and structural problems slowed the speed at which distressed assets in the euro area were resolved. The recovery of economic activity in the second half of the decade and a range of policy measures to tackle NPLs saw the euro area NPL ratio decline to 3.6% at the end of 2019. At the time of writing, however, the COVID-19 pandemic is expected to result in a renewed increase.

High NPL ratios in bank balance sheets can undermine the soundness of the banking system and its ability to lend to the real economy through three main channels. First, NPLs reduce bank profits. They require higher provisions, lead to lower interest income, generate higher expenses associated with their management and resolution, and increase funding costs, as risk-averse investors are less willing to lend to institutions with asset quality problems.[2]

[1] The authors thank participants of seminars at the European Central Bank, the Bank of England, at the ADB-ECB Workshop on NPL Resolution in Asia and Europe for helpful comments and suggestions. We also thank Bjorn van Roye, Dejan Krušec, Lorenzo Ricci, and Paolo Fioretti for useful discussions. Paola Antilici, Marija Deipenbrock, Marco Forletta, and Alexandros Kouris provided excellent research assistance. The authors are solely responsible for any errors that remain. The findings, views, and interpretations expressed herein are those of the authors and should not be attributed to the Joint Vienna Institute, the Croatian National Bank, the Eurosystem, and the European Central Bank and its executive board or its management.

[2] For example, Pancaro, Zochowski, and Arnould (2020) find that lower credit quality seems associated with higher banks' senior bond yields

Second, NPLs have higher risk weights, resulting in higher capital needs. To maintain or boost capital adequacy, banks may need to deleverage, leading to a contraction in credit supply. Finally, managing large NPL stocks can divert important managerial resources away from banks' more profitable core activities.[3] Given the importance of bank lending for the functioning of the euro area economy—as well as for most Asian economies—there is a clear need to study the feedback loop between NPLs, bank credit, and the real economy.

Empirical literature in this field can be grouped into three main strands: (i) the determinants of NPLs, (ii) the impact of NPLs on the real economy, and (iii) the feedback loops between NPLs and the macroeconomy. The first strand has identified three main groups of NPL determinants: bank-level, industry-specific, and macroeconomic. Bank-level determinants include exogenous factors such as a sudden drop in economic activity, poor management, excessive risk-taking, and a scarcity of resources allocated to underwriting and monitoring loans. The literature found support for all these factors, with bad management playing the most prominent role. Industry-specific drivers point mainly to the impact of competition on risk-taking, but there seems to be no consensus in the literature on whether bank competition increases or decreases stability in the banking system (Beck, De Jonghe, and Schepens 2013; Goetz 2018). Finally, regarding macroeconomic drivers, the literature has focused on economic activity, inflation, interest rates, and the exchange rate as the most relevant drivers of NPLs (Anastasiou, Dimitrios, and Tsionas 2016; Jimenez and Saurina 2006; Louzis, Vouldis, and Metaxas 2012).

The second strand of the literature studies the impact of NPLs on bank lending and economic activity, using both bank- and country-level data and deploying mainly single-equation estimation techniques. Balgova and Plekhanov (2016), using data for a global sample of 100 countries, quantified the (positive) effects of policy-induced declines in NPLs on the real economy. The authors find that foregone growth due to the overhang of NPLs can be large. Accornero et al. (2017), coupling bank-level data for Italy with borrower-based information for nonfinancial corporations, examine the influence of NPLs on the supply of bank credit. The study finds that the exogenous accumulation of new NPLs and an associated increase in provisions impair bank lending, although the impairment is not causally affected by the level of NPL ratios.

---

[3]   Grodzicki et al. (2015), Fell et al. (2016), and Fell et al. (2017) elaborate extensively on the challenges for banking systems stemming from the accumulation of NPLs, and illustrate macroeconomic and microeconomic policies that could be adopted to resolve the issue.

Do Nonperforming Loans Matter for Bank Lending and
the Business Cycle in Euro Area Countries?

113

The third strand of literature estimates the impact of NPL shocks using structural time series models, where aggregate NPL ratios and economic activity are included in a vector autoregression (VAR) together with a broader set of banking and macroeconomic variables. For example, Espinoza and Prasad (2010), Nkusu (2011), De Bock and Demyanets (2012), and Klein (2013) estimate panel VAR models for various groups of countries and use country-level data to investigate feedback interactions between NPLs and macroeconomic performance.[4] In addition to the expected countercyclical behavior of NPLs, these studies find significant feedback effects from NPLs to the real economy.

This chapter contributes to the empirical literature on the feedback effects between NPLs, the banking sector, and the macroeconomy by estimating a panel Bayesian VAR model with hierarchical priors (Jarocinski 2010). The analysis aims at estimating the impact of exogenous shocks to NPL ratios on bank lending and the macroeconomy. Exogenous shocks to NPL ratios, i.e., shocks that are not due to changes in economic fundamentals and the repayment capacity of borrowers, occur rather frequently—for example, due to regulatory and legal changes, including reporting requirements for distressed loans, sales of defaulted loans to investors, the creation of asset management companies, or when banks' risk appetites shift.

The chapter finds that exogenous increases in NPL ratios tend to depress bank lending (notably for company loans), widen lending spreads, lead to a fall in real gross domestic product (GDP) growth and residential real estate prices, and—as a consequence—an easing of monetary policy. Forecast error variance decomposition shows that exogenous shocks to NPLs explain a relatively large share of the variance of the variables in the VAR, particularly for countries with large increases in NPL ratios during the euro area sovereign debt crisis. Finally, a 3-year, structural out-of-sample scenario analysis assesses the impact of a decline in NPL ratios for the euro area countries with the most sizable increases in NPL ratios during the debt crisis.[5] The exercise shows that reducing NPL ratios can produce significant macroeconomic and financial benefits.

---

[4]   These groups of countries include the Gulf Cooperative Council countries; a group of 26 advanced economies; a large sample of emerging markets; and Central, Eastern, and Southeastern Europe, respectively.

[5]   These countries are Cyprus, Greece, Ireland, Italy, Portugal, and Spain.

In the next section, the chapter presents the empirical approach and the data used, followed by discussions of the various empirical analyses: the impulse response analysis, the forecast error variance decomposition, and the out-of-sample structural counterfactual analysis.

4.2 Empirical Approach and Data

The analysis here estimates a panel VAR model for 12 euro area countries[6] and 10 variables for the first quarter of 2006 until the third quarter of 2017.[7] The model allows for cross-subsection heterogeneity, hence capturing country-specific dynamics. More specifically, the analysis estimates the impact of exogenous shocks to changes in NPL ratios and real GDP growth on bank lending and economic developments, using the following panel VAR(p) model:

$$y_{i,t} = C_i + A_i^1 y_{i,t-1} + ... + A_i^p y_{i,t-p} + \varepsilon_{i,t} \qquad (1)$$

where i is an individual country (i = 1, ..., N), t is time (t = 1, ... , T), $y_{i,t}$ is a column vector of the 10 endogenous variables, C_i is a vector of constants, and $A_i^1, ..., A_i^p$ are matrices of coefficients for a different order of lags until lag p which are country-specific.

The panel VAR contains a larger set of variables than included in other related studies.[8] The variables included are the policy interest rate, economic activity, inflation, residential real estate prices, bank lending volumes and spreads (for mortgages and loans to nonfinancial corporations), ratio of capital and reserves over total assets, and change in NPL ratios. Employing a panel VAR with aggregate data allows us to estimate the dynamic interaction and feedback loops between NPLs, macroeconomic variables, and banking variables.

Table 4.1 provides information on data sources and summary statistics.

---

[6] These countries are Austria, Belgium, Cyprus, Estonia, France, Greece, Ireland, Italy, Lithuania, Spain, Netherlands, and Portugal.

[7] The estimations in this chapter were implemented relying on the BEAR toolbox and MATLAB codes developed by Dieppe, van Roye, and Legrand (2016).

[8] For example, the model in Espinoza and Prasad (2010) includes up to four variables, De Bock and Demyanets (2012) and Klein (2013) include five variables, and Nkusu (2011) includes nine variables.

Do Nonperforming Loans Matter for Bank Lending and
the Business Cycle in Euro Area Countries?

115

Table 4.1: Summary Statistics

Variable	Source	Obs	Mean	Std. Dev.	Min	Max
Real GDP growth	ECB SDW	564	1	4	-17.5	12
Inflation	ECB SDW	564	1.6	1.6	-3.1	10.6
RRE prices	ECB SDW	564	1.8	10.5	-40.3	57.5
Euribor	ECB SDW	564	1.4	1.7	-0.3	5.0
Corporate loans	ECB SDW	564	4.6	12.0	-20.2	67.5
Mortgage loans	ECB SDW	564	5.7	12.3	-33.0	87.4
Corporate spread	ECB SDW	564	2.5	1.4	0.2	6.6
Mortgage spread	ECB SDW	564	2.3	1.1	-0.3	5.0
Capital and reserves ratio	ECB SDW	564	12.3	10.9	2.7	68.8
Change in NPL ratio	See other sources below.	564	0.8	3.3	-8.2	27.2

ECB SDW = European Central Bank's Statistical Data Warehouse, GDP = gross domestic product,
NPL = nonperforming loan, RRE = residential real estate.
Sources: International Monetary Fund Financial Soundness Indicators, Banque de France, Banco de España,
Central Bank of Cyprus, Irish Central Statistics Office, Bankscope, and ECB SDW database.

Economic activity is measured by the annual rate of real GDP growth (adjusted for calendar and seasonal effects).[9] Inflation is defined as the annual rate of growth in the Harmonised Index of Consumer Prices, working day and seasonally adjusted. The 3-month Euribor rate is used as a proxy for the euro area policy interest rate.

Bank lending is defined as the annual rate of growth in bank lending to nonfinancial corporations and households (for house purchases). Originally, these two variables were defined as an index of notional stocks.[10] Bank lending spreads are defined as the difference between bank lending rates and Euribor. The lending rates used to compute the spreads are the interest rates on new business loans granted in euros, all maturities combined.[11] Including bank lending spreads among the endogenous variables in the VAR is important because the exogenous shocks might lead to a repricing of bank loans, and so affect the quantity of loans provided to the economy.

Residential real estate prices refer to new and existing dwellings for the whole country and are computed as the annual growth rate of the

[9] For Ireland, economic growth is computed as the annual growth rate of the nominal modified gross national income, deflated using the deflator of the modified domestic demand.

[10] Data for Estonia for nonfinancial corporation loans before 2008 is provided by the Central Bank of Estonia.

[11] The exception is lending rates to nonfinancial corporations in Greece, where the rates based on outstanding amounts are used because data on new business loans is not available.

underlying index. The series of residential real estate prices is included to account for the role that real estate markets play in business cycle fluctuations. Changes in real estate prices can have large real effects and welfare implications (Hartmann 2015).[12]

The ratio of bank capital and reserves over total assets is an index of notional stocks. Capital and reserves (the numerator) include total equity capital; non-distributed benefits or funds; and specific or general provisions against loans, securities, and other types of assets. The capital and reserves to assets ratio is then computed as the ratio between this series and total assets.[13]

Finally, the analysis includes in the VAR the annual change in NPL ratios, which is the most relevant variable in the analysis. NPL ratios are defined as nonperforming loans divided by total gross loans. The main source for this variable is the IMF Financial Soundness Indicators database.[14] For most countries covered in this chapter, however, the Financial Soundness Indicators series had to extended backward until the first quarter of 2006, using either bank-level information extracted from Bankscope (Austria, Belgium, Estonia, Greece, Ireland, Lithuania, and Portugal) or central bank data (Cyprus, France, and Spain).

Figure 4.1 displays the series of NPL ratios per country.

The set of countries in the sample exhibits rather different NPL dynamics over time. In some countries, the NPL ratio increased during the crisis and decreased thereafter, although to different degrees and from different starting levels (Austria, Belgium, and the Netherlands). In some countries, the NPL ratio increased significantly during the crisis and declined substantially afterward (Ireland and Spain), even to levels close to those before the crisis (Estonia and Lithuania). In other countries, the NPL ratio increased significantly without a significant subsequent decline (Greece), or with only a very recent reversal (Cyprus, Italy, and Portugal). In France, the NPL ratio remained unchanged throughout this period.

---

[12] Other studies that have included house prices in a VAR framework similar to this analysis include Bjornland and Jacobsen (2010), Iacoviello (2005), and Meeks (2017).

[13] Pre-2008 data for Estonia has been compiled by the Central Bank of Estonia and shared with the authors.

[14] The IMF recommends that loans be classified as nonperforming especially when: (i) payments of the principal and interest are past due by 1 quarter (90 days) or more; or (ii) the interest payments equal to 1 quarter (90 days) interest or more have been capitalized (reinvested into the principal amount), refinanced, or payment has been delayed by agreement (IMF 2006).

Do Nonperforming Loans Matter for Bank Lending and
the Business Cycle in Euro Area Countries?

117

Figure 4.1: NPL Ratios in Euro Area Countries

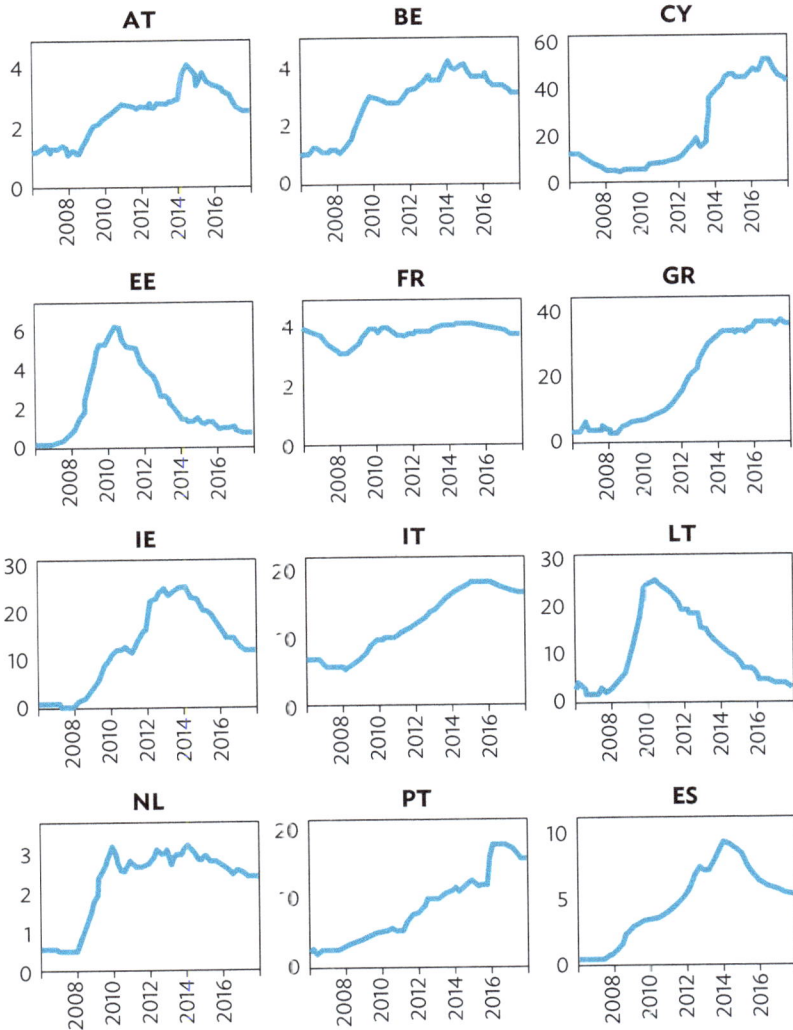

AT = Austria, BE = Belgium, CY = Cyprus, EE = Estonia, ES = Spain, FR = France, GR = Greece,
IE = Ireland, IT = Italy, LT = Lithuania, NL = Netherlands, NPL = nonperforming loan, PT = Portugal.
Note: The data sample spans from the first quarter (Q) of 2006 to 2017 Q3.
Sources: International Monetary Fund Financial Soundness Indicators, Banque de France, Banco de
España, Central Bank of Cyprus, and Bankscope.

Table 4.2 presents contemporaneous correlations among the variables in the panel VAR.

Table 4.2: Correlation Matrix among Variables Included in the Panel Vector Autoregression

	Real GDP Growth	Inflation	RRE Prices	Euribor	Corporate Loans	Mortgage Loans	Corporate Spread	Mortgage	Capital and Reserves Ratio	Change in NPL Ratio
Real GDP growth	1									
Inflation	0.15***	1								
RRE prices	0.79***	0.26***	1							
Euribor	0.15***	0.52***	0.25***	1						
Corporate loans	0.35***	0.57***	0.59***	0.69***	1					
Mortgage loans	0.40***	0.49***	0.62***	0.52***	0.78***	1				
Corporate spread	-0.29***	-0.30***	-0.32***	-0.47***	-0.36***	-0.27***	1			
Mortgage	-0.33***	-0.42***	-0.39***	-0.74***	-0.55***	-0.44***	0.69***	1		
Capital and reserves ratio	0.01	-0.27***	-0.11**	-0.37***	-0.26***	-0.25***	0.61***	0.42***	1	
Change in NPL ratio	-0.55***	-0.19***	-0.47***	-0.09*	-0.18***	-0.16***	0.39***	0.33***	0.15***	1

GDP = gross domestic product, NPL = nonperforming loan, RRE = residential real estate.
Note: The data sample spans the first quarter (Q) 2006 to Q3 2017. (***), (**) and (*) denote statistical significance at the 1%, 5%, and 10% levels, respectively.
Sources: Data based on the International Monetary Fund, European Central Bank, Banque de France, Banco de España, Banco de France, Central Bank of Cyprus, Central Statistics Office of Ireland, and Bankscope.

Do Nonperforming Loans Matter for Bank Lending and
the Business Cycle in Euro Area Countries?

119

Looking first at the banking sector variables, bank lending volumes are procyclical, while they are negatively associated with countercyclical bank lending spreads. Bank capital and reserves over total assets appears to be countercyclical only for lending, whereas the correlation with real GDP growth is not significant. Real estate prices move positively together with economic activity, inflation, monetary policy, and bank lending. By contrast, they are negatively related to the remaining variables. The change in NPL ratios, the variable of interest, correlates negatively with economic activity and bank lending. Finally, an increase in the change in NPL ratios is associated with a widening in bank lending spreads.

These simple correlations between changes in NPL ratios, macroeconomic, and banking sector variables do not allow disentangling the source of variation of these variables. On the one hand, an exogenous increase in economic activity is expected to boost bank lending, narrow spreads, and reduce NPLs (due to an improvement in the repayment capacity of economic agents). On the other, an exogenous decrease in NPL ratios may lead banks to boost lending and lower lending spreads, hence also boosting economic activity.

The next section uses Cholesky decomposition to disentangle the shocks to real GDP growth and the exogenous changes to NPL ratios (De Bock and Demyanets 2012, Espinoza and Prasad 2010, Klein 2013). This recursive identification approach implies that variables appearing earlier in the ordering are considered more exogenous than those appearing later.

The identifying assumptions are as follows. First, monetary policy is assumed to respond to many indicators (Bernanke and Boivin 2003; Ciccarelli, Maddaloni, and Peydró 2013; ECB 2011). Hence, this analysis ranks the monetary policy rate last in the VAR. Second, bank lending and lending spreads affect the capital and reserves-to-asset ratio within the same quarter. This assumption reflects the impact of the profit and loss account on capital in the same period as when the result was generated. Hence, the capital and reserves-to-asset ratio is ranked second-to-last in the system. Third, the analysis assumes that bank lending spreads move faster than macroeconomic variables (GDP and inflation). It thus ranks spreads after macroeconomic variables but before the capital and reserves-to-asset ratio. Fourth, the analysis follows Bjornland and Jacobsen (2010) in assuming that real estate prices react to macroeconomic developments within the same quarter. Fifth, the analysis assumes that macroeconomic variables do not simultaneously react to the policy rate, while policy reacts to the macroeconomic environment simultaneously. Also, it assumes that inflation is impacted simultaneously by a shock to economic activity (Bernanke and Gertler 1995; Christiano, Eichenbaum, and Evans 1996). Sixth, the analysis assumes that although it takes time to obtain a loan, it affects macroeconomic variables instantaneously once it is granted. The analysis thus places the macroeconomic variables (real GDP growth and inflation) after the lending variables and the change in the NPL ratio. Seventh, the change in the NPL ratio is placed after the loans because a shock to loans affects this ratio contemporaneously (through a change in its denominator). Last, the analysis assumes that changes in NPL ratios move slowly, meaning that GDP growth and inflation affect NPLs only with a lag.[15] Hence, the change in the NPL ratio is placed before the macroeconomic variables.[16]

In sum, the analysis uses the following ordering: growth in bank lending to nonfinancial corporations, growth in bank lending for mortgages, change in the NPL ratio, real GDP growth, inflation rate, real estate prices, lending spreads to nonfinancial corporations, lending spreads to households for house purchase, bank capital and reserves to assets ratio, and finally, monetary policy interest rate.

4.3 Empirical Findings

This section illustrates the impact of shocks to changes in NPL ratios, relying on three sets of results. First, the analysis presents impulse response functions. Second, it reports the share of the forecast error variance to assess the degree to which variables are driven by this shock. Third, the analysis implements an out-of-sample structural conditional forecast analysis to assess and quantify the macroeconomic and financial benefits stemming from a decline in NPL ratios.

4.3.1 Impulse Responses to Shocks in Nonperforming Loans and Real Gross Domestic Product

Based on the estimated VAR model in Equation (1) above, the analysis generates impulse responses of the endogenous variables to two structural shocks. More specifically, it reports the impulse responses to a (positive) one-standard-deviation shock to the change in the NPL ratio and to a (negative) one-standard-deviation shock to real GDP growth, respectively. For each variable, the analysis looks at the maximum impact recorded across

---

[15] As noted, loans are usually classified as nonperforming 1 quarter after the customer defaults.

[16] This ordering is similar to the ones used by Hancock, Laing, and Wilcox (1995); Klein (2013); and De Bock and Demyanets (2012).

Do Nonperforming Loans Matter for Bank Lending and
the Business Cycle in Euro Area Countries?

121

countries over a 4-year horizon (16 quarters) and reports the maximum, minimum, median, and the interquartile range of this distribution. Insignificant responses are excluded, based on 16% and 84% Bayesian credibility bands.[17]

The impulse responses to a one-standard-deviation positive shock to the change in NPL ratios are displayed in Figure 4.2. The size of the instantaneous shock ranges between 0.1 percentage point (for France) and 4.3 percentage points (Cyprus). While the median of the impact is relatively modest (0.3 percentage point), the countries hit hardest by the crisis (Cyprus, Greece, Ireland, Italy, Lithuania, Portugal, and Spain), not surprisingly, exhibit much larger shocks.

Figure 4.2: Response to a Shock to the Change in the NPL Ratio

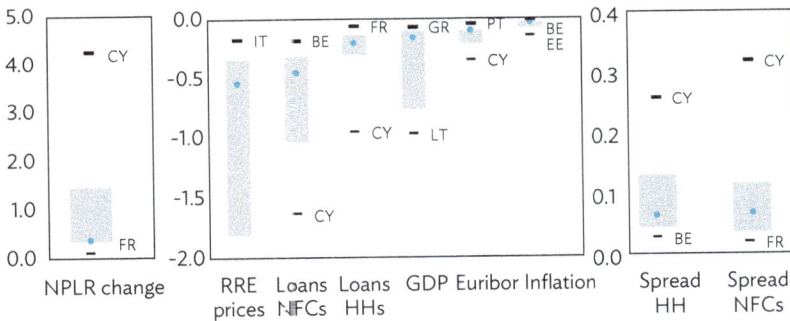

BE = Belgium, CY = Cyprus, EE = Estonia, FR = France, GDP = gross domestic product, GR = Greece, HH = households, IT = Italy, LT = Lithuania, NFC = nonfinancial corporations, NPL = nonperforming loan, NPLR = nonperforming loan ratio, PT = Portugal, RRE = residential real estate.
Note: The chart shows standard statistics for the maximum or minimum impact (depending on the variable) recorded across countries. The strongest response to the shock over a 16-quarter horizon is taken for all countries. Then the maximum, minimum, median, and interquartile range of this distribution across the 12 euro area countries are reported. Insignificant responses are excluded, based on 16% and 84% Bayesian credibility bands. The size of the shock considered is a one-standard-deviation shock to the relevant variable. Loans (to HHs and NFCs), real GDP growth, and RE prices are defined as annual percentage changes, while spreads (to HHs and NFCs) are defined in percentage points. The minimum impact on residential real estate prices is recorded for Cyprus at –3.4% but it is not reported in the chart.
Source: Authors' estimations.

---

[17] The analysis does not estimate impulse responses for the variable "capital and reserve ratios". The two components of this variable are expected to move in opposite directions when NPLs increase and GDP growth decreases, preventing a meaningful interpretation of the results.

The increase in the change in NPL ratios leads to a decline in bank lending. The annual growth of lending to nonfinancial corporations declines by up to 1.7 percentage points, while it decreases by up to 1 percentage point for mortgages. Also, the median response is stronger for nonfinancial corporations.[18] These responses suggest that banks materially deleverage their balance sheets following a negative shock to the change in the NPL ratio. The NPL shock also leads to a slight widening in bank lending spreads for nonfinancial corporations and mortgages (of up to around 0.3 percentage point in both cases) and to a decline in residential property prices (of up to 3.4 percentage points). The median impact for the spreads is very small, while that for residential real estate prices is 0.6 percentage point. For all these variables, the maximum impact is recorded for Cyprus, but strong effects can also be seen in Estonia, Ireland, and Lithuania.

The increase in the change in the NPL ratio also leads to a decline in real GDP growth in most countries (by between 0.07 and 1 percentage point), with a median response of 0.2 percentage point. The response to inflation is rather heterogeneous across countries. These findings are in line with those of other empirical papers like Klein (2013) and Espinoza and Prasad (2010),[19] as well as theoretical models like Curdia and Woodford (2010).[20]

Figure 4.3 reports the size of an exogenous negative one-standard-deviation shock to GDP growth. The absolute size of this shock varies across countries between –0.4 and –2.9 percentage points, with a median of –0.8 percentage point. The minimum impact is recorded for Lithuania, but some other smaller economies, which were strongly affected by the crisis (notably Estonia, Greece, Ireland) also record large, negative shocks.

---

[18] This result is consistent with Fell et al. (2018). Using bank-level data, the authors find a significant negative relationship between the ratio of NPLs over Tier 1 capital and loan origination. This relationship appears to be stronger for lending to nonfinancial corporations than for mortgages.

[19] These authors estimate the impact of much larger shocks, but their relative impact is comparable. Klein (2013) estimates that a 3-percentage-point instantaneous shock to the change in the NPL ratio leads to a decline in real GDP growth of about 2 percentage points after 1 year. Espinoza and Prasad (2010) find a relatively stronger impact.

[20] Curdia and Woodford (2010) develop a dynamic stochastic general equilibrium model with credit frictions and find that an increase in the loss rate of loans (i.e., the equivalent to nonperforming loans in the empirical model) leads to a widening in credit spreads, a contraction in credit, and to a substantial fall in real activity.

Do Nonperforming Loans Matter for Bank Lending and
the Business Cycle in Euro Area Countries?

123

Figure 4.3: Response to a Shock to Real GDP Growth

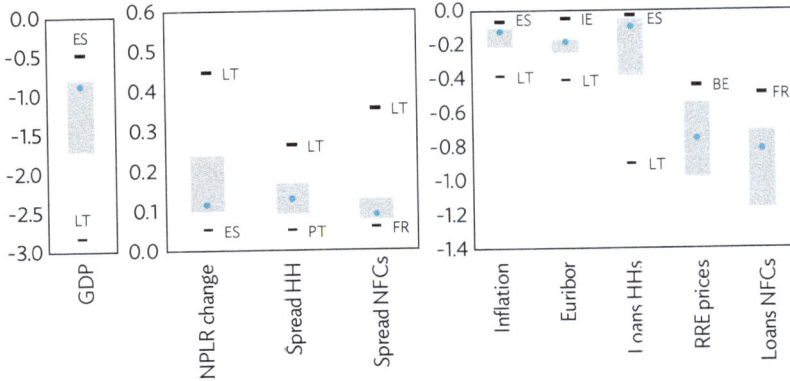

BE = Belgium, ES = Spain, FR = France, GDP = gross domestic product, HH = households, IE = Ireland,
LT = Lithuania, NFC = nonfinancial corporation, NPLR = nonperforming loan ratio, PT = Portugal,
RRE = residential real estate.
Note: The exogenous negative one-standard-deviation shock to GDP growth results in a change
in the repayment capacity of borrowers. The chart shows standard statistics for the maximum or
minimum impact (depending on the variable) recorded across countries. The strongest response to
the shock over a 16 quarter horizon is taken for all countries. Then the maximum, minimum, median
and interquartile range of this distribution across the 12 euro area countries is reported. Insignificant
responses are excluded, based on 16% and 84% Bayesian credibility bands. The size of the shock
considered is a negative one-standard-deviation shock to the relevant variable. Loans (to HHs and
NFCs), real GDP growth and RRE prices are defined as annual percentage changes, while spreads (to
HHs and NFCs) are defined in percentage points. The minimum impact for real estate prices and loans
to NFCs is recorded for Lithuania (4.65% and 2.5%, respectively, not reported in the chart).
Source: Authors' estimations.

Our results suggest a clear link between the exogenous negative one-standard-deviation shock to GDP growth and NPL ratios, with the latter increasing between 0.05 percentage point for Spain and 0.45 percentage point for Lithuania. The median increase in the change to the NPL ratio is 0.1 percentage point. These findings are consistent with a large body of empirical literature on the determinants of NPLs and the feedback loop between changes in NPLs and the economy.[21]

The negative shock to GDP growth negatively impacts annual inflation, which decreases between 0.06 and 0.4 percentage point. It also results in a decline of residential real estate prices of between –0.1 and –5 percentage

[21] See Quagliariello (2007); Louzis, Vouldis, and Metaxas (2012); and Anastasiou, Dimitrios, and Tsionas (2016) regarding the former. For the latter, Klein (2013) finds that a 3-percentage-point shock to real GDP growth is associated with a 0.5-percentage-point decline in the change in NPL ratios for Central, Eastern, and Southeastern European countries.

points, with a median response of −0.8 percentage point.[22] The negative shock to GDP growth also leads to a decline in bank lending. The response to the shock is again stronger for loans to nonfinancial corporations than for mortgage loans. The former declines between −0.5 and −2.5 percentage points (for France and Lithuania, respectively) with a median response of −0.8 percentage point. Mortgage loans decline only between −0.01 percentage point (for Spain) and -0.9 percentage point (for Lithuania), with a median response of −0.1 percentage point.[23] The stronger impact for corporate lending is likely to reflect the more flexible nature and on average shorter duration of nonfinancial corporation loans.

The negative shock to GDP growth increases lending spreads for nonfinancial corporations by between 0.07 percentage point (in France) and 0.35 percentage point (in Lithuania). Lending spreads for mortgages increase between 0.05 percentage point (in Portugal) and 0.26 percentage point (in Lithuania). The median responses in both cases are close to 0.1 percentage point.

4.3.2   Forecast Error Variance Decomposition

This section presents a forecast error variance decomposition (FEVD) to uncover further details about the relationships among variables included in the model. The FEVD shows for each variable the share of the forecast error variance that is explained by exogenous shocks to other endogenous variables. The results of this analysis are shown in Figures 4.4 and 4.5, which report the FEVD for shocks to the change in the NPL ratio and real GDP growth, respectively.[24] In both cases, the analysis presents the share of the variance for each variable and country over a 16-quarter horizon.

The FEVD suggests that exogenous shocks to changes in the NPL ratio are a powerful driver of real GDP growth, explaining between 10% and 33% of the forecast error variance in Cyprus, Estonia, Ireland, and Lithuania. For inflation, the share is below 7%, except for Cyprus.

---

[22] Bjornland and Jacobsen (2010) also find a stronger impact of monetary policy shocks on real estate prices than on inflation in Norway, Sweden, and the United Kingdom.

[23] Similar results are found by Kanngiesser, Martin, Maurin, and Moccero (2017) and Klein (2013) when estimating the impact of an aggregate demand shock in the euro area and the impact of a shock to GDP growth in Central, Eastern, and Southeastern Europe, respectively.

[24] Unlike the impulse responses above, FEDV analysis does not depend on the sign of the shock. Hence the analysis does not define shocks as "positive" or "negative" in this subsection.

Do Nonperforming Loans Matter for Bank Lending and
the Business Cycle in Euro Area Countries?

125

Figure 4.4: Forecast Error Variance Decomposition
(Shock to Change in NPL Ratio)

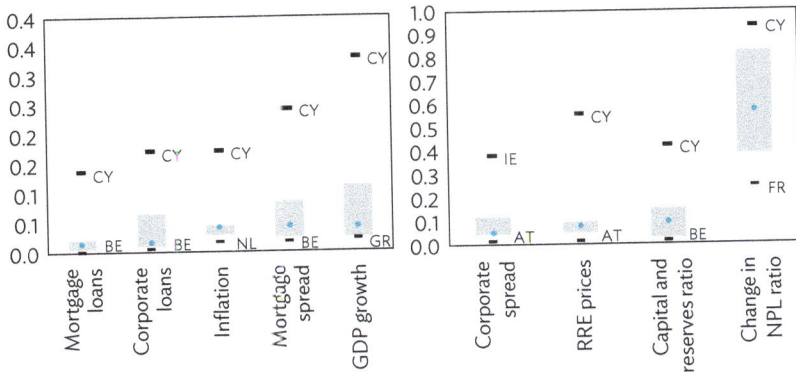

AT = Austria, BE = Belgium, CY = Cyprus, FR = France, GDP = gross domestic product, GR = Greece,
NL = Netherlands, NPL = nonperforming loan, RRE = residential real estate, VAR = vector
autoregression.
Note: The figure reports the share of the variance of the variables in the VAR which is explained by an
exogenous shock to the NPL ratio over a horizon of 16 quarters. The median of the accepted draws of
the variance decomposition from the posterior distribution is reported.
Source: Author's estimations.

For some countries, the shock to the change in the NPL ratio also explains a
non-negligible share of the variance of other variables included in the VAR.
For lending to nonfinancial corporations, the NPL shock explains, for example,
up to 17% of the variance for Cyprus. Relatively large values are also recorded
for Ireland, Italy, Lithuania, and Portugal. For mortgage lending, the share is
large for Cyprus, but less than 3% for the other countries. For corporate and
mortgage spreads, the explained share of the forecast variance is above 10%
for Cyprus, Ireland, Italy, and Lithuania.[25] For residential real estate prices,
the share is large for Cyprus, Estonia, and Ireland (between 12% and 56%).

These findings are broadly in line with those of previous related empirical
studies. Over long horizons (between 5 and 10 years), shocks to the change
in NPL ratios explain about 6% of the variance of GDP growth seen in the
sample of countries in Espinoza and Prasad (2010), 8% in De Bock and
Demyanets (2012), and 20% in Klein (2013). For the credit-to-GDP ratio
(the equivalent variable to bank lending in the model), the estimated share
stands at 13% in De Bock and Demyanets (2012) and at 8% Klein (2013).
Finally, Klein (2013) and De Bock and Demyanets (2012) find that 70% and
90% of the variance of the change in the NPL ratio is exogenously explained.

---

25 For Italy, the share is larger than 10% only for spreads on corporate lending.

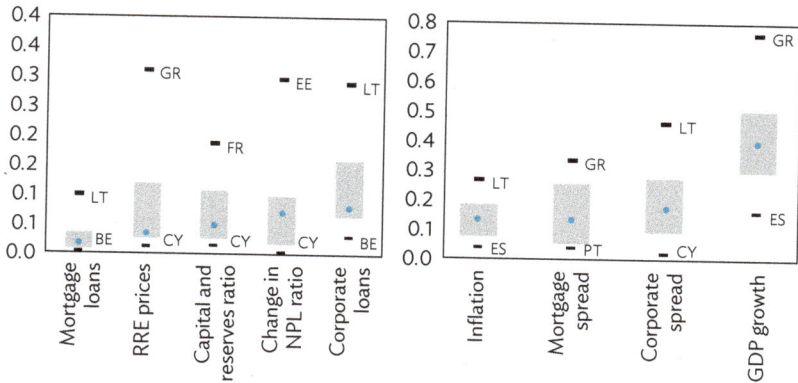

Figure 4.5: Forecast Error Variance Decomposition
(Shock to Real GDP Growth)

BE = Belgium, CY = Cyprus, EE = Estonia, ES = Spain, GDP = gross domestic product, GR = Greece,
LT = Lithuania, NPL = nonperforming loan, RRE = residential real estate, VAR = vector autoregression.
Note: The figure reports the share of the variance of the variables in the VAR which is explained by
a shock to real GDP growth over a horizon of 16 quarters. The median of the accepted draws of the
variance decomposition from the posterior distribution is reported.
Source: Authors' estimations.

Figure 4.5 shows that shocks to real GDP growth explain in some euro area countries a large share of the forecast error variance for bank lending, residential real estate prices, lending spreads, and inflation. For bank lending, the share is larger for nonfinancial corporation lending than for mortgage. For the former, it explains between 3% and 8% for most countries. However, the shock to GDP growth explains about 13% of the forecast error variance for Estonia and Italy, and more than 24% for Austria, Greece, and Lithuania. For mortgage loans, the shares are below 3% for most countries, except for Estonia, Greece, and Lithuania, for which the shares are between 6% and 10%.

For residential real estate prices, shocks to real GDP growth play the largest role in Lithuania and Greece, where they explain about 30% of the variance at the end of the forecast horizon. For France and the Netherlands, the shocks explain about 12%, and for other countries less than 7%. The variation is more homogeneously distributed for bank lending spreads (between 4% and 34% for nonfinancial corporation loans and 2% to 47% for mortgages). The same applies to inflation. Finally, for eight countries in the sample, the shock to real GDP growth explains more than 5% of the NPL forecast error variance.

Do Nonperforming Loans Matter for Bank Lending and
the Business Cycle in Euro Area Countries?

127

These results are also broadly in line with the related empirical literature. De Bock and Demyanets (2012) find that shocks to real GDP growth explain 4% of the growth rate in the ratio of private credit over GDP. Klein (2013) and De Bock and Demyanets (2012) find that over a long forecast horizon, shocks to real GDP growth explain between 5% and 7% of the variance in the change of the NPL ratio in Central, Eastern, and Southeastern European countries, as well as a large group of emerging economies. Hristov, Hülsewig, and Wollmershäuser (2012) find that demand shocks explain 13% of the variance of the GDP deflator and 16% of lending volumes over a 4-year horizon in a sample of euro area countries.

4.3.3   Structural Out-of-Sample Scenario Analysis

This section reports the results of a structural out-of-sample scenario analysis to assess the impact of two different paths of NPL ratios over the fourth quarter (Q) of 2017 to Q3 2020. This exercise provides a quantitative illustration of the possible economic and financial benefits associated with a decline in NPL ratios in euro area countries. For brevity, the analysis focuses on the six countries that exhibited the most sizable increase in NPL ratios during the crisis (Cyprus, Greece, Ireland, Italy, Portugal, and Spain) and the six most relevant variables in the VAR.

Under a "baseline scenario", the out-of-sample change in the NPL ratio for each country is assumed to equal the average change during the last 4 quarters of historical data.[26] Under an adverse scenario, the out-of-sample change in the NPL ratio is assumed to equal 0. Under both scenarios, the remaining variables in the VAR are projected conditional on the assumed evolution of the change in the NPL ratio, following the methodology proposed by Antolin-Diaz, Petrella, and Rubio-Ramirez (2018).[27] This approach implies assessing the most likely set of circumstances under which the change in the NPL ratio evolves.

The observed and out-of-sample evolution of the change in NPL ratios for the two paths and the six countries are depicted in Figure 4.6.

By construction, the gap between the baseline and the adverse changes in the NPL ratio depends on how strongly the variable evolved in the last

---

[26]   This implies an out-of-sample reduction in the NPL ratio of 3.6% for Cyprus, 0.5% for Greece, 3.2% for Ireland, 1.1% for Italy, 1.7% for Portugal, and 0.5% for Spain.

[27]   The forecasts are computed assuming that only the structural shock to the change in the NPL ratio adjusts to ensure the new path for the conditioning variable. See Dieppe, van Roye, and Legrand (2016) for more details.

Figure 4.6: Observed and Assumed Out-of-Sample Baseline and Adverse Change in NPL Ratios for the Structural Scenario Analysis

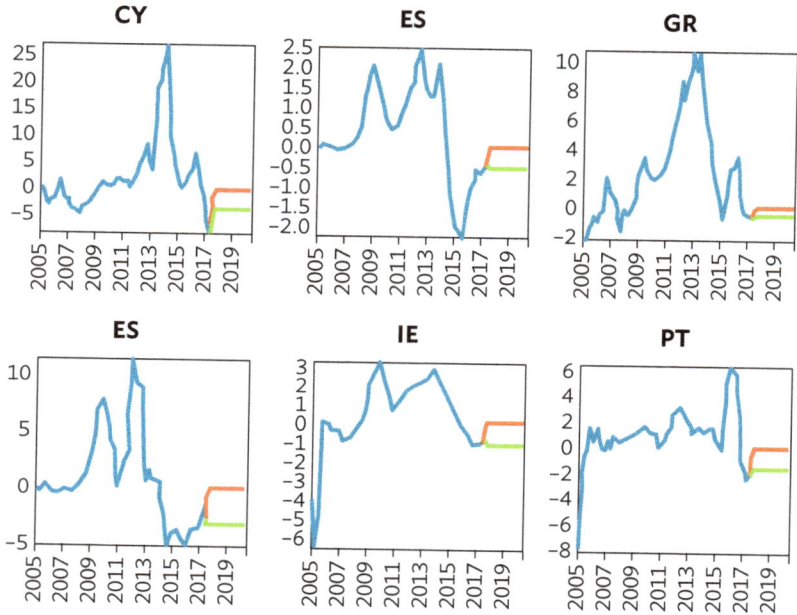

CY = Cyprus, ES = Spain, GR = Greece, IE = Ireland, IT = Italy, NPL = nonperforming loan, PT = Portugal.
Note: The data covers Q1 2006 to Q3 2017. The out-of-sample assumptions for the baseline and adverse paths for the change in NPL ratios span from Q4 2017 to Q3 2020.
Sources: International Monetary Fund Financial Soundness Indicators, Bank of France, Bank of Spain, Central Bank of Cyprus, Bankscope and authors' estimations.

4 quarters of the historical sample. This gap is the widest for Cyprus, followed by Ireland, Portugal, Italy, and then Spain and Greece. These assumptions result in different levels of the NPL ratio at the end of the forecast horizon.

The out-of-sample deviation between the baseline and adverse conditional forecasts of the variables is reported in Figure 4.7. The countries are reported in the columns, while the variables are depicted in the rows. A positive value implies that the baseline forecast exhibits a higher value than the adverse one.

The results show, as expected, that a further reduction in NPL ratios would have a positive impact on both the macroeconomic and the banking variables. At the end of the forecast horizon, the annual rate of growth of

Do Nonperforming Loans Matter for Bank Lending and
the Business Cycle in Euro Area Countries?

129

**Figure 4.7: Difference in Structural Scenario Forecasts between Baseline and Adverse Path
for Main Variables in the Panel Vector Autoregression**

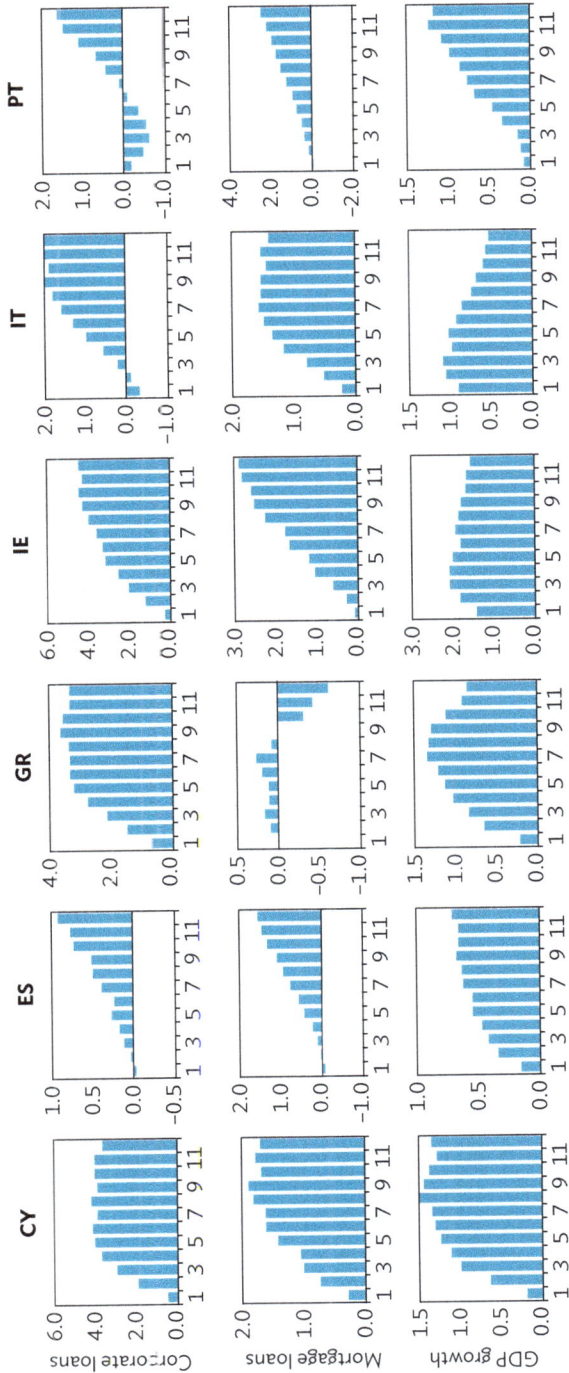

continued on next page

Figure 4.7 (continued)

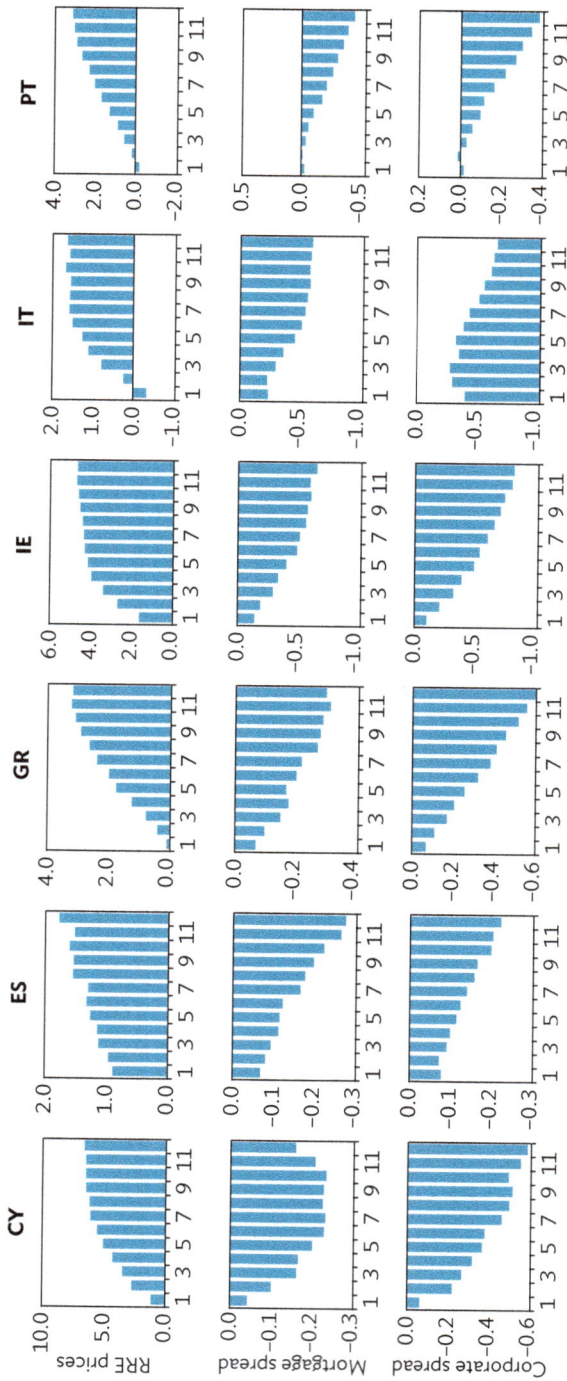

CY = Cyprus, ES = Spain, GDP = gross domestic product, GR = Greece, IE = Ireland, IT = Italy, PT = Portugal, RRE = residential real estate.
Note: The figure reports the difference between the baseline and the adverse structural scenario forecasts of the main variables in the panel VAR. Under both assumptions, the forecasts are computed assuming that only the structural shock to the change in NPL ratios adjusts to ensure the conditioning path for this variable. Real GDP growth, headline inflation, residential real estate prices, and corporate and mortgage loans are expressed in annual growth rates. The Euribor, bank lending spreads, change in NPL ratios, and capital and reserves-to-asset ratio are expressed in percentage points.
Source: Authors' estimations.

Do Nonperforming Loans Matter for Bank Lending and
the Business Cycle in Euro Area Countries?

131

mortgage lending under the baseline scenario is between 1.4 (Italy) and 2.9 (Ireland) percentage points higher than under the adverse scenario, while the annual rate of growth of corporate lending increases faster by between 0.9 percentage point (Spain) and 4.4 percentage points (Ireland). Bank lending spreads are narrower, by between 0.2 percentage point and 0.6 percentage point for mortgages, and by between 0.2 and 0.8 for loans to nonfinancial corporations under the baseline scenario. Stronger lending and lower spreads lead to higher residential real estate prices, with annual rates of growth being between 1.6 percentage point (Italy) and 6.7 percentage points (Cyprus) higher under the baseline scenario than under the adverse. Finally, the rate of real GDP growth is higher by between 0.5 percentage point (Italy) and 1.6 percentage points (Ireland). Overall, this structural out-of-sample forecast illustrates that a further reduction in NPL ratios can generate significant economic benefits in euro area countries.

4.4 Conclusion

NPL ratios increased substantially in many euro area countries from the onset of the global financial crisis. At the time of writing, NPL ratios remain an important problem in several euro area countries, despite a gradual decline from their peak in 2014. Moreover, the economic implications of the global COVID-19 pandemic are likely to undo recent successes in dealing with the stock of NPLs in the euro area.

High NPL ratios can impair the stability of the banking system and its ability to lend to the real economy. For highly bank-dependent economies such as the euro area, the necessity to deal with elevated NPL ratios is thus unquestionable, even as empirical papers analyzing the interlinkages between NPLs, bank lending, and economic growth are in short supply.

Given the relatively short time series available for NPLs and the large number of parameters to be estimated, a panel Bayesian VAR model with hierarchical priors, allowing for country-specific coefficients, was used in this chapter. The variables included in the panel VAR are those typically used in monetary policy analysis, supplemented by residential real estate prices and some aggregate banking sector variables.

The chapter illustrates the impact of an exogenous positive shock to the change in NPL ratio and an exogenous negative shock to real GDP growth through three sets of results. Looking first at impulse response functions, it finds that an exogenous increase in the change in NPL ratios depresses bank lending, widens lending spreads, and leads to a fall in real GDP growth and residential real estate prices. An exogenous decrease in GDP growth leads to an increase in the change in NPL ratios, reduction in bank lending, lower real estate prices, and increase in bank lending spreads. Forecast error variance decomposition shows that shocks to the change in NPL ratios, while being less relevant than shocks to GDP growth, explain a large share of the variance of the variables in the VAR, particularly for countries that exhibited a large increase in NPL ratios during the crisis. A 3-year structural out-of-sample forecast analysis clearly illustrates that a further reduction of NPL ratios can produce significant economic and financial benefits for euro area countries.

Overall, the results presented in this chapter provide clear empirical evidence for the economic merits associated with effective prudential and structural policy measures to speed up NPL resolution. Given the COVID-19 induced, expected rise in defaulting loans in the years ahead, the economic argument for the implementation of such policies is stronger than ever before.

Do Nonperforming Loans Matter for Bank Lending and
the Business Cycle in Euro Area Countries?

133

References

Accornero, M., P. Alessandri, L. Carpinelli, and A. M. Sorrentino. 2017. Non-Performing Loans and the Supply of Bank Credit: Evidence from Italy. *Questioni di Economia e Finanza (Occasional Papers)*. No. 374. Economic Research and International Relations Area. Rome: Bank of Italy.

Anastasiou, L., H. Dimitrios, and M. G. Tsionas. 2016. Non-Performing Loans in the Euro Area: Are Core-periphery Banking Markets Fragmented? *Bank of Greece Working Papers*. No. 219. Athens: Bank of Greece.

Antolin-Diaz, J., I. Petrella, and J. F. Rubio-Ramirez. 2018. Structural Scenario Analysis with SVARs. *CEPR Discussion Papers*. No.12579. Washington, DC: Center for Economic and Policy Research.

Balgova, M. and A. Plekhanov. 2016. The Economic Impact of Reducing Non-Performing Loans. *EBRD Working Paper Series*. No. 193. London: European Bank for Reconstruction and Development.

Beck, T., O. De Jonghe, and G. Schepens. 2013. Bank Competition and Stability: Cross-country Heterogeneity. *Journal of Financial Intermediation*. 22 (2). pp. 218–44.

Bernanke, B. S. and J. Boivin. 2003. Monetary Policy in a Data-rich Environment. *Journal of Monetary Economics*. 50 (3). pp. 525–46.

Bernanke, B. S. and M. Gertler. 1995. Inside the Black Box: The Credit Channel of Monetary Policy Transmission. *Journal of Economic Perspectives*. 9 (4). pp. 27–48.

Bjornland, H. C. and D. H. Jacobsen. 2010. The Role of House Prices in the Monetary Policy Transmission Mechanism in Small Open Economies. *Journal of Financial Stability*. 6 (4). pp. 218–29.

Christiano, L. J., M. Eichenbaum, and C. Evans. 1996. The Effects of Monetary Policy Shocks: Evidence from the Flow of Funds." *The Review of Economics and Statistics*. 78 (1). pp. 16–34.

Ciccarelli, M., A. Maddaloni, and J.-L. Peydró. 2013. Heterogeneous Transmission Mechanism: Monetary Policy and Financial Fragility in the Euro Area. *ECB Working Paper Series*. No. 1527. Frankfurt: European Central Bank.

Curdia, V. and M. Woodford. 2010. Credit Spreads and Monetary Policy. *Journal of Money, Credit and Banking*. 42 (1). pp. 3–35.

De Bock, R. and A. Demyanets. 2012. Bank Asset Quality in Emerging Markets; Determinants and Spillovers. *IMF Working Papers.* 12/71. Washington, DC: International Monetary Fund.

Dieppe, A., B. van Roye, and R. Legrand. 2016. The BEAR Toolbox. *ECB Working Paper Series.* No. 1934. Frankfurt: European Central Bank.

European Central Bank (ECB). 2011. The Monetary Policy of the ECB. Technical Report. Frankfurt: European Central Bank.

Espinoza, R. A. and A. Prasad. 2010. Nonperforming Loans in the GCC Banking System and their Macroeconomic Effects. *IMF Working Papers.* 10/224. Washington, DC: International Monetary Fund.

Fell, J., M. Grodzicki, D. Krušec, R. Martin, and E. O'Brien. 2017. Overcoming Non-Performing Loan Market Failures with Transaction Platforms. In *European Central Bank Financial Stability Review.* November. Frankfurt: European Central Bank.

Fell, J., M. Grodzicki, R. Martin, and E. O'Brien. 2016. Addressing Market Failures in the Resolution of Non-Performing Loans in the Euro Area. In *European Central Bank Financial Stability Review.* November. Frankfurt: European Central Bank.

Fell, J., M. Grodzicki, J. Metzler, and E. O'Brien. 2018. Non-Performing Loans and Euro Area Bank Lending Behaviour After the Crisis. In *Bank of Spain Financial Stability Review.* November. Madrid: Bank of Spain.

Goetz, M. R. 2018. Competition and Bank Stability. *Journal of Financial Intermediation.* 35 (PA). pp. 57–69.

Grodzicki, M., D. Laliotis, M. Leber, R. Martin, E. O'Brien, and P. Zboromirski. 2015. Resolving the Legacy of Non-Performing Exposures in Euro Area Banks. In *European Central Bank Financial Stability Review.* May. Frankfurt: European Central Bank.

Hancock, D., A. J. Laing, and J. A. Wilcox. 1995. Bank Capital Shocks: Dynamic Effects on Securities, Loans, and Capital. *Journal of Banking and Finance.* 19 (3–4). pp. 661–77.

Hartmann, P. 2015. Real Estate Markets and Macroprudential Policy in Europe. *ECB Working Paper Series.* No. 1796. Frankfurt: European Central Bank.

Hristov, N., O. Hülsewig, and T. Wollmershäuser. 2012. Loan Supply Shocks during the Financial Crisis: Evidence for the Euro Area. *Journal of International Money and Finance.* 31 (3). pp. 569–92.

Iacoviello, M. 2005. House Prices, Borrowing Constraints, and Monetary Policy in the Business Cycle. *American Economic Review*. 95 (3). pp. 739–64.

International Monetary Fund (IMF). 2006. Financial Soundness Indicators Compilation Guide (Guide). Technical Report. Washington, DC: IMF.

Jarocinski, M. 2010. Responses to Monetary Policy Shocks in the East and the West of Europe: A Comparison. *Journal of Applied Econometrics*. 25 (5). pp. 833–68.

Jimenez, G. and J. Saurina. 2006. Credit Cycles, Credit Risk, and Prudential Regulation. *International Journal of Central Banking*. 2 (2). pp. 65–95.

Kanngiesser, D., R. Martin, L. Maurin, and D. Moccero. 2017. Estimating the Impact of Shocks to Bank Capital in the euro area. *ECB Working Paper Series*. No. 2077. Frankfurt: European Central Bank.

Klein, N. 2013. Non-Performing Loans in CESEE; Determinants and Impact on Macroeconomic Performance. *IMF Working Papers*. 13/72. Washington, DC: International Monetary Fund.

Louzis, D. P., A. T. Vouldis, and V. L. Metaxas. 2012. Macroeconomic and Bank-Specific Determinants of Nonperforming Loans in Greece: A Comparative Study of Mortgage, Business and Consumer Loan Portfolios. *Journal of Banking and Finance*. 36 (4). pp. 1012–27.

Meeks, R. 2017. Capital Regulation and the Macroeconomy: Empirical Evidence and Macroprudential Policy. *European Economic Review*. 95 (C). pp. 125–41.

Nkusu, M. 2011. Non-Performing Loans and Macrofinancial Vulnerabilities in Advanced Economies. *IMF Working Paper Series*. WP/11/161. Washington, DC: International Monetary Fund.

Pancaro, C., D. Zochowski, and G. Arnould. 2020. Bank Funding Costs and Solvency. *ECB Working Paper Series*. No. 2356. Frankfurt: European Central Bank.

Quagliariello, M. 2007. Banks' Riskiness Over the Business Cycle: A Panel Analysis on Italian Intermediaries. *Applied Financial Economics*. 17 (2). pp. 119–38.

Country Case Studies
on Nonperforming Loan Resolution
in Asia and Europe

5   Country Case Studies on Resolving Problem Loans in Asia: Crises, Policies, and Institutions

Junkyu Lee, Peter Rosenkranz, and Edimon Ginting[1]

5.1 Introduction

The impact of the 1997–1998 Asian financial crisis warranted a proactive approach from crisis-affected countries in addressing the problem of nonperforming loan (NPL) proliferation. To manage and dispose of bad assets during the crisis, most Asian economies relied on centralized public asset management companies (AMC) as a key strategy. Authorities also restructured financial sectors at the onset of the crisis to facilitate effective government bank bailouts that only benefited solvent and healthy financial institutions. Also central to strategies for reducing NPLs, many Asian governments reformed insolvency laws and established out-of-court workout mechanisms to assist debt restructuring. Finally, governments strengthened financial institution supervisory bodies and tightened prudential regulations to curb the buildup of risks.

Despite substantial Asian NPL history, empirical studies on Asian resolution cases are lacking in documenting the effectiveness of the region's policies for reducing NPLs during banking crises and mitigating NPL growth amid banking stability. The Asian experience during and after the Asian financial crisis has been largely discussed through case studies, such as in Fung et al. (2004a); Kim, Kim, and Ryoo (2006); and Fujii and Kawai (2010).

This chapter contributes to the NPL reduction literature in two ways. First, it constructs case studies of Asia's NPL reduction policies implemented by selected ASEAN +3 economies resting on four main pillars: operation of AMCs, financial sector restructuring and bailouts, insolvency frameworks,

---

[1]   The authors acknowledge excellent research assistance from Mikko Diaz and Alyssa Villanueva.

and prudential measures during and after the Asian financial crisis.[2] These case studies are also the basis for constructing the novel dataset of NPL reduction policy dummy variables used in the analysis. Second, the study analyzes the effectiveness of reduction policies using a dynamic panel dataset of 78 financial institutions from six Asian countries during 2002–2017 in an effort to close the empirical gap in Asian NPL reduction studies.

The empirical results indicate that the most effective policy for reducing NPLs is to establish centralized public AMCs. Although government bank bailouts also have a significant impact, the results are not robust when analyzed using different bank-level indicators. The results suggest that public AMC operations are effective during banking crises as well as to reduce bank-level NPLs amid banking stability by providing a feasible platform for NPL transactions.

The next section reviews the literature on the determinants of NPLs and the effectiveness of reduction policies. The chapter summarizes the four main pillars of NPL resolution in Asia, and describes the data and provides the empirical and theoretical framework used to identify the best NPL reduction measures implemented in the ASEAN+3 region, and presents the results of the empirical analysis.

5.2 Literature Review

Empirical evidence on the effectiveness of NPL reduction programs and policies in Asia are relatively scarce in comparison to the traditional NPL literature, which studies the determinants of NPLs. Existing literature tells us that NPL cycles are closely related to external macroeconomic factors and micro-level bank-specific performance indicators. While many empirical studies examine the effect of macroeconomic factors (Quagliariello 2009; Mohaddes, Raissi, and Weber 2017) and bank-level indicators individually (Berger and De Young 1997), others have chosen to illustrate the interplay between the two factors. Salas and Saurina (2002) use the generalized method of moments (GMM) method to estimate the interplay of macroeconomic variables and bank-level indicators on the NPLs of commercial and savings banks in Spain from 1988 to 1997. They illustrate that while commercial bank NPLs are more susceptible to changes in the economic cycle, savings banks are more affected by bank-level indicators, due to the historical differences in the customer base of commercial banks (firms) and savings banks (families).

---

[2]   ASEAN+3 includes the members of the Association of Southeast Asian Nations plus the People's Republic of China, Japan, and the Republic of Korea.

Similarly, Louzis, Vouldis, and Metaxas (2012) replicate this methodology and apply it to the dynamic panel data of Greece's nine largest banks from the first quarter (Q1) of 2003 to Q3 2009. They show that management effectiveness (return on equity [ROE]), leverage (loans-to-assets [LA] ratio), and operating inefficiency were significant explanatory factors when applied alongside macroeconomic variables—gross domestic product (GDP) growth, unemployment, and real lending rates.

Klein (2013) extends the existing dynamic panel methodology regionally. Using difference GMM and system GMM, he analyzes 135 banks in Central, Eastern, and Southeastern Europe from 1998 to 2011. The chapter verifies the "bad management" and "moral hazard" hypotheses—originally proposed by Berger and De Young (1997)—by illustrating the negative relationship of ROE and the equity-to-assets ratio (EA) on NPLs, respectively. The study also verifies the positive relationship of increasing leverage on bank-level NPLs using LA and the loan growth rate.

Similar to previous studies, Ari, Chen, and Ratnovski (2019) highlight how a strong pre-crisis economy and well-managed and profitable banking and corporate sector lead to better NPL management. Using ordinary least squares (OLS) in conjunction with a "post rigorous least absolute shrinkage and selection operator" selection method, the study analyzes NPL dynamics in 88 banking crises since the 1990s. The study illustrates that GDP per capita alongside strong banking and corporate sector conditions reduce the likelihood of elevated NPLs. Findings also suggest that floating exchange rates help cushion real and financial shocks and help with banking sector and economic recovery. Finally, the study suggests that higher pre-crisis growth, exchange rate depreciation, and high bank profitability and good management aid the likelihood of NPL resolution.

However, the traditional NPL literature has been instrumental in the development of empirical studies on NPL reduction. Building on existing NPL determinant literature, Consolo, Malfa, and Pierluigi (2018) improve existing panel data models by including the quality of insolvency frameworks as an additional explanatory variable. The study constructs a novel Insolvency Framework Index based on the average of four variables from the World Bank's Doing Business Survey that measures: (i) the strength of legal rights in getting credits, (ii) the cost of resolving insolvency, (iii) the time needed to enforce contracts, and (iv) the cost of enforcing contracts. Using a simple time-fixed effects model, the study analyzes 41 countries from the European Union and Organisation for Economic Co-operation and Development.

The results illustrate that better insolvency frameworks expedite NPL reduction and lower NPL proliferation during severe economic crises.

Similarly, Wolski (2014) uses six resolving-insolvency and enforcing-contract variables derived from the World Bank's Doing Business Survey as additional NPL determinants. Using country-level data from 18 Economic and Monetary Union members, the study uses a fixed-effects estimation and finds that while all three enforcing contract variables are insignificant, resolving insolvency variables—cost of insolvency and recovery of insolvency—are positively and negatively related to the change in NPL stock, respectively.

Related studies by Balgova, Plekhanov, and Skrzypińska (2017) and Plekhanov and Skrzypińska (2018) construct a (i) novel database of NPL ratios from 1990 to 2015 covering more than 190 countries and a (ii) novel dataset of NPL reduction policies deployed to address NPL crises in many countries from 1990 to 2015. Using macroeconomic variables and bank performance indicators as control variables, both studies focus on analyzing the effectiveness of five NPL reduction policies: (i) establishment of AMCs, (ii) publicly funded bank recapitalization, (iii) macroprudential tightening, (iv) changes in loan classification, and (v) changes in provisioning stringency.

Plekhanov and Skrzypińska (2018) seek to capture (i) the effectiveness of NPL reduction policies, and (ii) the cross-border spillover effects of NPL reduction policies on foreign subsidiary branches. They do this using a fixed-effects regression that captures the interplay of foreign ownership dummies and policy variable dummies. Results indicate that AMCs and bailout packages deployed in the parent's home country, when implemented each by themselves, have no significant spillover effect on foreign subsidiary NPLs, but do have a significant negative relationship when deployed together. Likewise, the study indicates that macroprudential tightening, changes in loan classification, and provisioning stringency have no significant effects on foreign subsidiary NPLs. However, results also indicate a direct effect of AMCs only, macroprudential tightening, and loan classification tightening on reducing NPLs within the jurisdiction where they are implemented.

Balgova, Plekhanov, and Skrzypińska (2017) employ a novel approach in the NPL reduction literature, using a two-part model. The first part measures the likelihood of a sharp drop in NPLs within 3 years of the implementation of a policy and the second the magnitude of the subsequent NPL reduction conditional on a sharp drop.[3] The study finds that the best NPL reduction policies are a combination of AMCs and public bank bailouts. AMCs are associated with a significant increase in the likelihood of an NPL reduction and a greater magnitude of NPL reduction. While bank recapitalizations have no significant effects on NPL reduction likelihood and magnitude, AMCs are found to have a higher likelihood and magnitude when implemented together with bank recapitalization programs.

5.3 Case Studies on Asian Nonperforming Loan Resolution

Case studies reveal that Asian NPL resolution[4] measures rest on four main pillars: (i) operation of AMCs, (ii) financial sector restructuring and bailouts, (iii) insolvency reforms and resolution frameworks, and (iv) prudential tightening including loan classification and provisioning stringency.

5.3.1 Asset Management Companies

To address NPL problems in the aftermath of the Asian financial crisis, most economies in Asia established public AMCs as a key strategy for managing and disposing of impaired bank assets (Fung et al. 2004a). The crisis-affected countries—Indonesia, Japan, Malaysia, the People's Republic of China (PRC), the Republic of Korea, and Thailand—established public, centralized AMCs to clean up bad assets in financial institutions (Table 5.1). According to Terada-Hagiwara and Pasadilla (2004), a large and systemic NPL problem (and a weak banking sector and poor legal infrastructure) called for crisis-affected countries to choose a centralized AMC model.

---

[3] Balgova, Plekhanov, and Skrzypińska (2017) define a sharp drop as a 7-percentage-point decline in the NPL level.

[4] See also Appendix 1: Tables of NPL Resolution Cases.

Table 5.1: Summary of Asian Asset Management Companies' Operations

AMC Feature	PRC	Indonesia	Japan	Rep. of Korea	Malaysia	Thailand
Public asset management companies	Big 4 (Orient, Great Wall, Cinda, Huarong)	IBRA	RCC IRCJ	KAMCO	Danaharta	Thai Asset Management Company (TAMC)
Set up	1999	1998	RCC – 1999 IRCJ – 2003	1962 (Role expanded in 1997)	1998	2001
NPL acquisition period	1999–2000 2004	1999–2000	1999–2006	1997–2002	1998–2001	2001–2003
NPL acquisition (LCU billion)	1999 – 1,394.0 2004 – 320.1	391,870.0	9,800.0	111,400.0	47.7 (19.7 acquired NPL + 28 managed for government)	775.8
Peak NPL ratio (year - %)	1999 – 28.5	1998 – 48.6	2002 – 8.1	2000 – 8.9	1998 – 18.6	1998 – 42.9
NPL ratio + 5 years (year - %)	2004 – 13.2	2003 – 6.8	2007 – 1.5	2005 – 1.2	2003 – 13.9	2003 – 13.5
Sunset clause	No[1]	Yes	RCC – No IRCJ – Yes	No	Yes	Yes
Closing date/ Recovery period	-	2004	IRCJ – 2007	2012	2005	2006
Recovery rate (recovery/ acquisition, %)	20.84 (68.6% of portfolio sold)[2]	22 (60% of portfolio sold)	-	43.2 (100% of portfolio sold)	58.0 (96.4% of portfolio sold)	19.4 (~100% of portfolio sold)

AMC = asset management company, Cinda = Cinda Asset Management, Danaharta = Pengurusan Danaharta Bhd., Great Wall = Great Wall Asset Management, Huarong = Huarong Asset Management, IBRA = Indonesia Bank Restructuring Agency, IRCJ = Industrial Revitalization Corporation of Japan, KAMCO = Korea Asset Management Corporation, LCU = local currency unit, NPL = nonperforming loan, Orient = Orient Asset Management, PRC = People's Republic of China, RCC = Resolution and Collection Corporation.

Notes: Appendix 1 provides a more detailed comparison of Asian AMCs.

[1] The "Big 4" asset management companies were supposed to have a sunset clause of 10 years, but are still operating;

[2] Recovery value as of 30 June 2006 (Bihong 2006).

Sources: Authors' calculations using data from Haver Analytics; CEIC; World Bank, World Development Indicators; Bihong (2006); Cerutti and Neyens (2016); RCC (2019); Okina (2009); Financial Supervisory Service (Republic of Korea); Bank Negara Malaysia; Danaharta (2006); Bank of Thailand; and Santiprabhob (2003).

Indonesia

On 26 January 1998, Indonesia established the Indonesia Bank Restructuring Agency (IBRA) to assist in the country's restructuring and recapitalization program. IBRA acquired the NPLs of all banks recapitalized by Bank Indonesia and closed banks that were ineligible for the recapitalization program. During its acquisition period from 1999 to 2000, IBRA acquired Indonesian rupiah (Rp) 346.7 trillion in NPLs. Unlike most Asian AMCs established during the Asian financial crisis, the acquisition price for acquired NPLs was set at 0, as the capital injection provided by the government could be considered the payment. IBRA was relatively unsuccessful in the management of its NPL portfolio relative to other Asian AMCs established during the Asian financial crisis. IBRA's operations were constrained by the lack of strong political support, in particular conflicting views within the government on how best to maximize asset recovery and reluctance to sell assets at discounts. In its lifetime from 1999 to 2004,[5] IBRA only sold 60% of its NPL portfolio (Cerutti and Neyens 2016). At that time, this was one of the world's most costly bank recapitalization efforts, at 40% of GDP, causing a large increase in public debt and yielding an NPL recovery rate of 28.5% (IMF 2004).

Japan

On 1 April 1999, Japan established the Resolution and Collection Corporation (RCC). RCC was tasked to purchase NPLs from failed financial institutions and mortgage lenders. Loan purchases were focused on loans given to small to medium-sized enterprises and nonviable firms that were classified "bankrupt" or "in danger of bankruptcy." A special assessment of bank loans to large borrowers conducted in 2001 by the Financial Services Agency led to a large-scale reclassification of loans to 149 companies, causing a dramatic, 25% increase in NPL volume, from Japanese yen (¥) 33.6 trillion in 2000 to ¥43.2 trillion in 2001. In response, the government enacted the Program for Financial Revival, which aimed to accelerate bank loan restructuring through three main strategies: (i) reduce bank equity holdings equivalent to 100% of Tier-1 capital by 2006; (ii) strengthen NPL classification and provisioning; and (iii) reduce NPLs to half of 2002 levels (8.4% of total loans) by 2005. To facilitate the implementation of the program, the Financial Services Agency established a new AMC, the Industrial Revitalization Corporation of Japan (IRCJ),

---

[5] After the end of IBRA's sunset period in 2004, PT Perusahaan Pengelola Aset (Persero) absorbed its remaining assets.

in 2003. The IRCJ focused on higher-quality NPLs classified as those that "need special attention" extended to larger firms compared to RCC. IRCJ was designed to promote the restructuring of relatively large firms by purchasing NPLs from secondary banks.[6] It is estimated that RCC and IRCJ purchased approximately ¥9.8 trillion in nonperforming assets in face value (Fujiii and Kawai 2010). IRCJ liquidated all of its portfolio on 2 March 2007 (IRCJ 2007), while RCC is still operating (RCC 2019). Based on data from the Deposit Insurance Corporation of Japan, as of Q2 2020, RCC has managed a 103.9% collection rate, collecting a cumulative total of ¥10.2 trillion against a cumulative transfer of ¥9.8 trillion.

Republic of Korea

The reorganization of Korea Asset Management Corporation (KAMCO) and creation of the NPL resolution fund within KAMCO in November 1997 facilitated KAMCO's role as lead actor and purchaser of NPLs from financial institutions (Fung et al. 2004a). From 1997 to 2002, KAMCO acquired about Korean won (W) 111.4 trillion in NPLs in face value (more than 300,000 NPL accounts) at an average haircut of 64.8%, or W39.1 trillion (KAMCO 2010). KAMCO's acquisition program was 95% funded by KAMCO bonds, which were used to purchase NPLs from troubled financial institutions. KAMCO bonds were 100% guaranteed by the government and therefore have a 0% risk-weight, thereby having improved financial institutions capital bases to meet the 8% minimum capital adequacy ratio (CAR) requirements (Fung et al. 2004a). By the end of KAMCO's acquisition period in November 2002, it decreased domestic bank NPLs by 69.7% from their peak of W30.86 trillion in Q4 of 1999 to W9.2 trillion, or 2.38% of total loans by Q4 2002.[7]

Cerutti and Neyens (2016) report that KAMCO's overall performance was mixed. Unlike most Asian AMCs established during the Asian financial crisis, the AMC had no sunset period and the recovery of its NPL portfolio was relatively slow. By 2013, KAMCO was able to recover 100% of its NPL portfolio, gaining W48.1 trillion—122.70% of its NPL acquisition amount, or 43.18% of the face value of acquired NPLs (KAMCO 2014). However, KAMCO's disposal methods paved the way for the creation of a distressed debt market, which proved instrumental during the global financial crisis. KAMCO's resolution experience showed how a centralized AMC could play a role in market-making and market-promoting of distressed assets.

---

[6] Eligibility criteria for support relies on the feasibility of the company's submitted reorganization plan. The reorganization plan must include measures that enable a company to achieve at least one of the following: (i) increase in ROE of more than 2%; (ii) increase in turnover ratio of tangibles exceeding 5%; and (iii) increase in valued added per employee exceeding 6% (Takagi 2003).

[7] Data based on the Republic of Korea's Financial Supervisory Services.

Malaysia

Pengurusan Danaharta Bhd. (Danaharta)—established on 20 June 1998 to remove nonperforming assets from the banking system and manage them to maximize proceeds from recovery (Fung et al. 2004b)—was among Asia's most successful AMCs. During its acquisition period from September 1998 to December 2001, Danaharta was able to acquire Malaysian ringgit (RM) 19.71 billion from private financial institutions (priced at RM8.94 billion) and an additional RM27.96 billion NPL (no transfer price) managed on behalf of the government (Danaharta 2006). By the end of its operations in 2005, Danaharta managed a recovery rate of 58%.[8]

Thailand

Thailand's centralized AMC—the Thai Asset Management Company (TAMC)—was only established in June 2001, unlike other Asian centralized public AMCs which were established or strengthened within a year of the Asian financial crisis in 1997. Thailand originally favored a decentralized approach to addressing the Asian financial crisis, partly due to fiscal concerns (Terada-Hagiwara and Pasadilla 2004). At the onset of the crisis, the country enacted the Emergency Decree on Asset Management Company (1998), which facilitated the establishment of 12 private and 4 public AMCs. Its private AMC initiative was largely ineffective due to unfavorable situations,[9] but four decentralized AMCs—Bangkok Commerce AMC, Sukhumvit AMC, Petchburi AMC, and Radhanasin AMC—were more effective and removed Thai baht (B) 977.24 billion in NPLs from five of the country's state-owned corporate banks from 1998 to 2001 (Santiprabhob 2003).

A change in government in 2001, however, prompted the establishment of TAMC as an Emergency Decree on 8 June 2001 (Terada-Hagiwara and Pasadilla 2004). During its acquisition period from Q3 2001 to Q4 2003, TAMC acquired a total of B775.78 billion in NPLs, with an average transfer price of 34%. However, of the total acquisitions, only 19% were new NPL acquisitions from private institutions, with 81% of the NPL transfers mostly from old AMCs with significant NPL portfolios, such as Petchburi AMC and Sukhumvit AMC (Bank of Thailand 2004, 2007).

---

[8] Data are from Table 5.10 in Cerruti and Neyens (2016).

[9] Even though many private financial institutions had established AMCs, most of them could not transfer large amounts of their NPLs to AMCs after the Institution of Certified Accountants and Auditors of Thailand in 2001 issued a new operational guideline on the transfer of financial assets. Under the guideline, financial institutions would be worse off financially after transferring NPLs to their own AMCs because they would in effect be required to maintain capital adequacy against both the NPLs and AMCs' bonds issued to purchase the NPL. Excerpted from Santiprabhob (2003).

TAMC was successful in NPL resolution but, like IBRA, was relatively unsuccessful in its NPL recovery partly due to legal limitations in its ability to sell loans to third parties (Terada-Hagiwara and Pasadilla 2004).[10] By 2006, TAMC had resolved 99.98% of its NPL portfolio, but only managed to recover B150.12 billion—19.35% of the acquired NPL book value (Bank of Thailand 2007).

Viet Nam

In June 2003, Viet Nam established the Debt and Assets Trading Company under the Ministry of Finance. It was renamed as Vietnam Debt and Assets Trading Company (VDATC) in 2014 and was tasked with purchasing and disposing of distressed debt and assets from businesses, but mostly state-owned enterprises and state-owned commercial banks (VDATC 2018a). VDATC was also tasked to carry out the restructuring of state-owned enterprises in line with the Viet Nam government's roadmap. Over the years, VDATC has mainly implemented corporate restructuring. From 2004 to 2017, VDATC restructured nearly 180 enterprises, contributing significantly to restructuring and equitizing state-owned enterprises (VDATC 2018b). From the start of its operations in 2004 to November 2018, VDATC purchased approximately Vietnamese dong (D) 90 trillion in debt and supported more than 3,000 debt-processing enterprises in the process of equitization (Viet Nam News 2018).

Recent public, centralized AMCs in Asia

Initiatives since the global financial crisis by Asian economies to establish public and centralized AMCs include the establishment of the Vietnam Asset Management Company (VAMC) on 18 May 2013 to cope with the surge in NPLs in the aftermath of the global financial crisis in Viet Nam (Borst 2015). VAMC is a state-owned company established by the State Bank of Vietnam, the central bank, to address the NPLs of Vietnamese credit institutions. It was given broad power, such as to (i) purchase the bad debts of credit institutions by special bonds and market value; (ii) sell debts and collateral; (iii) restructure the debt; (iv) develop a roadmap to convert debt into capital; (v) guarantee loans; (vi) exploit, use, and lease collateral; and (vii) brokerage advice on the sale of debt and property.

---

[10] One of the key differences between TAMC and other AMC structures, however, is that the TAMC does not have the power to sell loans to third parties (Fung et al. 2004b).

VAMC buys bad debts paid for by special bonds at market value. The credit institutions may use the bonds as collateral for refinancing from the State Bank of Vietnam (VAMC 2018).[11] VAMC purchased all NPLs of banks with an NPL ratio greater than 3% (in a mandatory requirement for sales of NPLs by banks) and aimed to reduce total banking sector NPLs to 3% by 2015, playing an important role in reducing NPLs below 3% in recent years. Since its establishment and up to 2018, VAMC acquired D340 trillion ($14.7 billion) and D3.4 trillion through special bond instruments and market price purchases, respectively.[12] The AMC had recovered D119 trillion by 31 December 2018 (Vietnam Insider 2019).

Other established AMCs

Other Asian countries did not establish public and centralized AMCs during the Asian financial crisis. The PRC, for example, established four decentralized AMCs—Orient Asset Management (1999), Great Wall Asset Management (1999), Cinda Asset Management (1999), and Huarong Asset Management (1999)—to acquire the NPL of its four largest banks—Bank of China, Agricultural Bank of China, China Construction Bank, and Industrial and Commerce Bank of China. The approach of establishing four different AMCs may have well reflected the fact that the "Big 4" Chinese banks held nearly 70% of the market share and were specialized in different areas of business (Fung et al. 2004b).

The Philippines' NPL resolution measures were centered on private special purpose vehicles (SPV), due to lack of government funds and the seemingly non-systemic nature of the banking problem (Pasadilla 2005). In January 2003, the Philippines enacted the SPV Act of 2002, which facilitated the establishment of SPVs as the corporate vehicle to acquire NPLs and other nonperforming assets from banks' balance sheets. The SPV Act incentivized nonperforming asset transfers by providing lower taxes and fees on such transfers. By the end of its implementation period from 2003 to 2008, the SPV Act of 2002 facilitated the transfer of Philippine pesos (P) 119.98 billion NPLs from the banking system—P88.02 billion from its first implementation in 2003 to 2005, and an additional P31.96 billion from its second implementation in 2006 to 2008.[13]

---

[11] The special bonds are issued at zero coupon and have a maximum maturity of 5 years, no more than 10 years in the case of buying bad debts of credit institutions.

[12] IDS Argo's executive board member Akira Kondoh said Viet Nam's NPL market is bigger than estimated (Deal Street Asia 2019).

[13] Assessment of Republic Act No. 9343 Entitled "An Act of Amending Republic Act No. 9182, otherwise known as the Special Purpose Vehicle Act of 2002 for the Purpose of Allowing the Establishment and Registration of New SPVs and for other Purposes" (NTRC Tax Research Journal, XXII.6).

5.3.2 Financial Sector Restructuring and Bailout

Other pillars are instrumental in creating the enabling environment for the success of AMC operations. According to Balgova, Plekhanov, and Skrzypińska (2017), the best NPL resolution measures and strategies combine availability of public funds and establishment of specialized AMCs. Such was the case for Asian economies during the Asian financial crisis, where financial bailouts accompanied the transfer and acquisition of NPLs by AMCs (Table 5.2). Financial sector bailout programs were often preceded by or done in conjunction with a financial sector restructuring program to limit moral hazard and ensure the appropriate disbursal of important government funds. According to Santiprabhob (2003), financial sector restructuring through the separation of good financial institutions from bad mitigates the risk of moral hazard from bad banks and ensures that only solvent and healthy financial institutions remain to benefit from the government's expensive capital support schemes.

Table 5.2: Asian Recapitalization Programs

Feature	PRC	Indonesia	Japan	Republic of Korea	Malaysia	Thailand
Agency	State Council	Government	Deposit Insurance Corporation of Japan	Korea Deposit Insurance Corporation	Danamodal Nasional Berhad (Danamodal)	Financial Institutions Development Fund
Recapitalization Period	1999–2008	1997–2000	1997–2006	1997–2003	1998	1998–2002
Amount (LCU billion)	1999–270 2003–45 2005–15 2008–130	650,000	Direct injection–12,400 Monetary grant–18,900	160,400	6.15	Public–716.93 Private–0.71

LCU = local currency unit, PRC = People's Republic of China.
Note: Appendix Table A.2 provides a more detailed comparison of Asian recapitalization programs.
Sources: Bing (2005), Bihong (2006), Fung et al. (2004a), Sato (2005), Fujii and Kawai (2010), Lim and Hahm (2004), Lee (2017), and Santiprabhob (2003).

Indonesia

Indonesia had the most expensive financial sector bailout program among countries affected by the Asian financial crisis. Its banking sector exhibited the highest NPL ratio, at 48.6% at its peak in 1998. By the end of 2000, Indonesia's financial sector bailout program amounted to Rp650 trillion (31.6% of 2000 GDP), where Rp431 trillion was used for bank recapitalization, Rp144.5 trillion was used for emergency liquidity assistance, and Rp73.8 trillion was used for a temporary blanket deposit and liability guarantee issued from 1998 to 2004 to protect the banking sector from bank runs (Fung et al. 2004).

Due to the high cost of the program, the country implemented a comprehensive bank restructuring program to limit moral hazard in the banking sector. During this period, it closed 67 private banks; nationalized/ took over 12 private banks; and recapitalized 26 banks consisting of 7 state banks, 7 private banks, and 12 regional development banks. Although the program started in 1997, the country was only able to set up clear guidelines on closure and reconstruction in 1999. The guidelines established enforcement actions based on a banks' capitalization. Banks with a capital adequacy ratio (CAR) less than -25% were closed, while banks with a CAR between -25% and 4% were recapitalized under necessary conditions. An exemption was given to all seven state-owned banks, which were all recapitalized despite all having a CAR of less than -25% (Sato 2005).

Japan

The main actor during the Asian financial crisis was the Deposit Insurance Corporation of Japan. The revision of the Deposit Insurance Act and enactment of the Financial Revitalization Act and Early Financial Correction Law gave the Deposit Insurance Corporation of Japan measures to maintain stability of the financial system during significant turmoil. Measures include capital injection, full deposit protection, and temporary nationalization.

In 1998, a total of ¥60 trillion was allocated for financial support. ¥1.8 trillion were injected into the 21 major banks to meet the required capital adequacy standards. Japan temporarily nationalized two major banks, Long-Term Credit Bank of Japan and Nippon Credit Bank, and subsequently sold the banks to private investors. In 1999, Japan injected an additional ¥7.5 trillion into 15 of Japan's leading banks. The Program for Financial Revival enacted in 2002 implemented stricter loan classification and provisioning requirements, which prompted an additional public sector bailout amounting to ¥2 trillion to 4 banks. From 1997 to 2006, the Deposit Insurance Corporation of Japan deployed ¥12.4 trillion in direct injections and ¥18.9 trillion in monetary grants for the effective closure of failed institutions and blanket deposit guarantees deployed during the 1990 Japan Banking Crisis and extended until the resolution of the 1997 Asian financial crisis (Fujiii and Kawai 2010).

Republic of Korea

To address the collapse of the Korean banks during the Asian financial crisis, the government set up a public bailout package amounting to W160.4 trillion (30% of the Republic of Korea's GDP in 2002) released from November 1997 to June 2003 (Lim and Hahm 2004). W60.3 trillion of the package was used for direct recapitalization of troubled banks and other financial institutions, W17 trillion for liquidity support, W29.8 trillion for deposit insurance payoffs, W14.3 trillion for purchase of other assets, and W39.1 trillion for NPL purchases by KAMCO.[14] Unlike drastic measures developed in Indonesia, the Republic of Korea focused on rescuing— either through NPL purchase or capital injection—banking institutions and insurance companies. However, by the end of 2004, five weak banks had closed through purchase and acquisition and nine banks had merged with others (Lee 2017).

Malaysia

Danamodal Nasional Berhad (Danamodal) was established in 1998 to recapitalize insolvent but viable financial institutions. In 1998, Danamodal recapitalized 10 financial institutions through its purchase of the various financial institutions' subordinated capital loans, amounting to RM6.15 billion. Recapitalized institutions were then required to sell all NPLs to Malaysia's asset management company—Pengurusan Danaharta Bhd. (Danaharta). Unlike Indonesia, Malaysia's banking sector was less affected by the crisis—although NPLs were still high—exhibiting an NPL peak of 20.9% during Q1 1999. Malaysia elected not to implement a comprehensive banking sector restructuring, but rather collaborated with international specialists to identify viable financial institutions to ensure the best use of public money (Fung et al. 2004a).

Thailand

Before implementing its public sector recapitalization program on 14 August 1998, from March 1997 to August 1998, Thailand closed down 56 weak financial institutions and took over 7 failed banks in 1996.[15] According to Santiprabhob (2003), the Bank of Thailand's financial sector restructuring mitigated moral hazard from bad banking institutions and ensured that

---

[14]   The data are from Table 4 in Lim and Hahm (2004).

[15]   Bangkok Metropolitan Bank, Siam City Bank, First Bangkok City Bank, Union Bank, Laem Thong Bank, Nakornthon Bank, and Bangkok Bank of Commerce.

only solvent and healthy financial institutions remained to benefit from the government's capital support scheme. Thailand's comprehensive financial sector restructuring had similarities with Indonesia's, as Thailand's banking sector was one of the most affected in the region, with an NPL peak of 46% in Q1 1999.

Thailand's recapitalization program for public financial institutions started in 1998 to 2002. Of the B716.93 billion recapitalization effort (8.6% of 2002 GDP), only B16.57 billion was direct equity injections, while B429.57 billion was debt-equity conversions and B270.79 billion reserve reversals for accounting purposes.

Viet Nam

Viet Nam hoped that economic growth and banking sector improvement would resolve the country's bad debt problem without government involvement. However, as the necessary improvement in macroeconomic performance and bank management was slow after the Asian financial crisis, the government decided to intervene in clearing state-owned commercial bank balance sheets of the NPL problem. From 2001 to 2005, the government enacted a 5-year bank restructuring project that injected D10.9 trillion into Viet Nam's four largest state-owned commercial banks—Vietnam Bank for Agriculture and Rural Development, Vietnamese Bank for Investment and Development, Vietcombank, and Incombank (IMF 2006). The recapitalization program boosted the banks' equity against debt write-offs, which was the main form of NPL resolution then (World Bank 2006).

5.3.3 Insolvency Resolution Framework

Asian economies that were directly hit by the Asian financial crisis introduced legal and regulatory frameworks to create an enabling environment for the quick resolution of the AMC's acquired NPLs (Chapter 8). These policies included modernizing outdated insolvency frameworks and introduced out-of-court procedures to hasten and improve the corporate insolvency process (Appendix Table A.3).[16] In Thailand, the 1998 reform of the Thai Bankruptcy Act (Bankruptcy Act) introduced business reorganization procedures to rehabilitate financially distressed but viable businesses. Before this reform, the Thai Bankruptcy Act only dealt with liquidation proceedings. A 1999

---

[16] Prior to the Asian financial crisis, insolvency laws of many Asian economies were considered out of date and lacking in judiciary capacity (Carmer 2000).

reform of the Bankruptcy Act established the specialized Bankruptcy Court to have sole jurisdiction over all liquidation and rehabilitation cases and over all civil cases related to the aforementioned cases (Broude 2002). A specialized bankruptcy court allows a sufficiently trained judiciary to ensure efficiency and proper exercise of discretion in insolvency cases (IMF 1999).

Economies hit by the Asian financial crisis also developed out-of-court insolvency mechanisms to assist corporate restructuring. Indonesia developed the Jakarta Initiative Task Force in 1998 (Tomasic 2001), the Republic of Korea developed the Corporate Restructuring Coordination Committee in 1998 (Chan 2002), Malaysia established the Corporate Debt Restructuring Committee in 1997 (Abdullah, Keong, and Khuan 2016), and Thailand established the Corporate Debt Restructuring Advisory Committee in June 1998 (Broude 2002). In Thailand, in particular, out-of-court insolvency was more successful compared to its formal insolvency proceedings, with creditors attracted to its shorter processes than in court-mandated reorganizations caused by the inexperience and inefficiency of the judiciary (Broude 2002). By the end of the committee's operations on 1 October 2006, it had facilitated debt restructuring of 11,655 cases amounting to B1.5 trillion (Bank of Thailand 2007).

5.3.4 Strengthening Supervisory Framework and Institutions

A key problem during the Asian financial crisis was the ineffectiveness of supervisory bodies and prudential regulations. Asian economies hit by the crisis, such as the PRC, Indonesia, and the Republic of Korea enacted laws that strengthened the supervisory and executory powers of supervisory institutions. Indonesia amended the 1998 Banking Act and passed the new Central Bank Act of 1999 to strengthen Bank Indonesia's independence from other organizations, and centralized the bank licensing, revocation, supervision, and sanctioning powers (Sato 2005).

The Republic of Korea centralized its supervision framework in 1998 with the establishment of the Financial Supervisory Commission and the consolidation of existing financial supervisory agencies into the Financial Supervisory Services as the administrative body of the commission. Amendments to the Financial Industry Restructuring Act gave the Financial Supervisory Commission and Financial Supervisory Services statutory authority to order write-offs, mergers, and suspension and closure of troubled banks and financial institutions (Kim 2006). In the PRC, administrative measures on the supervision of the banking industry assigned the newly established China Bank Regulatory Commission (CBRC) to take over banking supervision and regulation from the decentralized handling of People's Bank of China, Ministry of Finance, and China Securities Regulatory Commission (Kossof 2014).

At the onset of the Asian financial crisis, supervisory bodies pressed for the implementation of stricter NPL classification. In the Republic of Korea, Financial Supervisory Services reclassified NPLs from 6 months in arrears to 3 months in arrears in September 1998. In December 1999, Financial Supervisory Services introduced forward-looking criteria in asset classification based on the borrower's capacity to pay (Kim, Kim, and Ryoo 2006). In March 2000, asset classification standards were strengthened, with the enhancement of forward-looking criteria classifying loans as NPLs when risks are significant even if interest payments have been made without a problem (Kim 2006). By the end of the first NPL reclassification in 1998, NPL estimates had grown to W118 trillion, almost double the W59.6 trillion NPLs valued using the old classification standards (Lim and Hahm 2004).

In Thailand, effective 1 July 1998, the definition of NPLs was changed to loans with unpaid principal and/or interest for 3 months or more, from 6 to 12 months or more. New rules on asset classification and provisioning were also implemented. Pass and special mention assets require 1% and 2% provisioning, respectively. Provisioning for substandard loans was increased to 20% from 15%. Doubtful loans decreased provisioning to 50% from 100% but loss loans maintained the 100% provisioning requirement (Santiprabhob 2003).

Other major reforms by Asian supervisory bodies at the onset of the Asian financial crisis included the establishment of prompt corrective action frameworks in Japan, the Philippines, the Republic of Korea, and Thailand, regulations on limiting short-term foreign borrowing and single-borrower limits, increased disclosure requirements of financial institutions, and increased capital requirements.

5.4 Data and Empirical Approach

Against the backdrop of these country case studies in Asia on resolving problem loans, the analysis empirically assesses the effectiveness of these measures quantitatively.

5.4.1 Data

The analysis uses panel data of (i) NPL resolution measure data from various sources, including case studies developed in conjunction with this report; (ii) individual bank-level indicators derived from S&P Global; and (iii) macroeconomic indicators from the World Bank's World Development Indicators. The analysis is based on annual data of 78 financial institutions from six Asian countries (Table 5.3).[17] Although most countries in the dataset implemented NPL resolution programs and policies at the onset of the Asian financial crisis, the analysis will only focus on the NPL resolution measures implemented by each country from 2002 to 2017 due to the lack of individual bank-level data before 2002.

The main concern of this study is illustrating the effectiveness of Asian NPL resolution measures and identifying the best policies and programs fit to address an NPL crisis. Based on the case studies, the analysis tests three main NPL resolution measures: (i) bank capital injection/bailout provided by the government, central banks, or deposit insurance companies; (ii) NPL purchases conducted by centralized public AMCs; and (iii) episodes of macroprudential tightening and increased banking supervision.

Data on bank bailouts is derived from the NPL resolution country case studies (Appendix 1) and cross-referenced with the contingent liability dataset from Bova et al. (2016). A bank bailout dummy variable is equal to 1 if the government conducted a financial sector capital injection/bailout program during the current year and 0 otherwise. Data on AMC NPL purchases is also derived from the country case studies and cross-referenced with the AMC database of Hallerberg and Gandrud (2015). Similarly, an AMC dummy variable is equal to 1 if a public centralized AMC is operating during the current year and 0 otherwise. Cerruti and Neyens (2016) is the source of data for macroprudential tightening. A dummy variable for macroprudential tightening is equal to one (1) if there is a positive change in the macroprudential index, negative one (-1) if there is a negative change, and 0 otherwise. This dataset is also cross-referenced with episodes of macroprudential reforms in the country case studies.

Based on existing NPL literature (e.g., Balgova, Plekhanov, and Skrzypińska 2017; Klein 2013; Louzis, Vouldis, and Metaxas 2012; Salas and Saurina 2002), the analysis also used two main factors in explaining the NPL ratio in Asian banks.

---

[17] The analysis is restricted to six Asian countries (Indonesia, Japan, Malaysia, the PRC, the Republic of Korea, and Thailand) due to data restrictions.

First are external factors such as macroeconomic indicators that affect debtors' capacity to repay loan obligations. Like the previous studies, GDP growth, unemployment rate, inflation rate, and exchange rate depreciation are used as the macroeconomic control variables. The NPL ratio is expected to exhibit a negative relationship with GDP growth, and a positive relationship with higher unemployment, increased inflation, and exchange rate depreciation.

Second are internal factors such as bank-level indicators that reflect bank efficiency and risk management, which influence bank NPL levels. Based on the cited literature, the analysis used the following bank-level indicators: return on equity (ROE), equity-to-assets (EA) ratio, loan-to-assets (LA) ratio, and loan growth rate as bank-level control variables. Equity-related financial indicators—ROE and EA—are associated with bank management effectiveness and are expected to have a negative relationship with NPL growth. Loan-related indicators—LA and loan growth rate—are contentious, but are associated with leverage and risk-taking and are expected to have a positive relationship with NPL movement (Louzis, Vouldis, and Metaxas 2012). Table 5.4 presents the descriptive statistics of all the macro and bank-level variables used in the study.

Table 5.3: Banks per Country

Country	Banks (number)
People's Republic of China	5
Indonesia	4
Japan	48
Republic of Korea	1
Malaysia	8
Thailand	12
TOTAL	**78**

Source: Authors' calculations using S&P Global (accessed August 2018).

Table 5.4: Control Variable Summary

Variable (%)	Observations	Mean	Std. Dev.	Min	Max
NPL ratio	1,248	4.8796	5.4322	0.324	93.606
GDP growth	1,170	3.9127	5.8498	-7.4149	25.2549
Unemployment	1,248	3.7237	1.4083	0.4900	8.0600
Inflation	1,248	1.2101	2.1568	-1.3528	13.1087
Exchange rate depreciation	1,170	-0.2500	8.3255	-12.5074	22.3211
Return on equity	1,248	-0.7015	132.1986	-4306.764	76.3291
Earnings-to-assets	1,248	6.9649	4.0797	-11.8310	42.4246
Loans-to-assets	1,248	64.4542	12.6598	11.3786	185.6251
Loan growth rate	1,170	8.5581	25.3982	-58.1459	516.1056

GDP = gross domestic product, NPL = nonperforming loan, Std. Dev. = standard deviation.
Source: Authors' calculations.

5.4.2 Empirical Approach

Following dynamic panel studies on nonperforming loans (e.g., Klein 2013; Salas and Saurina 2002; and Louzis Vouldis, and Metaxas 2012), the analysis estimates the dynamic panel data specification (I) below using a two-step difference generalized method of moments (GMM) popularized by Arellano and Bond (1991), Arellano and Bover (1996), and Blundell and Bond (1998). The analysis also estimates the data using pooled ordinary least squares (OLS) and fixed-effects regression as a test for good estimates. Since OLS estimates produce upward dynamic panel bias, while fixed effects result in downward dynamic panel bias, good estimates of the true parameter estimate should lie between the two values (Roodman 2009).

$$y_{i,t} = \alpha_0 y_{i,t-1} + \beta_1 BI_{i,t} + \beta_2 BI_{i,t-1} + \beta_3 MI_t + \beta_4 RSN_t + \beta_5 RSN_{t-1} + u_{i,t}$$

The dependent variable, $y_{i,t}$ denotes the logit transformation of the nonperforming loan ratio of bank i at year t. The logarithmic transformation of the ratio ensures that the dependent variable spans over $(-\infty, +\infty)$ and avoids generally nonsensical predictions for extreme values of the regressors when using proportions (Baum 2008). The dependent variable is further explained by its lag ($y_{i,t-1}$), bank-level indicators (BI), macroeconomic indicators (MI), and NPL resolution measures (RSN). Similar to Klein (2013), bank-level indicators are modeled as predetermined (instrumented GMM style similar to the lagged dependent variable), while the macroeconomic indicators are treated as strictly exogenous (instrumented IV style). The RSN will also be modeled as predetermined.

By adding RSN as an additional predetermined variable, the analysis runs the risk of overidentification caused by a higher number of GMM instruments compared to the number of groups or cross-sectional units. To account for this issue, the analysis implements a "restricted" GMM procedure to account for the limitations on the number of instruments that can be used on the limited cross-sectional units. Similar to Louzis Vouldis, and Metaxas (2012), the analysis uses only a limited number of GMM-style instruments by restricting the lags of the GMM instruments and using only one bank-level indicator at a time to reduce instrument proliferation.

5.5 Results

The results in Tables 5.5 and 5.6 confirm that both bank-level variables and macroeconomic conditions affect NPL movements. Starting with macroeconomic indicators, an increase in the unemployment rate has a significant positive relationship with NPL growth using the two-step difference GMM. Rising unemployment negatively affects household or business income, which leads to lower debt servicing capacity, and hence increasing bank-level NPLs. The analysis also finds that NPL ratios tend to be highly persistent, as indicated by a highly significant positive coefficient of the 1-year lagged NPL ratio, ranging between 0.69 and 0.85. This underpins the need for swift and preventive action in NPL resolution.

On bank-level indicators, ROE—as a measure of bank management effectiveness—exhibits a significant negative relationship with NPL movement during the current period and its 1-year lag (Table 5.5). This result confirms findings of previous studies, which indicate that effectively managed banks lead overall to better asset quality. Similarly, an increase in lending during the current period also leads to a statistically significant decrease in the NPL ratio (Table 5.6). This relationship is mainly associated with the effects of an increase in loans in the denominator of the NPL ratio.

Table 5.5: Effectiveness of NPL Resolution Measures, Bank Variable: Return on Equity

	Dependent Variable: Log of NPL Ratio		
Variable	OLS (1)	FE (2)	Two-step Diff. GMM (3)
Log of NPL ratio (t-1)	0.82447***	0.69096***	0.78066***
Macroeconomic variables			
GDP growth	-0.01047***	0.0023	-0.00151
Unemployment rate	-0.00889	0.04766**	0.06613*
Inflation rate	0.01355	-0.01804	-0.01643
Exchange rate	-0.0004	0.00004	-0.00007
Bank-level variables			
Return on equity (t-0)	-0.00017***	-0.00022***	-0.00023***
Return on equity (t-1)	-0.0001	-0.00016**	-0.00016***
Intervention variables			
AMC purchase (t-0)	0.0853**	0.09697**	0.07286
AMC purchase (t-1)	-0.03258	-0.05097	-0.0781*
Bank bailout (t-0)	0.07226*	0.08746*	0.09917
Bank bailout (t-1)	-0.08415**	-0.06424	-0.07837
Constant	-0.59604	-1.46424	
Observations	1,170	1,170	1,092
Number of banks	78	78	78
Number of instruments			74
A-B AR(1) test p-value			0.009
A-B AR(2) test p-value			0.168
Hansen test p-value			0.259

AMC = asset management company, FE = fixed effects, GDP = gross domestic product, GMM = generalized method of moments, NPL = nonperforming loan, OLS = ordinary least squares, ROE = return on equity.
Note: *** denotes significance at 1% level, ** denotes significance at 5% level, * denotes significance at 10% level.
Sources: Authors' calculations using data from Bova et al. (2016); Cerruti and Neyens (2016); Hallerberg and Gandrud (2015); S&P Global; World Bank's World Development Indicators (accessed August 2018).

Table 5.6: Effectiveness of NPL Resolution Measures, Bank Variable: Loans Growth Rate

Variable	Dependent Variable: Log of NPL Ratio		
	OLS (1)	FE (2)	2-step Diff GMM (3)
Log of NPL ratio (t-1)	0.84728***	0.69077***	0.80408***
Macroeconomic variables			
GDP growth	-0.01011***	0.0034	-0.00157
Unemployment rate	0.0009	0.05237***	0.08186**
Inflation rate	0.02479	-0.00305	-0.00339
Foreign exchange rate depreciation	-0.003	-0.0018	-0.00367
Bank-level variables			
Loan growth rate (t-0)	-0.00546***	-0.00488***	-0.00527***
Loan growth rate (t-1)	0.00048	0.00021	0.00021
Intervention variables			
AMC purchase (t-0)	0.12811***	0.13771***	0.09469*
AMC purchase (t-1)	-0.03802	-0.03191	-0.08573*
Bank bailout (t-0)	0.02901	-0.01748	0.0241
Bank bailout (t-1)	-0.06627**	-0.09385**	-0.10379**
Constant	-0.68378***	-1.41921***	
Observations	1092	1092	1014
Number of banks	78	78	78
Number of instruments			72
A-B AR(1) test p-value			0.000
A-B AR(2) test p-value			0.794
Hansen test p-value			0.099

AMC = asset management company, FE = fixed effects, GDP = gross domestic product, GMM = generalized method of moments, NPL = nonperforming loan, OLS = ordinary least squares.
Note: *** denotes significance at 1% level, ** denotes significance at 5% level, * denotes significance at 10% level.
Sources: Authors' calculations using data from Bova et al. (2016); Cerruti and Neyens (2016); Hallerberg and Gandrud (2015); S&P Global; World Bank's World Development Indicators (accessed August 2018).

On the main policy variable of interest, the 1-year lag of AMC operations, using both ROE and loan growth rate as bank-level indicators exhibited a significant negative relationship with bank-level NPL ratios. The results are similar for a 1-year lag of bank bailouts, using loan growth rate as a bank-level indicator, which resulted in a significant relationship with bank-level NPL ratios, though results were less robust when analyzed with ROE.

Table 5.7 presents a comparison of the results of four different bank-level indicators, confirming that for most specifications, AMC operations (1-year lag) were significantly associated with a reduction in bank-level NPLs. The other tested bank-level indicators—equity-to-assets ratio and loans-to-assets ratio—did not yield significant relationships with the movement of the bank-level NPL ratio.

Table 5.7: Comparison of Four Bank-Level Indicators

Variable	Dependent Variable: Log of NPL Ratio			
	ROE (1)	EA (2)	LOANS (3)	LA (4)
Log of NPL ratio (t-1)	0.73066***	0.78415***	0.80408***	0.79728***
Macroeconomic variables				
GDP growth	-0.00151	-0.0027	-0.00157	-0.00103
Unemployment rate	0.05613*	0.05832	0.08186**	0.06844**
Inflation rate	-0.01643	-0.00229	-0.00339	-0.00845
Exchange rate	-0.00007	-0.0012	-0.00367	0.00068
Bank-level variables				
Return on equity (t-0)	-0.00023***			
Return on equity (t-1)	-0.00016***			
Equity-to-assets (t-0)		0.03231		
Equity-to-assets (t-1)		-0.0275		
Loan growth rate (t-0)			-0.00527***	
Loan growth rate (t-1)			0.00021	
Loans-to-assets (t-0)				0.01354
Loans-to-assets (t-1)				-0.01075
Intervention variables				
AMC purchase (t-0)	0.07286	0.09006*	0.09469*	0.09599
AMC purchase (t-1)	-0.0781*	-0.0363	-0.08573*	-0.07021*
Bank bailout (t-0)	0.03917	0.04977	0.0241	0.05675
Bank bailout (t-1)	-0.07837	-0.09263	-0.10379**	-0.09852*
Observations	1092	1092	1014	1092
Number of banks	78	78	78	78
Number of instruments	74	74	72	74
A-B AR(1) test p-value	0.009	0.007	0.000	0.001
A-B AR(2) test p-value	0.158	0.145	0.794	0.171
Hansen test p-value	0.239	0.141	0.099	0.177

AMC = asset management company, EA = equity-to-assets ratio, GDP = gross domestic product, GMM = generalized method of moments, NPL = nonperforming loan, LA = loans-to-assets ratio, LOANS = loans growth rate, ROE= return on equity.
Notes: The estimation technique is a two-step difference GMM. *** denotes significance at 1% level, ** denotes significance at 5% level, * denotes significance at 10% level.
Sources: Authors' calculations using data from Bova et al. (2016); Cerruti and Neyens (2016); Hallerberg and Gandrud (2015); S&P Global; World Bank's World Development Indicators (accessed August 2018).

Finally, the analysis also tested macroprudential tightening as an additional NPL resolution variable, but the results were insignificant and shortened the dataset to 2002–2013 due to data availability constraints (Table 5.8). Additionally, using loan growth rate as a bank-level indicator also resulted in a positive relationship between the current period of AMC operations and bank-level NPLs. This relationship might reflect the ongoing turmoil that banks would experience during crises, which warranted the implementation of an NPL purchase program in the first place.

Table 5.8: Macroprudential Tightening

	Dependent Variable: Log of NPL Ratio	
Variable	ROE (1)	EA (2)
Log of NPL ratio (t-1)	0.75034***	0.77556***
Macroeconomic variables		
GDP growth	0.02074***	0.02338***
Unemployment rate	0.02753	0.03893
Inflation rate	-0.00614	0.00546
Exchange rate depreciation	0.04344	-0.31969
Bank-level variables		
Return on equity (t-0)	-0.00027***	
Return on equity (t-1)	-0.00019***	
Loan growth rate (t-0)		-0.00507***
Loan growth rate (t-1)		0.00014
Intervention variables		
AMC purchase (t-0)	0.05114	0.0862
AMC purchase (t-1)	-0.26715***	-0.2592***
Bank bailout (t-0)	0.11331	0.06092
Bank bailout (t-1)	-0.1297	-0.09192
Macroprudential tightening (t-0)	-0.0434	-0.07611
Macroprudential tightening (t-1)	-0.09329	-0.09966
Observations	780	702
Number of banks	78	78
Number of instruments	64	62
A-B AR(1) test p-value	0.013	0.000
A-B AR(2) test p-value	0.301	0.399
Hansen test p-value	0.287	0.046

AMC = asset management company, NPL = nonperforming loan, EA = equity-to-assets ratio,
GMM = generalized method of moments, ROE = return on equity.
Notes: The estimation technique is a two-step difference GMM. *** denotes significance at 1% level,
** denotes significance at 5% level, * denotes significance at 10% level.
Sources: Authors' computation using data from Bova et al. (2016); Cerruti and Neyens (2016); Hallerberg
and Gandrud (2015); S&P Global; World Bank's World Development Indicators (accessed August 2018).

Overall, the empirical results suggest public AMC operations are an effective tool to remove NPLs from the banking sector, as found in the case studies. Public AMCs established at the onset of the crisis were the key players in Asian NPL reduction efforts by giving banks an option to sell their NPLs to a readily accessible market or force these banks to offload problematic assets. Interestingly, due to time-period restrictions, most of the analysis is restricted to periods where AMCs established at the onset of the Asian financial crisis are at the tail end of their NPL acquisition period or their sunset date. Aside from Malaysia (2002–2005), Indonesia (2002–2004), and Thailand (2002–2003), AMC operations in the dataset are restricted to periods after the Asian financial crisis. The results therefore suggest that the continued operations of public AMCs—such as the ones operating in the Japan, the PRC, the Republic of Korea, and Thailand—contributed to a significant decrease in bank-level NPL ratios during periods of relative banking stability by providing a readily accessible platform for NPL transactions when markets were not efficiently functioning.

5.6 Conclusion

This chapter looked at case studies of Asian countries in resolving NPLs and examined best practices in NPL resolution by analyzing the most effective Asian NPL reduction policies implemented to remove bad assets in banking systems and maintain banking stability. The analysis used dynamic panel data methods to analyze the effectiveness of NPL reduction policies on bank-level NPLs in 78 banking institutions in six Asian countries from 2002–2017. The chapter investigated the effectiveness of three NPL reduction policies—(i) AMC operations; (ii) government bank bailout/ capital injections; and (iii) macroprudential tightening—implemented in 2002 as a crisis response during the tail end of the Asian financial crisis and as a bank stability measure after the crisis.

The NPL reduction literature has proposed novel methodologies in its analysis, such as the two-part model used in Balgova, Plekhanov, and Skrzypińska (2017) and the cross-border spillover effects of NPL reduction used by Plekhanov and Skrzypińska (2018). Other studies have sought to extend the simple literature on NPL determinants by adding new policy variables (Consolo, Malfa, and Pierluigi 2018; Wolski 2014). The study falls among the latter methods. The analysis builds on the dynamic panel data literature studying the determinants of NPL using difference GMM (e.g., Salas and Saurina 2002; Louzis, Vouldis, and Metaxas 2012; and Klein 2013) and include NPL reduction policy variables within the regression. The study contributes to the NPL reduction literature by analyzing the effects of NPL reduction policies in the Association of Southeast Asian Nations (ASEAN)—a region that implemented numerous policies at the onset of the Asian financial crisis, but with no studies of policy effectiveness aside from case studies.

Results indicate that AMC operations in selected Asian economies have a significant negative relationship with bank-level NPLs alongside macroeconomic factors and bank financial indicators. While bank bailouts have a significant relationship with bank-level NPLs, results are less robust when tested with different bank-level financial indicators. The analysis does not find evidence of a significant relationship between episodes of macroprudential tightening and bank-level NPL reduction. An interesting insight derived from the results is the effectiveness of AMC operations during periods of relative banking sector stability. Outside the closure of Danaharta in Malaysia in 2005 and IBRA in Indonesia in 2004, the continued operations of public AMCs in Japan, the PRC, the Republic of Korea, and Thailand—even after its mandated NPL acquisition period—appeared to have contributed to a significant decrease in bank-level NPLs. While AMC operations during the Asian financial crisis sought to clean bad assets from banking institutions, public AMCs that continued to operate after periods of banking crisis ensured that banks remained healthy and continued operations by providing a readily accessible market for NPLs.

These findings can have implications for Asian economies considering the implementation of public AMCs as a policy to develop and strengthen substantial NPL management and markets as well as a crisis resolution mechanism. The establishment of public AMCs as part of crisis prevention and resolution mechanisms becomes increasingly necessary due to the risks brought by rising Asian financial integration regionally and globally. Domestic banking sectors would likely be more vulnerable to external shocks, financial contagion, or liquidity risks from cross-border bank lending within the region. With decades of experience in bad asset management, existing Asian AMCs can easily facilitate the transfer of knowledge and expertise to new AMCs to increase stability in the Asian banking sector.

References

Abdullah, A., G. Keong, and T. Khuan. 2016. Recent Developments of Corporate Insolvency Law in Malaysia. *International Journal of Humanities and Social Science Invention.* 5 (12). pp. 33–37.

Akama, H., K. Noro, and H. Tada. 2003. Financial and Corporate Restructuring in South Korea. Paper. Bank of Japan.

Arellano, M. and S. Bond. 1991. Some Tests of Specification for Panel Data: Monte Carlo Evidence and an Application to Employment Equations. *Review of Economic Studies.* 58 (2). pp. 277–297.

Arellano, M. and O. Bover. 1996. Another Look at the Instrumental Variable Estimation of Error-Components Models. Journal of Econometrics. 68 (1). pp. 29–51.

Ari, A., S. Chen, and L. Ratnovski. 2019. The Dynamics of Non-Performing Loans During Banking Crises: A New Database. *IMF Working Paper WP/19/272.* Washington, DC: International Monetary Fund.

Balgova, M., A. Plekhanov, and M. Skrzypińska. 2017. Reducing Non-Performing Loans: Stylized Facts and Economic Impact. Working paper.

Bank of Thailand. 2004. *Bank of Thailand Supervision Report 2003.* Bangkok.

Bank of Thailand. 2007. *2006 Supervision Report.* Bangkok.

Baum, C. 2008. Stata Tip 63: Modeling Proportions. *The Stata Journal.* 8 (2). pp. 299–303.

Berger, A. and R. De Young. 1997. Problem Loans and Cost Efficiency in Commercial Banks. *Journal of Banking and Finance.* 21 (6). pp. 849–870.

Bihong, H. 2006. Non-Performing Loan of China's Banking System. Paper. http://kaahlsfiles.com/thesis/thesis%20papers/Unsorted%20More/23_asia%20east_4.pdf.

Bing, H. 2005. The Ways of Dealing with Non-Performing Loans in China: Challenges and Problems. Paper.

Blundell, R. and S. Bond. 1998. Initial Conditions and Moment Restrictions in Dynamic Panel Data Models. *Journal of Econometrics.* 87 (1). pp. 115–143.

Borst, N. 2015. Balancing the State and the Market: Banking Reform in China and Vietnam. Asia Program. Federal Reserve Bank of San Francisco.

Bova, E., M. Ruiz-Arranz, F. Toscani, and H. Ture. 2016. The Fiscal Costs of Contingent Liabilities: A New Dataset. *IMF Working Paper WP/16/14.* Washington, DC: International Monetary Fund.

Broude, R. 2002. Business Insolvency in Thailand: Reform and Rehabilitation.

Cerruti, C. and R. Neyens. 2016. *Asset Management Companies: A Toolkit.* Washington, DC: World Bank.

Chan, H. S. 2002. Korea's Corporate Restructuring since the Financial Crisis: Measures and Assessment. Paper for the conference Promoting Growth and Welfare: Structural Changes and the Role of Institutions in Asia. 29 April.

Collectius. 2018. Collectius Is Pioneering into Indonesia with a 300 Million USD Non-Performing Loan (NPLs) Portfolio Transaction. 18 September. https://www.collectius.com/news-post/collectius-is-pioneering.

Consolo, A., F. Malfa, and B. Pierluigi. 2018. Insolvency Frameworks and Private Debt: An Emperical Investigation. *ECB Working Paper Series.* No. 2189. Frankfurt: European Central Bank.

Danaharta. 2006. Final Report: 1998–2005. Kuala Lumpur.

Deal Street Asia. 2019. Vietnam's NPL Market Is Bigger than Estimated, says IDS Argo's Kondoh. 21 March. https://www.dealstreetasia.com/stories/vietnam-npl-market-135691/.

Fujiii, M. and M. Kawai. 2010. Lessons from Japan's Banking Crisis, 1991–2005. *ADBI Working Paper Series.* No. 222. Tokyo: Asian Development Bank Institute.

Fung, B., J. George, S. Hohl, and G. Ma. 2004a. Public Asset Management Companies in East Asia - Case Studies. Basel: Bank for International Settlements.

_____. 2004b. Public Asset Management Companies in East Asia: A Comparative Study. *BIS Occasional Papers.* No. 3. Basel: Bank for International Settlements.

Hallerberg, M. and C. Gandrud. 2015. Building Better Bad Banks: The Political Economy of Public Asset Management Companies for Resolving Financial Crises. http://fgch.github.io/amc-site/.

Harmer, R. W. 2000. *Law and Policy Reform at the Asian Development Bank.* Manila.

International Monetary Fund (IMF). 1999. Orderly and Effective Insolvency Procedures. Key Issues. Washington, DC: IMF.

_____. 2004. "Was IBRA Successful?" Chapter 3 in Indonesia Selected Issues, IMF Country Report 04/189 (July). Washington, DC: IMF.

_____. 2006. Vietnam: 2005 Article IV Consultation. Box 3. Washington, DC: IMF.

Industrial Revitalization Corporation of Japan (IRCJ). 2007. Dissolution of the IRCJ. Press release. 5 March. https://www8.cao.go.jp/sangyo/ircj/en/pdf/ircj_news_20070315.pdf.

Kim, K. 2006. The 1997–98 Korean Financial Crisis: Causes, Policy Response, and Lessons. The High-Level Seminar on Crisis Prevention in Emerging Markets. Singapore.

Kim, S., J. Kim, and H. Ryoc. 2006. Restructuring and Reforms in the Korean Banking Industry. *BIS Papers.* No. 28. Basel: Bank for International Settlements.

Klein, N. 2013. Non-Performing Loans in CESEE: Determinants and Impact on Macroeconomic Performance. *IMF Working Paper WP/13/72.* Washington, DC: International Monetary Fund.

Korea Asset Management Corporation (KAMCO). 2010. KAMCO 2009 Annual Report: Building a Hope. Busan.

_____. 2014. KAMCO 2013 Annual Report: A Stepping Stone of Hope Toward Happiness. Busan.

_____. 2016. KAMCO 2015 Annual Report: Creating Hope for Tomorrow. Busan.

Kossof, P. 2014. China's Non-Performing Loans: History, Current Infrastructure, and the Future of Bad Debt in China. *International Journal of Law and Legal Jurisprudence Studies.* 1 (6). pp. 1-35.

Lee, J-W. 2017. Twenty Years after the Financial Crisis in the Republic of Korea. ADBI Working Paper Series. Tokyo: Asian Development Bank Institute.

Lim, W. and J. Hahm. 2004. Financial Globalization and Korea's Post-Crisis Reform: A Political Economy Perspective. *KDI Working Paper Series.* No. 2004-1. Chungcheongnam-do: Korea Development Institute.

Louzis, D., A. Vouldis, and V. Metaxas. 2012. Macroeconomic and Bank-Specific Determinants of Non-Performing Loans in Greece: A Comparative Study of Mortgage, Business and Consumer Loan Portfolios. *Journal of Banking and Finance*. 36 (4). pp. 1012–1027.

Macroeconomic Policy Program. n.d. Financial Reforms in Thailand.

Mohaddes, K., M. Raissi, and A. Weber. 2017. Can Italy Grow Out of Its NPL Overhang? A Panel Threshold Analysis. *IMF Working Paper WP/17/66*. Washington, DC: International Monetary Fund.

Okina, Y. 2009. Activity of IRCJ and Banking Crisis in Japan. *Public Policy Review*. 5 (2). pp. 151–200. Tokyo: Policy Research Institute, Ministry of Finance.

Pasadilla, G. 2005. Special Purpose Vehicles and Insolvency Reforms in the Philippines. *PIDS Discussion Paper Series*. No. 2005-06. Manila: Philippine Institute for Development Studies.

Plekhanov, A. and M. Skrzypińska. 2018. Cross-Border Spillovers from Reducing Non-Performing Loans. *EBRD Working Paper Series*. London: European Bank for Reconstruction and Development.

Putih, D. 2005. Malaysia's Experience with Corporate Restructuring. In M. Pomerleano and W. Shaw, eds. *Corporate Restructuring: Lessons from Experience*. Washington, DC: World Bank.

Quagliariello, M. 2009. Macroeconomic Uncertainty and Banks' Lending Decisions: The Case of Italy. *Applied Economics*. 41 (3). pp. 323–336.

Resolution and Collection Corporation (RCC). 2019. Fiscal Year 2019 Overview of the RCC's Activities. https://www.kaisyukikou.co.jp/.

Roodman, D. 2009. How to do Xtabond2: An Introduction to Difference and System GMM in Stata. *The Stata Journal*. 9 (1). pp. 86–136.

Salas, V. and J. Saurina. 2002. Credit Risk in Two Institutional Regimes: Spanish Commercial and Savings Bank. *Journal of Financial Services Research*. 22 (3). pp. 203–224.

Santiprabhob, V. 2003. *Lessons Learned from Thailand's Experience with Financial-Sector Restructuring*. Bangkok: Thailand Development Research Institute.

Sato, Y. 2005. Bank Restructuring and Financial Institution Reform in Indonesia. *The Developing Economies*. 43 (1). pp. 91–120.

Takagi, S. 2003. Inauguration and First stage of the Industrial Revitalization Corporation of Japan.

Terada-Hagiwara, A. and G. Fasadilla. 2004. Experience of Asset Management Companies: Do They Increase Moral Hazard? - Evidence from Thailand. *ERD Working Paper Series*. No. 55. Manila: Asian Development Bank.

Tomasic, R. 2001. Some Challenges for Insolvency System Reform in Indonesia. Insolvency Reform in Asia: An Assessment of the Recent Developments and Role of the Judiciary. Bali.

Tong, Z. and S. Zhou. 2014. Local Asset Management Companies in China: The Next Frontier to Tackle China's Local Debt Problem. Orient Capital Research.

Vietnam Asset Management Company (VAMC). 2018. Role of VAMC in Dealing with Bad Debts. Presentation material prepared for the 4th IPAF Summit and Conference. Hanoi. 14-15 November.

Vietnam Debt and Assets Trading Company (VDATC). 2018a. Situation and Mechanism of Dealing with Bad Debt to Ensure National Financial Security from VDATC. Presentation material prepared for the 4th IPAF Summit and Conference. Hanoi. 14-15 November.

_____. 2018b. VDATC's Role in Developing the Debt Trading Market in Vietnam. Presentation material prepared for the 4th IPAF Summit and Conference. Hanoi. 14-15 November.

Vietnam Insider. 2019. Vietnam Asset Management Company announced its plan for 2019. 20 May.

Viet Nam News. 2018. Vietnam and Partners Discuss Bad Debts Handling. 17 November.

Wolski, M. 2014. Box 6: Institutions and NPLs. In Unlocking lending in Europe. Luxembourg: European Investment Bank.

World Bank. 2006. Vietnam Business: Vietnam Development Report 2006. Chapter 5. p. 64.

Zhou, Y. 2016. Establishing a Deposit Insurance System in China: A Long-Awaited Move Toward Deepening Financial Reform. *Chicago-Kent Journal of International and Comparative Law*. 16 (2). pp. 46–97.

Appendix 1: Tables of Nonperforming Loan Resolution Cases

Table A1.1: Summary of Asian Asset Management Companies' Operations

AMC Feature	China, People's Rep. of	Indonesia	Japan	Republic of Korea	Malaysia	Thailand
Public asset management companies	Big 4 (Orient, Great Wall, Cinda, Huarong)	IBRA	RCC IRCJ	KAMCO	Danaharta	Thai Asset Management Company (TAMC)
Set up	1999	1998	RCC – 1999 IRCJ – 2003	1962 (Role expanded in 1997)	1998	2001
Governing agency/ body	Ministry of Finance, CBRC	Ministry of Finance, Financial sector Policy Committee	RCC – DICJ IRCJ – FSA	Ministry of Finance, Financial Supervisory Commission	Bank Negara Malaysia (BNM)	Bank of Thailand (BOT), Financial Institutions Development Fund (FIDF)
Enabling laws/ programs	Executive Order via State Council	Presidential Decree	RCC – Financial Revitalization Law IRCJ – Program for Financial Revival	KAMCO Act	Danaharta Act	Royal Decree via TAMC Act
Official mandate	Restructuring	Restructuring	RCC – Nonperforming loan (NPL) collection IRCJ – Restructuring	Restructuring/ Rapid Asset Disposition	Restructuring/ Rapid Asset Disposition	Restructuring
Special power	No explicit power	Special power to seize assets of noncooperative debtors without court approval	RCC – Assisted by DICJ special powers IRCJ – No explicit power	No explicit power	Special power to purchase and resolve nonperforming loans (NPLs) w/o court process	Special power to force debtors to enter into negotiation for loan repayment

continued on next page

Table A1.1 (continued)

AMC Feature	China, People's Rep. of	Indonesia	Japan	Republic of Korea	Malaysia	Thailand
Centralized	No	Yes	Yes	Yes	Yes	Yes
Financing	AMC bond, and Govt. and Central Bank contribution	–	RCC – DICJ	KAMCO bonds	Government guaranteed bonds	BOT, Financial Institutions Development Fund
Source of NPL	Four state-owned banks (SOBs)	Banks with CAR = –25% to 4% SQR	RCC – Mortgage Lending (Jusen) IRCJ – Troubled financial institution	Troubled financial institution	Troubled financial institution and SOB	81% are old NPL from decentralized AMC
Asset selection	47% manufacturing 6% agriculture 16% commercial 7% real estate	84% corporate 9% commercial 7% SME	RCC – Small to Medium firms IRCJ – Large corporations	–	–	–
Pricing	Book value	Payment can be considered as the capital injection provided by the government	Market Value RCC – 24.6% avg. IRCJ – 36.0% avg.	Market value (35.2% average transfer price)	1. Value of collateral 2. Percentage of outstanding principal (10% for regular loans)	Market value (34% average transfer price)
Disposition and Resolution	Debt collection, portfolio sales, auctions, joint ventures, debt-for-equity swaps, and lease of collateral	Bank restructuring was the main priority resulting in delays in asset disposition and pursuit of shareholders	Bulk sale, asset securitization, and revitalization of firms	Bulk loan resolution, foreclosure, public auctions, loan sales, JV partnerships, rescheduling	Loan restructuring for viable loans. Loan sale for nonviable loans	Debt restructuring, business reorganization, or dispose/write off the asset and foreclose on the collateral
NPL acquisition period	1999–2000 2004	1999–2000	1999–2006	1997–2002	1998–2001	2001–2003

continued on next page

Table A.1 (continued)

AMC Feature	China, People's Rep. of	Indonesia	Japan	Republic of Korea	Malaysia	Thailand
NPL acquisition (LCU billion)	1999 – 1,394.0; 2004 – 320.1	391,870.0	9,800.0	111,400.0	47.7 (19.7 acquired NPL + 28 managed for government)	775.8
Peak NPL ratio (year – %)	1999 – 28.5	1998 – 48.6	2002 – 8.1	2000 – 8.9	1998 – 18.6	1998 – 42.9
NPL ratio + 5 years (year – %)	2004 – 13.2	2003 – 6.8	2007 – 1.5	2005 – 1.2	2003 – 13.9	2003 – 13.5
Sunset clause	No[1]	Yes	RCC – No; IRCJ – Yes	No	Yes	Yes
Closing date/ Recovery period	–	2004	IRCJ – 2007	2012	2005	2006
Recovery rate (recovery/ acquisition, %)	20.84 (68.6% of portfolio sold)[2]	22 (60% of portfolio sold)	–	43.2 (100% of portfolio sold)	58.0 (96.4% of portfolio sold)	19.4 (~100% of portfolio sold)

AMC = asset management company, CAR = capital adequacy ratio, CBRC = China Bank Regulatory Commission, Cinda = Cinda Asset Management, Danaharta = Pengurusan Danaharta Bhd, DICJ = Deposit Insurance Corporation of Japan, FSA = Financial Services Agency, Great Wall = Great Wall Asset Management, Huarong = Huarong Asset Management, IBRA = Indonesia Bank Restructuring Agency, IRCJ = Industrial Revitalization Corporation of Japan, KAMCO = Korea Asset Management Corporation, LCU = local currency unit, Orient = Orient Asset Management, RCC = Resolution and Collection Corporation.

Notes:

[1] The "Big 4" asset management companies were supposed to have a sunset clause of 10 years but are still operating;

[2] Recovery value as of 30 June 2006 (Bihong 2006).

Sources: Authors' calculations using data from Haver Analytics; CEIC; World Bank, World Development Indicators; Bihong (2006); Cerutti and Neyens (2016); RCC (2019); Okina (2009); Financial Supervisory Service (Republic of Korea); Bank Negara Malaysia; Danaharta (2006); Bank of Thailand; and Santiprabhob (2003).

Table A1.2: Asian Recapitalization Programs

Features	China, People's Republic of	Indonesia	Japan	Republic of Korea	Malaysia	Thailand
Enabling Laws/Programs	Executive Order via State Council	Comprehensive bank sector restructuring and recapitalization program	Financial Revitalization Act, Early Financial Correction Law, Program for Financial Revival	Financial sector restructuring program	National Economic Recovery Plan	Public sector recapitalization program
Agency	State Council	Government	Deposit Insurance Corporation of Japan	Korea Deposit Insurance Corporation	Danamodal Nasional Berhad (Danamodal)	Financial Institutions Development Fund
Recapitalization Period	1999–2008	1997–2000	1997–2006	1997–2003	1998	1998–2002
Amount (LCU billion)	1999–270 2003–45 2005 – 15 2008–130	650,000	Direct injection–12,400 Monetary grant–18,900	160,400	6.15	Public–716.93 Private–0.71
Recipient Institutions	Bank of China, Agricultural Bank of China, China Construction Bank, Industrial and Commerce Bank of China	Banks with CAR between –25% to 4%. Exemptions were made for seven state-owned banks.	Troubled financial institutions	Troubled banks and other financial institutions	10 insolvent but viable financial institutions	Bangkok Bank of Commerce, Bangkok Metropolitan Bank, First Bangkok City Bank, Krung Thai Bank, Siam City Bank, Union Bank

CAR = capital adequacy ratio, LCU = local currency unit.
Sources: Bing (2005), Bihong (2006), Fung et al (2004a), Sato (2005), Fujii and Kawai (2010), Lim and Hahm (2004), Lee (2017), and Santiprabhob (2003).

Table A1.3: Insolvency Resolution Frameworks in Asia

	Asian Financial Crisis Legal and Regulatory Reforms	Current Legal and Regulatory Framework
People's Republic of China (PRC)		• Jun 2007: The PRC implemented its first comprehensive bankruptcy law, Law of the People's Republic of China on Enterprise Bankruptcy "Bankruptcy Law" (2006). The Bankruptcy Law also introduced provisions for out-of-court workout (OOCW). • From 2007–2017, the PRC introduced specialized liquidation and bankruptcy trial court. As of Feb 2017, there are 73 specialized liquidation and bankruptcy courts in the country. • Financial Institution Insolvency: Article 38-39 of Law of the People's Republic of China on Banking Regulation and Supervision • Recovery and Resolution Planning: China Banking Regulatory Commission required the four globally systemically important banks to prepare and submit recovery plans annually for review, with resolvability assessment being conducted for three.
Indonesia	• Sep 1998: Reform of the court supervised insolvency process, Bankruptcy Act, in September 1998 – introduced measures for debt restructuring and establishment of specialized court for insolvency, Commercial Court. • Sep 1998: Establishment of Jakarta Initiative Task Force as facilitator of OOCWs.	• Court procedure: Law No. 37 of 2004 on Bankruptcy and Suspension of Payment (Bankruptcy Law) dated 18 October 2004. • Financial Institution Insolvency: Article 17 to 31 of the PPKSK Law (Law No. 9 of 2016 on Prevention and Resolution of Financial System Crisis) and Chapter V of the DIC Law (Law No. 24 of 2004 Concerning Deposit Insurance Corporation) • Recovery and Resolution Planning: OJK Regulation No. 14/POJK.03/2017 on Recovery Plan for Systemic Banks
Japan	• 1999: Civil Rehabilitation Law (1999) replaces Composition Law (1927). The new law is debtor friendly in nature. • 2001: Establishment of OOCW guidelines. • 2003: Reform of Corporate Reorganization Proceedings in 2002, which amended the previous version in 1967.	• 2007: Establishment of Turnaround Alternative Dispute Resolution as OOCW for medium and large companies. • 2013: Establishment of Regional Economy Vitalization Corporation of Japan as OOCW for small and medium-sized enterprises.

continued on next page

Table A1.3 (continued)

Republic of Korea	• Feb 1998: Reform of the court-based insolvency system and revised the bankruptcy law. • Jul 1998: Start of the Republic of Korea's out-of-court restructuring program. • 2000: Introduced the Corporate Restructuring Promotion Law (effective until 2005) to efficiently dispose of and reduce the nonperforming loans of financial institutions. • Mar 2001: Introduced a pre-packaged bankruptcy system that allowed creditors to negotiate out-of-court settlement with borrowers prior submission to court.	• Court procedure: Debtor Rehabilitation and Bankruptcy Act • Out-of-court procedure: Corporate Restructuring Promotion Act
Malaysia	• Schemes of Arrangement • 1998: Establishment of OOCW framework, Corporate Debt Restructuring Committee	• Court procedure: Companies Act (2016) • Financial Institution Insolvency: by Bank Negara Malaysia under the Financial Services Act 2013 or Perbadan Insurans Deposit Malaysia under the Malaysia Deposit Insurance Corporation Act 2011.
Thailand	• 1998: Reform of the Thai Bankruptcy Act • 1998: Establishment of Corporate Debt Restructuring Advisory Committee • 1999: Establishment of specialized Bankruptcy Court with sole jurisdiction over liquidation and rehabilitation cases	• Financial Institution Insolvency: Chapter 5 and 6 of the Financial Institutions Business Act B.E. 2551 (2008)

OJK = Financial Services Authority (Indonesia), POJK = OJK rules.
Source: Compiled by authors.

6

Country Case Studies on Resolving Problem Loans in Europe: Crises, Policies, and Institutions

Alexander Lehmann

6.1 Introduction

European Union (EU) countries feature some of the most developed banking systems worldwide. European banks have supported growth within economies primarily reliant on small and medium-sized enterprises, and increasingly established linkages across the EU's integrated financial market. Yet, on the back of the apparent stability in the early years of the euro area, several banking systems became highly reliant on international wholesale funding. In 2008, Europe was impacted by a "sudden stop" in capital flows, a phenomenon well-known to emerging market policy makers. This brought to light unsustainable private sector debt, and quickly resulted in widespread nonperforming loans (NPLs).

The ensuing rise in loan delinquency and excess private debt primarily affected the countries of the euro area periphery that had drawn on unsustainable debt flows within the currency union that suffered from growth imbalances. High NPLs undermined bank profitability and lending growth (IMF 2015a). Failure to resolve unsustainable corporate and household debt undermined growth more broadly, in turn perpetuating loan delinquency (Caracea et al. 2015). In the euro area periphery, NPL resolution therefore quickly emerged as a central element in national bank recovery policies, including in the five joint European Commission and International Monetary Fund (IMF)-led programs between 2008 and 2018.

However, it quickly became apparent that excessive NPL burdens in individual countries affected financial stability within the entire currency area due to cross-border exposures and tight links between sovereign and bank balance sheets (Council of the EU 2017a).

Once the financial and macroeconomic adjustment of the immediate post-crisis period was dealt with, EU bank regulation was therefore tightened, including to recognize problem loans more quickly and set aside provisions for future loan losses. Within the euro area, the European Central Bank (ECB) in 2014 took on its new role as supervisor of the largest banks in the currency area. Tentatively, and perhaps belatedly, Europe adopted an action plan for NPL resolution to contain risks from unsustainable private debt in bank assets.

It is often overlooked that success in NPL resolution was not just due to reformed EU regulation and newly established euro area supervision, but also depended on supportive national reforms, the subject of this chapter. Dealing with poor asset quality and write-offs required buffers in capital and profitability which were absent in banking systems that were undergoing profound structural change. Key areas of the resolution framework remained the prerogative of national policies, including legal frameworks for insolvency and debt restructuring, principles of provisioning and collateral valuation, and the restrictions in NPL sales and workout by third-party loan servicers. Some reforms were dealt with in IMF/EU financial adjustment programs with euro area countries, others were subject to diverging national policies. Europe thus offers a rich set of national resolution strategies, and some common principles for workout are now emerging that may be relevant for Asia.

Following the country case studies in Asia in Chapter 5, this chapter examines differing national approaches in NPL resolution in EU countries and derives policy implications for Asian economies. Seven case studies offer insights into the relative effectiveness of resolution strategies. This will address three key questions. To what extent were NPL resolution strategies well defined and a priority in individual EU countries? What have been the respective roles of bank-led resolution, systemic asset management companies, and of market solutions? What has been the relative success of such strategies in financial sector health and a recovery in lending? Throughout this study, the focus will be on national, not EU or euro area, policies. Making this distinction is crucial, even though absence of quantifiable indicators and identification problems prevent a clear attribution of success.

National impediments to NPL resolution in the EU remain significant, and section 6.2 offers a classification of such obstacles and reviews two surveys of national regimes. Section 6.3 then reviews the experience in addressing such national impediments in five euro area countries and two other EU countries with earlier NPL crises.

Section 6.4 assesses the impact of resolution policies. On the surface, the reduction in NPL ratios and stocks seems to be evidence that policies have been effective, though it is hard to attribute this reduction to any one actor—EU, IMF, or national authorities. The section therefore focuses on NPL markets and insolvency processes as two aspects on which policy effectiveness can be assessed directly. Section 6.5 then concludes and examines implications for emerging markets in Asia.

6.2 National Nonperforming Loan Resolution Frameworks

Why national obstacles to NPL resolution persist within common EU regulation and euro area supervision

NPL resolution has been an increasingly central aspect of the post-crisis agenda for European financial regulation and supervision since at least 2016, when clearer standards for banks were first published. Common policies emerged primarily at the euro area level, in preparation for the supervision established by the ECB in 2014, and the euro area bank resolution framework that was established in 2015. However, based on its powers to regulate within the single market for financial services, the EU also legislated in ways that made delinquent exposures more transparent, expedited more significant provisioning, and facilitated the transfer of loans. By early 2019, the following elements of the EU framework had been put in place.

- Common definition for nonperforming exposures and forbearance issued by the European Banking Authority in 2014 (EBA 2014).

- ECB guidelines for NPL management, issued to the about 120 euro area banks under direct ECB supervision in 2017, which put in place clear expectations for banks' internal management of NPLs. This was subsequently replicated in guidance by the EBA to smaller banks and non-euro area countries (ECB 2017a).

- Since 2018, International Financial Reporting Standard (IFRS) 9, which forces banks to adopt forward-looking provisioning (Lehmann 2017).

- Accelerated provisioning, through the ECB's supervisory expectations for the banks under its supervision, and in similar form for loans originated after April 2019 through the capital requirements regulation that applies across the EU, both significantly discouraging the renewed accrual of under-provisioned NPLs (the "prudential backstop").

- Other measures to stimulate the EU secondary loans market relating to data transparency and disclosure by banks, transfer of claims, and activities of loan servicers.

In mid-2017, the EU Council adopted a comprehensive NPL Action Plan, tasking various agencies with completing the framework (Council of the EU 2017b; see also Chapter 7). The EU law and common ECB standards in supervision have therefore considerably strengthened the framework for NPL resolution. This framework emerged relatively late after the crisis and as such could not prevent the significant buildup in NPLs and subsequent slow reduction in the stock of NPLs. Resolution policies were initially constrained by deep recessions in key crisis countries and the resulting weak banking sector capitalization and profitability. As the euro area recovered from 2014, NPL resolution and associated private debt restructuring moved to center stage.

This EU process ran up against numerous obstacles, arising in particular from national legal and tax regimes and the often poor quality of accounting information. These obstacles persisted because EU law derives from competencies relating to the single market, including through a common framework for bank regulation. EU law barely touches various areas of national law, importantly, principles for debt restructuring, enforcement, and insolvency law.[1]

National obstacles typically arise where investors and other financial institutions seek to acquire and service distressed assets and in banks' foreclosure or enforcement of collateral (the demand side). Investor appetite and valuations of NPLs offered in the market are constrained by the legal framework for insolvency and restructuring and poorly functioning or uncertain processes in national judiciaries.[2]

In addition, structural factors impede loan sales. National tax regimes, for instance, often do not offer tax relief for loan write-offs or for net present value reductions in the context of corporate debt restructuring. Bank supervision within the euro area remains a shared competency between the ECB and national authorities, which are responsible for less significant

---

[1] Two proposals in corporate debt restructuring and insolvency are not yet adopted though have reached political agreement: a 2016 proposal for enhanced preventive restructuring and the "fresh start" for entrepreneurs; and the March 2018 European Commission proposal for a directive for the extrajudicial enforcement of collateral and harmonized rules for credit servicers and purchasers.

[2] IMF (2015a) identified a clear negative correlation between the foreclosure periods and NPL stocks, and significantly higher expected rates of return and hence lower valuation can be imputed from such problems.

institutions. Common supervisory standards for the treatment of NPLs, including collateral valuation, have only been in effect since about 2017. Standards for less significant banks, let alone for EU banks outside the euro area, still vary significantly.[3]

These obstacles were identified, and to some extent addressed, in the financial support programs which the IMF and EU institutions jointly oversaw in the euro area crisis countries: in Ireland (2010–2013), Portugal (2011–2014), Spain (with a more focused financial sector program 2012–2014), Cyprus (2013–2016)—and of course in Greece, where the NPL ratio remains in excess of 40% in three programs between 2010 and 2018. All five countries underwent comprehensive bank restructuring and recapitalization essential for the write-down of delinquent claims or restructuring of private debt by banks.

However, no agreed inventory of national obstacles to NPL resolution exists and sufficiently comparable and comprehensive information is only available in two one-off surveys.

Stocktaking of national NPL frameworks

The first cross-country evidence emerged in a survey the IMF conducted in 2015 (IMF 2015a, 2015b). This was based on responses from national authorities in 9 euro area countries and 10 other jurisdictions in the EU and neighboring countries which had displayed high NPL ratios following the European debt crisis.[4]

The functioning of the judiciary and lengthy insolvency procedures were a recurring concern. Corporate insolvency law was seen as inadequate in numerous countries, suffering from poorly functioning resolution or rehabilitation procedures and an absence of simplified and cost-effective frameworks for small and medium-sized enterprises (SMEs) which constituted the bulk of corporate sector NPLs. Insolvency frameworks for households were often missing entirely, a particular concern in non-euro countries. These obstacles were, on the whole, more severe in the non-euro area countries which had less developed local debt markets. The inefficiency detected in this area broadly matched World Bank indicators for the efficiency and costs in national insolvency proceedings.

---

[3]   EBA (2016) shows the variation in NPL levels across different types and sizes of banking institutions.

[4]   Country responses were verified based on a survey of cross-border banking groups operating in these jurisdictions, though in the published version countries could not be identified.

The ECB also published a comprehensive stocktaking of national provisions and obstacles in NPL resolution in the 19 euro area countries in March 2016 and updated it in 2017 (ECB 2017b). Both exercises were designed as input to the then-emerging ECB NPL guidance to banks. Questionnaires were considerably more detailed than those in the IMF survey. Unlike in the IMF survey, the ECB drew only on responses from the authorities.

Ineffective supervisory regimes for NPLs emerged as a key concern (Box 6.1 lists the key aspects of such regimes). Most high-NPL jurisdictions had specific supervisory regimes for NPL resolution, though these often lacked teeth, for instance due to the absence of on-site inspections. The wide-ranging and fairly intrusive ECB guidance to banks on NPLs was drafted at the time of the survey and superseded national regimes when the ECB took over the supervision of the significant institutions in 2015.[5]

Country responses are highly detailed and do not lend themselves to aggregation across the 19 countries that responded. The IMF's finding that legal impediments have frustrated NPL resolution, however, seems to be reflected in the relatively poor indicators of some countries with persistent high NPL levels, such as Cyprus and Greece. A finding similar to that of the IMF was that reforms of legal, judicial, and out-of-court restructuring frameworks were progressing only slowly, and that inadequate capacity (for instance, specialist judges or insolvency experts) was a key obstacle.

Recent trends in NPL resolution policies

The IMF and ECB assessments of national obstacles to NPL resolution take stock at two points in time and have not been updated. Looking at recent trends in such policies, the European Commission found that more than half of the EU's then 28 member states had undertaken some steps to reduce NPLs. These were focused on NPL sales (at least six countries); establishment of central asset management agencies (in Ireland, Slovenia, and Spain); securitization schemes (Italy); and improved capacity within banks. Initiatives in NPL management are part of a broader package of measures aimed at risk reduction in the financial system, also comprising legal and judicial reforms and micro and macroprudential policies. Such measures are now regularly and comprehensively monitored, albeit based on diverging understanding among the authorities of what reforms

---

[5] As with other documents issued by the supervisor, such guidance is not legally binding, though it has become a key part of the ECB's supervisory review and evaluation process, the second pillar of banking supervision.

should comprise. Appendix 2 lists recent reforms in the five case study countries as they were reported by national authorities.[6]

Box 6.1: Main Elements of the 2017 European Central Bank Stocktaking

Supervisory regime regarding credit risk and nonperforming loans (NPLs)

- Is there specific guidance on the treatment of NPLs and forborne exposures; data collection requirements and exit criteria?
- Guidance on provisioning beyond accounting standards.
- Guidance on collateral valuation, and requirements for appraisers and data collection.
- Guidance on NPL governance and workout, covering internal strategy and internal governance, operational targets; outsourcing of NPL management and role of nonbanks.
- On-site inspections and thematic reviews of NPL management.

Legal, judicial, and extrajudicial framework

- Development of the NPL markets, impediments to the transfer of loans and to sales to nonbanks and foreign investors; presence of asset management companies.
- Out-of-court enforcement of collateral; sales of repossessed assets and bans on foreclosures.
- Quality of corporate insolvency and restructuring framework.
- Quality of the household insolvency and restructuring framework.
- Features of the judicial system (e.g., specialized judges, time requirements)
- Main features of the tax regime.

Information framework

- Central credit registries and asset registers, debt counselling, and impediments through excessive data and consumer protection.

Source: European Central Bank (2017b).

---

[6]   For a stocktaking of recent reforms based on such a classification, see EU Commission, ECB, and Single Resolution Board (SRB) (2018).

6.3 Case Studies of Resolution Strategies

The detailed case studies of national NPL resolution strategies in this section review two countries outside the euro area with relatively independent policy design in the early post-crisis period, and five euro area countries afflicted by high NPL levels with more protracted resolution histories. Table 6.1 summarizes indicators on the evolution of NPLs and private debt, and Table 6.2 the principal dimensions of resolution strategies.

Table 6.1: NPL Ratios and Private Debt in Case Study Countries

	NPL Ratio[a]		Coverage Ratio[b]	Corporate Debt, % of GDP[c]		Household Debt, % of GDP[c]	
	2012	2017	2017	2012	2017	2012	2017
Euro Area Economies							
Greece	23.3	45.6	46.9	65.9	60.6	64.6	56.4
Italy	13.7	14.4	50.6	73.6	60.3	43.3	40.8
Portugal	9.7	13.3	48.6	99.1	76.3	88.8	67.7
Spain	7.5	4.5	41.9	105.6	75.0	80.2	60.7
Slovenia	15.2	3.2	62.9	79.3	46.2	30.6	27.0
Ireland	25.0	11.5	29.5	175.1	190.1	98	47.2
Germany	2.9	1.5	41.3	40.7	40.9	55.8	52.2
Other EU Countries							
Romania	18.2	6.4	67.6	51.4	34.8	20.6	16.1
UK	3.6	0.7	31.9	68.3	65.7	87.5	84.6

EU = European Union, GDP = gross domestic product, NPL = nonperforming loan, UK = United Kingdom.
Sources: [a]World Bank, based on IMF Financial Soundness Indicators; [b]European Banking Authority Risk Dashboard; [c]Eurostat, based on consolidated reporting.

Table 6.2: Dimensions of Resolution Strategies in Case Study Countries

	Supervisory Guidance[a]				OECD Indicator on Quality of the Insolvency and Restructuring Regime[b]		AMC		Cumulative NPL Sales
	NPL Recognition	Provisioning	Collateral Valuation	NPL Governance	2010	2016	Year Established	Initial Portfolio, Gross (€ billion)	2015–2017 (€ billion)
Euro Area Economies									
Greece	2	0	1	5	0.63	0.38			7.5
Italy	1	0	3	0	0.53	0.44			119.0
Portugal	2	4	4	0	0.52	0.31			4.8
Spain	3	2	4	1	0.39	0.31	2012	€106	43.0
Slovenia	3	2	3	5	0.58	0.33	2013	€5.5	1.4
Ireland	3	2	4	5	0.39	0.31	2009	€74	36.0
Germany	0	0	3	1	0.44	0.28	2010	€252[c]	15.0
Other EU Countries									
Romania									5.6
UK					0.10	0.10	2010	£75[c]	53.0

AMC = asset management company, EU = European Union, NPL = nonperforming loan,
OECD = Organisation for Economic Co-operation and Development, UK = United Kingdom.
Notes: [a] The indicators represent the number of additional requirements in force in addition.
[b] Lower indicators represent better regimes.
[c] Bank-specific asset wind-down entity; in the case of Germany, two entities were set up in 2010 with initial portfolios of €77 billion and €175 billion, respectively.
Source: European Central Bank. 2017b. Stocktake of National Supervisory Practices and Legal Frameworks Related to NPLs. Frankfurt.

6.3.1 Two Early Resolution Experiences in European Union Countries outside the Euro Area

United Kingdom

The United Kingdom (UK) was the first EU country to be impacted by a full-blown banking crisis, in 2008. Unlike in the later crises in the euro area periphery, two midsized failing UK banks (Northern Rock and Bradford & Bingley) were swiftly resolved and the funding and capital position of others protected through the state. The emerging NPLs were separated relatively quickly, primarily through a government-owned resolution agency.

In 2009, the UK Treasury established an asset protection scheme into which the Royal Bank of Scotland as the largest distressed bank placed assets valued at pound sterling (£) 282 billion. The bank guaranteed a first loss of 6% of assets. The protection by the state of the remaining portfolio value represented considerable contingent liability to the taxpayer but was conditional on the bank's commitment to increase lending (Baudino and Yun 2017). In 2010, an asset management company (AMC) was established (UK Asset Resolution) which initially took over £75 billion in gross value of residential mortgage assets from the two failed banks, making it one of the earliest, though by no means largest, "bad banks" in Europe.

Even though the UK's banking crisis was severe and unexpected, three factors helped in NPL resolution. First, highly liquid capital markets for NPLs, other distressed debt, and banks' noncore portfolios assisted considerably in bank restructuring. For many years following the crisis the UK market was the most liquid, whereas other European countries encountered considerable delays in making NPL sales an effective resolution tool. NPLs were concentrated in real-estate backed loans, which could be easily absorbed in UK distressed debt markets. Second, insolvency law, and out-of-court workouts of corporate debt, were always reasonably efficient in the UK. This was evident in the courts' processing of insolvency, but also in the UK's world leading standard in out-of-court restructuring (the INSOL Principles), which helped in saving distressed but viable enterprises. Third, the government's resolution scheme was relatively swiftly approved in compliance with EU state aid rules (which resulted in significant delays in later crisis countries). By early 2020, the UK Asset Resolution had wound down its balance sheet to £6.3 billion, from £116 billion at the time of formation.

Romania

Romania, as many other formerly socialist transition economies, saw a period of extremely rapid financial sector growth leading up to, and immediately following, its accession to the EU in 2007.[7] The majority of banking sector assets was under the control of foreign-owned subsidiaries. While foreign subsidiaries brought much-needed banking skills and technology to the country, they also engaged in some risky funding practices and in foreign-exchange-based lending, for which loan quality later deteriorated most rapidly. Weak credit standards and lending to the overly buoyant real

---

[7] Between 2004 and 2010 (the year immediately following the crisis), Romania's credit-to-GDP ratio increased from 16.6% of GDP to 40%. In 2007, the year of EU accession, real credit growth stood at 50%.

estate sector proliferated. The steep recession of 2008–2010 was then followed by a period of foreign bank deleveraging and a brief contraction in domestic credit.

By 2013, Romania's NPL ratio had reached a peak of nearly 22%, one of the highest ratios in emerging Europe. The stock of delinquent loans was predominantly owed by nonfinancial corporations, in particular by microenterprises and SMEs. Until about 2011, nearly half of corporate lending was in foreign exchange, resulting in risky unhedged exposures within enterprises and households.

Nevertheless, the banks' capital coverage was at an ample 14.7%, and the provisioning ratio at 63% under IFRS standards. This provided buffers with which the banking industry could implement NPL resolution. Underpinned by a rapid economic recovery, Romania then saw one of the steepest reductions in the NPL ratio of any country in the EU (Figure 6.1).

Under the 2013 IMF program, the government and central bank had already committed to a package of measures, which subsequently was articulated in a so-called NPL resolution action plan (IMF 2013). This plan clarified the supervisory powers of the National Bank of Romania in this area, set clear standards for supervised banks, and put in place prudential incentives to divest NPLs with no chance of recovery.

Between 2014 and 2016, the National Bank of Romania then adopted a series of recommendations on provisioning and write-offs:

- to write off uncollectable NPLs fully covered by provisions;
- to fully cover with provisions the exposures having debt service overdue by more than 360 days where no legal action had been taken against borrowers, followed by their removal;
- to establish 90% provision coverage of NPLs for exposures against insolvent borrowers;
- to carry out an external audit on the IFRS provisions established by banks to cover losses for the existing loans and on the banks' collateral; and
- to fully cover by provisions the unsecured NPLs overdue for more than 180 days, followed by their write off (Voinea 2017).

Collateral valuation was also strengthened between 2013 and 2015 and shortfalls had to be swiftly corrected through additional provisioning.

These measures implemented by the supervisor were backed by reforms to bankruptcy proceedings, which were typically very lengthy, and resulted in low recovery values (World Bank 2014). An inefficient court system did not allow swift processing of cases. The government committed to the establishment of a specialized court and the training of judges for such cases. Out-of-court workouts were relatively rare and only subsequently became part of the program.

The central bank also adopted measures to open the secondary market for distressed debt. This market had been held back by discrepancies in how debt sales were treated in the tax code and in accounting terms. Together with the stricter rules for provisioning and write-offs, this resulted in a temporary boom in NPL sales, even though by 2016 government measures aimed at the protection of mortgage borrowers raised uncertainty over enforcement and valuation.[8]

While this program of measures was initiated under the MF program, the National Bank of Romania subsequently continued implementing it. Ownership and policy will to deal with NPLs seemed very strong. Success was underpinned by a rapid recovery in growth and property values and by a number of successful NPL transactions that attracted the interest of international investors. Until today, relatively high corporate debt lingers, and insolvency cases remain protracted.

In late-2017, Romania adopted an innovative systemic risk buffer, which set higher capital requirements for high-risk institutions with either elevated NPL ratios or inadequate loan-loss coverage. This is expected to equip banks to deal with a future rise in NPLs (European Systemic Risk Board [ESRB] 2019).

---

8   These initiatives refer to limiting the tax deductibility of write-offs arising in loan sales and to limiting the amounts that can be collected from debtors to, at most, double the purchase price of the loan. The National Bank of Romania expressed concern that these measures would limit supply of NPLs for market sales and reduce prices for such sales (also see Cloutier and Montes-Negret [2014]).

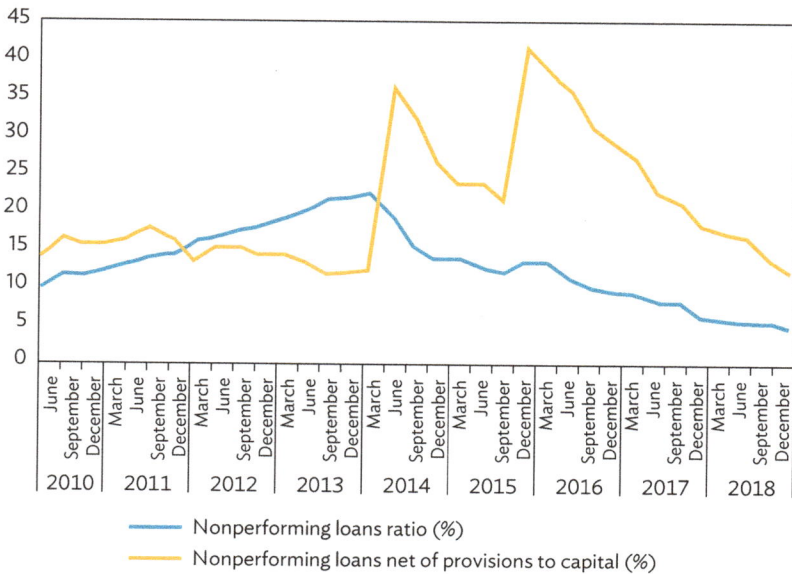

Figure 6.1: NPL Ratio and Provisioning Ratio in Romania

Nonperforming loans ratio (%)
Nonperforming loans net of provisions to capital (%)

NPL = nonperforming loan.
Note: A new European Union standard for the classification of nonperforming exposures and forbearance came into effect in 2013 and led to a one-time upward revision in reported NPL figures.
Source: National Bank of Romania.

6.3.2 Nonperforming Loan Resolution in Five Euro Area Countries

The euro area crisis of 2010 to 2013 was as much a financial sector crisis as a sovereign one. The crisis exposed flaws in the architecture of the currency union which had fostered large credit flows to the periphery of the region but featured no tools to deal with country-specific shocks or the resulting banking fragilities. Until 2014, banking sector policy was firmly in national hands and the coordination of macroprudential policies between EU countries had only just begun.

Protection of large national banking institutions and deep exposures by banking sectors to the respective sovereigns therefore endured in the first decade of the currency union. Regulatory forbearance that tolerated poor asset quality was widespread. With the crisis, booming property prices came to a sudden halt in Ireland and Spain as credit flows reversed. Protracted corporate debt crises lingered for much longer in other euro area countries, such as Italy and Portugal, and national insolvency regimes did not facilitate the necessary reductions in excess debt.

The rise in euro area NPLs was the predictable result of the abrupt tightening in financial conditions and the ensuing recession of 2009–2010. The very tepid recovery, and a second recession in Italy in 2012, led to a protracted worsening of private sector debt distress. For the euro area as a whole, the NPL ratio peaked at about 8% in 2013, though NPL stocks were heavily concentrated in just six countries (Chapter 1).

Ireland epitomized the earliest resolution experience within the currency union, and some key elements preceded the IMF/EU program initiated in 2010. The valuation and speedy divestment of commercial real estate and other business lending is still regarded as exemplary. The National Asset Management Agency was set up in 2009 and acquired property loans with a gross value of €74 billion from Irish banks, valuing the assets at 43% of gross value. The agency has successfully recovered value and, in fact, returned a surplus over the acquisition value to the state.[9] Banks themselves also enforced on collateral of delinquent corporate loans on their books. At the same time, the workout of residential mortgages proceeded much more slowly. Restructuring solutions were offered only much later, and the arrears reduction targets set by the central bank were based on restructuring solutions with questionable value for borrowers (Coffey 2018). As would later become evident in other euro area countries, public opposition would make enforcement in this sector very difficult.

In other euro area countries, banking distress was more contained and the public sector balance sheet more comfortable, allowing more leeway in designing resolution strategies. Germany in 2009 and 2010, for instance, created two sizable state-owned AMCs to assist in the wind-down of two failed banks. Political considerations in saving regional savings banks outweighed the significant impact on public debt (8% of GDP in the case of the larger AMC).

It was not until 2014, when the ECB took over bank supervision, that the significant threat from the "legacy debt" to the financial stability in the entire euro area was recognized. Together with the so-called sovereign-banking nexus, NPLs quickly became the main focus of risk reduction within the currency area. The stocks of NPLs were seen as the main obstacle to further financial integration and to the establishment of joint tools for stabilization, most notably the common bank resolution fund and the attempt to create

---

[9] The National Asset Management Agency was initially set up as a private entity to comply with new statistical rules on state support to the banking sector. This private nature subsequently came to an end when important shareholders were nationalized (Medina Cas and Peresa 2016).

a deposit insurance system. While NPL problems were concentrated in only six countries, negative spillovers across the entire currency area were evident in discouraging financial integration through cross-border credit or bank mergers, and in perpetuating sovereign risks from contingent liabilities.[10]

In 2014, the EU-wide definition of NPLs became the basis for the asset quality review and stress test, and subsequent assumption by the ECB of microprudential supervision of the largest banks. Under the supervision of the ECB, banks improved their internal procedures and documentation standards, and this effort is now gradually mirrored by national supervisors elsewhere in the EU. Ultimately, a more comprehensive strategy was articulated in the EU-wide "NPL action plan" of 2017.

Common bank supervision in the euro area was only gradually backed by more consistent national policies, importantly in insolvency law and debt restructuring. Efforts in the key countries built on reforms in earlier IMF/EU programs in Cyprus, Ireland, Portugal, and Spain, where the fund as well as European institutions were engaged between 2010 and 2014, and the second and third programs in Greece. In the euro area, the IMF also made NPL resolution a key element of its supervision through the periodic Financial Sector Assessment Programmes and additional research (IMF 2015a).

Five country cases illustrate how national policies underpinned, or frustrated, common euro area financial policies. The marked drop in euro area NPLs, and a somewhat less pronounced fall in excess private debt, are evidence that this effort has partially succeeded, barring remaining problems notably in Greece.

Spain

Spain illustrates a national resolution strategy that was closely guided and supported by the IMF, the European Commission, and the ECB. The combination of thorough asset quality reviews in 2012 and comprehensive bank restructuring contained the costs of bank equity and liquidity support borne by the government and brought an end to the credit contraction. Spain's AMC, SAREB, was established in 2012 and remains Europe's largest.

---

[10] The ECB first designated Cyprus, Greece, Ireland, Italy, Portugal, Slovenia, and Spain as high-risk jurisdictions through more in-depth coverage in its stocktaking of national supervisory practices (2017b).

Problems in the Spanish banking sector resulted to a large extent from poor governance in savings banks, the so-called *cajas*. These institutions benefited from a more lenient regulatory regime but suffered from poor risk management and often thin capital coverage of questionable quality. Control by local foundations and other stakeholders exposed these banks to political interference, and in many cases a culture of forbearance took hold (also see Garicano 2012).

Asset quality problems were concentrated in commercial property.[11] This sector had concerned the supervisor for some time. Innovative regulation, such as the system of dynamic provisioning, however, proved insufficient in the face of the ultimate capital shortfall once the bubble in commercial and residential real estate had burst.

The Spanish banking sector benefited from an as-yet unique financial assistance for recapitalization obtained by the Spanish government from the European Stability Mechanism.[12] The agreement with the EU, with the IMF participating as observer, put in place the key elements of the financial sector adjustment program an asset quality review and a stress test, bank resolution, recapitalization and consolidation of the cajas sector, and the establishment of an AMC. As a result of this review in late-2012, a capital gap of €59 billion was identified for the sector in total, and this was bridged largely through public capital injections and a limited bail-in of bond holders (Véron 2016). This provided relative certainty for the valuations of property portfolios in a rapidly declining market.

SAREB, the systemic AMC, was established relatively swiftly in late 2012. The transfer of distressed real estate assets of €106 billion at book value, was subject to an average 52% "haircut" and compulsory for banks receiving public capital injections. With a relatively long-life horizon of 15 years, the institution could focus on valuation and recovery in the real estate sector and is phasing divestments as the property market recovers. SAREB also catalyzed a market for distressed assets. It played a key role in attracting investors and in developing four servicers with restructuring expertise, making Spain one of the most significant distressed loan markets in Europe, with SAREB as a key source of supply.

---

[11] Construction and real estate accounted for 60% of defaulted exposures in mid-2012.

[12] At the insistence of some euro area countries, the IMF supported this program through advice, though not additional finance

Bank restructuring was supported by a number of reforms to the legal framework and supervision, including:

- upgrades in the framework for provisioning and collateral valuation;

- legal amendments facilitating debt restructuring for both enterprises and households, offering a "fresh start" to those previously insolvent (IMF 2015c);

- amendments to the insolvency law which appears to have been effective in taking nonviable companies into liquidation (EU Commission 2019);

- requirements set by the Bank of Spain for strengthened disclosure of distressed assets by individual banks; and

- stronger internal audit functions and procedures for dealing with impaired assets.

By 2017, the ECB had assessed the NPL resolution framework as superior to the average in the euro area (ECB 2017b). Overall, the Spanish adjustment program, through an early recovery and policies aimed at NPL resolution, has succeeded in reducing the aggregate NPL ratio from a peak of 13.6% of gross loans in 2013 to 4.1% by mid-2018. The domestic enterprise sector still showed a slightly elevated ratio of 6.8%, though debt ratios were improving. By the third quarter of 2018, corporate debt had fallen to 75% of GDP from a peak of 116% in 2009, as buoyant GDP growth reduced the debt servicing burden for enterprises that increasingly took on new credit to fund investments.

By 2018, the period of banking sector deleveraging appears to have come to an end. Credit to the corporate sector was still declining as NPLs were divested, in the construction and property sectors in particular. Bank profitability indicators were improving, as were indicators of credit availability. This was a striking contrast with the situation in early 2013, when credit to enterprises had been falling at an annual rate of almost 8%, and the risk premium over lending rates in Germany had exceeded 2 percentage points. A significant share of delinquent real estate related debt remained within SAREB. Given the losses incurred over recent years and the ongoing recovery in property prices, the latest SAREB business plan foresaw a back-loading of divestments toward the end of the institution's lifetime (Medina Cas and Peresa 2016).

Portugal

Portugal's NPL problem has proved more intractable than that in Spain. After Greece and Cyprus, the country in 2018 showed the third-highest NPL ratio in the currency union. The country's experience underlines how the absence of early and comprehensive asset quality review, and inadequate private debt restructuring processes can undermine NPL reduction.

Portugal did not experience a major property boom, as was the case in Ireland or Spain. However, unlike other countries in the euro area periphery, a period of low growth and rising private sector debt distress started already in about 2000 and was more wide-ranging across sectors, as it exposed a profound lack of productivity growth well ahead of the later euro area crisis. Despite a rapid rise in external bank funding following accession to the currency union at its inception in 1999, capital inflows were channeled to a narrow part of the economy and funded largely unproductive firms in the domestic services sector. As the real exchange rate appreciated, resources were channeled away from export-oriented sectors (Reis 2013).

Portugal therefore experienced a very rapid rise in corporate sector debt in the years leading up to the financial crisis of 2008–2009. By 2012, the ratio of corporate debt on a consolidated basis had peaked at 99% of GDP. This ratio was extremely high in the EU context, and well above the threshold level identified in the empirical literature beyond which damaging effects to growth set in (Table 1) (Cecchetti, Mohanty, and Zampoli 2011). Excess leverage rendered firms vulnerable to the post-crisis phase of consolidation and low growth and resulted in a rapid further deterioration in company finances and loan performance.[13] Bank asset quality problems therefore were more protracted than in other euro area countries (Figure 6.2).

Addressing excessive private sector indebtedness was one of the key objectives under the IMF/EU program, as coordinated with the ECB and EU within the troika. As agreed with the IMF, the authorities reformed court-led and out-of-court corporate debt restructuring, and in 2014 a strategic plan for corporate debt restructuring was launched. Changes to the commercial code promoted the issuance of equity-type instruments, encouraging private restructuring schemes rather than liquidation of over-indebted companies. Also, a new debt restructuring mechanism was added to the bankruptcy

---

[13]   The debt stock of the nonfinancial corporate sector peaked at about 213% on an unconsolidated basis in 2013. The unconsolidated corporate debt figures do not net out claims within the sector. This is a more accurate reflection of the likely debt burden of individual enterprises.

Figure 6.2: NPLs and Private Debt in Portugal

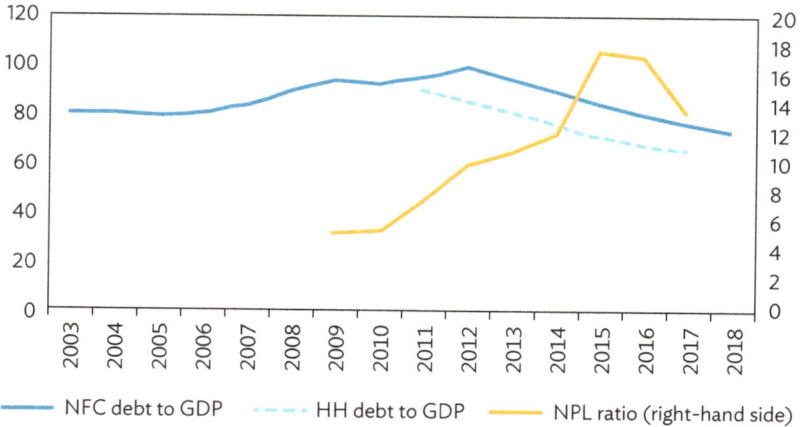

GDP = gross domestic product, HH = household, NFC = nonfinancial corporation,
NPL = nonperforming loan.
Sources: International Monetary Fund Global Financial Soundness Indicators (NPL ratios) and
Eurostat.

code, facilitating out-of-court procedures. Courts could now enforce out-of-court agreements concluded between creditors representing a majority of claims. A public mediator facilitates such out-of-court agreements with micro and small enterprises, supported by an electronic platform to reduce paperwork (EU Commission 2016).

Still, by the end of the program period (2011–2014), the IMF assessment found progress to be inadequate (IMF 2014a). Creditor coordination was still poor, the government agency tasked with out-of-court procedures seemed inefficient, and agreed restructuring schemes did not entail sufficient write-downs, rendering borrowers prone to relapse into delinquency. A strategy for the numerous SME cases was lacking.

For these reasons the banking sector remained fragile. Reliance on ECB liquidity provision was not meaningfully reduced, NPLs remained very high, and the banking sector remained loss-making. No significant private investors could be attracted into the sector. Unlike in Greece and Spain, no independent balance sheet review had been undertaken, and the IMF did not seem to press for equity injections, possibly from new owners, even though the state held significant stakes in the sector. Also, the central bank in its role as supervisor did not exert sufficient pressure to address forbearance in delinquent private sector loans

(Véron 2016 and IMF 2014a). The resolution of two systemic banks shortly after the conclusion of the IMF program underlined this rather poor outcome in restoring banking sector health.[14]

More recently, the authorities seem to have become more ambitious. A comprehensive strategy for NPLs adopted by the Banco de Portugal in 2017 mirrored the ECB guidance (Banco de Portugal 2017). The main elements envisaged that:

- banks need to report impairments in specific asset types and in assets with longer-running impairment history;

- there would be more intense information requests of banks with NPL ratios above a certain threshold, leading to in-depth diagnostics of such portfolios;

- reduction targets were set by asset class and time horizon; and

- supervisory pressure would be stepped up on banks to develop strategic and operational plans in the internal management.

The government also appeared to support corporate deleveraging. Tax and social security authorities took common decisions in corporate restructuring negotiations and write-offs were made tax-deductible under certain conditions.

The problem of multiple credit relationships of distressed borrowers was also being addressed. In early 2018, a private coordination platform was launched by the three largest banks which aims to expedite restructuring.[15] The platform negotiates restructuring solutions with delinquent borrowers on behalf of the lenders, and it is also open to represent the claims of other lenders. It may also sell the joint claims to investors. The platform aims to attract both public and private funds and offers technical assistance to restructure debt-distressed but viable businesses (EU Commission 2018a).

In sum, the Portuguese supervisor began to scrutinize NPLs and excess corporate leverage relatively late and did not seem to coordinate sufficiently with the government. Government support emerged only in 2016, when excessive corporate leverage was clearly holding back the recovery materializing elsewhere in Europe.

---

[14] Banco Espirito Santo, Portugal's third-largest bank, was resolved through a good bank–bad bank split in August 2014. Banif, a smaller bank, was resolved in December 2015.

[15] The Integrated Bank Credit Trading Platform was launched in early 2018 by Portuguese lenders Caixa Geral de Depositos, Banco Comercial Português Millennium, and Novo Banco.

Slovenia

As a former Yugoslav Republic, Slovenia showed a historically large state-ownership of the corporate sector, with the largest three banks also in state hands.[16] These close linkages, and the fragilities that they entailed, remained intact following EU accession in 2004. From that point, EU law constrained state aid though did not result in ownership separation or changed lending practices by state banks.

The otherwise sound macro policies then allowed accession to the euro area in 2007, making Slovenia the first of the EU's "new" member state to take this step. Membership in the currency area resulted in a compression in country risk premiums and a surge in wholesale funding directed to the banking sector (the loan-to-deposit ratio similarly doubled). Loans were mainly directed to the corporate sector, while household indebtedness remained relatively low. The total credit-to-GDP ratio increased from 90% to over 170% of GDP in 2008, while corporate debt remained above 80% of GDP until 2011 (Figure 6.3).

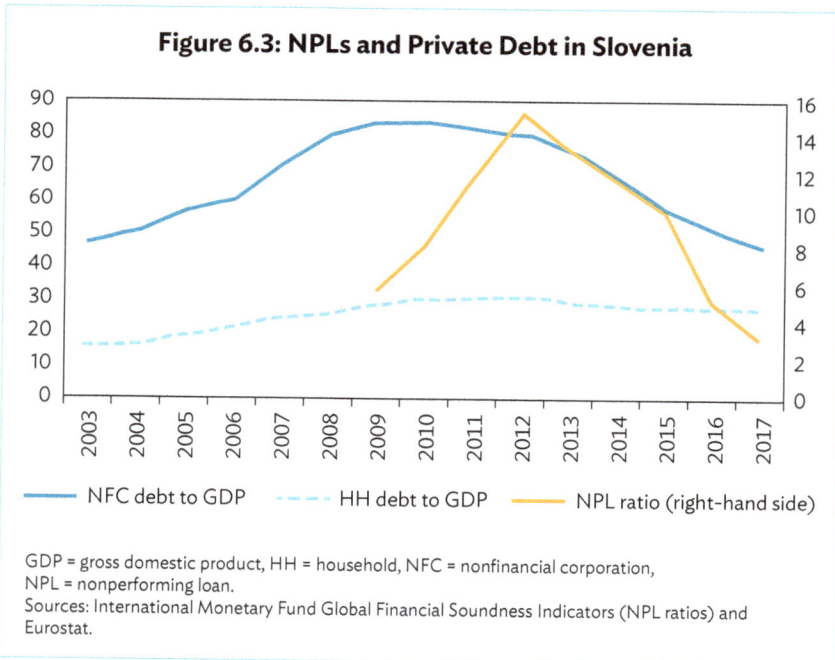

Figure 6.3: NPLs and Private Debt in Slovenia

GDP = gross domestic product, HH = household, NFC = nonfinancial corporation, NPL = nonperforming loan.
Sources: International Monetary Fund Global Financial Soundness Indicators (NPL ratios) and Eurostat.

---

[16] In 2013, state-owned enterprises in Slovenia were estimated to generate one-sixth of value added.

As elsewhere in the euro area, the 2008 crisis resulted in rapid deleveraging by the largely domestically owned banking sector. This was reinforced by high leverage of the corporate sector, an abrupt tightening of risky lending practices by state banks, and a rapid rise in NPLs to 19% in 2012, which eroded bank profitability.[17]

Despite the sharp macroeconomic and financial sector deterioration, with GDP contracting by nearly 10% in the 4 years to 2013, the adjustment in the following years took shape without a formal support program of the IMF, EU, and ECB. The concerted resolution strategy was designed by the government and central bank from 2013, and was closely coordinated with the EU to address concerns over state aid. In effect, the central bank's asset quality review was the first under the new EU standards.

Stress tests and asset quality reviews of the eight largest banks in late 2013 exposed large gaps in capital. The three largest state-owned banks were recapitalized by the state following a write-down of subordinated claims and of previous shareholders. State support to the banking sector was subject to commitments to the EU that two banks would be fully privatized, and that state ownership would be significantly reduced.[18] Along with the imminent transfer of supervision of significant institutions to the ECB, this raised incentives for NPL resolution within the banks.

A key element of bank restructuring was the establishment of the Bank Asset Management Company. In 2013 and 2014, this AMC took over distressed corporate loans from six banks valued at €1.7 billion (or €5 billion in gross value). But takeover of these portfolios suffered lengthy delays. New EU rules for determining state aid to banks had just come into effect, requiring valuation of portfolios at market prices. In addition, documentation of loans within the banks was often poor.

The asset transfers were comprehensive and equivalent to 60% of NPLs to domestic enterprises, or about 16% of Slovenian GDP. Two-thirds of this portfolio consisted of loans in foreclosure, where the AMC acquired collateral, mostly real estate. However, the portfolio also included a substantial portion of about 100 cases of potentially viable companies, where the AMC initiated restructuring. This restructuring work was supported by

---

[17] Damijan (2014) found half of the firms to have unsustainable leverage ratios, undermining firm performance and survival rates. However, this debt, and particular debt within unviable firms, was also highly concentrated in the largest firms. Focused restructuring efforts were hence easier to design.

[18] The three largest banks were recapitalized by the state with €3.7 billion, of which €700.0 million was in the form of the bail-in of certain creditors.

special powers under Slovenian law, which allowed it to acquire exposures from other banks, thereby attaining a critical vote in restructuring decisions. Unlike Europe's two other system-wide AMCs, in Ireland and Spain, which acquired large real estate portfolios, the Slovenian AMC was confronted with significant challenges in recovering value through corporate restructuring. The work of the Slovenian AMC, and that of the banks with the remaining exposures, was facilitated through the revision of the Slovenian insolvency code in 2013, and the related out-of-court restructuring principles, agreed within the banking industry.

Despite the protracted restructurings and changes in the Bank Asset Management Company management directed by the government, its financial performance has been positive. In the 5 years following its inception, the AMC generated cumulative cash flows of nearly €1.1 billion, representing nearly 60% of the fair value of the loans transferred. Most of these cash flows arose from maturing loans, and in recent years loan sales also picked up. The guarantee exposure of the state to the AMC was substantially reduced and through guarantee fees and interest payments an annual average return of 25% on equity has accrued (Balogh 2018).

Supervision was considerably tightened, building on the asset quality reviews and stress tests of 2013. In 2015, the Bank of Slovenia issued guidance to banks on the organizational structure of NPL management and debt workout, and annual reduction targets, foreshadowing a similar approach by the ECB relative to the largest banks in the euro area. Following the transfer to the AMC, the NPL ratio fell to 13%, with most delinquent loans concentrated in the corporate sector. The affected banks significantly stepped up their efforts in corporate debt restructuring.[19]

The case of Slovenia underlines that a program for banking sector recovery needs to comprise a framework for restructuring of corporate exposures, possibly extending into operational and financial restructuring. Even for the more complex asset types among larger enterprises in Slovenia, this restructuring could proceed once the legal framework and capacity in the judiciary had been upgraded. Close coordination between the government and central bank as financial sector supervisors was essential to tackle long-standing and risky lending practices. Slovenia's corporate debt crisis came to a head as the euro area was already recovering, benefiting the highly export-oriented corporate sector.

---

[19] Under the new EU classification for nonperforming exposures, even restructured and newly performing loans would remain classified as NPLs for at least another year.

Italy

Italy, which accounted for roughly a third of the stock of euro area NPLs in 2018, remains a focus of European efforts to deal with the stock of so-called legacy debt. NPL workout is intricately linked to the complex and long-delayed reform of the Italian banking system, which will require tackling chronically low profitability and excessive fragmentation of the sector and the destructive links between bank and sovereign balance sheets. Banking sector reform has been slow and intermittent. Yet, Italy's experience is instructive, given the recent dynamism in its NPL market and a government scheme to support this market, until 2018 without the help of an asset management entity.

Unlike in other euro area countries, Italy did not experience a credit or property boom ahead of the crisis. Household debt and credit quality were not excessive. Yet, economic growth had been chronically weak throughout Italy's membership in the Economic and Monetary Union. NPLs rose quickly once the 2009 recession hit and in the subsequent very weak recovery and further recession (Table 1). Bank capital buffers were thin (at 11.7% capital adequacy in 2009), discouraging write-offs, and the Bank of Italy exerted only limited pressure on banks. A complex insolvency law, obstacles in the tax system, and lengthy processes in the judiciary further impeded a workout led by the banks. The ECB (2017b) assessment found the framework to be weaker in most dimensions than the average of jurisdictions with high NPL levels.

Without the more comprehensive support awarded in the IMF/EU programs in other countries, and given continued political uncertainty, concerted measures aimed at NPL resolution in Italy came relatively late.

In the summer of 2015, the government adopted a package of measures that shortened the length of insolvency procedures, accelerated the tax deductibility of provisions, strengthened debt enforcement, and reformed the civil justice system. In 2016, there were also reforms to out-of-court enforcement through exercising real estate collateral and other measures to enhance transparency of insolvency procedures (Garrido, Kopp, and Weber 2016). The Italian law on loan securitization has been reformed to allow more flexible use, including by simplifying loan sales and allowing special purpose vehicles (SPVs) to engage in loan restructuring. By 2016, supervisory pressure on the largest banks, including through the setting of reduction targets, brought considerable additional supply of NPLs to the distressed loan market.

In addition, several measures have been aimed at a consolidation of smaller banks, strengthening of bank governance, and liquidation of various smaller banks. Consolidation and resolution of smaller banks moved a considerable stock of distressed debt into markets and removed inherently fragile institutions from the sector.

As in other countries, the Italian NPL market has historically displayed large gaps between valuations offered by investors and those demanded by the originating banks. To bridge this gap, the Italian government in 2015 proposed establishing a publicly backed AMC. This scheme could not be agreed with the EU Commission, however, as the acquisition of portfolios by the AMC at valuations above the market price would have triggered state aid procedures.

An alternative scheme (GACS) was agreed in early 2016.[20] Government guarantees are provided for securitizations of NPLs. Each participating bank establishes an SPV which funds the portfolio acquisition by issuing bonds in different risk tranches. The most senior tranche could be guaranteed by the government in return for a guarantee fee that is based on market prices for comparable credit default swap instruments, though this is only possible once at least half the junior tranches have been placed with private investors. Until September 2018, 14 transactions with a total gross value of €59 billion had been concluded. The scheme appears to have been of limited use to the smaller banks in Italy which face more difficulties in pooling assets of sufficient size, and in providing detailed loan-level data.

Also, in early 2016, a bank recapitalization fund (Atlante) was set up. This was funded by several private Italian banks, with only minority participation by a public fund, but emerged only after state pressure on the banks. Atlante was to act not only as a buyer of last resort of bank equity, but also of junior tranches of NPL securitizations. The fund has been criticized for elevating the role of the state and raising the risk of contagion between key banks (Merler 2016).

By mid-2018, the Italian NPL ratio had decreased to under 10%. This relatively rapid decline from a peak of 18% in 2018 reflects a number of large NPL sales and securitizations by the largest banks. The rapid emergence of a dynamic NPL market in Italy in recent years came on the back of a fairly well-developed loan servicing industry and through the

---

[20] GACS is the Italian scheme, Fondo di Garanzia sulla Cartolarizzazione delle Sofferenze, for the securitization of NPLs.

engagement of a small number of specialist investment funds. Nevertheless, the market has been mainly in foreclosed assets offered by the largest banks, rather than those with payment delays where borrowers may still be viable but require restructuring. In future, valuations and investor interest are susceptible to renewed economic weakness and the associated rise in risk sovereign premiums.

Greece

With €87 billion in NPLs in June 2018, equivalent to 48% of gross loans, Greece remained the euro area's most severely affected country by a crisis in banks' loan delinquency and the underlying excess private debt.

Economic growth resumed in 2017 following the steep and protracted economic recession in which GDP fell by over 25%. NPL resolution and a resumption of bank lending then became the focus of efforts aimed at a recovery in bank credit, which is seen as essential for macroeconomic stabilization.

Unlike in some other countries in the euro area periphery, the crisis in Greece was at root a fiscal one that spread to the financial sector. Concerns over sovereign solvency that emerged in 2009 led to rapid deposit withdrawals, as bank capital deteriorated amid a deep recession. The second IMF/EU program from 2012 then put in place a strategy for the recapitalization of Greek banks, as bank funding relied increasingly on emergency facilities from the ECB.

The economic recession that extended over almost a decade showed an early and dramatic impact on sovereign as well as private debt. Household and corporate debt each increased to about 65% of GDP and have declined only marginally since then. Corporate debt is concentrated in firms that remain loss-making and exhibit significant excess leverage. The OECD estimated that in 2013 "zombie firms" in Greece accounted for 28% of the capital stock and 18% of employment.[21] These estimates underline that a significant amount of debt write-off would be required in the resolution of bank NPLs.

---

[21] These firms are defined as aged more than 10 years and showing an interest-coverage-ratio less than 1 for more than 3 consecutive years (McGowan, Andrews, and Millot 2017).

While the recession was the principal cause of the NPL problem, structural problems also clearly aggravated loan delinquencies.[22] In 2016 (6 years after the initiation of IMF/EU support), the ECB survey still found significant impediments. In most of the surveyed dimensions of supervision, the legal framework and the information provision Greece scored worse than other euro area jurisdictions with high NPLs (ECB 2017b).

In addressing the NPL overhang following the banks' recapitalization, the second and third financial programs (extending between 2012 and 2018) therefore relied on a combination of measures in regulation, judicial reform, and supervision. An important objective was the creation of a market for NPL sales and a better targeting of debtor protection through streamlined insolvency codes.

Over the course of the second financial adjustment program, the government committed to several legal reforms that support NPL resolution, including:

- an out-of-court debt restructuring framework, which also included a write-down of tax arrears;
- a reform of the insolvency regime for households and enterprises;
- acceleration of the sale by banks of collateral in defaulted loans through electronic auctions;
- the simplification of the sale of NPLs through the liberalization of the loan servicing regime; and
- a strengthening of efficiency in the courts to deal with NPL-related cases and improved staffing in the judiciary (EU Commission 2018b).

Over the 2 years to mid-2018, the absolute stock of NPLs fell by over €20 billion. This occurred largely through write-offs, and, in its assessment, the EU Commission does not as yet see sustainable restructuring solutions designed by either banks or the acquirers and servicers of NPLs (EU Commission 2018b).

Implementation of the reform measures has been slow, and the impact of the various legal reforms has been limited. For instance, the reformed out-of-court mechanism, including an electronic platform for the submission

---

[22] See speech by Governor Stournaras (Stournaras 2017) pointing to the ineffectiveness of judicial procedures, excessive borrower protection, preferential claims of the state and pension funds on the proceeds of liquidations as against other classes of creditors, unfavorable tax treatment of provisioning and write-offs, lack of an out-of-court-workout framework, and absence of a secondary market for distressed debt.

and processing of cases, only started in 2017, and required a further upgrade in late 2018 to collect data on claims from all creditors. The previous system for auctions of collateral faced aggressive public resistance and was replaced by an electronic platform in late 2017. The rate of liquidations remains very low compared to the pre-crisis period. Auctions often fail or result in the bank reacquiring the collateral due to a lack of bids.

Excessive borrower protection has continuously impeded resolution efforts. As in other euro area countries, this is primarily a problem in residential real estate. The "Katseli" law of 2010 initially provided near universal protection from foreclosure on primary residences. Despite a number of attempts to better target the law, until 2019, protection remains very comprehensive and has prevented NPL reduction in the household mortgage sector. What was intended as a temporary measure amid the acute crisis has in effect become a permanent and blanket protection (IMF 2019). Moreover, estimates suggest that at least one-sixth of firms are in a situation of a strategic default (Stournaras 2017). The recent major reform of the corporate insolvency code and the strengthening of the profession of insolvency administrators does not seem to have led to an increase in new cases.

By contrast, the emergence of NPL markets and securitizations are encouraging. At the end of 2017, Greece saw the first significant NPL sales, which was much later than in other euro area countries. Transactions are now facilitated by a new framework for nonbank credit servicing firms. Completion of announced transactions could bring the total volume to €20 billion over the course of 2019. The four largest banks already established a common platform (Project Solar) which aims at maximizing recoveries from SMEs that are in default, and a similar platform that is primarily designed for larger borrowers.

In addition, the ECB and the Bank of Greece (as the supervisor of the smaller banks) have become much more assertive. In line with the ECB's NPL guidelines, targets for NPL reduction were agreed between the four largest banks and the ECB. NPL ratios were to fall to 35% at the end of 2019 and possibly to 20% at the end of 2021. These targets were set for all banks under ECB supervision in a dialogue with bank management and revised on a rolling basis. While the national legal framework is gradually improving, it is clear that these targets cannot be accomplished through the banks' own restructuring work.

In early 2020, an asset protection scheme (Plan Hercules) was to be implemented. This will result in the establishment of a number of SPVs by each of the four systemic banks. Each SPV would purchase NPL portfolios from an individual bank, funded by the sales of asset-backed securities to private investors. The most senior tranches of these securities would be guaranteed by the government for a fee once a large enough share of the riskier tranches has been sold to other investors (only then would the NPL portfolios no longer require capital coverage by the bank). This proposal is very similar to the Italian scheme GACS, which the EU Commission approved in 2016 as complying with state-aid rules. The key idea is that government backing helps bridge wide gaps between the pricing of NPL portfolios sold by the banks and prices offered by investors in very illiquid local markets. Limitations will be the low credit rating of the government, which will result in a relatively high guarantee fee, and the underdeveloped servicing industry in Greece.

6.4 Impact of National Reforms in the Euro Area

6.4.1 National Resolution Policies and Success in Nonperforming Loan Reduction

By the end of 2019, just ahead of a new and sharp recession triggered by the COVID-19 pandemic, the aggregate EU NPL ratio had declined to 2.7% (from 6.5% 5 years earlier), and for the largest euro area banks subject to ECB supervision this ratio stood at 3.2%.[23] With the exception of Greece and Portugal, NPLs have declined substantially in most countries studied in the previous section, both in absolute and ratio terms.

In early 2019, the NPL crisis legacy seemed to be squarely concentrated in just a handful of countries which experienced sharp recessions or protracted stagnation: Cyprus, Greece, Italy, and Portugal (Table 6.3, based on Georgosouli et al. 2019).

Lower aggregate euro area NPL levels coincided with a recovery in growth and asset prices in the currency area from 2014 (ESRB 2019). Yet, the decline was due to active policy efforts in reducing NPL stock, rather than passively growing out of NPLs.[24] Common standards in euro area supervision and the

---

[23] Data reported for such significant institutions supervised by the ECB differ from the data the European Banking Authority reported for entire banking systems. As the EU-wide NPL definition only came into effect in 2014, earlier national data are not comparable.

[24] Also see the distinction between active and passive periods of NPL reduction in Balgova, Nies, and Plekhanov (2016).

new ECB guidance on NPL management became effective in 2016. National reforms were necessary for this common framework to be effective. Above all, banking sector restructuring and recapitalization allowed write-downs and portfolio sales at market prices. Such reforms explain relatively early successes in Ireland, Slovenia, and Spain, all of which created system-wide AMCs. Conversely, delays in bank restructuring explain persistently high NPL levels. Italy in particular has long delayed corporate governance reforms and consolidation in its banking sector, reducing banks' willingness to write down and dispose of distressed assets.

Table 6.3: Turning Points in NPL Levels in Euro Area Countries

No Significant NPL Accumulation	Moderate Increases, Relatively Swift NPL Resolution	Sharp Increase, Persistently High NPL Ratios
Germany (Q1 2010)	Lithuania (Q2 2010)	Slovenia (Q3 2013)
Belgium (Q4 2013)	Estonia (Q3 2010)	Spain (Q4 2013)
France (Q4 2013)	Latvia (Q4 2010)	Ireland (Q4 2013)
Netherlands (Q4 2013)	Austria (Q4 2010)	Malta (Q2 2014)
Luxembourg (Q4 2016)	Slovakia (Q4 2010)	Italy (Q4 2015)
Finland (Q2 2017)		Cyprus (Q2 2016)
		Portugal (Q2 2016)
		Greece (Q3 2017)

NPL = nonperforming loan, Q = quarter
Source: Georgosouli et al. (2019).

Large parts of the NPL framework remain under national prerogative, rather than subject to EU-wide regulation or ECB supervision. Crucially, this concerns the legal framework for insolvency and restructuring and the process for loan sales. Early reforms in these aspects of the framework helped. NPL sales in Spain boomed due to, inter alia, the activity of its AMC and a conducive environment for loan servicers, though only on the back of the bank restructuring already noted. By contrast, the inefficient corporate restructuring framework in Portugal and excessive protection of household borrowers in Greece explained delays in these countries, aggravating the effects of inadequate capital in the banking sector.

In terms of the policy process and ownership, NPL resolution was rarely a distinct agenda, but rather formed part of a broader crisis recovery program. Few countries coordinated well between macrofinancial policies, such as bank consolidation and resolution, and microeconomic reforms, such as of insolvency laws and loan sales. IMF/EU programs forced such a coordination between different policy fields, though Slovenia, which in 2012/2013 came close to the point where it would have required a program, illustrated that this may well happen independently.

The evolution of the NPL stock is clearly only partially under the control of national policy makers. Macroeconomic and financial market factors play key roles, in particular in the integrated EU financial market. Two narrower aspects of NPL resolution frameworks, distressed loan markets and restructuring and insolvency frameworks, offer more direct evidence of whether national reforms have worked.

Policies to develop secondary loan markets

All national reforms have sought to facilitate NPL sales as an alternative to bank-internal restructuring. Based on the ECB guidance to banks on NPL management, from 2016 supervisors began to set NPL reduction targets for the most affected banks under ECB supervision. Supervisory guidance on internal governance and data standards was in principle not biased toward either internal workout or sales, though it was increasingly clear that capacity within banks to restructure or foreclose on a large scale was inherently limited (ECB 2017a, 12–15).

Therefore, the rapid emergence of NPL markets in Spain and Ireland, and, belatedly, in Italy, was reassuring. In 2017, loans with a gross value of about €130 billion were transacted in the euro area (Figure 1.10 in Chapter 1).[25] Transactions remain concentrated in Ireland, Italy, Spain, and the UK, while NPL sales in other markets have not matched the severity of the loan distress (Figure 6.4) (Lehmann 2018).

A number of factors contributed to the rise of NPL sales. Policies included more assertive provisioning policies, as in Romania, market engagement by an AMC, as in Ireland, Spain, and Slovenia, or government risk-sharing, as in Italy.

Euro area countries have consistently supported NPL disposals by banks through national reforms. By 2016, the ECB's stock taking of national legal frameworks (ECB 2017b) did not identify formal restrictions in the legal and regulatory frameworks that would impede the entry of NPL investors and their acquisition of assets. All 19 euro-area jurisdictions allowed the transfer of loans without the borrower's consent, and all countries allowed their banks to sell NPL assets to foreign investors and nonbanking institutions. Several countries liberalized the activity of loan servicers, and the initial transactions in Greece in 2017 underlined that this liberalization can unlock sales. Government guarantees offered for securitized portfolios was key

---

[25] Deloitte estimates.

to market development in Italy. Transactions with a gross value of nearly a fifth of the total NPL stock were securitized in this way. In early 2020, the onset of the COVID-19 crisis in Europe substantially widened the spreads on high-yield bonds and made access to bond markets for other issues highly uncertain.

Figure 6.4: NPLs and Cumulative Loan Sales as a Share of Gross Loans

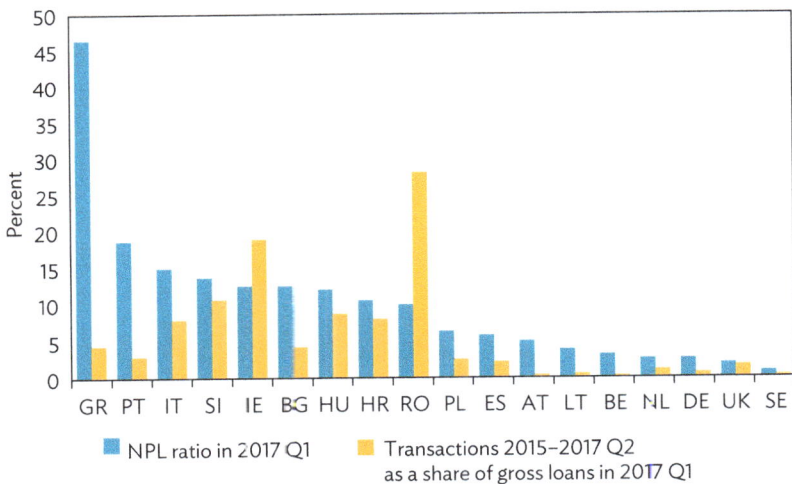

AT = Austria, BE = Belgium, BG = Bulgaria, DE = Germany, ES = Spain, GR = Greece, HR = Croatia, HU = Hungary, IE = Ireland, IT = Italy, LT = Lithuania, NL = Netherlands, NPL = nonperforming loan, PL = Poland, PT = Portugal, Q = quarter, RO = Romania, SE = Sweden, SI = Slovenia, UK = United Kingdom.
Source: Lehmann (2018), based on European Banking Authority and KPMG data on loan transactions.

Market development is still impeded by differing licensing and regulatory regimes, poor data quality, tax disincentives, and difficulties for loan servicers to move between markets. This motivated an EU directive in this area, which was adopted in 2019.[26] Going forward, more complex asset classes (viable enterprises and SMEs in need of restructuring) or country cases (Greece) may require a different type of investors. Market failures, due to poor transparency of loan quality or inadequate investor incentives to engage in restructuring, explain persistent gaps between valuations sought

---

[26] See the Eur-Lex website for more information: https://eur-lex.europa.eu/legal-content/en/TXT/?uri=CELEX%3A52018PC0135.

by the originating banks and those offered by investors (ECB 2017c).[27] EU policy makers have therefore initiated work on a pan-European transaction platform (EU Commission 2018c).

Reforms of corporate insolvency and restructuring frameworks

For many countries in the EU periphery, accession to the euro area resulted in a substantial expansionary demand shock as interest rates and risk premiums became inordinately compressed. In several countries, high corporate and household debt were vulnerable to the subsequent shock from the financial crisis. In the ensuing protracted period of low growth and high unemployment, NPLs quickly rose. In some countries debt was concentrated in specific sectors, such as property and residential real estate in Ireland and Spain. In others it was more widely spread, as in Greece and Italy (ESRB 2019).

National NPL resolution strategies therefore typically comprised a reform of insolvency legislation. About half the EU's members states with active NPL resolution policies have implemented legal reforms in this area (EU Commission, ECB, and SRB 2018). Unlike supervisory regimes that guide banks' management of distressed exposures, national insolvency frameworks have remained squarely within national law (efforts to set a common EU standard on foreclosure and insolvency law have stalled due to fundamental differences in legal systems). Progress in corporate insolvency has been more significant than for households, which remain generally sheltered from foreclosure.

A corporate insolvency framework is efficient if excess debt in viable companies is quickly restructured, while debt in nonviable companies is resolved through foreclosure and liquidation. The law defines conditions for restructuring and the respective rights of creditors and borrowers in a court-led procedure, in turn setting incentives for private restructuring. In a court case, proceedings need to be transparent and speedy, maximizing value recovered (Consolo, Malfa, and Pierluigi 2018).

Targeting this aspect of the law within national NPL policies has been justified by a number of empirical studies examining the connection between insolvency law and loan defaults. For instance, Consolo, Malfa, and Pierluigi (2018) show that countries with better insolvency frameworks

---

[27] See the special feature "Overcoming Nonperforming Loan Market Failures with Transaction Platforms" in ECB (2017c).

deleverage faster and reduce NPLs more quickly than countries with weaker frameworks. A similar result is obtained for the level of NPLs, with more efficient frameworks associated with lower levels. Good insolvency laws will also speed up *reductions* in NPL ratios once an adverse macroeconomic shock has occurred, and will otherwise limit the rise in NPLs.[28] Reforms in this area were also motivated by evidence that valuation gaps arising in NPL sales are largely explained by costs of enforcing claims within national legal systems (ESRB 2019, ECB 2017c).

An indicator developed by the OECD suggests that national reforms have been effective on the whole. Figure 6.5 shows an aggregate index for eight euro area countries for 2010 and 2016. All euro area crisis countries appear to have made progress, including Greece, Portugal, and Slovenia.

Figure 6.5: OECD Composite Indicator for Corporate Insolvency for Selected Euro Area Countries

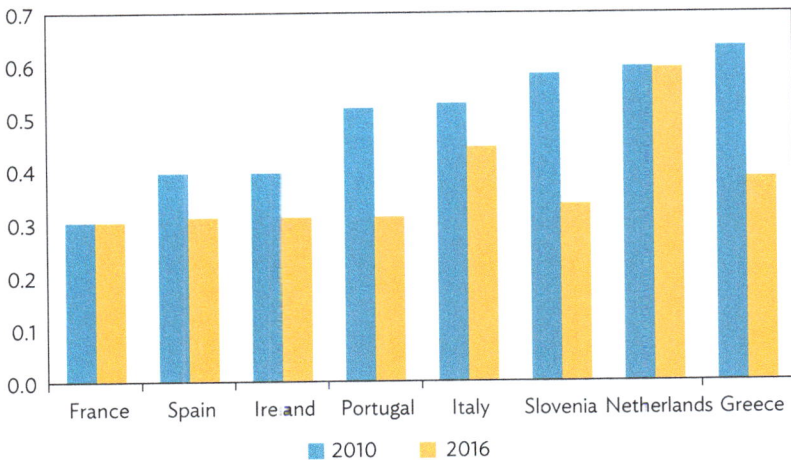

OECD = Organisation for Economic Co-operation and Development.
Note: Lower scores represent better regimes. The composite indicator is based on a quantification of four aspects of insolvency laws, including treatment of failed entrepreneurs, prevention and streamlining regimes, and restructuring tools.
Source: OECD.

---

[28] Also see Caracea et al. (2015).

Effective and sustainable nonperforming loan resolution

NPL markets in the euro area expanded rapidly, and loan sales have become a significant resolution tool, alongside loan restructuring performed within banks. Yet, it is not clear that investor interest is sustainable. Large swathes of distressed assets, in particular among SMEs, will require reform of legal frameworks and development of local capital markets. In most markets only foreclosed assets have transacted. NPLs of delinquent enterprises, though in principle viable following a financial restructuring, are no more than a negligible part of this market.

Insolvency laws have been reformed, but in practice a more mixed picture emerges, evident for instance in the World Bank indicators on resolving insolvency. This can reflect constraints in the actual implementation of the law, including in the functioning of the judiciary, and ineffective private restructuring. The number of successful debt restructurings of midsized and large European enterprises is small, as most legal systems retain a bias toward liquidation.

As debt resolution, in particular within enterprises, is essential for NPL resolution, effective national NPL policies have been implemented only in countries that coordinated well between these two reform areas. Progress in both aspects, as evident in Table 1, allows the grouping of euro area countries into three distinct categories.

- *Effective NPL reduction mechanisms, supported by corporate debt deleveraging.* Of the case study countries, Slovenia and Spain have made impressive progress in both aspects, and policy reforms were well coordinated. NPL resolution is sustainable in that even a renewed recession would not likely lead to widespread or protracted corporate loan delinquencies, as corporate debt vulnerabilities have been addressed to a significant extent.

- *NPL reduction, though continued vulnerabilities from corporate debt.* Italy clearly still belongs in that category. Despite sizable NPL sales, largely of foreclosed loans, corporate debt distress remains significant, in particular among SMEs.

- *Marginal NPL reduction, combined with continued excess debt in the corporate sector.* Greece still belongs to this category, even though a tentative banking recovery and some loan sales are encouraging.[29]

---

[29] The specter of undercapitalized banks and debt distressed enterprises has given rise to several empirical studies, though most other euro countries seem to have escaped this scenario (McGowan Andrews, and Millot 2017).

6.5 Conclusions and Implications for Emerging Asia

Europe confronted a dual challenge of a rise in NPLs and excess private debt following the dramatic financial crisis and recession of 2009–2010. Five countries benefited from the IMF/EU financial support to bank recapitalizations. These adjustment programs guided and disciplined structural reforms. AMCs at bank-level and system-wide, as in Ireland, Spain, and Slovenia, were an important element of these adjustment programs. As the case studies in this chapter demonstrate, national reforms played a key role in this process, sometime accelerating it, for example in Slovenia but sometime also slowing it down, e.g., through excessive debtor protection (in Greece) or lack of a comprehensive strategy for banking sector restructuring, as in Italy, could easily frustrate loan restructuring within the sector.

By 2016, it was clear that excess private debt and loan delinquencies within national banking systems undermined sovereign credit quality and integration and risk-sharing within the currency union as a whole. Common policies quickly became imperative.

Concerns over state aid have made public support to distressed banks more difficult over time, whereas the workout process has benefited from much more intrusive supervision by the ECB. It was quickly recognized that internal bank capacity for workout is inherently limited, so the rapid expansion of the NPL market played an important part in delivering on ambitious reduction targets. The market failures that are inherent in loan sales by banks, such as asymmetric information about loan quality, have to some extent been addressed through better standards in documentation. More wide-ranging innovations, such as regulatory incentives for private transaction platforms, remain on the drawing board (see Chapter 6 for more details).

This experience cannot be easily transferred to Asian emerging markets. Macroeconomic and private sector financial balances are sounder and would offer more buffers to withstand a liquidity shock as it occurred in Asia 20 years ago.

Yet, Europe offers a number of lessons.

A first is that a clear and comparable asset quality definition is a precondition for supervisory action. Spain and Slovenia underlined how on the basis of such a standard, set by the IMF and the EU, respectively, a wider bank restructuring can proceed. The EU-wide definition for NPLs and forbearance of 2013 was a precondition for the ECB assuming supervision of the largest euro area banks from 2014. This standard has been adapted by the Basel Committee on Bank Supervision (BCBS) and could be a relevant best-practice benchmark for a number of Asian emerging markets (BCBS 2017). Where an asset quality review reveals that an NPL crisis has resulted in a deep undercapitalization of the banking system, and external support to the financial sector, as in Spain in 2012, may need to be part of a regional financial safety net.

Second, banks will not sufficiently resource internal workout, and are typically poorly equipped to engage with investors in a loan sale process. They do not take the economy-wide effects of persistent excess debt and loan default into account, presenting a clear case for supervisory guidance. In Europe, a key change came with the ECB guidance on NPL management in 2016. This only applied to the largest euro area banks and was a priority in those with the highest NPL burdens, where ambitious reduction targets were set. By now, this document has set a standard for bank-internal processes in handling delinquent assets, alongside supervisory scrutiny of business models, risk policies, and corporate governance.

Third, NPL sales can be an important relief mechanism. While supervisory guidance can stimulate the supply side, numerous structural reforms need to facilitate the engagement of investors and loan servicers. European banks have worked with an international investor base that is also engaged in Asian markets. These investors will apply the same due diligence standards, and will seek similar standards in loan documentation, and in local frameworks for loan transfers and servicing.

Fourth, policy must address the market failures that are inherent in the process of loan sales. Asset management companies (AMCs) offered crucial support in systemic crises in several countries but inherently raise concerns over state aid in asset transfers. For important parts of the European NPL stock, including in Italy, and possibly in the future in Greece, a public guarantee for a low-risk tranche of securitized NPL structures was sufficient to stimulate loan sales. The private sector by itself has not overcome such market failures. Creditor coordination of common exposures, setting standards for loan documentation, and establishing a joint platform for loan transactions are now being developed and may help addressing remaining issues.

Lastly, the legal framework for insolvency and debt restructuring is part and parcel of sustainable NPL resolution. The emerging empirical literature on insolvency regimes and NPL resolution has confirmed this link. Unless the process to deal with excess private debt is transparent and efficient, and recovers value, delinquent exposures will accumulate within banks. Once cured, restructured loans would then likely relapse into delinquency.

In these areas, Europe and its emerging common financial market have accumulated valuable policy experience. The risks of excess debt and widespread loan delinquency are now better understood, also internationally, and will hopefully be preempted in future.

References

Balgova, M., M. Nies, and A. Plekhanov. 2016. The Economic Impact of Reducing Non-Performing Loans. *EBRD Working Paper Series.* No. 193. London: European Bank for Reconstruction and Development.

Balogh, I. 2018. Lessons Learned from Work of DUTB. Presentation to World Bank Conference. May 2018.

Banco de Portugal. 2017. Financial Stability Report. June.

Basel Committee on Banking Supervision. 2017. Guidelines – Prudential Treatment of Problem Assets – Definitions of Non-Performing Exposures and Forbearance. Basel: Bank for International Settlements.

Baudino, P. and H. Yun. 2017. Resolution of Non-Performing Loans – Policy Options. *FSI Insights on Policy Implementation.* No. 3. Basel: Bank for International Settlements.

Caracea, M., D. Ciriaci, C. Cuerpo, D. Lorenzani, and P. Pontuch. 2015. The Economic Impact of Rescue and Recovery Frameworks in the EU. *European Economies Discussion Papers.* No. 4. Brussels: European Commission.

Cecchetti, S. G., M. S. Mohanty, and F. Zampolli. 2011. The Real Effects of Debt. *BIS Working Paper.* No. 352. Basel: Bank for International Settlements.

Cloutier, E. and F. Montes-Negret. 2014. What Lessons from Romania's Early Success in NPL Reduction?

Coffey, S. 2018. Non-performing Loans in Ireland: Property Development versus Mortgage Lending. In P. Monokroussos and C. Gortsos. eds. *Non-Performing Loans and Resolving Private Sector Insolvency.* London: Palgrave Macmillan.

Consolo, A., F. Malfa, and B. Pierluigi. 2018. Insolvency Frameworks and Private Debt: An Empirical Investigation. *ECB Working Paper Series.* No. 2189. Frankfurt: European Central Bank.

Council of the European Union (EU). 2017a. Report of the FSC Subgroup on Non-Performing Loans.

———. 2017b. Council Conclusions on Action Plan to Tackle Non-Performing Loans in Europe. Press release 459/17. July.

Damijan, J. 2014. Corporate Financial Soundness and Its Impact on Firm Performance: Implications for Corporate Debt Restructuring in Slovenia. *EBRD Working Paper Series.* No. 168. London: European Bank for Reconstruction and Development.

European Banking Authority (EBA). 2014. EBA Final draft implementing technical standards on supervisory reporting on forbearance and non-performing exposures. EBA/ITS/2013/rev1.

_____. 2016. EBA Report on the Dynamics and Drivers of Non-Performing Exposures in the EU Banking Sector. European Banking Authority. Paris.

European Central Bank (ECB). 2017a. Guidance to Banks on Non-Performing Loans. Frankfurt: ECB.

_____. 2017b. Stocktake of National Supervisory Practices and Legal Frameworks Related to NPLs. Frankfurt: ECB.

_____. 2017c. *Financial Stability Review.* November 2017. Frankfurt: ECB.

_____. 2018. *Financial Stability Review.* May 2018. Frankfurt: ECB.

European Systemic Risk Board (ESRB). 2019. Macroprudential Approaches to Non-Performing Loans. Frankfurt am Main: European Systemic Risk Board.

EU Commission. 2016. Country Report Portugal 2016. Brussels.

_____. 2018a. Third Progress Report on the Reduction of Non-Performing Loans and Further Risk Reduction in the Banking Union. COM (2018) 766. Brussels.

_____. 2018b. Enhanced Surveillance Report – Greece. Brussels: EU Commission.

_____. 2018c. European Platforms for Non-Performing Loans. Staff Working Document. Brussels.

_____. 2019. Country Report – Spain. Brussels: EU Commission.

EU Commission, European Central Bank (ECB), and Single Resolution Board (SRB). 2018. Monitoring Report on Risk Reduction Indicators. November.

Garicano, L. 2012. Five Lessons from the Spanish Cajas Debacle for a New Euro-Wide Supervisor. *VOX.* 16 October.

Garrido, J., E. Kopp, and A. Weber. 2016. Cleaning up Bank Balance Sheets: Economic, Legal, and Supervisory Measures for Italy. *IMF Working Paper Series.* No. 16/135. Washington, DC: International Monetary Fund.

Georgosouli, A., R. Giacon, C. Macciarelli, and M. Monti. 2019. Why Non-Performing Loans Are Still Putting the European Banking Union at Risk. *LSE blog.*

International Monetary Fund (IMF). 2013. Romania: Request for a Standby Program, Memorandum of Economic and Financial Policies. March 2013.

_____. 2014a. Portugal Eleventh Review under the Extended Arrangement. Washington, DC.

_____. 2015a. A Strategy for Resolving Europe's Problem Loans. *IMF Staff Discussion Note* 15/19. Washington, DC: International Monetary Fund.

_____. 2015b. Technical Background Notes. *IMF Staff Discussion Note* 15/19. Washington, DC: International Monetary Fund.

_____. 2015c. Spain - Selected Issues. Washington, DC.

_____. 2018. Euro Area Policies - Financial System Stability Assessment. Washington, DC.

_____. 2019. Greece – Selected Issues. Section "Primary Residence Protection in Greece". Washington, DC.

Lehmann, A. 2017. Accounting for True Worth: The Economics of IFRS9. Bruegel blog, 13 November.

_____. 2018. Risk Reduction through Europe's Distressed Debt Market. *Bruegel Policy Contribution* Issue 2.

McGowan, M., D. Andrews, and V. Millot. 2017. The Walking Dead – Zombie Firms and Productivity Performance in OECD Countries. *Economics Department Working Paper.* no. 1372. Paris: OECD.

Medina Cas, S. and I. Peresa. 2016. What Makes A Good 'Bad Bank'? The Irish, Spanish and Germany Experience. *Discussion Paper.* 036. Brussels: European Commission.

Merler, S. 2016. Italy's Atlas Bank Bailout Fund: The Shareholder of Last Resort. *Bruegel.* 22 April.

Reis, R. 2013. The Portuguese Slump and Crash and the Euro Crisis. *Brookings Papers in Economic Activity.*

Stournaras, Y. 2017. Entrepreneurship, NPL Resolution Policies and Economic Growth Prospects in Greece. Speech by Yannis Stournaras, Governor of the Bank of Greece. Event hosted by Piraeus Bank. Athens. 28 March.

Véron, N. 2016. The IMF's Role in the Euro Area Crisis: Financial Sector Aspects. Independent Evaluation Office. Washington, DC.

Voinea, L. 2017. Breaking the back of NPLs – the Romanian experience, presentation by Deputy Governor, IMF. April.

World Bank. 2014. Report on the Observance of Standards and Codes: Insolvency And Creditor/Debtor Regimes, Romania. Washington, DC.

Appendix 2: Risk-Reducing Measures Adopted Nationally in Selected Euro Area Countries

Ireland

Legal/Judicial, Tax, or Other Reforms	Prudential Supervisory Actions	NPL Management Initiatives	Macroprudential Measures
- A mortgage-to-rent scheme has been announced, which allows qualifying homeowners in arrears to remain in their homes as social tenants of a housing association which buys the property from the lender. - Code of Conduct on Mortgage Arrears established to provide statutory safeguards for financially distressed borrowers in arrears or at risk of falling into arrears. A review of the code was concluded. - Personal insolvency legislation introduced in 2012 significantly modernized the regime by providing a range of debt resolution options which balances the rights of creditors and debtors. - Enhanced money advice and budgeting service introduced for distressed borrowers.	- Mortgage Arrears Restructuring Targets encouraged restructuring efforts by banks to move from a short-term forbearance model to one where longer-term sustainable restructuring products were offered to borrowers. These targets were a contributing factor to the reversal in the Irish banks' NPL ratio since 2013. - Legislation introduced to regulate credit servicing firms in 2015 introduced a new regulatory regime for credit servicing firms to clarify that consumers maintained the same protections when their loans are sold to an unregulated purchaser. - Ongoing supervisory focus on addressing NPL levels in Irish banks.	- Centralised Credit Register introduced in 2017 - Asset Management Company established (National Asset Management Agency) -Dedicated NPL workout units established by banks	- Authorities introduced macroprudential measures to limit the high loan-to-value and loan-to-income ratios on new residential mortgage loans in February 2015. The aim was to lower risks to vulnerable borrowers and dampen cyclical dynamics between house prices and lending volumes. The rules have been revised in 2016 (i.e., introduction of a sliding loan-to-value limits) and in 2017 (i.e., stricter rules for second and subsequent buyers).

NPL = nonperforming loan.

Spain

Legal/Judicial, Tax, or Other Reforms	Prudential Supervisory Actions	NPL Management Initiatives	Macroprudential Measures
- Establishment of a new legal framework for savings banks and banking foundations - Introduction of new personal and company insolvency regimes - Enhancement of consumer protection legislation for financial instruments	- Spain implemented a financial assistance program between July 2012 and January 2014 which resulted in the cleaning-up and transfer to an AMC of legacy assets of former savings banks and the restructuring and recapitalization of those entities.	- NPLs remain on a solid downward trend, supported by the announcement of large portfolio disposals by the two largest banks, Santander and Banco Bilbao Vizcaya Argentaria. In addition, smaller operations for the sale of NPLs and foreclosed assets have already been finalized or are ongoing. - Following the resolution of Banco Popular, other banks have accelerated the cleaning-up of their balance sheets.	- Creditors' preferential claim on secured collateral increased to 70% in 2015 and 90% in 2018.

AMC = asset management company, NPL = nonperforming loan.

Italy

Legal/Judicial, Tax or Other Reforms	Prudential Supervisory Actions	NPL Management Initiatives	Macroprudential Measures
- Reform of the insolvency and foreclosure frameworks in 2015 and 2016 to shorten the recovery period for collateral and foster the repossession of collateral - Reform of large cooperative banks (*banche popolari*) and small mutual banks (*banche di credito cooperativo*); once fully implemented, these reforms are expected to also impact positively on the arrears management capacity of those banks - Introduction of immediate tax deductibility for loan loss provisions	- Enhanced reporting by all banks on nonperforming exposures and collateral reporting template introduced in 2016 by the Italian central bank	- Establishment of an NPL securitization scheme with state guarantees (GACS) to support banks' resolution of NPLs. That scheme, which was introduced in 2016, was extended several times. - Establishment of a private sector backstop facility to invest in NPLs sold or securitized by banks (i.e., Atlante Fund II, renamed the Italian Recovery Fund in 2017)	

NPL = nonperforming loan.

Portugal

Legal/Judicial, Tax, or Other Reforms	Prudential Supervisory Actions	NPL Management Initiatives	Macroprudential Measures
- Expedited insolvency proceedings: technology used to (i) accelerate proceedings, and (ii) ensure transparency in judicial sales procedures - Flexibility for tax credit to be restructured and creation of a common decision-making body between social security and tax authority to participate in company restructuring negotiations - Creation of an early warning mechanism for entrepreneurs—compares various indicators to past levels and industry benchmarks to create awareness and promote preventive approach - Measures to facilitate the transfer of NPL portfolios – regime allowing mass registration of the transfer of collateral and mass communication to courts in insolvency proceedings	- In line with Single Supervisory Mechanism recommendations, Portuguese banks have submitted 5-year NPL reduction plans forecasting at least a 50% reduction in NPL stocks over the coming years. - On-site and off-site inspections to segment banks' NPL portfolios by type, vintage, size, and sector of activity	- Initiatives to promote coordination between creditors to accelerate credit restructuring and/or NPL sales; the flagship measure is a "coordination platform." - Financing lines and/or guarantees for viable companies that go through the restructuring process. - Creation of credit recovery funds, which allow banks to dispose of bad assets through dedicated marketable investment funds, boosting the secondary market for bad assets. - Creation of incentives to develop the secondary market for NPLs by enabling new servicing companies to enter the market	- Recommendation on new credit agreements for consumers, which places limits on new credit relating to residential immovable property, credit secured by a mortgage or equivalent guarantee, and consumer credit agreements concluded as of July 2018; this measure aims to promote the adoption of prudent credit standards in order to enhance the resilience of the financial sector and the sustainability of households' financing, thereby minimizing defaults. i. Maximum loan-to-value ratios: (i) 90% for credit for own permanent residence, (ii) 80% for credit for purposes other than own permanent residence, and (iii) 100% for credit for purchasing immovable property held by credit institutions and for property financial leasing agreements.

continued on next page

Appendix 2 (continued)

Legal/Judicial, Tax, or Other Reforms	Prudential Supervisory Actions	NPL Management Initiatives	Macroprudential Measures
- Creation of new insolvency practitioners acting as mediators for companies in "recovery" mode and assisting debtors in both in-court and out-of-court restructuring procedures - Framework allowing majority creditors (holding at least two-thirds of debtor's liabilities) to convert their credit into share capital without the consent of shareholders, outside of insolvency proceedings (in certain strictly specified situations) - Framework for voluntary out-of-court restructuring for recovery of companies - Ability for banks to fiscally recognize write-offs (to a larger extent than before)			ii. Maximum debt-service-to-income ratio of 50%, with the following exceptions: (i) up to 20% of the total amount of credit granted by an institution in a year may have a maximum debt-service-to-income ratio of 60%; and ii) up to 5% of credit granted may exceed that 60% limit. For variable and mixed interest rate agreements, the impact of an interest rate rise should be taken into account, as should a reduction in the borrower's net income if the borrower will be aged 70 or over at the end of the contract. iii. Original maturity of loans: (i) maximum of 40 years for new credit agreements secured by a mortgage; (ii) average maturity of new credit agreements should be 30 years by 2022; and (iii) maximum of 10 years for new consumer credit agreements. All credit agreements must have regular principal and interest payments. The relevant limits must be observed simultaneously. The recommendation follows the principle of "comply or explain", and its implementation will be monitored on at least an annual basis.

NPL = nonperforming loan.
Note: The document on which this is based is, in turn, based on responses by the authorities which may be partial and reflect different time horizons. No specific date of adoption of individual measures is available.
Source: Excerpts from EU Commission, European Central Bank, and Single Resolution Board (2018).

PART

4

Policy Strategies for
Nonperforming Loan Resolution
and Market Development
in Asia and Europe

7   Resolution of Nonperforming Loans in the Euro Area

John Fell, Maciej Grodzicki, Reiner Martin, and Edward O'Brien[1]

7.1   Introduction: The Nonperforming Loan Problem in the Euro Area

In the wake of the global financial crisis and the euro area sovereign debt crisis, the large stock of nonperforming loans (NPLs) became an important cause for concern for policy makers in the euro area. Addressing this matter effectively remains a priority for the European Central Bank (ECB) and for the Council of the European Union. Although the average NPL ratio has gradually declined from a peak of 8% in 2013 to 2.9% by end-2020, it remains almost three times above the equivalent ratios in the United States, the United Kingdom, and Japan. Moreover, differences across euro area countries remain stark, with four countries having NPL ratios above 5%—significantly so in some cases.[2]

Large NPL stocks are problematic for a number of reasons. First, bank resources are tied up by assets that tend to produce—at best—less income than initially envisaged and at worst no income at all, which adds to bank profitability challenges.[3] At the same time, high stocks of NPLs create uncertainty about the health and prospects of the banking sector, increasing bank funding costs and the costs of new credits. Ultimately, this impedes

---

[1] This chapter should not be reported as representing the views of the European Central Bank (ECB) or the Joint Vienna Institute (JVI). The views expressed are those of the authors and do not necessarily reflect those of the ECB or the JVI.

[2] As of end-2020, these countries are Cyprus, Greece, Italy, and Portugal. The source is European Central Bank Supervisory Banking Statistics.

[3] On productivity developments in the euro area banking sector, see for example ECB (2016) and Huljak, Martin, and Moccero (2019).

the scope for new lending to productive ventures and undermines the transmission of monetary policy.[4]

Second, high stocks of NPLs usually indicate underlying solvency and debt overhang issues affecting both households and the corporate sector. Excessive indebtedness often implies that corporate investment remains below the desirable level to support recovery in the real economy.[5] Moreover, keeping over-indebted and ultimately nonviable firms alive by not resolving NPLs in a timely fashion generates artificial and unhealthy competition for firms that are actually viable.

Third, given the strong financial and economic interlinkages between euro area countries, the high NPL stock gives rise to euro-area-wide financial stability and macroprudential concerns. This is notwithstanding substantial variability across countries and the fact that not all euro area countries have significant NPL problems.

Against this backdrop, the case for swift resolution of NPLs is clear. Caution is needed to avoid NPL fire sales, however, which are not conducive to recovering maximum value from the underlying assets and thus put additional pressure on bank capital.

Following the global financial crisis, accelerating the initially unsatisfying speed of NPL resolution in the euro area required a comprehensive approach comprising supervisory, macroprudential, and structural measures and, involved some degree of coordination at the European level. Appropriately robust supervisory guidance, as published by ECB Banking Supervision (ECB 2017), was essential to improving banks' NPL management. However, this must be complemented by structural reforms to enhance recoveries and increase the net present value of NPLs and by complementary measures to facilitate the development of NPL markets. Work on many of these reforms has been completed under the umbrella of the European Council Action Plan on NPLs, which—among other objectives—aimed to review licensing requirements for NPL investors, addressing transferability restrictions, and to create a harmonized legal instrument to enforce collateral out of court. Only when banks have the full set of potential NPL resolution tools available can they optimize the speed of resolution.

---

[4] See Aiyar et al. (2015) for discussion of the possible impact of NPL resolution on bank capital and lending capacity.

[5] For example, see Goretti and Souto (2013), Nkusu (2011), Balgova and Plekhanov (2016) for evidence that a high stock of NPLs is associated with weaker economic growth.

The rest of this chapter reviews in more detail the main obstacles to NPL resolution in the euro area and the elements of a comprehensive NPL resolution strategy, with a particular focus on asset management companies (AMCs) and the benefits of regional cooperation.

7.2 Why Was Nonperforming Loan Resolution So Slow in the Euro Area?

A striking aspect of NPL developments in the last decade in the euro area is that secondary NPL markets were initially not very active, although they gained traction over the years, driven among other things by the strong cyclical upswing in the euro area economy. Around the time NPLs peaked in the euro area, Deloitte (2016) and KPMG (2016) highlighted that even with a stock of some €2,000 billion in noncore assets on bank balance sheets (of which about 50% were NPLs), annual transactions only amounted to slightly more than €100 billion.

ECB analysis (ECB 2018) and market intelligence suggest that investors had considerable interest in acquiring bank-held NPLs, but that the prices they were willing to pay tended to be substantially lower than what would be at least neutral for the capital positions of banks. This so-called "bid-ask spread" can be explained by a number of factors. First, investors may have faced market frictions and more significant information challenges than better-informed banks, which significantly increased their required returns and discount rates.[6] Second, differences in the contractual position between banks and investors may have contributed to this spread, as banks usually cannot adjust lending rates in line with the deteriorating creditworthiness of a borrower. However, this can be captured by investors who buy loans at a discount. Finally, many banks may not have fully incorporated the costs of working out impaired assets in their provisioning, while bid prices on the secondary NPL market reflected such costs.

In sum, seen through the lens of Akerlof (1970), the secondary market for NPLs in Europe can be characterized as a "market for lemons" (where investors have insufficient knowledge of the quality of the assets), and as a situation where informational asymmetries impede market functioning because buyers know less about asset quality than sellers. Buyers therefore fear that the assets are of low quality and bid at a correspondingly low price. The sellers, being able to distinguish between low- and high-quality assets, trade only the former—the lemons—whereas the market for the remaining

---

[6]   The cost of overcoming the information challenges will ordinarily reduce the price bid by the investor.

good-quality assets fails. In the NPL context, sellers may also not have perfect information about their assets, but the informational asymmetry remains because buyers cannot know whether sellers are revealing all available information.

Akerlof shows that in a "market for lemons," demand depends not only on price, but also on the average quality of the goods. As a result, the demand curve contains a kink so that multiple equilibria can arise (Figure 7.1). The figure shows that the NPL supply curve positively intercepts the price–quality axis at a level commensurate with banks' ability to dispose NPLs at a given price—in effect, the intercept represents banks' price floor.

The "bad" market equilibrium depicted as "A" is consistent with market conditions in which only a small quantity of "lemons"—low-quality NPLs—is traded at low prices. In this framework, improving supply (i.e., a rightward shift of the supply curve), such as by exerting supervisory pressure on banks to dispose of NPLs, leads to an improved market equilibrium (labeled as "B") but the overall gains remain limited because additional NPL supply will not be fully absorbed.[7]

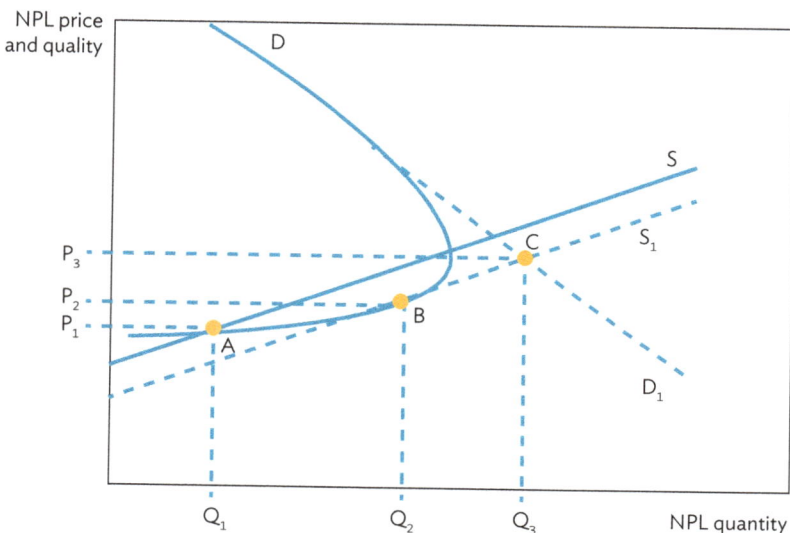

Figure 7.1: Asymmetric Information and the NPL Market

NPL = nonperforming loan.
Source: Fell et al. (2016).

---

[7]   See Fell et al. (2016), for example.

Overcoming informational asymmetries has greater potential to respond to the market failure. If these asymmetries are addressed, the shape of the demand curve changes from "D" to the more standard "D_1," and equilibrium "C" can be achieved. Akerlof shows that mechanisms which restore buyers' "trust"—for example, guarantees, licensing, and branding—can reduce informational asymmetries and improve demand.

A number of key impediments are at the heart of the "trust" problem between buyers and sellers n euro area NPL markets. First, the absence of high-quality NPL data can compromise valuation methods, resulting in heightened uncertainty about asset values and additional data collection costs.

Second, ineffective legal frameworks for debt recovery and collateral enforcement can create additional information asymmetries. To the extent that buyers and sellers have diverging views about the merits of such frameworks, buyers may require steep discounting of future NPL cash flows to offset the risks of inordinately long and unpredictable recovery times and rates, penalizing the original asset owners in jurisdictions where legislation is least effective.

Asymmetric information may also give rise to imperfect excludability, which forms another source of market failure. Investors may not be able to gain access to the full resources—cash flows or assets—of the debtor, which may have been financed by other parties, such as banks or suppliers. This further increases uncertainty about future recovery rates and may restrict the range of workout options available to an investor. The resulting creditor coordination prob em, with often misaligned incentives between various classes of creditors, may even bring workout efforts to a standstill.

These impediments to NP_ transactions point to a number of levers that can be used to lower information asymmetries, restore buyers' trust, and ultimately lower bid-ask spreads. First, improved data availability for buyers is key to enabling a better distinction between "lemons" and good assets, thereby attracting more buyers. Second, credible actions that increase market confidence in NPL valuation by instilling more certainty about cash flows and recovery values could be useful.[8]

---

[8] Improved recovery rates may also be achieved through reforms that increase the transparency of procedures related to repossessions and insolvency. Furthermore, benefits may be derived from increased transparency in collateral auctions, measures that lower transaction costs for properties purchased under foreclosure or insolvency, and creditor-friendly measures that encourage out-of-court restructuring in a value-maximizing manner. Faster cash flow may result from shorter in-court judicial processes and related administrative insolvency procedures, out-of-court debt restructuring, and faster enforcement of collateral.

7.3 Elements of a Comprehensive Solution

The resolution of NPLs in the euro area that followed the global financial crisis required a comprehensive, multipronged approach that took country-specific circumstances into account. Generally speaking, a wide range of possible, often complementary, responses to address large NPL stocks is available (Figure 7.2).

Figure 7.2: Elements of a Comprehensive Approach to NPL Resolution

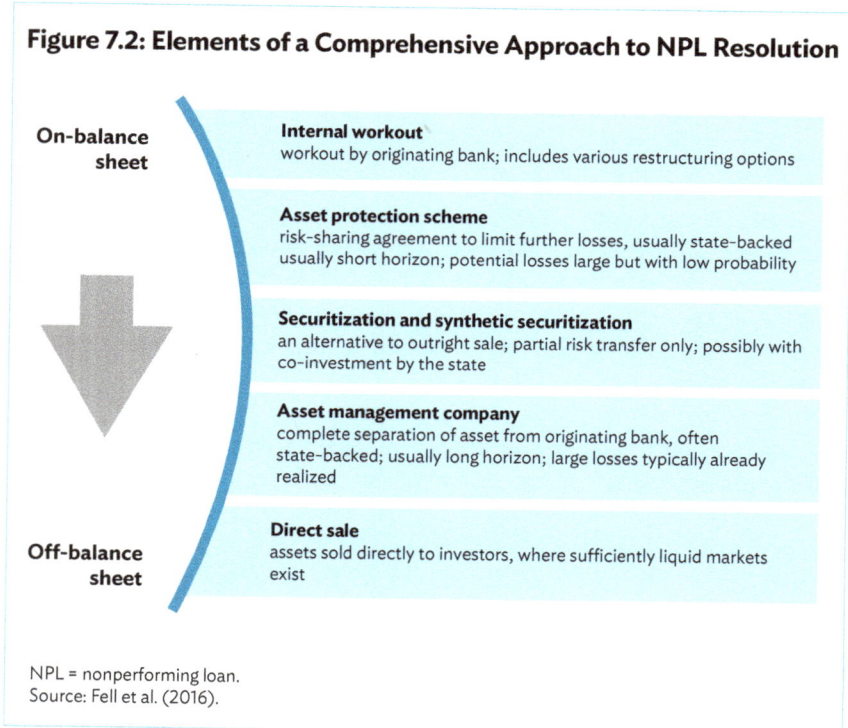

On-balance sheet

Internal workout
workout by originating bank; includes various restructuring options

Asset protection scheme
risk-sharing agreement to limit further losses, usually state-backed
usually short horizon; potential losses large but with low probability

Securitization and synthetic securitization
an alternative to outright sale; partial risk transfer only; possibly with co-investment by the state

Asset management company
complete separation of asset from originating bank, often state-backed; usually long horizon; large losses typically already realized

Direct sale
assets sold directly to investors, where sufficiently liquid markets exist

Off-balance sheet

NPL = nonperforming loan.
Source: Fell et al. (2016).

The internal workout by the bank originally holding the impaired asset marks one end of the spectrum of options and should feature highly in any comprehensive resolution scheme. It requires banks to maintain or build necessary expertise but, at the same time, may allow them to recover more value for themselves than from an asset disposal and maintain potentially profitable client relationships. Notably, highly granular, small-ticket retail exposures may be best worked out internally or sold directly to investors. Bespoke products, which require detailed knowledge of borrowers and their business, may also be best kept on the balance sheet, given the sunk costs of acquiring that knowledge.

At the other end of the spectrum, the direct sale of NPLs to investors is the most rapid resolution mechanism for banks, but it is also the costliest. The extent to which direct sales can be used depends, among other things, on provisioning levels relative to market prices, the size of banks' capital buffers, and the presence of liquid NPL markets. In between, a range of options exists. These include asset protection schemes, securitization, the creation of AMCs (which are often referred to as "bad banks"), and the development of NPL platforms with little or no involvement of the state. Each of these options has different requirements, costs, and benefits.

Asset protection schemes are not discussed in detail here, given that they have proven particularly useful when potential losses from declining asset valuation and the associated uncertainty about the health of the financial sector are large but are unlikely to actually occur. Broadly speaking, such schemes are more useful in the early stages of a financial crisis than in the aftermath.

Turning to securitization schemes, Akerlof shows that one solution to the "market-for-lemons" problem is for sellers of "good" assets to offer a performance guarantee to create or restore trust in the quality of the goods sold. Appropriately structured securitization schemes, with an element of public support, could deliver this guarantee and help overcome the "lemons" problem. For these schemes to be effective, public support should target the riskiest tranche in a securitization structure.[9] This can have two important effects. First, it signals that the underlying asset quality may be better than currently perceived. Second, it signals a commitment of the state to structural reforms that can influence NPL valuations (for example, through the time and costs to recovery), given that the state becomes exposed to risk.

A junior guarantee on securitization could be offered bilaterally on the equity tranche in a true-sale NPL securitization.[10] It may be structured as a total return swap, essentially exposing the state to the same risk/return profile as a private investor. The scheme closely aligns the interests of investors and the state and offers investors the possibility of an enhanced risk/return profile due to the state's direct exposure to the same risks and its resulting vested interest in avoiding losses. It can be offered flexibly, allowing investors in the junior tranche to choose their own level of protection, if any.

[9] By tranching funding across different risk categories, securitization generally achieves a lower average cost of funding.

[10] For further details, see Fell, Moldovan, and O'Brien (2017).

It may also open the way to increasing the number and types of investors in the junior tranche by allowing a partial de-risking of that tranche.[11] The scheme also offers important advantages from the state's perspective— it requires no upfront investment, it is priced at market levels, and the fact that the tranche investor remains exposed to the performance of the underlying NPL portfolio ensures that moral hazard and the risk to the state remain contained.[12]

AMCs have often been used to manage distressed assets arising from systemic financial sector stress (Cerruti and Neyens 2016; Medina Cas and Peresa 2016) and have a proven record in making significant contributions to the clean-up of banking sectors suffering from NPL problems. Examples include AMCs established in the aftermath of banking crises in Sweden in the early 1990s (Jonung 2009); in the Republic of Korea in the late 1990s (He 2004); and, more recently, in the euro area countries Ireland (2010), Spain (2012), and Slovenia (2013). One of the common features of these banking system-wide AMCs is that governments have been deeply involved in their creation by providing capital, facilitating funding, and passing legislation that governs their design and operations.[13]

The main function of systemic AMCs is to "bridge" the intertemporal pricing gaps that emerge when market prices for NPLs and the underlying collateral are temporarily depressed due to heightened risk aversion and reduced liquidity in the market. The gap is bridged by removing a significant share of NPLs—usually belonging to a specific asset class such as commercial real estate or residential property development—from bank balance sheets and working them out over a specific period to maximize their recovery value. The transfer price that a government-sponsored AMC pays a bank is usually set at long-term ("real economic") value, thus avoiding a fire sale when NPLs are sold into illiquid markets. Shielding banks from fire sale conditions can be especially beneficial if several banks are attempting to resolve their NPLs at the same time. In other words, systemic AMCs can provide an important coordination role. Other benefits of AMCs are related to a swift reduction in uncertainty surrounding the profitability and solvency of banks once NPLs are transferred to the AMC. This has a positive impact on banks' funding and capital costs.

---

[11] In particular, the scheme could play a catalyst role in widening the investor base in the junior NPL securitization tranches.

[12] Pricing at market levels is a key element for smooth implementation of the junior guarantee. This also opens up the possibility of using it free of state aid, subject to assessment by the European Commission.

[13] AMCs may also be created in the process of restructuring or resolving a single bank, often without government support. Such bank-specific AMCs do not normally have a systemic reach and do not offer the benefits discussed in this chapter and, as such, are not covered here.

Despite these advantages, AMCs are no panacea for systemic NPL problems. Their success depends on their design and the prevailing economic circumstances. Experience suggests that several success factors should be present for an AMC to accomplish its objectives. First, AMCs tend to be best suited for particular asset classes. Second, asset valuations and the resulting transfer prices should be realistic. A well-designed governance structure, with a strong mandate, is another essential ingredient. Finally, a basic premise for the success of AMCs is that asset values start to recover in the medium term. This, in turn, implies that authorities pursue sound macroeconomic and financial policies.

In the EU, the scope for establishing banking system-wide, government-sponsored AMCs is restricted by the EU legal framework governing state aid to the financial sector, as well as by other institutional and—notably in some countries—fiscal constraints. More specifically, the Bank Recovery and Resolution Directive and the state aid communications of the European Commission[14] regulate the participation of governments in AMCs. The complexity of these rules and their interplay was one of the reasons for the initiative launched by former ECB Vice-President Vítor Constâncio (Constâncio 2017) to develop a joint European Commission, ECB, and European Banking Authority (EBA) blueprint for banking-system-wide, government-sponsored AMCs in the EU (European Commission 2018).[15]

Looking in more detail at considerations for setting up successful AMCs, the main issues are the asset perimeter, the participation perimeter, the asset valuation, the capital and funding structure and, last but certainly not least, the governance of AMCs. The description below is cross-country in nature and accounts for the interconnectedness between the various issues, international best practices, and EU-specific legal constraints.

Considering first the assets, a strong argument can be made to limit transfers to asset classes where AMCs have a track record of having recovered value, such as commercial real estate, large corporate exposures, and syndicated

---

[14] See Communication from the Commission on the treatment of impaired assets in the community banking sector (Impaired Assets Communication, 2009/C 72/01) and Communication from the Commission on the application, from 1 August 2013, of state aid rules to support measures in favor of banks in the context of the financial crisis (Banking Communication), OJ C 216, 30.7.2013, 1–15.

[15] Besides clarifying relevant EU legislation, the "AMC blueprint" discusses, based on international experience, many important aspects that are relevant for successfully setting up and running of system-wide AMCs.

loans.[16] The volume of asset transfers should balance the benefits from economies of scale with the risk that the AMC may be overburdened by having to work out too many assets within a relatively short time, particularly if they are insufficiently homogenous. It would appear useful that only assets above a predetermined gross book value are transferred to avoid burdening the AMC unduly with the administrative challenge of too many small exposures. Finally, it is often very useful to transfer all loans of a (partially) nonperforming debtor to the AMC.[17]

Participation in the AMC should not normally be left entirely to the discretion of banks. The case for AMCs rests on gaining a critical mass of assets, and a fully voluntary approach is unlikely to achieve this. First, a voluntary approach may result in inaction due to first-mover disadvantages. Voluntarily participating banks may endanger their client relationships by being seen as unduly tough. There may also be a cherry-picking of NPLs, with participating banks trying to transfer their lowest-quality NPLs to the AMC, while keeping on their balance sheets those bad loans with the best chance of being cured. Fully voluntary participation may also jeopardize the advantages of the debtor approach already mentioned. If a debtor is making good on loans to some banks but not to others, no (apparent) incentive exists for the banks holding the "good" loans to transfer them to the AMC. The authorities should therefore introduce sufficiently strong incentives to transfer assets to the AMC, be it through moral suasion, supervisory or accounting measures, or by sharing gains resulting from recovery values above the transfer price with the banks.

Conducting a valuation exercise is an indispensable part of the setup process. Generally, the aim of this exercise is to establish both the market value and the real ("long-term") economic value of the assets. The valuation should start once the possible asset and participation perimeters have been determined. The assumptions of the valuation should be realistic, and the valuation should include a viability test on the underlying assets and debtors to identify assets that need to be liquidated rather than transferred to the AMC for recovery. In the EU, state aid rules require that a valuation exercise be conducted in agreement with the European Commission, as the relevant competition authority, before the transfer of assets to the AMC.

[16] Recent AMCs in the euro area have often been set up and associated with particular asset classes, such as the National Asset Management Agency in Ireland and the SSociedad de Gestión de Activos Procedentes de la Reestructuración Bancaria in Spain.

[17] Experience has shown that such a debtor-specific approach is warranted. A debtor may have an NPL with one bank but performing loans with another. By taking all of the outstanding debt of a specific debtor, subject to respecting the perimeter of the AMC, the positions may be quickly resolved.

The valuation is a key input into the approval of the state aid that the commission gives to either the AMC or participating banks.

The amount of capital of the AMC should be calibrated to ensure that the equity layer is sufficient to absorb unexpected losses on assets. Equity requirements when setting up an AMC should, however, normally remain well below those typically required for a troubled bank. As long as the asset transfer price is based on a thorough valuation, the AMC should not be expected to endure major losses during its lifetime.

A public–private partnership model may also help. First, it can alleviate some of the burden for countries with limited fiscal space, where a majority private ownership may allow the deconsolidation of the AMC from the balance sheet of the public sector.[18] Second, the scope for government interference in operations of the AMC is considerably reduced when the private sector holds an equity stake of more than 50%. That is the case for the National Asset Management Agency in Ireland, and for *Sociedad de Gestión de Activos Procedentes de la Reestructuración Bancaria*, Spain's banking-sector-wide AMC.

The AMC funding structure should minimize costs and liquidity risks. This can be achieved by issuing government-guaranteed senior bonds, which can be used as payment-in-kind to buy NPLs from banks. Senior bonds may be short-dated (1-year), with restrictions on transferability and an implicit guarantee to mitigate rollover risks. In the euro area, senior bonds may be structured to meet eligibility criteria for Eurosystem credit operations. Other central banks may consider a similar arrangement.[19]

Strong and sound governance is critical to the success of an AMC. The right balance is needed between business flexibility and constraints that prevent diversion from the core AMC mandate. It appears best to establish the AMC through legislation laying down its objectives, the form of its decision-making bodies, and its rules on transparency and accountability. Experience suggests that AMCs should be free from political interference and budgetary

---

[18] In a European Union context, a majority of privately owned AMC, may be classified outside the government sector, and therefore not drive an increase in government debt, provided a number of conditions are met. According to the rules by which Eurostat compiles government deficit and debt statistics, an AMC which is majority privately owned, may be classified as outside the government sector even if its liabilities have received a government guarantee, provided that it is established for a temporary duration, has the sole purpose of addressing the financial crisis, and that its expected losses are small in comparison with the total size of its liabilities. For further details, see O'Brien and Wezel (2013).

[19] The scope of central bank involvement in the funding of an AMC depends crucially on the mandate and legal framework governing the permissible activities of the central bank. In the EU, Article 123 of the Treaty on the Functioning of the European Union prohibits monetary financing by the ECB.

pressures, although public authorities should oversee some aspects of their operations, in particular those relating to compliance with its mandate and applicable regulations.

The AMC should have a clear primary mandate to maximize the recovery values of NPLs on a commercial basis. Its operational overheads should remain light and, wherever possible, the AMC should be allowed to outsource services such as property management, legal services, or collections to independent providers at market prices. More generally, it should be permitted to use any relevant legal tool or workout strategy to achieve its goals, regardless of political or vested interests.

Turning to NPL trading platforms, these may be a way to realize some of the benefits of an AMC while avoiding the costs—notably the upfront fiscal costs and financial risks for the public sector—that tend to be associated with the setting up of systemic AMCs, even though a well-designed and well-managed AMC may not result in a net loss for the taxpayer once the AMC has completed its task.

Like AMCs, trading platforms, can be designed in different ways and for different purposes. As a minimum, an NPL platform can serve as a vehicle to collect NPL-related information from different banks. This provides a number of advantages, which, returning to Akerlof's concept above, are likely to narrow bid-ask spreads in NPL markets by reducing information asymmetries.[20]

First, "shoe-leather" costs for potential investors are reduced by having a centralized port of call for information about (parts of) the NPL supply. This is particularly useful in countries with a large share of multi-lender and/ or syndicated loans, which are often particularly difficult to resolve.

Second, and very importantly, NPL platforms will require standardized information from banks that would like to use their services. High quality, standardized data will, in turn, reduce the time and cost of due diligence for potential investors, likely increasing the investor pool interested in acquiring such assets. As the value of NPLs becomes clearer, the rate of return expected by NPL investors should also decline. Participation in such a platform may also provide a welcome push for banks to solve possible NPL data problems.

---

[20] See Fell, Grodzicki, Krušec, Martin, and O'Brien (2017) for a more detailed exposition of the transaction platform concept.

In principle, NPL platforms can provide additional services, for example, selling assets on behalf of participating banks or acting as an interface between the banks and third-party NPL service firms.

Operationally, NPL platforms will face a number of challenges, for example, data confidentiality restrictions have to be overcome. Banks will normally be required to finance the platform, so they have to be convinced of its merits. Encouragement from bank supervisors to participate in the platform may be very helpful in this regard. On the positive side, the government will not normally have to commit resources. In the EU context, this has the added benefit that states aid rules do not apply—although general competition rules may come into play. A precedent for such a platform already exists in the EU, with a rather similar rationale, even though it does not directly relate to NPLs.[21]

At the time of writing, several private companies were already operating NPL platforms in a number of EU Member States. However, they offered limited geographic scope and the loan data used is not standardized across the market. Despite significant investor interest, the supply of NPLs to these existing platforms has thus been rather limited so far and the potential benefits of a European NPL platform remained largely unrealized.[22]

7.4 The Benefits of European Regional Cooperation

The EU—and even more so, the euro area—is a closely integrated group of countries: financially, economically, politically, and institutionally. This needs to be kept in mind when assessing the challenges associated with NPL resolution in the euro area and when designing appropriate approaches to speed up NPL resolution.

In recent years, high NPL ratios were present only in a subset of euro area countries. This notwithstanding, high NPLs in one country can impose significant externalities on others due to important cross-border spillover channels within and beyond the banking sector. Banking spillover channels relate to banks' cross-border lending and cross-border ownership links. Spillover channels to the real economy relate to the potential deterioration of

---

[21]   The ECB led an initiative to improve transparency in asset-backed securities markets by requiring loan-by-loan information to be made available and accessible to market participants and to facilitate the risk assessment of such securities as collateral to be used by Eurosystem counterparties in monetary policy operations. The asset-backed securities loan-level initiative sought to enhance access to more timely information about the underlying loans and their performance in a standard format.

[22]   For further details on this, see European Commission (2019a).

the macroeconomic environment in countries with high NPLs, which affects other countries through lower import demand (the trade channel), and a loss of value of equity and debt claims on residents in the affected countries (the financial channel). Finally, the differences in supply and demand of credit and the stigma attached to some EU countries with high NPL ratios may impede the transmission of monetary policy (European Systemic Risk Board 2017).

Whereas these spillovers increase the negative impact of the NPL problem in the EU and the euro area, the close institutional cooperation between the euro area countries is an important asset when it comes to solving the problem.

Looking first at cooperation among bank supervisors, the European Banking Authority (EBA), the EU agency in charge of coordinating banking sector regulation and supervision across the EU, agreed in 2014 to a uniform definition of NPLs (also called nonperforming exposures or NPEs) across all EU jurisdictions. This significantly strengthened the measurement and comparability of NPLs, even though the application of the EBA's NPL concept may not yet be fully harmonized across all countries and banks.[23]

The comprehensive assessment conducted by the ECB in 2014—before the launch of the Single Supervisory Mechanism (also known as ECB Banking Supervision), which unified banking supervision across all member states of the euro area—already applied the EBA NPL concept (ECB 2014). Comprising an asset quality review and a solvency stress test for 130 significant euro area banks (81.6% of the total euro area balance sheet at the time), the comprehensive assessment identified €135.9 billion of previously unaccounted NPLs across the banks it covered. This was a significant step toward creating transparency in the euro area banking system and strengthening its resilience to adverse developments.

In March 2017, the Single Supervisory Mechanism published its guidance to banks on nonperforming loans (ECB 2017). This document outlines the measures, processes, and best practices banks should incorporate when tackling NPLs and urges banks with high NPL ratios to treat this as a priority. More specifically, the guidance calls on banks to implement realistic and

---

[23]   Any exposure that is at least 90 days past due, or unlikely to be repaid without recourse to collateral, is considered to be nonperforming. Additionally, exposures which have been restructured, or forborne, may be classified as nonperforming subject to common criteria laid down by the EBA. Forborne nonperforming exposures remain classified as such for a cure period of at least 1 year, even if the debtor complies with the new schedule of payments and all the criteria for a loan to be classified as performing.

ambitious strategies to work toward a holistic NPL approach, including areas such as governance and risk management. For instance, banks should ensure that managers are incentivized to carry out NPL reduction strategies. The ECB Banking Supervision did not stipulate quantitative top–down targets to reduce NPLs but asked banks to devise strategies that include internal targets, based on a range of policy options such as NPL workout, servicing, and portfolio sales. In 2018, the ECB Banking Supervision published an addendum to its 2017 guidance document, clarifying supervisory expectations for prudential provisioning of nonperforming exposures. Without prejudice to accounting or Pillar 1 prudential standards, unsecured (secured) exposures are expected to be fully provisioned when older than 2 (7) years. Divergence from these expectations is to be discussed with banks as part of the annual supervisory review and evaluation process and may lead to the adoption of supervisory measures under the Pillar 2 framework. A similar time-bound provisioning requirement was introduced for loans originated after April 2019 in the Pillar 1 framework.

Looking beyond banking supervision, the ECB has published contributions focusing on the secondary market for NPLs, including an analytical framework to look at information asymmetries between potential buyers and sellers (Fell et al. 2016, 2017a), the possible role of national AMCs (Fell et al. 2017b), and securitization schemes (Fell, Moldovan, and O'Brien 2017).

In July 2017, the European Systemic Risk Board, the EU agency in charge of coordinating macroprudential policy across the EU, published a report on resolving NPLs in Europe. The report identifies NPL-related macroprudential policy issues and develops ideas on possible macroprudential responses. Specific areas addressed include incentives for and potential impediments to the resolution of NPLs, policy experiences regarding AMCs, and the conditions of secondary markets for distressed assets in the EU (ESRB 2017).

That was preceded in May 2017 by a report on NPLs from a subgroup of the EU's Financial Services Committee (FSC 2017) which contained a range of policy objectives and recommendations covering supervisory tools, structural reforms relating to insolvency and debt recovery, development of secondary NPL markets, and restructuring of banks and the EU banking sector as a whole.

The range of discussions across EU and euro area bodies and in forums that preceded the publication of these reports helped raise awareness of the "systemic" dimension of the NPL problem in the euro area, in particular in those countries where NPL ratios are relatively low and where the negative repercussions of high NPLs occur mainly through spillover effects. Moreover, these discussions helped to ensure that all relevant parts of European and national administrations, micro and macroprudential supervisors, competition authorities, finance and economics ministries, and so on, were involved. This is crucial for ensuring sufficiently broad-based political support to implement comprehensive solutions to the NPL problem.

The conclusions of the Financial Services Committee report have been endorsed by the Council of EU Finance and Economics Ministers and gave rise to the EU Council Action Plan, published in July 2017.[24] Since then, European institutions and governments have been engaged with follow-up activities such as the development of a blueprint for national AMCs in the EU. In fact, at the time of writing this document, the implementation of the large majority of the measures outlined in the EU Council Action Plan was either completed or well advanced, with the exception of actions related to benchmarking and improving insolvency frameworks.

7.5 Conclusions

The high stock of NPLs in the euro area over the last decade is largely a legacy of the economic and financial crisis as well as the euro area sovereign debt crisis. However, it also exposed long-standing structural weaknesses in euro area countries, including, for instance, their insolvency and debt-recovery regimes. Although the NPL landscape varies considerably across the euro area, NPL problems are a source of concern for the euro area as a whole due to important cross-border spillover channels within and beyond the banking sector. These concerns are particularly relevant in the context of the COVID-19 pandemic.

Significant progress has been made by microprudential supervisors in improving NPL measurement and management by banks. That said, although internal workouts by banks and pressure by micro-supervisors are always necessary, these are unlikely to be sufficient to solve future problems. Comprehensive solutions, making full use of the various NPL resolution options and taking country-specific situations into account, offer the most promising approach. In particular, banking system-wide national AMCs may contribute to swifter reduction of large, systemic NPL stocks in Europe. In addition, other tools, including NPL transaction platforms and securitization schemes, could be usefully deployed.

---

[24] See European Council (2017) and for a recent update on the implementation of the Action Plan of the European Commission (2019b).

The COVID-19 outbreak and the associated recession in the euro area are likely to lead to resurgence of NPLs. This will put the newly developed frameworks to test. It is important to keep in mind that all of these tools can only be successful if they are supported by appropriate legal and administrative framework conditions that facilitate debt enforcement and access to collateral by sound lending standards that prevent the creation of new NPLs beyond a level that is customary and unavoidable in banking and by sound macrofinancial policies promoting economic recovery. Regional cooperation can help raise awareness of the euro-area-wide nature of the NPL problem, in establishing the right framework conditions, and in designing the best-suited instruments to solve it. Last but not least, regional cooperation can also help prevent a re-emergence of the problem.

References

Aiyar, S., W. Bergthaler, J. M. Garrido, A. Ilyina, A. Jobst, K. Kang, D. Kovtun, Y. Liu, D. Monaghan, and M. Moretti. 2015. A Strategy for Resolving Europe's Problem Loans. *Staff Discussion Note SDN/15/19*, International Monetary Fund, Washington, DC.

Akerlof, G. 1970. The Market for 'Lemons': Quality Uncertainty and the Market Mechanism. *Quarterly Journal of Economics*. 84 (3). pp. 488–500.

Balgova, M. N. and A. Plekhanov. 2016. The Economic Impact of Reducing Non-Performing Loans. *Working Paper 193*. London: European Bank for Reconstruction and Development.

Cerruti, C. and R. Neyens. 2016. Public Asset Management Companies: A Toolkit. World Bank Studies. Washington, DC: World Bank.

Constâncio, V. 2017. Resolving Europe's NPL Burden: Challenges and Benefits. Keynote speech at conference on Tackling Europe's Non-Performing Loans Crisis: Restructuring Debt, Reviving Growth. Brussels, 3 February.

Deloitte. 2016. *Deleveraging Europe 2015–2016*. London: Deloitte.

European Central Bank (ECB). 2014. *Aggregate Report on the Comprehensive Assessment*. ECB Banking Supervision, October 2014. Frankfurt: European Central Bank.

———. 2016. *Report on Financial Structures*. October 2016. Frankfurt: European Central Bank.

———. 2017. *Guidance to Banks on Non-Performing Loans*. ECB Banking Supervision, March 2017. Frankfurt: European Central Bank.

———. 2018. *Financial Stability Review May 2018 (Box 7)*. Frankfurt: European Central Bank.

European Commission. 2018. *AMC Blueprint – SWD (2018)72final*. Brussels: European Commission.

———. 2019a. *European Platforms for Non-Performing Loans – SWD (2019)472final*. Brussels: European Commission.

———. 2019b. *Fourth Progress Report on the Reduction of NPLs and Further Risk Reduction in the Banking Sector, COM(2019)278final*. Brussels: European Commission.

European Council. 2017. *Council Conclusions on Action Plan to Tackle Non-Performing Loans in Europe*. Brussels: European Council.

European Systemic Risk Board (ESRB). 2017. *Resolving Non-Performing Loans in Europe*. European Systemic Risk Board, July 2017. Frankfurt: European Central Bank.

Fell, J., M. Grodzicki, R. Martin, and E. O'Brien. 2016. Addressing Market Failures in the Resolution of Loans in the Euro Area. *Financial Stability Review*. European Central Bank. November. pp. 134–146.

———. 2017a. Addressing the Eurozone's 'Lemons' Problem. *Quarterly Journal of Central Banking*. 28 (1). pp. 62–68.

———. 2017b. A Role for Systemic Asset Management Companies in Solving Europe's Non-Performing Loan Problems. *European Economy—Banks, Regulation, and the Real Sector*. Rome.

Fell, J., M. Grodzicki, D. Krušec, R. Martin, and E. O'Brien. 2017. Overcoming Non-Performing Loan Market Failures with Transaction Platforms. *Financial Stability Review*. European Central Bank. November. pp. 130–144.

Fell, J., C. Moldovan, and E. O'Brien. 2017. Resolving Large Stocks of NPLs: A Role for Securitisation and Other Financial Structures? Special Feature in *Financial Stability Review*. ECB. May 2017. Frankfurt: European Central Bank.

Financial Services Committee (FSC). 2017. *Report of the FSC Subgroup on Non-Performing Loans*. Council of the European Union, Financial Services Committee, May 2017. Brussels: European Union.

Goretti, M. and M. Souto. 2013. Macro-Financial Implications of Corporate (De)leveraging in the Euro Area Periphery. *IMF Working Paper 13/154*. Washington, DC: International Monetary Fund.

He, D. 2004. The Role of KAMCO in Resolving Nonperforming Loans in the Republic of Korea. *IMF Working Paper 04/172*. Washington, DC: International Monetary Fund.

Huljak, I., R. Martin, and D. Moccero. 2019. The Cost Efficiency and Productivity Growth of Euro Area Banks. *ECB Working Paper*. No. 2305. Frankfurt: European Central Bank.

Jonung, L. 2009. The Swedish Model for Resolving the Banking Crisis of 1991–93. Seven Reasons Why It Was Successful. *Economic Papers 360*. Brussels: European Commission.

KPMG. 2016. *European Debt Sales Report*. Amstelveen, Netherlands: KPMG International Cooperative.

Medina Cas, S. and I. Peresa. 2016. What Makes a Good 'Bad Bank'? The Irish, Spanish and German Experience. *European Economy Discussion Paper 036*. Brussels: European Commission.

Nkusu, M. 2011. Non-Performing Loans and Macrofinancial Vulnerabilities in Advanced Economies. *IMF Working Paper*. 11/161. Washington, DC: International Monetary Fund.

O'Brien, E. and T. Wezel. 2013. Asset Support Schemes in the Euro Area. *Financial Stability Review*. 1 (May). pp. 112–120. Frankfurt: European Central Bank.

8 Strategies for Developing Asia's Nonperforming Loan Markets and Resolution Mechanisms

Junkyu Lee, Cyn-Young Park, Daekeun Park, and Peter Rosenkranz

8.1 Introduction

A buildup of nonperforming loans (NPLs) poses a risk to banks' balance sheet health and financial soundness. NPLs reduce interest income, lower profitability, and deplete banks' capital bases. They also require higher risk weights and minimum loss coverage in banks' capital requirements, straining liquidity and increasing funding costs. With less money available to extend new loans, banks' capacity to lend and make profits is further constrained. NPLs also have negative impacts on bank management as their resolution takes time and effort which could be better utilized on core business. In addition, NPLs may cause banks to lose business relationships with customers.

Unresolved NPLs not only inflict direct damage on banking systems, but also eventually cast long shadows on entire economies by keeping banks from adequately performing the role of financial intermediaries, slowing overall economic activity. The adverse effects of NPLs on overall macroeconomic activities are well established in theoretical models and empirical regularities. A broad spectrum of theoretical and empirical studies offers a good background for the interactions between NPLs and the macroeconomic performance of an economy through the role of financial intermediation.

The economic literature investigating the role of financial intermediation in macroeconomic outcomes has increased significantly in the past several decades. Some theoretical models have focused on the amplifying effects of financial institutions and markets on broader economic activity and business cycles when a real or financial shock affects access to finance. Bernanke, Gertler, and Gilchrist (1996) coin the term "financial accelerator," building on the pioneering work of Bernanke (1981, 1983) and Bernanke and Gertler (1989). A variety of the financial accelerator models offer a theoretical basis to explain the link between the financial system and the real economy. For example, asymmetric information and financial market imperfection can amplify and propagate a shock to affect broad economic conditions through sudden changes in credit market conditions and limit firms' access to finance. The financial accelerator literature further developed in Bernanke, Gertler, and Gilchrist (1999) and Kiyotaki and Moore (1997) provides one of the most prominent theoretical frameworks for thinking about the macrofinancial linkages of NPLs.

Empirical studies also confirm adverse macrofinancial feedback effects of NPLs. The magnitude differs depending on the sample group of countries and the sample period. However, these studies demonstrate that an increase in NPL ratios generates a strong, albeit short-lived negative response in economic activities such as output growth, employment, and credit growth (Espinoza and Prasad 2010, Nkusu 2011, De Bock and Demyanets 2012, Klein 2013, Lee and Rosenkranz 2019). In that vein, Chapter 4 also discusses the negative impact of NPLs on bank lending and macroeconomic conditions in 12 euro area countries.

More than anything else, a large and sustained buildup of NPLs may signal the specter of a banking crisis that could develop into a nationwide financial crisis, levying a heavy toll on the entire economy. Moreover, such a crisis is likely to spread across borders as impacts spill into broader economies given closer connections through international banking and financial activities.

Noting the key role that NPLs play in financial crises, Caprio and Klingebiel (1996), Drees and Pazarbasioglu (1998), and Kaminsky and Reinhart (1999) suggest a large increase in NPLs as a signal that might directly or indirectly help predict financial crises. A credit crunch that accompanies a financial crisis often exerts disproportionately large influence on small and medium-sized enterprises (SMEs), households, and infrastructure financing, hindering inclusive growth.

Once NPLs occur, they can be resolved by internal workout efforts of banks, including debt collection, debt restructuring, and debt write-off. NPL markets provide banks with additional means of resolving NPLs by enabling them to remove NPLs from loan portfolios through direct sale to NPL investors or through securitization. NPL markets and NPL resolution frameworks enable banks to sustain financial soundness and to adequately perform their role of financial intermediation. They serve as financial stabilizers and crisis management tools, and contribute to financial development, which justifies the adoption of strategies to develop NPL markets nationally.

Developing NPL markets and NPL resolution frameworks, in addition, can help strengthen international financial safety nets. Since the economies in Asia and the Pacific depend heavily on US-dollar-denominated funding and depend on banks as the major channel for such funding, the interplay between NPLs and their macrofinancial impacts are important in the cross-border spillover of financial instability. On one hand, a large buildup of NPLs in a banking system raises the possibility of a currency crisis as international investors withdraw their investment from banks for fear of bankruptcy. On the other, a sharp currency depreciation is likely to deteriorate the quality of banks' assets and eventually lead to a banking crisis. Besides, as demonstrated by ADB (2017), the cross-border linkage of Asian financial markets has grown within the region and around the globe. This leaves Asian financial markets more vulnerable to cross-border spillover of financial shocks and means that the region's policy makers should pay attention to the bank balance sheet channel of cross-border contagion.

As the experience of the Asian financial and the global financial crises highlighted the importance of an international financial safety net for emerging economies in coping with currency and financial crises, emerging economies in Asia have built up theirs. Nationally, they enlarged foreign reserve holdings, while introducing and strengthening macroprudential regulations on financial institutions. Regionally, they have also built up financial safety nets, as exemplified by the Chiang Mai Initiative Multilateralization and the Asian Bond Market Initiative. The latter intends to reduce dependence on bank loans and foreign-currency-denominated external liabilities by fostering markets for local-currency-denominated bonds. Introducing NPL resolution frameworks and developing NPL markets can help strengthen Asia's international financial safety nets by complementing these existing measures.

There is no doubt that developing NPL markets and NPL resolution frameworks will be beneficial in Asia and the Pacific. This is because banks that are the key source of financing in most of the region already hold a large amount of legacy NPLs and are likely to be an important channel of cross-border spillover of financial crises. NPL markets and NPL resolution mechanisms will allow economies to enhance financial stability, manage financial crises, and promote financial development.

Yet, NPL markets are not well developed or do not even exist in some countries in Asia and the Pacific. And even where they do, they are not liquid enough to be of significant help in resolving NPLs. In Europe, too, NPL markets are not well developed even though financial markets and financial industries are well advanced, and NPL resolution after the global financial crisis has been slow and heterogeneous. As Fell et al. (2018) point out, this weighed heavily on bank profitability and ability to make new loans.

These observations demonstrate the inherent difficulties of developing NPL markets. Factors including information asymmetry, tax and accounting impediments, and inefficiency in debt and collateral enforcement hinder their development, and will continue to do so until development strategies are carefully designed to remove these fundamental impediments.

Although many of these strategies can be devised nationally, regional strategies are also needed. One reason for this is the systemic importance of foreign banks and regional banks engaged in cross-border banking activities. A more important reason arises from the negative externalities of financial crises. As the financial interconnectedness in the region deepens, it is more likely that a financial crisis in one economy will spill over to others. Regional strategies and frameworks for NPL resolution are needed to handle these negative externalities. In this regard, regional frameworks for NPL resolution serve as regional public goods.

This chapter suggests strategies to build NPL resolution frameworks and develop NPL markets in Asia based upon the experience of Asian economies to foster NPL markets. Section 8.2 assesses the status of NPLs and NPL markets in Asia, showing that those markets and NPL resolution mechanisms remain inadequate despite persistently high NPL ratios in some economies. Section 8.3 discusses structural impediments due to demand, supply, and institutional factors that hinder the development of NPL markets. Section 8.4 draws lessons from cases of developing NPL markets in Asia, and section 8.5 suggests strategies to develop NPL markets and NPL resolution frameworks based on findings. Section 8.6 concludes.

8.2 Nonperforming Loan Markets in Asia and the Pacific

8.2.1 Nonperforming Loan Ratios

Economies in the region display a wide range of NPL ratios (Table 8.1), low in some and high and rising in others. NPL ratios are persistently high in economies in Central and West Asia and in South Asia. The 2019 figures in Table 8.1 were collected from the International Monetary Fund (IMF) or official sources. However, it is likely that in some economies, these official figures understate the true nature of their NPL problems. Lack of capital to support NPL provisioning and weak supervision are creating incentives for banks to hide NPLs using practices including manipulation of loan classification and "ever-greening,"[1] among others. As such, independent estimates adjusted for differences in loan classification report much higher numbers than those in Table 8.1.

Table 8.1: NPL Ratios in Asia and the Pacific

Economy	2019	2015	Economy	2019	2015
Below 5%			**5% to below 10%**		
New Zealand	0.5	0.6	Armenia	5.4	7.9
Hong Kong, China	0.6	0.7	Kyrgyz Republic	8.1	7.1
Korea, Republic of	0.9	0.6	Kazakhstan	8.6	8.0
Australia	1.0	1.0	Pakistan	8.8	11.4
Japan	1.1	1.6	India	8.9	5.9
Singapore	1.4	0.9	Maldives	9.6	14.1
Uzbekistan	1.5	0.4	**Above 10%**		
Malaysia	1.6	1.6	Azerbaijan	10.1	4.9
Viet Nam	1.8	2.9	Bhutan	10.9	11.9
PRC	1.8	1.5	Bangladesh	11.5	9.3
Cambodia	2.1	1.6	Afghanistan	12.7	12.3
Philippines	2.1	1.9	Tajikistan	31.5	19.1
Georgia	2.6	2.7			
Thailand	3.1	2.7			
Fiji	3.5	1.8			
Samoa	3.9	5.3			
Brunei Darussalam	4.1	0.4			
Sri Lanka	4.8	3.2			

NPL = nonperforming loan, PRC = People's Republic of China.
Note: All of the 2019 figures as of September 2019, except for Armenia, Cambodia, the PRC, Fiji, Samoa, Thailand, and Uzbekistan (as of June 2019), and Bhutan, Japan, and Kazakhstan (as of March 2019). Figures for New Zealand and Viet Nam are as of December 2018.
Sources: All of the 2015 figures are from World Development Indicators. Most of the 2019 figures are from the International Monetary Fund (IMF) Financial Soundness Indicators; Azerbaijan: Central Bank of the Republic of Azerbaijan, Statistics. Monetary Indicator, Sectoral Breakdown of Loans. Table 2.8.; Republic of Korea: Financial Supervisory Service. Financial Statistics Information System; New Zealand: 2019 Article IV Consultation – Press Release and Staff Report. IMF Country Report. No. 19/303. Washington, DC; Tajikistan: National Bank of Tajikistan. Financial Soundness Indicators.

---

[1] "Ever-greening" is a practice in which a bank defers the losses that are associated with an NPL by rolling the loan over and keeping it classified as performing.

In the historical trend of NPL ratios for the eight economies in Asia in Figure 8.1, two spikes are evident: one during the Asian financial crisis and one after the global financial crisis. Since the Asian financial crisis of 1997–1998, NPL ratios have been trending downward in most of these economies. Improvement in banks' asset quality in the region can be attributed to stronger growth in nominal income and credit as well as supervisory efforts to improve banks' credit risk management and underwriting practices. In most emerging Asian economies, however, NPL ratios spiked during and/or after the global financial crisis.

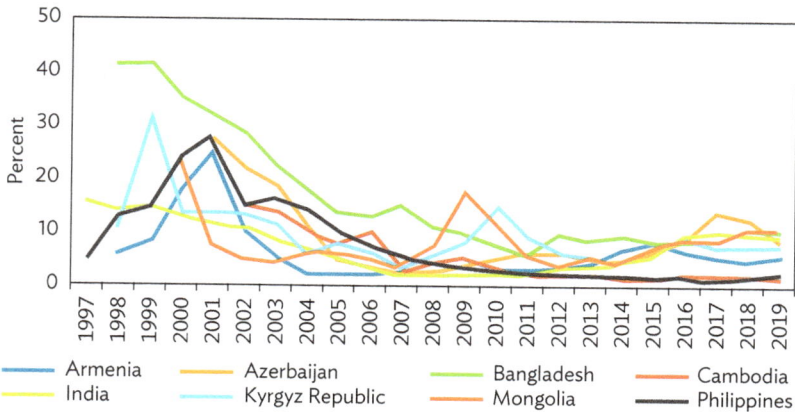

Figure 8.1: NPL Ratios of Selected Asian Countries

NPL= nonperforming loan.
Note: All figures in 2019 are based on September data, except for Armenia, Cambodia, and Mongolia.
Sources: International Monetary Fund (IMF) Financial Soundness Indicators; World Bank Development Knowledge Open Data; and IMF Country Report. Azerbaijan: Central Bank of the Republic of Azerbaijan, Statistics. Monetary Indicator, Sectoral Breakdown of Loans, Table 2.8.; Bangladesh's figures from 2008 through 2010: Bangladesh Bank. Annual Report for 2009–2010, Table 5.3; and for 2010–2011, Appendix 4; Kyrgyz Republic figures from 1999 through 2009: National Bank of the Kyrgyz Republic. Historical Data from 1993 to 2007, Table 4.3.4., and Statistical Bulletin for 2017. Table 4.3; Mongolia: Staff Calculations based on data from Bank of Mongolia. Banks Outstanding Loan Report.

The coronavirus disease (COVID-19) pandemic raises the specter of a global debt crisis. A pandemic-induced economic slowdown implies lower corporate earnings and greater debt servicing burdens on companies, leading to increasing defaults, loss of investor confidence, and potentially widespread credit crunch. With the economic slowdown due to the COVID-19 outbreak, concerns are rising that a considerable number of corporate borrowers could default on their loans, setting off chain reactions in global financial systems.

Developing countries are often vulnerable to a global credit crunch. Countries with large current account deficits, high external debt, and low international reserves typically face financing problems during a global credit crunch. With the prolonged global trade tensions, many Asian economies have experienced a squeeze in their current account surpluses, while some endured the deficits. The external debt-to-GDP ratio for developing Asia was at 33% in 2018, only slightly lower than 34% during the global financial crisis.

As considerable global headwinds continue to exert downward pressure on the region's economic growth—particularly exacerbated by the recent COVID-19 outbreak—NPL ratios in many Asian economies in recent years have begun a trend reversal. Since 2013, NPLs—in level and as a percentage of total amount of loans—have been picking up in many economies, particularly Cambodia, India, and Kazakhstan. Moreover, NPL ratios in 2019 were more than 5% in countries including Bangladesh, India, and Kazakhstan. As jittery market sentiments and a stronger US dollar have accelerated capital outflows from emerging market economies, there are concerns that the NPL problem in these economies will worsen.

NPL ratios in Indonesia, Malaysia, the Republic of Korea, and Thailand, the four Asian economies at the center of the Asian financial crisis, have decreased substantially over the past two decades (Figure 8.2). All of these countries relied on public asset management companies (AMCs) to remove NPLs from banks. The success of these countries in managing NPLs, however, cannot be ascribed to the establishment of public AMCs alone (Chapter 5). Accompanying measures were legal and institutional arrangements designed to help AMCs and banks resolve NPLs as well as NPL resolution measures such as securitization and corporate restructuring.

Figure 8.2: NPL Ratios of Asian Countries with Public Asset Management Companies

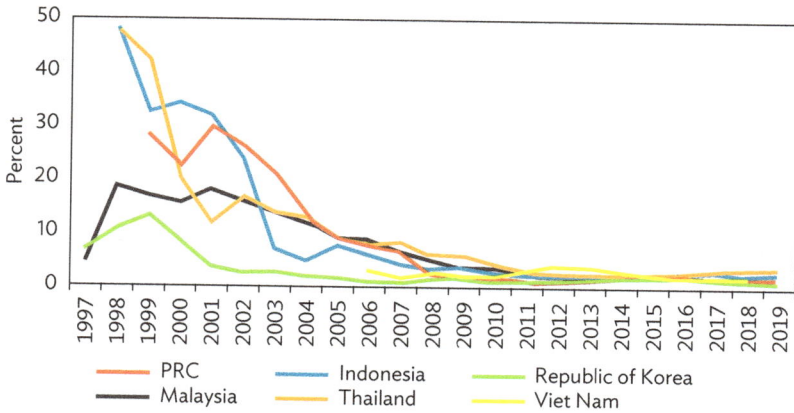

NPL = nonperforming loan, PRC = People's Republic of China.
Note: Figures for Indonesia, Malaysia, and the Republic of Korea in 2019 are based on September data and for the PRC and Thailand on June data. No 2019 data are available for Viet Nam.
Sources: International Monetary Fund (IMF) Financial Soundness Indicators; World Bank Development Knowledge Open Data; and IMF Country Report. Korea: Financial Supervisory Service. Financial Statistics Information System; Thailand's figures from 1998 through 2005: Bank of Thailand. Financial Soundness Indicators. 1998–2018.

8.2.2 Nonperforming Loan Markets and Resolution Frameworks in Asia

NPL markets in which banks can dispose of NPLs are yet to be developed in Asia. Only a few economies in the region have NPL markets in which financial institutions and NPL investors trade NPLs and other distressed assets. In these economies, diverse tools of NPL resolution are also available. In many economies in Asia, however, NPL markets do not exist at all. Even when they exist, they are illiquid and resolution of distressed assets then must rely on global NPL investors who are willing to participate in local NPL markets only at a discount so large that it could be called a fire sale.

No public data is available to show and compare the size of NPL markets in Asian economies in consistent quantitative measures. This chapter presents qualitative measures that give rough estimates of NPL market developments in Asia. Table 8.2 describes some of the AMCs operational in Asian countries. In most of these countries, AMCs were first introduced as a public entity, such as in the four Asian countries directly hit by the Asian financial crisis that established public AMCs to restructure their banking sectors. Some of these public AMCs then ceased to operate as required by sunset clauses. Later, the People's Republic of China (PRC) introduced four public AMCs to deal with NPLs in its four largest state-owned commercial banks. Table 8.2 also demonstrates that private AMCs operate, especially in countries that introduced public AMCs earlier. The Republic of Korea and Thailand are good examples. The public AMCs, together with government efforts to create an enabling legal and regulatory environment for these public AMCs, laid the ground for the development of NPL markets and the emergence of private AMCs.

Table 8.2: Asset Management Companies in Asian Economies

Economy	Asset Management Companies
China, People's Republic of	Four public asset management companies (AMCs) for each of the four largest state-owned commercial banks—China Great Wall Asset Management (for the Agricultural Bank of China); China Orient Asset Management (for the Bank of China); China Huarong Asset Management (for the Industrial and Commercial Bank of China); and China Cinda Asset Management (for the China Construction Bank)—and many local and provincial AMCs are in operation.
Indonesia	After dissolution of Indonesian Bank Restructuring Agency (IBRA), PT Perusahaan Pengelola Aset was established as a state-owned AMC in charge of managing the assets of IBRA, restructuring state-owned enterprises and managing state-owned assets. Indonesian banks rely on private, in-house methods. Foreign banks establish asset management units as nonperforming loan (NPL) warehousing entities.
Japan	Private AMCs as well as public AMCs (Resolution and Collection Corporation and Industrial Revitalization Corporation of Japan) were established to purchase NPLs.
Kazakhstan	Fund of Problem Loans (a public AMC) and OUSAs[a] (private AMCs) are in operation.
Malaysia	After the closure of Danaharta in 2005, private AMCs and debt collection agencies became NPL market players.
Philippines	Privately owned special purpose vehicles and global (multinational) AMCs like Collectius are used to deal with NPLs.
Korea, Republic of	Korea Asset Management Corporation and private AMCs (United Asset Management Corporation, Daishin F&I, etc.) are major NPL market players.
Thailand	Four public AMCs removed NPLs from state-owned commercial banks and Thai Asset Management Corporation (TAMC) acquired NPLs from distressed financial institutions. After TAMC's last acquisition in 2003, Bangkok Commercial Asset Management Company and Sukhumvit Asset Management Company Ltd dominate the NPL market together with small private AMCs.
Viet Nam	Vietnam Asset Management Company purchases NPLs from banks but its NPL resolution function is limited. The Debt and Asset Trading Corporation is in charge of restructuring state-owned enterprises. Bank AMCs and private debt trading companies also participate in the NPL market.

[a] In accordance with Article 11 of the Law of the Republic of Kazakhstan on Banks and Banking Activities, commercial banks may acquire approval from the National Bank of Kazakhstan to establish and operate a subsidiary called OUSA as the sole investor for prompt resolution of NPLs in their possession.
Source: Authors' compilation.

Table 8.3 presents the insolvency resolution framework for some Asian countries, which for many are comparable to international standards. The actual problem, however, may lie with inefficiencies in the judicial system that delay insolvency resolution, thereby increasing the cost of resolving insolvency, as will be discussed later. Table 8.3 also demonstrates that out-of-court corporate reorganization frameworks are available only in a few countries including Japan, Malaysia, the Republic of Korea, and Thailand. Out-of-court corporate reorganization frameworks make it possible to achieve corporate restructuring without going through a lengthy court process.

Table 8.3: Insolvency Resolution Frameworks in Selected Asian Countries

Economy	Insolvency Resolution Framework
Brunei Darussalam	Insolvency Order introduced the Company Voluntary Arrangement, a debtor rehabilitation scheme.
Cambodia	Insolvency Law, a modern framework but hampered by ineffective implementation and an underdeveloped judicial framework.
PRC	Enterprise Bankruptcy Law allows two insolvency proceedings: bankruptcy and rehabilitation. Specialized bankruptcy courts allow a sufficiently trained judiciary to resolve insolvency proceedings efficiently.
Indonesia	The Bankruptcy Law provides two procedures: a debt restructuring procedure through suspension of payment and a bankruptcy procedure.
Japan	Court supervised insolvency mechanisms consist of bankruptcy and corporate reorganization. Out-of-court workout procedures also exist.
Lao PDR	No separate liquidation or rehabilitation proceeding. Upon the company or creditor's petition, the court will convene the creditor meeting, which will ultimately decide if the company will be rehabilitated, liquidated, or sold to prospective investors.
Malaysia	The Companies Act introduced Judicial Management, a formal restructuring facility and Corporate Voluntary Arrangement, a pre-insolvency mechanism.
Republic of Korea	Two corporate rehabilitation programs are available, the Debtor Rehabilitation and Bankruptcy Act rehabilitation proceeding and the Corporate Restructuring Promotion Act workout program, an out-of-court proceeding.
Thailand	In the early days of reform, due to inexperience and inefficiencies in the judicial system, most creditors relied on debt restructuring frameworks formed through the Corporate Debt Restructuring Committee. The Bankruptcy Act has two court insolvency proceedings: business reorganization and business liquidation.
Viet Nam	Unlike other Asian insolvency laws, the Law on Bankruptcy has only one general procedure, which can branch out to either restructuring or liquidation.

ASEAN = Association of Southeast Asian Nations, PRC = People's Republic of China, Lao PDR = Lao People's Democratic Republic.
Source: Lee and Rosenkranz (2018).

Table 8.4, meanwhile, shows that in Bangladesh, Cambodia, Mongolia, and Viet Nam, it takes 4 years or more to resolve insolvency through the court process. Two years ago, India would have belonged to this group, but time and cost of resolving insolvency have been reduced dramatically through reform of the insolvency law and framework. The table also demonstrates that recovery rates are very low in many Asian economies. Longer insolvency resolution and lower recovery rates translate into higher costs of debt and collateral enforcement. This high cost of debt enforcement makes it difficult for financial institutions to resolve NPLs and for those economies to develop NPL markets, because NPL investment is unprofitable for NPL investors.

Table 8.4: Time and Cost of Resolving Insolvency in Asian Economies

Economy	Time (years)	Recovery Rate (cents on the US dollar)	Cost of Recovery (% of estate)
Afghanistan	2.0	26.7	25.0
Armenia	1.9	39.2	11.0
Azerbaijan	1.5	39.7	12.0
Bangladesh	4.0	29.1	8.0
Brunei Darussalam	2.5	47.2	3.5
Cambodia	6.0	14.6	18.0
China, People's Republic of	1.7	36.9	22.0
Hong Kong, China	0.8	87.2	5.0
India	1.6	71.6	9.0
Indonesia	1.1	65.5	21.6
Japan	0.6	92.1	4.2
Kazakhstan	1.5	39.8	15.0
Korea, Republic of	1.5	84.3	3.5
Kyrgyz Republic	1.5	40.6	9.5
Malaysia	1.0	81.0	10.0
Maldives	1.5	50.2	4.0
Mongolia	4.0	18.2	15.0
Pakistan	2.6	42.8	4.0
Philippines	2.7	21.1	32.0
Singapore	0.8	88.7	4.0
Sri Lanka	1.7	43.0	10.0
Tajikistan	1.7	29.6	17.0
Thailand	1.5	70.1	18.0
Uzbekistan	2.0	34.4	10.0
Viet Nam	5.0	21.3	14.5

Source: World Bank Doing Business 2020 Database.

8.3 Impediments to Nonperforming Loan Market Development

As noted, Asia and the Pacific is not the only region where active NPL markets have failed to emerge. In Europe, where financial markets and financial industries are more developed, NPL markets are also not fully developed and efficient (Chapters 6 and 7). This suggests that demand-side and supply-side impediments as well as structural problems often inhibit proper functioning of NPL markets and NPL resolution frameworks.

8.3.1 Demand-Side Factors of Market Failure

Fell et al. (2016), discussing why secondary markets for NPLs are not active in Europe, point out that the low volume of NPL transactions despite heavy buildup of NPLs in European banks and wide bid-ask spread are indicative of typical market failure. They argue that all of the three fundamental sources of market failure, information asymmetry, lack of competition, and insufficient control, are applicable to European NPL markets. First of all, NPL markets are characterized by information asymmetries in that banks have an information advantage over investors about the quality of NPLs and collaterals. This causes a large gap between the prices that investors are willing to pay for NPLs and the prices that banks are willing to accept. Second, barriers to entry arising from institutional factors, such as licensing requirements as well as from established capacity to value NPLs, make NPL markets dominated by a few large investors, giving them the characteristics of oligopsony. Third, investors in NPLs may have to compete with other creditors if multiple creditors extended loans to the same debtor. It is likely that all of these three sources of market failure apply to economies in Asia and the Pacific region as well. Many of these economies do not have active NPL markets despite a large buildup of NPLs on the balance sheet of their banks.

8.3.2 Supply Factors

The reluctance of banks to dispose of NPLs from their balance sheets also hinders development of active NPL markets by limiting the supply of NPLs to the market. A steady supply is essential for developing NPL markets in that domestic NPL investors need business volume during normal times as well as during financial crises. A few reasons may explain why banks are reluctant to sell their NPLs. First, large bid-ask spreads typical of NPL markets imply that banks are likely to realize a loss when they dispose of NPLs through the market, which hurts capital adequacy ratios and the evaluation of the incumbent management (Fell et al. 2016; Ciavoliello et al. 2016). Instead of realizing a loss, banks would rather hold or to their NPLs and wait for a possible recovery in asset prices. Banks are also afraid of the stigma associated with NPL sales.

Second, in Europe, accounting standards or regulations that do not allow the cost of debt recovery to be fully recognized in the book value of NPLs may create a large discrepancy between the economic value and the book value of NPLs. This in turn creates disincentives to increase the supply of NPLs, which will be stronger in countries where the cost of debt recovery is significant due to an inefficient legal system for debt and collateral enforcement. In some Asian countries, the cost of debt recovery could be significant, as it takes several years to enforce a claim through the judicial system.

Third, legal and regulatory restrictions on loan sales may further hinder the market supply of NPLs. For example, in 2012, the Indonesian Constitutional Court issued a ruling prohibiting state banks (but not private banks) from restructuring or selling NPLs at a discount. This represented a significant challenge to NPL resolution in the banking industry, where the main overhang of NPLs was within state banks. Until 2015, the Vietnamese AMCs were prohibited from selling NPLs at a price lower than their book value, making it difficult for secondary markets for NPLs to appear.

8.3.3 Structural Factors: Legal and Institutional Elements

Structural factors such as inefficiency in debt and collateral enforcement may also impede the development of NPL markets. In some countries, the legal procedure needed to enforce debt and collateral may take too long and costs too much, increasing debt recovery cost. In some cases, it is not the insolvency law but the capacity of the judicial system that is responsible for inefficiency in debt and collateral enforcement. For example, the World Bank's Doing Business 2015 report states that Cambodia's Insolvency Law is a modern framework comparable to international standards but resolving insolvency in Cambodia has been hampered by ineffective implementation and an underdeveloped judicial framework. The insolvency process is criticized for lacking judicial experience as well as established precedents.

Faced with high legal cost and uncertainty, investors with limited information would use a much higher discount rate in evaluating the value of NPLs, creating a wider bid-ask spread. Adopting the same framework as in Fell et al. (2016), Figure 8.3 illustrates three key sources of the bid-ask spread arising from inefficiency in debt enforcement. The gray segment of the bars represents the reported average cost of enforcing claims through individual legal systems, the yellow segment represents the net present value (NPV) loss from the bank perspective arising from delays in debt recovery, and the blue segment represents the additional NPV loss from the investor perspective. The NPV loss from the bank perspective is computed using the average bank lending rate of each economy in 2019 as the discount rate. The NPV loss from the investor perspective is computed using a discount rate of 25%, assumed to represent the premium required by investors for the risk of acquiring NPLs.[2] The blue segment is the difference between the NPV loss from the investor perspective and that from the bank perspective.

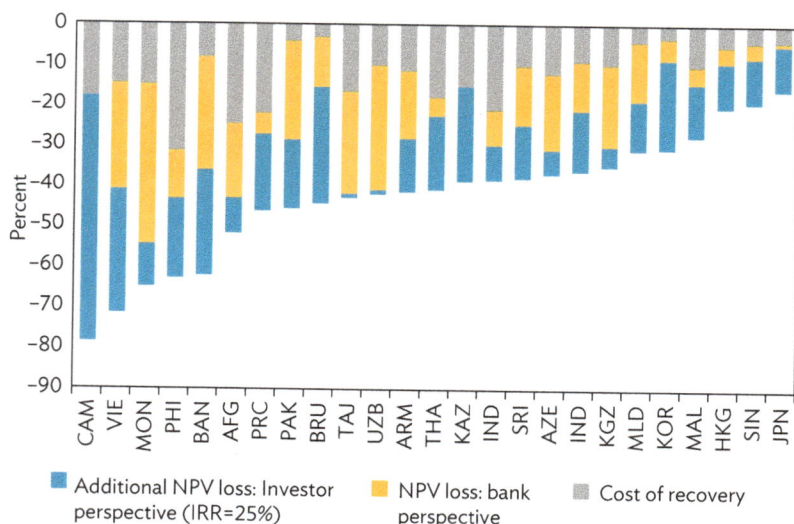

Figure 8.3: Bid-Ask Spreads Caused by Inefficient Insolvency Framework

■ Additional NPV loss: Investor perspective (IRR=25%)   ■ NPV loss: bank perspective   ▨ Cost of recovery

AFG = Afghanistan; ARM = Armenia; AZE = Azerbaijan; BAN = Bangladesh; BRU = Brunei Darussalam; CAM = Cambodia; HKG = Hong Kong, China; IND = India; INO = Indonesia; IRR = internal rate of return; JPN = Japan; KAZ = Kazakhstan; KOR = Republic of Korea; KGZ = Kyrgyz Republic; MAL = Malaysia; MLD = Maldives; MON = Mongolia; NPV = net present value; PAK = Pakistan; PHI = Philippines; PRC = People's Republic of China; SIN = Singapore; SRI = Sri Lanka; TAJ = Tajikistan; THA = Thailand; UZB = Uzbekistan; VIE = Viet Nam.
Note: For Cambodia and Kazakhstan, only the total NPV loss is reported without being separated between bank perspective and investor perspective. The bank lending rate data is not available in these economies.
Source: Authors' calculations based on data from World Bank Doing Business 2020.

---

[2]   Based on available anecdotal evidence, Ciavoliello et al. (2016) suggest using an internal rate of return (IRR) between 15% and 25%. Since the average bank lending rate exceeds 20% in some Asian economies, an IRR of 25% is adopted. Using a higher IRR increases the net present value loss.

Under the assumption of a discount rate of 25%, the bid-ask spread is likely to exceed 30% in 21 of these 25 economies.[3] In six economies, the spread exceeds 50%. Inefficiency in debt and collateral enforcement not only deters potential investors from participating in NPL markets, but also makes it difficult for AMCs to resolve the NPLs they acquire from banks. It is because AMCs, like other potential investors in NPLs, will be facing longer resolution times and higher costs. This will certainly deter the emergence of private AMCs. Even if governments establish public AMCs, in the absence of a special legal framework for efficient debt enforcement, these are likely to end up as NPL warehouses as they would likely be unable to find investors to purchase NPLs.[4]

Legal uncertainty about the transferability of NPLs and collateralized properties also deters the development of NPL markets. For example, in the PRC, NPL transactions can be ruled invalid on various grounds, including the existence of a broad "pub ic interest." And local governments in the PRC retain the first right of refusal in selling NPLs out of AMCs. Foreign NPL investors are required to obtain the consent of the National Development and Reform Commission, in a process that can take up to 3 months or more. In Viet Nam, legal uncertainty about registration of property ownership for foreigners makes foreign NPL investors reluctant to acquire NPLs to which real properties are attached as collateral. In Mongolia, a large portion of NPLs in the mining sector are collateralized by mining licenses, but Mongolian banks find it difficult to recover NPLs by disposing of mining licenses because of the regulation that allows acquisition of mining licenses by qualified firms only.

8.3.4 Sector-specific Factors and Unfavorable Macrofinancial Conditions

Sector-specific factors may also contribute to increases in NPLs and negatively affect their resolution. The concentration of NPLs in a specific sector may make it difficult to recover NPLs through the disposal of collateral. Since collateral in real estate sector loans is mostly property, the concentration of NPLs in the real estate sector makes it difficult to recover NPLs by disposing of collateral because such attempts by banks will put

---

[3] Even with the modest discount rate of 15%, the bid-ask spread is likely to exceed 30% in 15 of these 25 economies.

[4] For the National Asset Management Agency in Ireland, for example, a strong legal mandate with an objective of rapid enforcement put it in a position to quickly sell assets, not loans.

further downward pressure on property prices.[5] In Mongolia, NPLs have been concentrated in the mining sector as the bust in global commodity prices depressed the mining industry. Collateral for NPLs of mining companies includes heavy machinery and mining licenses. Heavy mining machinery, however, is specialized for mining use only and given that the sector was depressed in general, banks found it difficult to dispose of mining equipment.

Unfavorable macrofinancial conditions and the failure of macroeconomic and financial market policies to achieve economic stability and deliver plausible economic prospects may also delay NPL resolution and deter NPL market development. This is because macrofinancial conditions can have a direct impact on future cash flows from NPLs, both from the operations of the borrower and from the sale of collateral. Thus, policies that stabilize the economy and deliver plausible economic prospects will help secondary NPL market development and functioning. This positive impact can accrue not only through increases in asset values and economic expansion, but also through reduced uncertainty.

8.4 Case Studies of Developing Nonperforming Loan Markets in Asia

Despite impediments to developing NPL markets, some countries in Asia tried to build NPL resolution frameworks and develop NPL markets. Most of these attempts were motivated by the need to have their banks restructured in the middle of a banking crisis. This section discusses a few country cases of developing NPL markets and NPL resolution frameworks. The case study begins with the four Asian countries directly hit by the Asian financial crisis. This will be followed by the cases of three other Asian countries, the PRC, Viet Nam, and Kazakhstan. These countries were not directly hit by the Asian financial crisis but tried to introduce NPL resolution frameworks and develop NPL markets to deal with their own banking problems.

8.4.1 Countries Directly Hit by the Asian Financial Crisis

The banks in the four Asian countries hit directly by the Asian financial crisis—Indonesia, Malaysia, the Republic of Korea, and Thailand—were suffering from rapidly ballooning NPLs and rapidly depleting foreign exchange reserves and had difficulties in resolving NPLs in the absence of

---

[5] In this case, a public AMC might be an appropriate policy response, to act as a warehouse of property related loans, which can be hoarded and released to the market at the appropriate time.

NPL markets. In response, these countries introduced and strengthened their NPL resolution frameworks to have their banking sectors restructured. Developing NPL resolution frameworks was part of the holistic approach to restructure the banking sector, which also included mergers and acquisitions, purchase and assumption, and bank recapitalization. AMCs were one of the main pillars of the NPL resolution framework in these countries (Chapters 2 and 5). All of these countries established centralized public AMCs to remove NPLs and other distressed assets from the balance sheets of the banking sector.

In addition to establishing public AMCs, these countries took measures to improve the legal and institutional environment for NPL resolution with a view to facilitating AMCs' operations, including in acquisition and disposal of NPLs. The adoption of these measures was motivated by the necessity to promptly remove massive amounts of NPLs from financial institutions with limited public funding. To achieve this goal while minimizing taxpayers' burden, AMCs had to promptly recover as much value as possible from the NPLs they acquired. The measures to provide AMCs with an enabling environment for NPL resolution included introducing legal and regulatory frameworks to strengthen bank supervision, introducing and revising legislation on insolvency, embarking on judicial reforms to improve the efficiency of court-driven debt enforcement processes, and introducing out-of-court corporate restructuring mechanisms.

For instance, Malaysia undertook legal and judicial reforms to enhance efficiency in court-driven insolvency process. The Bankruptcy Law and the Foreclosure Law were amended a few times between 1988 and 2000. Judicial reforms included the introduction of a pretrial case management scheme intended to reduce unnecessary delay in court processes and the creation of new commercial courts and new civil courts to reduce the backlog of insolvency cases. In addition, the Thai government established the Corporate Debt Restructuring Committee to assist financial institutions with out-of-court corporate restructuring. A framework was established that provided regulatory and tax inducements to contractually bind debtors and creditors. Indonesia also amended the Bankruptcy Law to promote prompt and fair resolution of commercial disputes and to provide a framework to encourage out-of-court debt settlements. To facilitate the rapid disposal of NPLs, the Republic of Korea government adopted diverse NPL resolution measures, namely asset-backed securities and corporate restructuring vehicles. Legal foundations for these new measures were established and tax benefits were introduced to provide tools with tax neutrality.

It turned out that not only were AMCs helpful in resolving NPLs of the banking sector, but the legal and institutional environment created to facilitate the operation of these AMCs were also helpful in fostering NPL markets that did not exist before the Asian financial crisis. Operations of the AMCs also contributed to developing the NPL market ecosystem by creating business opportunities for NPL market service agencies such as debt servicing agencies, asset appraisers, credit rating agencies, lawyers, and brokers. Diverse NPL investors, including domestic private AMCs, private equity funds, and foreign investors, appeared and participated in their NPL markets, utilizing diverse tools of NPL resolution. The NPL markets and the ecosystems developed in these countries not only contributed to financial development but may also have helped these countries avoid massive NPL accumulation during periods of financial market turbulence. For example, as can be seen in Figure 8.2, Indonesia, Malaysia, the Republic of Korea, and Thailand, unlike other Asian countries, did not experience a hike in the NPL ratio during the global financial crisis and its aftermath.

8.4.2 The People's Republic of China, Viet Nam, and Kazakhstan

The PRC, Viet Nam, and Kazakhstan tried to build NPL resolution frameworks and NPL markets to deal with their own banking problems. They adopted public AMCs as the main component of their NPL resolution frameworks. But initially they failed to create active secondary NPL markets because of restrictions on the operation of AMCs, the absence of an enabling environment for AMCs and NPL investors, and inefficient legal and a judicial framework for debt enforcement. Realizing the limitations of the government bailout approach, the PRC and Viet Nam began adopting a more market-friendly approach, removing restrictions on the operation of AMCs and reforming the legal and judicial systems to create an enabling environment for NPL market development.

People's Republic of China

The PRC established four public AMCs—Cinda, Huarong, Orient, and Great Wall—to resolve NPLs held by the four largest state-owned commercial banks. Though these AMCs were helpful in resolving NPLs held by state-owned commercial banks, resolution of the NPLs acquired by these AMCs was slow. This was because secondary NPL markets were not active, due to restrictions on the operation of these AMCs. For example, in the beginning, these AMCs had to acquire NPLs from their partner state-owned commercial bank at book values, making it difficult for them to recover

NPLs through sale to other investors. Besides, efforts to resolve NPLs by financial institutions and AMCs were hindered by inefficient insolvency resolution frameworks.

As the amount of NPLs of the Chinese banking system began growing rapidly from 2012, the PRC government stepped up its efforts to resolve NPLs. This time, however, the policy toward NPL resolution changed from the previous government bailout approach to the multipronged market-based approach. New measures were adopted to create and improve the NPL market environment. These measures included enhancing the role of AMCs, establishing a conducive legal system, and strengthening the regulation on NPL recognition and provisioning.

First, the role and number of AMCs were expanded. More provincial and local AMCs were established. As of October 2018, 174 AMCs including 53 local AMCs were in operation, serving as conduits between banks and NPL markets. Although NPL investors were still required to acquire NPLs through AMCs, restrictions on the operation of AMCs were removed so that these could recover NPLs by selling them to other NPL investors. NPL transfers from financial institutions to AMCs changed from acquisition at book value to auctions, allowing AMCs to acquire NPLs at market prices rather than book values.

The legal system for insolvency resolution and debt enforcement has continuously been improved through amendments and modifications to the related laws and the judicial system. As a result, the entire legal process to enforce NPLs now takes approximately 2 years, much shorter than the 5 years of a decade ago. Fanger (2018) states that predictability and enforceability pertaining to NPL resolution have improved significantly as the quality of legal practitioners has improved and as regulations provide clear protection of creditor rights.

The China Banking and Insurance Regulatory Commission[6] also stepped up regulatory efforts to enforce recognition and resolution of NPLs. For example, Circular 46 issued in April 2017 listed and prohibited over 50 accounting practices that financial institutions had used to understate their credit exposure and to warehouse their problem loans. Similar to the outcomes in Europe (Chapter 7), the regulatory efforts, together with

---

[6]   The China Banking Regulatory Commission and the China Insurance Regulatory Commission were merged into the China Banking and Insurance Regulatory Commission in March 2013.

extensive on-site examinations and heavier penalties, have increased the amount of NPLs recognized and have accelerated the flow of NPL supply to NPL markets.

Viet Nam

The NPL resolution framework in Viet Nam before 2015 consisted of two public AMCs, Debt and Asset Trading Corporation and Vietnam Asset Management Company, and bank AMCs. The Debt and Asset Trading Corporation was established in 2003 to restructure state-owned enterprises, and later mandated also to resolve NPLs held by credit institutions. Although it contributed significantly to restructuring and equitizing state-owned enterprises, its debt purchases from banks have been very modest. The Vietnam Asset Management Company was established in 2013 by the State Bank of Viet Nam to deal with the NPL problem. In addition, bank-specific AMCs were introduced to deal with the NPL problem caused by the Asian financial crisis. These AMCs dealt with the NPLs of the parent bank only.

Before the global financial crisis, domestic credit in Viet Nam rapidly expanded, fueled by widespread policy lending. The economic downturn and the decline in real estate prices, however, resulted in rapid growth of NPLs. The Vietnam Asset Management Company purchased NPLs from banks in exchange for special Vietnam Asset Management Company bonds. These bonds could be used as collateral to borrow money from the State Bank of Viet Nam. All banks with an NPL ratio of above 3% were required to sell NPLs to the asset management company. However, the company was not allowed to purchase NPLs at market prices nor was it allowed to resell NPLs at a discount. Because of these restrictions, the NPL resolution efforts of the Vietnam Asset Management Company were limited to such activities as urging repayments, restructuring debts, and disposing of collateral.

Although 2 public AMCs and about 20 private AMCs were in operation, secondary market NPL transactions were not active in Viet Nam. This was because AMCs were not able to trade the NPLs they acquired due to restrictions that prohibited these AMCs from purchasing NPLs from banks at a discount from book value. The legal system for debt enforcement in Viet Nam was not favorable to NPL market development either. Enforcement of debt in Viet Nam used to demand a lengthy and costly court process to settle disputes. According to the World Bank's Doing Business Index in 2018, Viet Nam's bankruptcy procedures ranked 129th in the world. The insolvency process in Viet Nam took 5 years on average, compared with an average of 2.8 years in Southeast Asia.

Faced with a rapid buildup of NPLs in the financial sector, however, the Vietnamese government began taking a market-based approach to NPL resolution in 2015. To enhance the function of the Vietnam Asset Management Company, the government allowed it to purchase NPLs from financial institutions at market prices. This was expected to facilitate the sale of NPLs to foreign investors, activating secondary NPL markets. In addition, Resolution No. 42 introduced several measures to remove difficulties in dealing with NPLs, creating a favorable environment for NPL market development. These measures included allowing financial institutions and the Vietnam Asset Management Company to foreclose collateral to enforce debt, reducing the procedures to resolve disputes related to collateral by introducing a shortcut court procedure, and allowing banks and the Vietnam Asset Management Company to sell NPLs and distressed assets to organizations and individuals. These measures removed difficulties in dealing with NPLs and collateral by affirming the creditor rights of banks and the Vietnam Asset Management Company to seize collateral.

The market-based measures seem to have contributed to developing the NPL market in Viet Nam, which has grown in number and diversity of market participants. Yet, room for improvement still exists. Tuan (2018) argues that although Resolution No. 42 created the legal framework to induce debt trading business and to strengthen creditor rights, the development of NPL markets has been slow because regulations and decrees to support Resolution No. 42 are still incomplete and some of the measures are in conflict with existing laws and regulations.

For example, Tran (2019) points out that Resolution No. 42 specifically states that the Vietnam Asset Management Company, Debt and Asset Trading Corporation, and bank AMCs can seize collateral without court arbitration after a certain period. But it does not clearly state whether other investors can also seize collateral without a court process. In addition, enforcement of court decisions remains lengthy, taking up to 2 years.

Kazakhstan

Kazakhstani authorities have taken policy measures to remove NPLs from the banking system since 2012. These measures include establishing AMCs such as the Fund of Problem Loans and OUSA (subsidiary established by commercial banks to manage NPLs), strengthening supervision of NPLs, and amending the tax code to encourage NPL resolution by banks. In 2015, the tax code was amended to eliminate tax barriers to NPL provisioning and to encourage NPL divestment and write-off. Before the amendment, the tax code had strictly restricted the tax deduction effect from loan-loss provision.

These policy measures, however, have not been an effective solution to the NPL problem in Kazakhstan. Nor have they been effective in fostering NPL markets there. According to Chae (2015), the number of NPL transactions by the Fund of Problem Loans has been limited and the cooperation between banks and the fund has been passive. Banks' reluctance to sell NPLs, disagreement over price and acquisition structure, limitations on the types of collateral subject to acquisition, and inadequate Fund of Problem Loans capital are noted as the main reasons.[7] For instance, banks were required to share the risk of further asset impairment with the AMC and compensate potential losses when disagreement occurred between banks' ask price and the AMC's bid price, which made banks reluctant to sell NPLs to the fund. Besides high transfer prices, the limited scope of the AMC's activities is regarded as the reason why it has been ineffective in NPL resolution. The range of the Fund of Problem Loan's activities has been too narrow relative to the scope of the activities of AMCs in other economies and even compared to the range of OUSA activities. Lack of autonomy is also responsible for the unsatisfactory performance of the Fund of Problem Loans in NPL resolution. So far, all internal and external procedures and activities of the AMC have been fully controlled and supervised by the National Bank of Kazakhstan to maintain the safety of transactions and debt collection possibility.

8.4.3 Lessons

Case studies of the Asian countries that attempted to establish NPL resolution frameworks demonstrate that a holistic approach is needed to develop NPL markets. The four countries directly hit by the Asian financial crisis—Indonesia, Malaysia, the Republic of Korea, and Thailand—had modest success in developing NPL markets because the establishment of public AMCs was accompanied by efforts to create an enabling legal and institutional environment to facilitate the operations of AMCs so that they could promptly recover NPLs. Other Asian countries' efforts to develop NPL markets were not so successful, because they did not add to such efforts to create an enabling environment. These countries even imposed restrictions on AMC operations, including restrictions on the prices at

---

[7]   In 2014, the Fund of Problem Loans was provided with additional capital of tenge 500 billion (about $2.73 billion as of end-2014).

which they could acquire NPLs from banks. It was only when the PRC and Viet Nam adopted a market-based approach by removing restrictions on AMC operations and by reforming the legal system for debt and collateral enforcement that their NPL markets became active.

8.5 A Strategy to Develop Nonperforming Loan Markets and Resolution Frameworks

8.5.1 Two Approaches to Nonperforming Loan Resolution

Financial institutions and policy makers have adopted a variety of tools to cope with NPL problems. These tools reflect a debtor-focused approach and a bank-focused approach to NPL resolution. The debtor-focused approach supports NPL resolution by enhancing the repayment capacity of debtors and by preserving the value of the debtors' business. Debt restructuring by individual banks, a court-driven insolvency framework, and an out-of-court corporate workout mechanism belong to this approach. The bank-focused approach, on the other hand, focuses on removing NPLs from the balance sheet of banks. Debt write-offs, asset protection schemes, AMCs, securitization, and direct sales belong to this approach. Among these, debt write-offs and asset protection schemes resolve NPLs while these remain on banks' balance sheets. The other tools resolve NPLs by removing these from banks' balance sheets.

Baudino and Yun (2017) argue that the choice of the NPL resolution tool among a set of options should reflect the country-specific characteristics including macroeconomic conditions, fiscal space, legal and judicial constraints, and type of underlying assets. While the creation of centralized public AMCs is favored to deal with a sudden economic shock that rapidly and widely undermines the asset quality of the banking sector, debt restructuring and debt write-offs are suitable options if the NPL problem is driven by protracted slow growth that erodes asset quality gradually and repeatedly.[8] Table 8.5 elaborates on NPL resolution methods contingent on country-specific characteristics.

For countries with limited fiscal space, resolution tools that do not require heavy upfront government expenditure are recommended. An asset protection scheme is a good example, as governments do not disburse real resources in advance, but provide guarantees instead. It is only when the

---

[8]   An AMC is also a useful option in clearing up the legacy NPLs built up from a period of slow growth.

guarantees are called that governments need to disburse real resources. Legal and judicial constraints on debt enforcement not only make it difficult for banks to enforce debt and collateral, but also for NPL investors and AMCs. The composition of the assets underlying NPLs also matters for the choice of NPL resolution tools and policies. AMCs are known to be good in handling commercial real estate loans but not in handling household mortgages,[9] because of the high administrative costs required for managing these assets.

Table 8.5: Country Characteristics and Resolution Methods

		APS	Public AMCs	Securitization	Direct Sales	Debt Restructure	Out-of-Court Workout
Nature of shock	Slow growth			√		√	√
	Crisis	√	√	√	√	√	√
Asset types	Mortgages			√		√	
	SME loans		√	√	√	√	√
	Large corp. loans		√		√		√
	Unsecured loan		√	√	√	√	
Fiscal space	Limited	√	√	√	√	√	
Legal constraint	Strong						√

AMC = asset management company, APS = asset protection scheme, SME = small and medium-sized enterprise.
Source: Adopted from Baudino and Yun (2017) and modified by the authors.

NPL markets where banks and NPL investors including AMCs trade NPLs, if well developed, can help banks resolve NPLs through direct sales. The benefits from developing NPL markets, however, are not confined to enabling direct sales of NPLs. A wide and deep investor base formed by active NPL markets can also support NPL resolution through AMCs and securitization. In particular, active NPL markets allow AMCs to raise funds by disposing of the NPLs acquired from banks with which AMCs can acquire more NPLs from banks. The success of AMCs depends heavily on their ability to recover value from the NPLs they acquire. NPL markets can also complement other NPL resolution tools, such as debt write-off and debt restructuring, by allowing banks to dispose of NPLs before they grow to an amount large enough to become a threat to capital adequacy. Besides, they can help banks dispose of performing noncore assets, markets for which may also not always be developed.

---

[9] Public AMCs dealing with mortgages are quite problematic in Europe owing to the political sensitivity of governments managing residential mortgages, and possibly throwing voters out of their homes.

As was already mentioned, however, NPL markets are difficult to develop because of various impediments. Consequently, to develop NPL markets, carefully designed strategies and action plans to address these impediments are a must. The first step in developing the strategies and action plans is to identify the impediments that obstruct transactions between main participants in NPL markets. As Figure 8.4 shows, the main players in NPL markets are banks, AMCs, and NPL investors. In addition, there are other stakeholders such as debtors, service providers, financial supervisors, and other public authorities. The next step is to examine if NPL transactions between each of these participants can be made without difficulty. Transactions between each of these market participants may be impeded for various reasons, including information asymmetry, regulatory restrictions, legal and judicial constraints, economic costs, and inadequate tax rules and accounting principles. Identifying the impediments and taking reform measures to remove these impediments should be the natural next step.

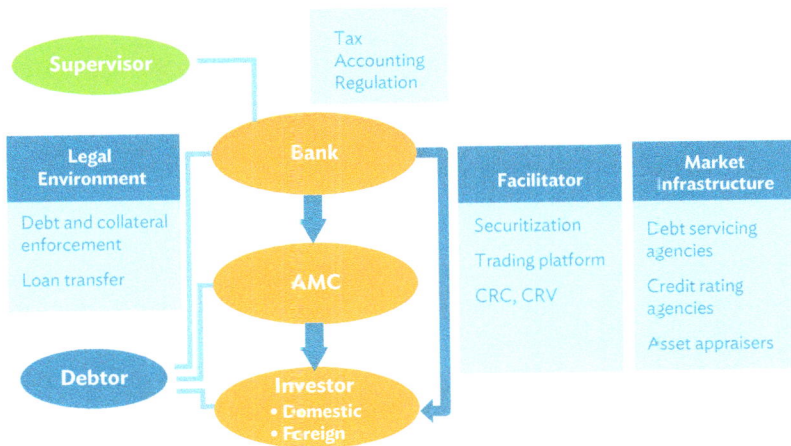

Figure 8.4: A Strategic Framework to Develop NPL Markets

AMC = asset management company, CRC = corporate restructuring company, CRV = corporate restructuring vehicle, NPL = nonperforming loan.
Source: Authors' compilation.

Developing active NPL markets cannot be achieved by removing regulatory and legal constraints alone. Well-functioning market infrastructure and ecosystems are also needed for NPL markets to operate efficiently. First, NPL trading platforms are needed to reduce information asymmetry, as discussed in Chapter 7. And diverse means of NPL disposal should be available to financial institutions including securitization and corporate restructuring. However, these means require a legal basis and financial expertise. In addition, NPL market participants need services from debt servicing agencies, credit rating agencies, and asset appraisers.

8.5.2 Strategic Framework for Developing NPL Markets

Despite the potential benefits of NPL markets, most countries in Asia and the Pacific do not have a well-developed NPL market. One of the main reasons lies in the impediments to developing NPL markets discussed in section 8.4 as well as the fact that large stocks of NPLs mostly occur during crisis periods, while it may be costly to maintain adequate market infrastructure during times of low NPL incidence. In consequence, implementing a strategy designed to address these impediments is a must. This section suggests some of the elements of a strategy to develop NPL markets and NPL resolution frameworks.

Supervisory efforts for NPL recognition and resolution

In general, bank managers are reluctant to recognize, make provisions for, and sell NPLs for fear that these will deteriorate their management performance. As a result, regulatory and supervisory efforts are needed to provide banks with incentives to engage in NPL resolution and debt restructuring. For example, several European countries, such as Ireland, have overlaid their accounting standards with guidelines on provisioning. Measures, such as imposing a higher capital charge on NPLs and adopting the European Union (EU) approach on calendar provisioning to introduce a time-limit on NPL write-offs, can also motivate banks to resolve their NPLs. Supervisory agencies may have to identify and prohibit the measures and the practices used by financial institutions to avoid recognition of NPLs.

Tightening supervisory guidelines on NPLs to force banks to resolve NPLs, however, will only end up penalizing banks unless they are accompanied by improvement in the legal, tax, and accounting environment for NPL resolution. To avoid penalizing banks, strengthening supervisory guidelines on NPLs and imposing time limits for NPL write-offs should be combined with a parallel strategy that addresses the length of judicial proceedings for debt and collateral enforcement. In addition to legal and judicial inefficiency, various kinds of impediments to NPL resolution exist, including tax and accounting rules that do not recognize the cost of NPL resolution in excess of the provisions. These impediments should be taken care of to improve the environment for NPL resolution. For example, a cap on tax deductibility may make banks reluctant to make provisions for NPLs or write off NPLs. Raising the cap or allowing provisions and write-offs to be fully deductible in the same fiscal year will strengthen the incentive for provisioning and write-offs. The introduction of IFRS 9[10] and more forward-looking provisioning rules conducive to faster recognition of losses may also provide incentives for banks to quickly resolve NPLs.

Providing incentives to banks for NPL resolution and debt restructuring not only contributes to enhancing soundness of banks and their lending capacities, but also contributes to developing and maintaining NPL markets by maintaining a steady supply of NPLs to the market thereby helping maintain a domestic base of NPL investors. Without a steady supply of NPLs to the market, domestic NPL investors including AMCs will not be able to sustain their business. And without a domestic NPL investor base, NPL resolution should rely on large global NPL investors that are capable of searching for investment opportunities in the global NPL market. In times of crisis when a large amount of NPLs should be resolved at a large discount, a country without a domestic investor base must endure a huge loss of national wealth.

Improving the legal and judicial system for debt enforcement

It goes without saying that the legal and institutional environment should be addressed in designing a strategy to develop NPL markets and NPL resolution frameworks. Enhancement in structural inefficiency in debt and collateral enforcement allows financial institutions and NPL investors to promptly redeem their investment in NPLs with reasonable returns and improves NPL market liquidity by reducing bid-ask spreads.

Inefficiency in debt enforcement is usually caused by a legal system that requires several lengthy rounds of court decisions to enforce debt and makes debt enforcement through collateral disposal difficult and costly. Inefficient debt enforcement is also caused by limited court capacities delaying decisions, and even when court decisions are made, enforcing them may take a long time. As a result, it takes more than 5 years to enforce debt through the judicial process in some economies, as Table 8.4 shows. Enhancement of judicial system capacity and legal system reform are

[10] International Financial Reporting Standards (IFRS) are the accounting standards issued by the IFRS Foundation and the International Accounting Standards Board. IFRS 9 addresses the accounting for financial instruments and covers classification and measurement of financial instruments, impairment of financial assets, and hedge accounting.

needed to strengthen creditor rights and improve efficiency in debt and collateral enforcement. A few countries tried to improve debt and collateral enforcement by introducing shorter court processes. Viet Nam introduced a shortcut procedure that allows financial institutions to seize collateral without court arbitration after a certain period, strengthening protection of the creditor rights of financial institutions (Tran 2010). In some cases, however, such a legal reform may be constrained by constitutional law considerations, or face opposition based on the need to protect debtors.

Asset management companies

Centralized public AMCs have proven useful in promptly resolving massive amounts of NPLs from the banking system during a systemic banking crisis as well as in resolving legacy NPLs accumulated on the balance sheet of banks through an extended period of lackluster growth. For example, the four Asian economies directly hit by the Asian financial crisis relied on centralized public AMCs to promptly remove NPLs from the banking system. The Indonesian Bank Restructuring Agency, the Korea Asset Management Corporation,[11] Danaharta (Malaysia), and the Thai Asset Management Corporation are representative cases. AMCs have also been used by a few European countries to cope with banking crises during the global financial crisis. Prominent cases include Ireland's National Asset Management Agency, SAREB in Spain, and Bank Assets Management Company in Slovenia. Recognizing the benefits of AMCs in NPL resolution, the EU Action Plan for NPL resolution also includes the AMC Blueprint as a core element.

An alternative to establishing public AMCs is to place NPLs with the internal restructuring unit of the originating bank in conjunction with appropriate recapitalization. However, AMCs have several advantages over such an alternative. First, asset support through an AMC delivers relief in time. A forced workout of NPLs, especially during a banking crisis, drives down the market price of assets and collateral. Consequently, distressed assets can be sold only at fire-sale prices, which in turn requires a larger amount of capital injection. Since AMCs in general have a longer time horizon for asset disposal, they can wait until market conditions improve. Public AMCs purchasing NPLs from banks at long-term economic values rather than current market prices enable banks to remove NPLs from their balance sheets without taking huge losses.

---

[11] The Korea Asset Management Corporation was established by converting a public company in charge of managing government properties into an AMC.

Second, AMCs can provide banks with much-needed liquidity during times of distress. A large portfolio of non-paying illiquid claims implies reduced cash flows for banks that may lead to funding problems, particularly in the wholesale market. Third, banks may lack resources to work out large amounts of NPLs at the same time during a banking crisis. But AMCs can attract the needed skills and be more productive in management, workout, and sale of nonperforming assets. Fourth, if the internal workout process of banks is protracted owing to the leniency of banks toward their borrowers to protect business relationships or owing to the reluctance of bank management to materialize losses, AMCs can help speed up the process with more decisive action in the public interest.

Recent research tends to support the potential benefits of AMCs for banks, notably better access to funding and enhancement in lending capacities, but it also points to challenges. First, establishing and operating AMCs entail significant costs. Even though use of public AMCs can be justified by their role as a public good to deal with the negative externalities of financial crises, their mandate requires minimizing the burden to taxpayers. This implies that AMCs must have the expertise to extract the full value of NPLs transferred from banks and that the expertise should be available at a reasonable cost. If this is not the case, a lump-sum subsidy in the form of a capital injection may achieve the same result at a lower cost.

The ability of AMCs to extract the full value from NPLs at a reasonable cost also depends on the composition of assets they acquire from banks. Historically, AMCs have been most successful when tasked with resolving real assets, typically commercial real estate and land (Fell et al. 2016, p. 144). Such assets are relatively straightforward to value and as a result AMCs can manage them with relatively thin staffing. Real estate valuations are also likely to track macroeconomic trends, recovering value as the economy grows. It is somewhat unclear, however, that an AMC could efficiently resolve other assets such as household mortgages that burden AMCs with managing a large number of small-sized loans.

Governance is another critical issue for the success of public AMCs. Poor governance and political influence may force an AMC to be used as a tool to bail out banks or bank owners, causing them to end up as financial failures (see European Commission (2018) and Chapter 7 for further discussion). For example, the Mongolian Asset Realization Agency, established to deal with the NPLs of Mongolian banks during the 1996 banking crisis, ended up as a financial failure because of poor governance and political influence (Enoch, Gulde, and Hardy 2002).

AMCs also need an enabling legal and judicial environment for debt enforcement to promptly resolve NPLs. Otherwise, AMCs will be faced with the same difficulty banks have in recovering the value of the NPLs they acquire from banks and will end up as a warehouse for NPLs. This is why the Asian countries hit directly by the Asian financial crisis tried to improve the legal and judicial environment for debt enforcement when they established public AMCs. There were also cases in which AMCs were given special rights through special AMC laws to overcome an inefficient legal and judicial environment.

Besides removing toxic assets from banks, public AMCs can help foster NPL markets. AMCs create demand for NPL market services and thereby support market infrastructure and ecosystems. In addition, AMCs can help establish NPL information and validation standards, thereby reducing information asymmetry. As Box 8.1 discusses, the Republic of Korea did not have an NPL market before the Asian financial crisis and had to rely on the Korea Asset Management Corporation (KAMCO), a centralized public AMC, to remove NPLs from the banking sector when it was hit by the Asian financial crisis. In addition to removing NPLs from banks, KAMCO paved a way to develop NPL markets in the Republic of Korea. Now, private AMCs and private NPL investors actively participate in the Korean NPL market. Governments may even utilize public AMCs as a strategic tool to create and foster NPL markets. The impact of public AMCs on secondary NPL markets depends on the size of AMCs, restrictions on transfer prices, and asset disposal strategies of AMCs. Martin (2019), argues, however, that governments should not burden AMCs with secondary NPL market development, as this task is likely to create conflicting objectives. Instead, policy makers should design AMCs and their operations so that these could contribute to secondary market development.

Nonperforming loan trading platforms to reduce information asymmetry

Information asymmetry between banks and NPL investors has repeatedly been identified as a key impediment to NPL market development, and thus measures to address it should be taken. Fell et al. (2017) and Chapter 7 propose that such market failure can be overcome by introducing NPL trading platforms. An NPL trading platform, an electronic transaction platform combined with a data warehouse and a trade repository, is expected to resolve market failure arising from information asymmetry and coordination failure by providing transparent and validated information about the credit quality of NPLs to potential investors.

Box 8.1: Korea Asset Management Corporation and NPL Market Development in the Republic of Korea

To help restructure the ailing banking sector by resolving nonperforming loans (NPLs) from financial institutions, the Government of the Republic of Korea converted the Korea Asset Management Corporation (KAMCO) into a public asset management company (AMC). Since the government had to achieve bank restructuring with limited amount of public funding, KAMCO had to resolve the NPLs acquired from banks as quickly as possible.

At the early stage of the Asian financial crisis, a domestic NPL market where KAMCO could dispose of the NPLs it acquired from banks did not exist. Nor was there a domestic investor base for NPLs. As a result, KAMCO tried to utilize diverse tools of NPL resolution, including international auctions to attract foreign investors, NPL securitization, and corporate restructuring. To facilitate rapid disposal of NPLs, the government took reform measures to improve the legal and institutional environment.

The measures taken to improve NPL resolution and to facilitate acquisition and disposal of NPLs not only facilitated the operations of KAMCO, but also contributed to developing NPL markets. Private AMCs such as UAMCO and Daishin F&I, and Hana F&I have emerged, specializing in NPL acquisition and disposal. Commercial banks use asset-backed securities issuance to dispose of their NPLs. The development of NPL markets seems to have facilitated NPL disposal by commercial banks and as a result helped maintain a stable NPL ratio, despite economic turbulence.

NPLs Resolution Tools Used by Republic of Korea Banks, 2007–2019
(%)

Tool	2007	2009	2011	2013	2015	2017	2019
Write-offs	24.6	32.0	30.9	35.2	33.6	27.1	26.7
Sales[a]	7.4	13.8	24.8	25.4	23.3	20.3	22.8
Asset-backed securities	14.8	12.8	...	...	...	...	...
Sale of collateral	31.1	19.5	23.8	22.5	22.9	34.3	22.8
Credit normalization	18.9	16.8	18.5	12.7	15.7	11.6	22.2
Others	3.3	4.7	2.0	4.1	3.6	6.8	5.6

AMC = asset management company, F&I = finance and insurance, NPL = nonperforming loan, UAMCO = United Asset Management Corporation.
Note: [a] From 2011, the resolution through issuing asset-backed securities is included in the sales category.
Source: Authors' calculations based on the press release of the Financial Supervisory Service.

To fully exploit its advantages, an NPL trading platform should perform the following functions: (i) collect and provide loan-level data; (ii) enhance comparability of NPL data across banks by harmonizing data templates for loan tapes; (iii) provide qualitative information such as the legal position of the lender vis-à-vis the borrower, the attitude of the borrower, the past history of interactions with the borrower, and qualitative information on collateral and act as a repository of key legal documents; and (iv) provide independent validation of the reported NPL data.

The European DataWarehouse GmbH, established by the European private sector as a part of the European Central Bank's asset-backed securities Loan Level Data Initiative, provides a possible benchmark for NPL trading platforms. It provides an open platform for users to access asset-backed securities data and is the first centralized data repository in Europe for collecting, validating, and making accessible specific loan-level data for asset-backed securities transactions. In addition, a few private ventures have recently begun providing NPL trading and data warehousing services based on electronic platforms.

Besides introducing NPL trading platforms, strengthening supervisory regulations to induce frequent asset quality reviews by financial institutions and to promptly report the results to shareholders and stakeholders can also help reduce information gaps between NPL investors and banks.

Securitization

Securitization is a form of structured financing in which securities are issued through repackaging of a series of assets that generate cash flows in a way that separates these assets from the credit profile of the company that originally owned them. The credit assessment of asset-backed securities is made solely based on cash flows created by the underlying assets.

Securitization can take on a large variety of attributes depending on the structure, the underlying assets, the way underlying assets are managed, and the types of securities issued. Securities issued through securitizing loans as underlying assets are called collateralized loan obligations. NPLs as well as performing loans can be used as the underlying assets for collateralized loan obligations. Securitization would be useful in disposing of a large number of small-sized assets: NPLs from household loans, SME loans, and unsecured loans.

Collateralized loan obligations can be beneficial in resolving NPLs for several reasons. First, they reduce the overall credit risk of the pool of underlying assets by diversifying the idiosyncratic credit risk of each borrower. Second, securitization can expand the universe of distressed debt investors by creating securities whose credit risk profile is tailored to the risk preference of diverse investors. In particular, collateralized loan obligations with a higher credit rating than the average credit rating of the underlying assets can be issued by using senior/junior tranches. Generally, senior bonds can receive credit ratings higher than the average credit rating of the pool of collateralized assets, and hence can be more easily absorbed by the market. Third, in addition to utilizing senior/junior tranches, other credit enhancement methods such as credit guarantees, over-collateralization, spread accounts, cash collateral accounts, and credit swaps can be used to enhance the creditworthiness of the asset-backed securities and make them attractive to an even greater range of investors.

In addition, securitization provides governments with means to help banks resolve NPLs and develop NPL markets. Governments may provide guarantees on senior (as in GACS, Chapter 6) or junior tranches of NPL securitization. Securitization, with this sort of guarantee, can achieve results similar to asset protection schemes except that securitization removes NPLs from the balance sheet of originating banks, while in asset protection schemes NPLs remain on the balance sheet of originating banks. Instead of providing guarantees on securitization, governments can also facilitate NPL resolution through securitization by purchasing a certain portion of junior bonds.

Fell, Moldovan, and O'Brien (2017) point out that large-scale co-investment by governments in NPL securitization could not only facilitate NPL securitization deals but may help activate NPL sales by aligning the incentives of the government with those of private investors. While banks and private investors have little control over factors such as structural inefficiencies, frictions, and uncertainties that impede NPL workout, governments can use legislative measures on these factors that can have a consequential effect on the asset values.

Securitization requires enabling legal infrastructure. First, the true sale nature of the underlying assets should be guaranteed by the legal system and recognized by the accounting principle. Second, special purpose vehicles (SPVs) in which underlying assets are grouped together should be available without much extra cost. In common law jurisdictions, such a vehicle is available in the form of trust and, as a result, no additional legislation is needed. In civil law jurisdictions, however, such a vehicle should be given legal foundation together with tax transparency. For example, the Republic of Korea enacted the Law on Asset Backed Securities in 2008 to facilitate resolution of NPLs through securitization.

In addition to legal infrastructure, securitization requires financial market infrastructure. For example, accurate pricing of the senior bonds and the mezzanine bonds depends on the capacity of credit rating agencies. Since different tranches of bonds with different credit ratings are issued based on diverse underlying assets, credit rating for securitization is more difficult than that for ordinary corporate bonds. That means credit rating agencies must have the capacity to evaluate and analyze securitization deals with diverse structures and underlying assets. In addition to credit rating agencies, a wide investor base with different preferences on risk–return profile should be available, which is not the case for many countries whose financial markets are at a nascent stage of development.

Out-of-court corporate workouts

Enhancing the repayment capacity of debtors through debt restructuring is also a tool banks use frequently. While debt restructuring is simple when there is a single creditor, it is difficult with multiple creditors who do not agree with others. Court-driven insolvency procedures can overcome this difficulty by binding interested parties to the court decision. Despite this advantage, court-driven corporate restructuring often faces limited capacity and limited specialty of courts, causing delays in decisions. Although improving the capacity of insolvency courts is the solution to this problem, it takes time and money to achieve this goal. And during a financial crisis when the number of insolvency cases soars, the burden on the judicial system becomes unbearable.

One way to speed up the process of corporate restructuring under limited court capacity is to utilize out-of-court corporate workouts, which are generally more time efficient, more flexible, and carry less stigma.[12] Initially, corporate workouts adopted the so-called London approach in which participation in the workout plan was voluntary. Later, to expedite corporate workouts, some countries made participation mandatory once the majority

---

[12]   Out-of-court corporate workouts are useful as a corporate restructuring tool in countries with efficient legal and judicial systems for debt enforcement as well. It is sometimes argued that out-of-court corporate workouts work better it there is a properly functioning legal system available as a 'threat' to ensure compliance.

of creditors had decided on a workout plan. In the Republic of Korea, for example, the Corporate Workout Law allows a majority rule of three-quarters of the credit amount to facilitate decision-making among creditors in the workout process. And the Thai government established the Corporate Debt Restructuring Committee to assist financial institutions with out-of-court corporate restructuring during the Asian financial crisis.

Debt restructuring can also be achieved by private equity funds that specialize in corporate restructuring. These funds acquire the majority of shares of the firm to be restructured by purchasing equities or by swapping debt into equities and turn the firm around through corporate restructuring. To facilitate corporate restructuring by private equity funds, corporate restructuring vehicles with tax transparency should be available.

Regional strategies to establish regional framework for nonperforming loan resolution

Most strategies suggested so far can be adopted as national strategies. In developing NPL markets, there is also room for regional strategies. In Europe, for example, EU-wide financial regulations and widespread use of cross-border loans made it necessary to introduce an EU-wide framework for NPL resolution. In Asia and the Pacific, region-wide financial regulations do not exist, and cross-border loans are not so common as in Europe, but room exists.

One reason regional strategies and frameworks are needed lies in the systemic importance of international banks and regional banks engaged in cross-border banking activities. Cross-border operations of these banks are conducted through local branches, local subsidiaries, or direct cross-border loans. A more important reason, however, is in the negative externalities associated with financial crises. As financial interconnectedness among countries in the region deepens, it is more likely that financial crisis in one country will spill over into another. To deal with such negative externalities, regional strategies and frameworks for NPL resolution are needed. Regional frameworks for NPL resolution thus serve as regional public goods, as noted in the introduction.

Supervision of regional systemically important financial institutions should be strengthened. The systemic importance of international banks and regional banks engaged in cross-border banking activities in Asia has been growing. For many host economies, these banks function as the main source of external funding. Maintaining stable funding to the host economies through credit supply channels of these banks has thus become crucial to financial stability in the region. Since these regional, systemically important financial institutions conduct business in multiple countries, there is the risk of regulatory arbitrage by these cross-border banks, which cannot be properly supervised by a host economy alone. In this regard, supervisory colleges for regionally active banks can be an effective form of regional cooperation to strengthen cross-border supervision and to solidify regional financial safety nets. Supervisory colleges can contribute to resolving regional NPLs by strengthening supervisory guidelines to provide regional financial institutions of this nature with stronger incentives to recognize and resolve NPLs.

While strengthening supervisory efforts through supervisory colleges may help maintain the fiscal soundness of regional, systemically important regional financial institutions and prevent the accumulation of NPLs, it cannot completely prevent the occurrence of NPLs. As a result, regional frameworks to resolve NPLs should be discussed and developed. Efficient resolution of NPLs held by such regional institutions in different countries requires regional frameworks for NPL resolution. Regional multinational companies with loans from multiple regional banks are another reason a regional framework for NPL resolution is needed. In resolving and restructuring NPLs, these regional and international banks must deal with differences in the legal and regulatory environment as well as differences in the tax and accounting rules. Such a difference should be taken care of when developing a regional framework for NPL resolution. In this regard, the approach of the Vienna Initiative could be appropriate. This initiative was launched at the height of the first wave of the global financial crisis to provide a forum for decision-making and coordination to safeguard the financial stability of emerging Europe. It brought together all relevant public and private sector stakeholders of EU-based cross-border banks active in emerging Europe.

Fostering a regional NPL market in which regional NPL investors and global NPL investors participate and trade regional NPLs not only supports the development of domestic NPL markets in Asia and the Pacific but also can enhance operations of other tools of NPL resolution. Home bias in an investment portfolio is one reason for the need for regional NPL markets in which regional NPL investors actively participate. This bias was initially recognized by French and Poterba (1991) as home bias in equity investment. One explanation for home bias is in the informational advantage of home investors that translates into lower costs and higher rates of return. Likewise, regional investors may have an information advantage over global investors for NPLs in the region. When this is the case, NPLs can be disposed of at more favorable terms if regional NPL markets are well developed. A regional NPL trading platform can be created by linking national NPL data warehouses or by establishing a separate entity. Reducing information asymmetries will help develop regional NPL markets for regional and global NPL investors.

The multilateral development banks should take part in regional efforts to build regional NPL markets and regional NPL resolution frameworks. They, together with international financial institutions, have been providing technical assistance and program loans to member economies to promote financial stability. In addition, they can serve as focal points for soliciting regional knowledge and experience. The International Public AMC Forum can also contribute to regional efforts to build up regional NPL resolution frameworks by sharing knowledge and expertise of member AMCs.

8.6 Conclusion

The potential benefits of active NPL markets are huge. They help banks resolve NPLs through direct sales and complement other means of NPL resolution. Challenges to the development of NPL markets include information asymmetry, inadequate tax and accounting rules, inefficient debt and collateral enforcement system, and other structural impediments. To develop NPL markets, carefully designed policy strategies and action plans are a must to address these impediments. No one-size-fits-all strategy exists, however, so each country or territory should design and adopt strategies appropriate to local economic conditions and the nature of the NPL problem as well as subject to its legal and institutional environment and fiscal space.

References

Arner, D. W., E. Gibson, and E. Avgouleas. 2016. A Comparative Analysis of NPL Resolution Strategies during the Asian Crisis, the GFC, and the Eurozone Debt Crisis. Consultation report for TA-8370: *Establishment of the International Public Asset Management Company Forum*. Manila: ADB.

Asian Development Bank (ADB). 2017. The Era of Financial Interconnectedness: How Can Asia Strengthen Financial Resilience? *Asian Economic Integration Report*. pp. 96–136.

Baudino, P. and H. Yun. 2017. Resolution of Non-performing Loans – Policy Options. *FSI Insights on Policy Implementation No. 3*. Financial Stability Institute of Bank for International Settlements.

Bernanke, B. S. 1981. Bankruptcy, Liquidity and Recession. *American Economic Review*. 71 (2). pp. 155–159.

_____. 1983. Nonmonetary Effects of the Financial Crisis in the Propagation of the Great Depression. *American Economic Review*. 73 (3). pp. 257–276.

Bernanke, B. S. and M. Gertler. 1989. Agency Costs, Net Worth, and Business Fluctuations. *American Economic Review*. 79 (1). pp. 14–31.

Bernanke, B. S., M. Gertler, and S. Gilchrist. 1996. The Financial Accelerator and the Flight to Quality. *The Review of Economics and Statistics*. 78 (1). pp. 1–15.

_____. 1999. The Financial Accelerator in a Quantitative Business Cycle Framework. In J. B. Taylor and M. Woodford, eds. *Handbook of Macroeconomics*. Vol. 1. Ch. 21. pp. 1341–1393.

Caprio, G. and D. Klingebiel. 1996. Bank Insolvencies: Cross-Country Experience. *World Bank Policy Research Working Papers*. No. 1620. Washington, DC: World Bank.

Chae, S. 2015. Enhancing the Legal Framework for NPL Management in Kazakhstan by Sharing and Adapting the Korean Model. In *2014/2015 Knowledge Sharing Program with Kazakhstan II: Policy Consultation for Enhancing Divestment of NPLs to Fund of Problem Loans and the Establishment of Effective NPL Acquisition Regimes*.

Ciavoliello, L. G., F. Ciocchetta, F. M. Conti, I. Guida, A. Rendina, and G. Santini. 2016. What's the Value of NPLs? *Notes on Financial Stability and Supervision*. No. 3. pp. 1–6. Bank of Italy.

De Bock, R. and A. Demyanets. 2012. Bank Asset Quality in Emerging Markets: Determinants and Spillovers. *IMF Working Paper.* WP/12/71. Washington, DC: International Monetary Fund.

Drees, B. and C. Pazarbasioglu. 1998. The Nordic Banking Crisis Pitfalls in Financial Liberalization. *IMF Occasional Papers.* No. 161. Washington, DC: International Monetary Fund.

Enoch, C., A. Gulde, and D. Hardy. 2002. Banking Crises and Bank Resolution: Experiences in Some Transition Economies. *IMF Working Paper.* WP/02/56. Washington, DC: International Monetary Fund.

Espinoza, R. and A. Prasad. 2010. Nonperforming Loans in the GCC Banking System and their Macroeconomic Effects. *IMF Working Paper.* WP/10/224. Washington, DC: International Monetary Fund.

European Commission. 2018. AMC Blueprint. *Commission Staff Working Document.* Brussels.

Fanger, B. 2018. Asia's NPL Markets: Opportunities and Challenges in PRC. A presentation at the 4th IPAF International Conference. 15 November. Hanoi.

Fell, J., C. Moldovan, and E. O'Brien. 2017. Resolving Non-performing Loans: A Role for Securitisation and Other Financial Structures? *Financial Stability Review.* May. pp. 158–174. Frankfurt: European Central Bank.

Fell, J., M. Grodzicki, D. Krušec, R. Martin, and E. O'Brien. 2017. Overcoming Non-performing Loan Market Failures with Transaction Platforms. *Financial Stability Review.* November. pp. 130–144. Frankfurt: European Central Bank.

Fell, J., M. Grodzicki, R. Martin, and E. O'Brien. 2016. Addressing Market Failures in the Resolution of Non-Performing Loans in the Euro Area. *Financial Stability Review.* November. pp. 134–146. Frankfurt: European Central Bank.

Fell, J., M. Grodzicki, J. Metzler, and E. O'Brien. 2018. Non-performing Loans and Euro Area Bank Lending Behavior after the Crisis. *Banco de España Financial Stability Review.* November. pp. 7–28.

French, K. and J. Poterba. 1991. Investor Portfolio and International Equity Markets. *American Economic Review.* 81 (2). pp. 222–26.

Kaminsky, G. L. and C. M. Reinhart. 1999. The Twin Crises: The Causes of Banking and Balance-of-Payments Problems. *American Economic Review.* 89 (3). pp. 473–500.

Kiyotaki, N. and J. Moore. 1997. Credit Cycles. *Journal of Political Economy*. 105 (2). pp. 211–248. Chicago: University of Chicago Press.

Klein, N. 2013. Non-Performing Loans in CESEE: Determinants and Impact on Macroeconomic Performance. *IMF Working Paper*. WP/13/72. Washington, DC: International Monetary Fund.

Lee, J. and P. Rosenkranz. 2018. Case Studies on NPL Reduction Measures in the ASEAN+3 Region. Unpublished.

Lee, J. and P. Rosenkranz. 2019. Nonperforming Loans in Asia: Determinants and Macro-Financial Linkages. *ADB Economics Working Paper Series*. No. 574. Manila: Asian Development Bank.

Martin, R. 2019. NPL Market Development – Challenges, Opportunities and Lessons from Europe. Presentation material.

Nkusu, M. 2011. Nonperforming Loans and Macrofinancial Vulnerabilities in Advanced Economies. *IMF Working Paper*. WP/11/161. Washington, DC: International Monetary Fund.

Park, C.Y. and K. Shin. 2017. A Contagion through Exposure to Foreign Banks during the Global Financial Crisis. *ADB Economics Working Paper Series*. No. 516. Manila: Asian Development Bank.

Thang, D. V. 2018. The Role of VAMC in Dealing with Bad Debts. Manuscript presented at the 4th IPAF International Conference. 14–15 November. Hanoi.

Tran, D. 2019. Vietnamese Legal Framework on Nonperforming Loans. Manuscript presented at the 6th IPAF Training Seminar on Strengthening Regional Financial Stability through Effective Legal and Operational Frameworks for NPLs Resolution. 27–28 May. Hanoi.

Tuan, D. A. 2018. Environmental Business Reform and Requirement of Developing the Debt Trading Market in Viet Nam. Manuscript presented at the 4th IPAF International Conference. 14–15 November. Hanoi.

www.ingramcontent.com/pod-product-compliance
Lightning Source LLC
Chambersburg PA
CBHW041144230326
41599CB00039BA/7156